· THE ·
SACRED
TABLE

Creating a Jewish Food Ethic

Edited by

MARY L. ZAMORE

CCAR Challenge and Change Series

Library of Congress Cataloging-in-Publication Data

The sacred table : creating a Jewish food ethic / edited by Mary L. Zamore.
p. cm—(CCAR challenge and change series)

ISBN 978-0-88123-170-0 (pbk. " alk. paper)
1. Food—Religious aspects—Judaism.   2. Jws—Dietary laws.   3. Kosher food.
4. Reform Judaism.   I. Zamore, Mary L., 1969–
BM710-.S244   2011
296.7´3—dc22   2010053913

10 9 8 7 6 5 4 3 2 1

CCAR Press, 355 Lexington Avenue, New York, NY 10017
(212) 972-3636
www. ccarpress.org

Sacred Table Task Force

SURELY, THIS COMMAND WHICH I ENJOIN UPON YOU THIS DAY
IS NOT TOO BAFFLING FOR YOU, NOR IS IT BEYOND REACH.
IT IS NOT IN THE HEAVENS, THAT YOU SHOULD SAY, "WHO
AMONG US CAN GO UP TO THE HEAVENS AND GET IT FOR US
AND IMPART IT TO US, THAT WE MAY OBSERVE IT?" NEITHER IS
IT BEYOND THE SEA, THAT YOU SHOULD SAY, "WHO AMONG US
CAN CROSS TO THE OTHER SIDE OF THE SEA AND GET IT FOR US
AND IMPART IT TO US, THAT WE MAY OBSERVE IT?" NO, IT IS
VERY CLOSE TO YOU, IN YOUR MOUTH AND IN YOUR HEART,
TO OBSERVE IT. (DEUTERONOMY 30:11-14)

DEDICATED TO THOSE WHO SHARE THIS WONDERFUL JOURNEY
WITH ME, ESPECIALLY TERJE AND ARYEH.

Contents

Acknowledgments

I gratefully acknowledge Rabbi Hara Person and the CCAR Press for believing in me and my vision. It was a gift to work with Hara and Deborah Smilow, as well as publishing interns Jillian Cameron and Sara Newman. I also thank the book's task force members for their input and support of this project: especially Richard Levy and Carole Balin for their thorough reviewing of our manuscript. Thank you to Rabbi Ellen Greenspan for her editing support. Thank you to Rabbi Rob Scheinberg for being my phone-a-friend. Thank you to Rabbi Amy Schwartzman for her inspired title suggestion. And the deepest thanks to the writers—I am so blessed to have such talented, passionate people give of their time and talent.

The work reflected in this book has its roots in many places and projects, including the 1998 CCAR President's Kallah under Rabbi Chuck Kroloff's leadership, the CCAR Taskforce on Kashrut under Rabbi Bennett Miller and Rabbi Steve Kushner's leadership, and the URJ Commission on Religious Living under Rabbi Sue Ann Wasserman's leadership. Thank you to all who have joined me in the sacred conversation regarding food.

Thank you to all of my teachers and mentors, especially Chuck Kroloff for his ongoing encouragement and guidance of my rabbinate. Thank you for the sisterhood of my peer mentoring group: Rabbis Debbie Bravo, Helaine Ettinger, Ellen Greenspan, Randi Musnitsky, and Amy Small. Thank you to Sue Fishkoff for her enthusiastic support of my work. Thank you to Rabbi Donald Rossoff and all the staff and temple family at Temple B'nai Or for their encouragement. I am blessed to be surrounded by a wonderful community of Jewish professionals who strive for excellence.

I thank Hazon, especially Hazon's Jewish Food Educators Network, for their ongoing creation of food talk, thought, and learning. I thank the Covenant Foundation for their funding, which allowed me to participate in Hazon's Jewish Food Educators Network training.

There are many at the CCAR who helped the book move forward in different ways. These include Rabbi Ellen Weinberg Dreyfus, CCAR President; Rabbi Steven A. Fox, CCAR Chief Executive; Rabbi Lance Sussman, Chair of the Press Committee; and Rabbi Elaine Zecher, Chair of Worship and Practice, as well as copy-editor Debra Hirsch Corman and cover designer Barbara Leff.

This working mother could not do everything I do without the help of caring friends. My gratitude goes to Elana Altzman for keeping me sane and Lillie Bryen and Maxine Schwartz for driving, feeding, and watching my son when I could not. In addition, I continued to be inspired by all my friends, who are the most talented and caring bunch.

Thank you to my mother Ellen Zamore, for her talented proofreading help and all her loving support, and to my brother Phillip Zamore and his family, Catherine Colinvaux, Hannah, and Eli for their love and good food. I remember my father, Leonard, knowing that he would have been proud.

Finally, the most important thank-yous: to my love and partner in everything, Terje, for supporting me and my dreams, and to my favorite and most-beloved foodie, Aryeh, for being so proud of me and understanding when I had to work on the book. I could not do this without both your support and love.

Foreword

ERIC H. YOFFIE

The publication of *The Sacred Table* is a historic event for Reform Judaism. It is a proclamation that we have entered a new era of Reform Jewish practice and belief. It is an assertion that we are finally opening doors that have been closed for more than a century.

Since the mid-1950s, North American Reform Judaism has been undergoing a process of "re-ritualization." Reform Jews, led by their rabbis, have begun to embrace rituals and traditions that were once discarded as obsolete. In a movement that has proudly emphasized its ethical commitments and its quest for justice in the world, there has been a growing awareness that the realms of ritual and ethics are intimately intertwined and that it is simply impossible to embrace one without the other. And individual Reform Jews, yearning to embrace *k'dushah* (sanctity) and God, have come to realize that ritual practice is a means of giving structure to the holy. In particular, long-ignored rituals connected to aspects of worship and holiday practice have become popular in Reform homes and synagogues.

Nonetheless, there have been limits—places that we simply do not go. Kashrut is the primary example, and all Jewish traditions that involve restrictions on what we eat have been treated with suspicion, if not contempt. They have been seen as lacking in ethical content, as a wall between Jews and their neighbors, and as an instrument used by an often corrupt religious establishment to derive profit for itself and to control others.

Yet, remarkably, all of this has recently begun to change. The broad interest in ethical eating that exists in Western culture is surely a factor. Our society's focus on eating has sent us back to our own sources. The Passover seder, of course, with its message that we cannot enjoy the food of affluence while others eat the bread of affliction, is the supreme example of a ritual practice focused on eating that is constructed on an ethical foundation. If Reform Jews find meaning in the seder, should we not seek other opportunities to impart ethical content to our eating?

Even more important is the desire that exists in the Reform Movement to bring elements of sanctity into our day-to-day existence. Judaism is not only about grand ideas. It is also about finding wonder and mystery in the texture of our everyday acts. It is about inviting God into our homes, our family life, and our tables. Since we eat at least three times a day, Reform Jews now understand that if we are to sanctify our most mundane acts, we must begin to see eating as a gateway to holiness.

In a Shabbat morning sermon that I delivered at the URJ Biennial in Toronto in 2009, I argued that the time had come for the topic of sacred eating to be a high-priority item on the personal agenda of Reform Jews. I called on the Reform Movement and Reform synagogues to think carefully about how they could encourage a Jewish way of eating that is right for our bodies and our souls. I did not, however, use the word "kashrut," largely out of concern that the negative associations that the term still retains for so many would stop the discussion before it even began.

In retrospect, I regret my excessive caution, and I applaud this volume for putting kashrut at the center of its deliberations. I now realize that to discuss Jewish eating without reference to kashrut is an impossibility. Of course, I recognize that kashrut will mean something very different for Reform Jews than it means for others and that inevitably there will never be a single system of Reform kashrut; there will be many. The virtue of this book is that it provides a guide—practical, theological, and historical—that will enable Reform Jews to arrive at thoughtful decisions on an approach to kashrut that will make sense for them.

Finally, it is important to note that the trends referred to above encompass only a modest number of people in our Movement. Kashrut and sacred eating are concerns confined to a relatively small minority of Reform Jews. Nonetheless, Rabbi Zamore and the CCAR have been wise to comprehend that as more and more Reform Jews commit themselves to a Torah-centered Reform Judaism rooted in Jewish *doing*, this minority is certain to grow. By producing this collection of thoughtful and creative essays, they have helped it to do so.

Preface

Nigel Savage

The Sacred Table and the New Jewish Food Movement

Ten minutes after I began writing this foreword, on a train in England, my phone rang. It was a rabbi calling from suburban New Jersey—far away, in its demographic, from the presumed eco-hippies of Brooklyn and Berkeley. She said, "Nigel, I'm giving the sermon on *Shabbat B'reishit*, and it's the story of Creation, the story of our relationship with the world, and I'm going to tell my congregants that we need to launch our own CSA, a community-supported agriculture program. Can you help me with a few questions I have?"

Years from now it will be clear that this conversation must have taken place in or around 2010. Six years ago, when Hazon launched the first CSA in the American Jewish community, few people had really heard of a CSA or knew what it was. Today there are forty-five CSAs in Hazon's network (the largest faith-based CSA network in the United States), and there is enormous interest in how to launch one, strengthen one, use it to do good in all sorts of ways. Twenty years from now I think most synagogues and temples will have CSAs, or else they'll be growing some food themselves, or their members will, or they'll have a farmers' market at the synagogue—or maybe these things won't even be a big deal, because America's supermarkets will have shifted from industrial monoculture to local, healthy, sustainable, ethical produce.

But today we live in a moment of transition, a tipping point in which food has gone from the restaurant page to the front page. And the Jewish community is part of that transition. At the cusp of World War I, there were a quarter of a million Jewish farmers in the United States. Their kids headed out to the elite universities and became doctors and lawyers and academics; in the 1960s people might have heard of "growing your own," but it wasn't food they were growing. Today we're back to the future: this year the new farm manager at Adamah, a Jewish farming program in Connecticut, dropped out of Harvard Medical School to become a farmer. I trust her grandparents are kvelling.

Food is in transition in our society, and so too, Jews are in transition in relation to food. But how do these things fit together? This question, also, is not new.

The *t'reifah* banquet took place on July 11, 1883. It heralded two or three generations in which Reform Jews rejected kashrut. The promise of America was the promise of freedom; the possibility of America was truly to fit in, not to be rejected or stigmatized; and the pathway to success and integration was through the abandonment of food customs that might in any way separate an American Jew from his or her neighbor. The *t'reifah* banquet symbolized a deep change in attitude toward food, and its echoes last to this day.

One hundred and twenty-five years later, the topic of American Jews and food was back on the nation's front pages. On May 12, 2008, federal authorities raided the Agriprocessors kosher meat plant in Postville, Iowa. If the *t'reifah* banquet heralded a century of we-don't-believe-in-keeping-kosher, what does the raid on Agriprocessors symbolize? On the face of it, nothing to do with liberal Jews. The plant was owned by Lubavitcher Chasidim, and most of its customers were presumed to be Orthodox or ultra-Orthodox. Carole Balin, in her article in this collection, accurately quotes Rabbi Eric Yoffie, head of the Union for Reform Judaism, speaking at the 2009 Biennial, saying that his new initiative around food guidelines in Reform communities "is not about kashrut; we as a Movement have put kashrut aside. We do not accept the authority of the kashrut establishment, and its problems are for others to resolve."

But the raid on Agriprocessors will I think throw a long shadow, and not just in the Orthodox world. The modernist love affair with uniformity, scale, mass production, a car any color so long as it is black, has steadily given way to the postmodern riot of choice and color and possibility. In relation to food, the contours of this encounter challenge us on a daily basis. Mass production in food seems to offer uniformity of quality and color and size (think tomatoes) and availability year-round (think strawberries) and high quality that is also convenient (think Starbucks). Yet we have learned steadily, from Wendell Berry and Michael Pollan and others, that we pay an unseen price for all of this: Industrial monoculture robs the soil of its vitality, reduces variety, and drives down farm wages. Industrial meat production means animals living unnatural lives of misery, enormous and problematic waste runoff, and—as in the case of Agriprocessors—389 illegal immigrants employed and subsequently arrested, because few local and legal workers were willing to do such dangerous and unpleasant work for such a low wage.

Sue Fishkoff's recent *Kosher Nation* makes clear that the number of consumers who in this country buy products that are certified as kosher far exceeds the number of Jewish people who keep kosher. Going back to the famous sixties' ad campaign "We Answer to a Higher Authority," the widespread presumption has been that kosher means purer, cleaner, somehow better. But the Agriprocessors raid made clear that this was not necessarily so—certainly in relation to meat.

Thus many Jewish people find themselves in a place with more questions than answers. What does it mean to be Jewish in the twenty-first century? How can I eat in a way that's healthy, not only for me and my family, but also for the world itself? If I have the choice between meat that is kosher, but not local or grass-fed, or grass-fed but not kosher, which should I choose, and why? If my food choices are only informed by contemporary wisdom, in what sense am I distinctly

Jewish? What does it mean to choose to celebrate Jewish food traditions in a postmodern society? What does it mean to eat sustainably, and how do I do it? Can Jewish tradition offer wisdom that is relevant to the choices I make today? And can my engagement with food help to strengthen my understanding of Jewish tradition and my commitment to Jewish life?

If you're asking these questions you're in the right place. Read on . . .

New York, Rosh Chodesh Kislev 5771

Introduction:
A Buffet of Educated Choices

Kosher—this word evokes strong reactions and images. For some of us, it brings to mind fond memories of delicious family meals at a grandparent's table; for others, it conjures up images of inedible prepackaged airline meals. We recall ugly headlines announcing embarrassing abuses in a midwestern meat factory; we hear a clarion call for higher standards of ethical treatment of workers and animals. We wonder if keeping the laws of kashrut can draw us closer to God and our Judaism.

The world of kashrut is filled with contradictions and challenges. Each one of us brings to this discussion all of the complexities of our relationships with food, each other, and Judaism. After all, food defines our first relationship with our caregivers when we are children; food defines our view of culture and civilization. Throw in our religion and we create quite a conversation! And yet, the reality is that despite (or perhaps, compelled by) the complexities, many liberal Jews are talking and thinking about kashrut and food.

For too long, Reform Jews have felt alienated from the laws of kashrut. The assumption is, in fact, that Reform Jews do not keep kosher. Richard N. Levy and Marc Gertz's "Is Dietary Practice Now in the Reform Mainstream? A Survey of Attendees at the 2005 Houston Biennial" quickly breaks that stereotype, and Carole Balin illustrates the history of kashrut in the Reform Movement in "Making Every Forkful Count: Reform Jews, Kashrut, and Mindful Eating, 1840–2010." In the past, kashrut, with its all-or-nothing ritual approach, did not seem to fit with Reform Judaism's ideology and worldview. After all, Reform Judaism treasures educated individual choice, modern education and science, and social integration and emphasizes ethics, social action, and social justice. Yet, within the Reform and greater liberal Jewish world, there is growing interest in revisiting traditional rituals, including a strong curiosity about traditional ritual kashrut. This is mixed with our secular culture's growing passion about the numerous, multifaceted issues surrounding our relationship to food and its production. Our Reform community is deeply influenced by secular thinkers like Alice Waters, Michael Pollan, Mark Bittman, and Barbara Kingsolver. These two trends join together in a vibrant, Reform discussion of kashrut.

The Sacred Table: Creating a Jewish Food Ethic, an anthology of essays on Reform dietary practice, seeks to accomplish two goals. The first is to create a rich dialogue about the intersection of Reform Judaism and food while daring to use the term "kashrut." As Richard N. Levy wisely points out in "Kashrut: A New Freedom for Reform Jews":

> Just as we have set forth models of Shabbat observance for our people, so we can create models of dietary practice, and just as they are free to follow our Shabbat examples, reject them, or find models of their own, so, of course, are they free to do the same with kashrut.

We Reform Jews do not shy away from using the term "Shabbat" even though our ritual practices differ greatly from those of halachic Judaism. *The Sacred Table* challenges our Reform community to do the same for kashrut. We can embrace the term "kashrut" as we navigate through our choices, using an authentically Reform approach.

As our community reappropriates the word "kashrut," we will broaden its definition, Reforming it as we have with so many aspects of Judaism. This second goal challenges us to view kashrut not only as a ritual practice, but also as a multifaceted Jewish relationship with food and its production, integrating values such as ethics, community, and spirituality into our dietary practice. Please note that I do not use the term "eco-kashrut" or "ethical kashrut," as I believe that kashrut must be a holistic approach to eating and food production. From a Reform point of view, ritual cannot be orphaned from ethics. (I will address this further in the introduction to part 3, "Environmental Ethics: *Bal Tashchit.*")

Liberal Jews want to shape the discussion about kashrut so that we can consider questions such as the following: Does kashrut represent a facade of religiosity, hiding immorality and abuse, or is it, in its purest form, a summons to raise the ethical standards of food production? How does kashrut enrich spiritual practice by teaching intentionality and gratitude? Can paying attention to our own eating practices raise our awareness of the hungry? Can kashrut inspire us to eat healthfully? Can these laws draw us around the same table, thus creating community? Is keeping kosher all-or-nothing?

As we set out to explore these complexities and challenges, we, in turn, redefine our understanding of the term "kosher." When we broaden the definition of kosher to mean "Jewish sacred eating," we discover that many liberal Jews are already engaged in an exciting process of keeping kosher. As we stretch our personal views of kashrut, we challenge our movement to ask, "What is our Jewish relationship with food?" And in so doing, we discover that Reform Judaism and kashrut go together quite naturally.

Ultimately, *The Sacred Table* celebrates the ideology of educated choice, which is the backbone of the Reform Movement. As Reform Jews explore traditional ritual and laws, we synthesize them with our passion for ethics, social action, and living among neighbors of all backgrounds. Expanding beyond the traditional, narrow definition of ritual kashrut, this book includes topics such as agricultural workers' rights, animal rights, food production, the environment, personal health, the spirituality of eating and fasting, and the challenges of eating together.

The Sacred Table presents voices, opinions, and options as diverse as the Reform Movement itself. For example, Mark Sameth challenges us to rethink meat in "'I'll Have What She's Having': Jewish Ethical Vegetarianism." In contrast to the vegetarian model, Karen R. Perolman's "Meat Minimalism: Were We Meant to Be Ethical Omnivores?" encourages us to think about the role of meat in our diets in a new light. Lest we quickly substitute fish for meat, Joel Mosbacher explores the downfalls of the fishing industry in "Fish: A Complex Issue." Neal Gold ("Let All Who Are Hungry Come and Eat: Food Ethics, *Tzedakah*, and How We Celebrate") asks us to consider the role of excess food consumption and waste in light of hunger issues; William Cutter ("Palates, Pilates, Politics: A Prophetic Vision for Eating") explores similar issues but layers in questions of *sh'mirat haguf* (protecting our health). Michael Namath and Rachel Cohen ("Raising Our Voices for Food Justice") dare our lawmakers to think differently when addressing food production, health, and hunger in America. As exemplified by these chapters, *The Sacred Table* highlights Jewish values with its corresponding vocabulary to create a rich, challenging discussion that focuses on the joy, spirituality, challenges, and controversies of keeping kosher (however the individual Jew defines it).

This book also supplies the basic how-tos of keeping kosher so that each of us can adopt these practices into our lives; it provides guidance on incorporating these choices into our religious practice as an individual, family, or community. These resources will be helpful if we are new to kashrut or if we are teaching or counseling others. Each part of this book defines an important food value through an anchor chapter directly addressing the headline value and through accompanying chapters that flesh out the value; each part ends with a thought piece under the heading "Real Life / Real Food." In this manner, *The*

Sacred Table creates a rich, multifaceted discussion of the possibilities of Reform kashrut.

So, picture a beautiful buffet of choices from which you can shape your personal kashrut. Read, educate yourself, build on those practices that you already follow, and eat well.

Voices: Small Bites

These short statements reveal the passion for Jewish dietary practice that exists in our Reform Jewish community. They provide a taste of what is to be shared in the pages of this volume. May they spur thought and conversation, and whet the appetite for more.

Studying the kashrut laws yielded compelling personal reasons for my decision to keep kosher. Kashrut is a meaningful way to share quality time with God in my personal Temple, my home. Inviting God to my table through the selection, preparation, serving, and blessing of my meals and through my conversations with my table companions makes eating a sacred act, a holy ritual. My table becomes a Holy Altar, connecting me to the ancient Israelites and to Jewish history. Along with prayer, Torah study, and engaging in acts of *g'milut chasadim*, eating provides another cherished opportunity to connect with God daily.

Dr. Dev Smith, Long Valley, NJ

One can be a Reform Jew and accept all of the mitzvot of kashrut. I have always taught this. The key point is that an Orthodox Jew observes these mitzvot because s/he believes that God has commanded him/her to do so. The Reform Jew observes these mitzvot because s/he has chosen to do so.

Rabbi Dan Pernick, Pearl River, NJ

Three years ago, to deepen my connection to Shabbat, I set out on the "Great Challah Experiment." I have baked a different recipe every Shabbat—over 150 recipes so far. Yet, the greatest discovery is that by baking challah weekly, I set aside time to nourish my family and my soul. I have come to enjoy measuring the ingredients, mixing, and kneading in silence. It's my meditation, *bubbe*-style, and it means more to me with each passing week. I connect to generations of mothers in the past and, God willing, a link to the future, too, as my son and daughters bake their own bread and someday bake with their children.

Mindy Knapp, Randolph, NJ

There was a brief time in my life when I ate *t'reif*, rebelling against my family and the kosher household in which I grew up. Since then, I have developed my own version of kashrut that fulfills me both intellectually and Jewishly. By not eating pork or shellfish, I restrict myself from something that at one time I loved to eat. This forces me to exercise control over my impulses and to think about everything I put in my body. That constant self-analysis, to me, is a crucial part of living as a Jew.

Joe Eglash, Tulsa, OK

We are equipped to perform mitzvot when our bodies, minds, and souls are nourished. Human beings crave oxygen, water, sunlight, nutrients, love, community, and inner peace. God has created a world for us with these elements. Healthy air, water, spirituality, relationships, work, exercise, and food are our sustenance. (If we don't satisfy these needs through natural means, we turn to less effective methods.) Nourishing meals are balanced in flavors and nutrients, prepared humanely and in moderate quantity. Like our liberal faith, our diets are dynamic and based on one's unique constitution. As our lives change, so does our need for sustenance. When we feel balanced and nourished, we can then bring meaning and joy to ourselves and others.

Sarah Kroloff Segal, Montclair, NJ

My father, *z"l*, always used to say that seafood is *t'reif*, but pork is anti-Semitic. No Jew was ever tied up and forced to eat lobster thermidor; only pork was used to hurt or taunt us. He recalled that the Maccabees cleansed and rededicated the Temple after the Romans desecrated it with pigs. He never ate pork and none entered our home. In our modern age we choose what to eat, not as a matter of convention, but mostly for reasons of health, taste, and ethics. Perhaps, we should add to that list the voice that inspires us stemming from the history of our people.

Rabbi Morley T. Feinstein, Los Angeles, CA

I'm actually a strict lacto-vegetarian at home, and I also never use sugar or anything unhealthy but non-fat dairy in my own kitchen. I don't even know how to cook meat, as I've eaten always like this as an adult. Yet, like the pick-and-choose Jew I am at heart (as in Jews who keep kosher at home but eat bacon in the streets), I will lapse and eat all kinds of meat and other unhealthy things excluded in my daily life when I eat in restaurants and at friends' homes.

Robert H. Rosenberg, Miami Beach, FL

In 5770, 26,413 sandwiches were made by the volunteers of the Mandy Reichman Feeding Program. Every Tuesday night, the kitchen is home to a joyful assembly line of bread and cold cuts and and cookies and fruit and eager hands. Hours later, a truck carries the lunch bags a few miles away, to a neighborhood in Elizabeth. With this program, Temple Emanu-El honors the memory of a big-hearted young woman who died far too young. And it carries on her good works, recognizing that the hungry are not relegated to far-off places like the Sudan or Somalia, or to the slums of the cities or the hollows of rural poverty; they are our neighbors, and they are our responsibility.

Written by Jerry Schwartz on behalf of Barry and
Meryl Reichman, Westfield, NJ

In Poland, we face many challenges because of the limited availability and exceedingly high prices of kosher food items, particularly meat and any packaged items bearing a *t'udah* (certification) from outside the country. At Beit Warszawa, we have resolved our problem by making our kitchen fish, vegetarian, and dairy only. With respect to cheese, we treat rennet as *d'var chadash* (a new substance). Many in our community follow this pattern in their homes. Many others observe a biblical kashrut, as do I. There is concern over environmental and social justice issues and interest in eco-kashrut.

Rabbi Burt E. Schuman, Warsaw, Poland

Since my ordination, I've served as the *mashgichah* (kashrut supervisor) of an elder-care facility where fewer than half of the residents, and no members of the kitchen staff, are Jewish. I'm constantly amazed and inspired by how willing and eager these staffers are to maintain the rules of kashrut—even though they are not tied to them by religious law, historical memory, or culture. My Christian and Muslim cooks don't view kashrut as a burden; rather, they see it as an interesting culinary challenge to prepare tasty meals for a multicultural clientele within these parameters. I often wish my fellow Jews could approach kashrut with such "fresh" eyes.

Rabbi Ellen Flax , New York, NY

I decided to become a vegetarian well before I knew the word *tzimchonit* (vegetarian, in Hebrew). My mother, who remembered hunger and the lack of meat during the siege on Jerusalem in 1948, agonized about my uncommon choice at first but nevertheless became supportive with time. As a five-year-old, I didn't think in philosophical, theological terms, or halachic terms; I just knew that it is not right to eat meat. My choice led to endless heated discussions with friends at camp and school. Since I became a mother, I have stopped my proselytizing about vegetarianism, but I still hold my position—for me, there is no kosher meat.

Rabbi Dalia Marx, Jerusalem, Israel

I do not, in any form, keep kosher. This is a moral choice based on my understanding of Reform Judaism. From the Torah, I perceive kashrut as a method to separate the Jewish people from social contact with others. I believe in the Reform ideal of being a light among the nations, of the importance of social interaction with those outside my religion. I find other Jewish values that speak to what and how I eat, without having to redefine kashrut. For me this is an ethical Reform position. Therefore, my conviction is marginalized when a Reform event offers only kosher food, in the belief that "anyone can eat kosher."

Rabbi Joel N. Abraham, Fanwood, NJ

Without sun, rain, earth, and seed, which we didn't create, there is no food. Forgetting our dependence on God's contributions, we blithely harm our environment. *Motzi* helps us remember why we should be grateful and reverent to God. Those who live by these mitzvot dine with God: "This is the table, which is before God" (Ezek. 41:22).

Rabbi Allen S. Maller, Culver City, CA

For me, keeping kosher is not a burden but a daily reminder that I am blessed to live as a Jew. It moves some of the seemingly non-Jewish moments of my life into sacred terrain. Many years ago, my wife and I were driving across the country on vacation and spent Friday night in a small New Mexican town far from any Jewish community. As we scanned the menu of this loud Mexican restaurant, we noticed there was only one item that did not have meat or lard in it. As we ordered our meal and shared Shabbat together in this most unusual of places, we felt as intensely Jewish as we have at any other Shabbat meal before or since.

Rabbi Brian Zimmerman, Dallas, TX

I adhere to few biblical commandments—not praying daily, counting the Omer, or observing kashrut. I do, however, draw upon the spirit of halachah in my efforts to eat ethically. A few examples: Beginning in 1973, I boycotted table grapes in support of Cesar Chavez and the United Farm Workers. While visiting the Midwest with a kashrut-observant friend in 2008, I ate vegetarian fare over Agriprocessors' *glatt* kosher meat. And when in Maine, I will skip the lobster—not because it's inherently *t'reif*, but because plunging it alive into boiling water renders it *t'reif* according to my personal ethics.

Jane E. Herman, New York, NY

My grandfather and father were non-kosher butchers. I was nourished on succulent baby back ribs. Today, I no longer eat pork or shellfish, and I don't mix milk and meat, though I don't impose my choices on others. I had attended a retreat featuring eco-kashrut food: vegetarian, free trade, fair trade. My work-study job: placing food meditation cards on the tables. After the retreat, I wanted a practice. I realized that if a food choice wasn't for taste alone (pork ribs taste good) or nutrition (salmon is very healthy), then non-reasoned choices could increase space for meaning, devotion, and God.

Rabbi Owen Gottlieb, Brooklyn, NY

When I started to consider kashrut, I asked everyone I knew who kept kosher why they did so. Most answered, "Because it's tradition." This didn't work for me. The tradition I grew up in placed no value on dietary restrictions; boneless spare ribs were a favorite Shabbat meal. A batch of cookies changed my mind. I realized that my kashrut-observant friends couldn't eat the hamantaschen I'd prepared in my non-kosher kitchen. I began to move toward keeping kosher so that all Jews could eat in my home. This dream may never become a reality:

there are ways I cannot bend and ways other people cannot bend, there are always new restrictions to consider. But whether it's cooking vegetarian, shopping locally, or working around food allergies, my goal is still the same: a table that welcomes all people, a kitchen where I can express my love for friends and family with a home-cooked meal.

Rabbi Leah R. Berkowitz, Durham, NC

People often laugh at our kosher practice.

"It's so hypocritical to only keep kosher at home!"

"What's the point of having plates for take-out *t'reif?*"

But this is what has worked for us. This is, for us, what distinguishes our home as Jewish. This is our way of being conscious of our history, heritage, culture, and community as we make our way through what is otherwise the banality of everyday events. So, no, it's not halachic. No, it's not accessible to the broadest population of Jews. But it is a daily reminder that we are committed to a specific community.

Jenni Person, Miami, FL

My passion for Judaism and my enjoyment of food intersect in many ways, but none better than in my baking thematic challah for our Torah study group at Congregation Sherith Israel in San Francisco. I bake a challah that complements each weekly parashah. For example, when Joseph interprets Pharaoh's dream, I baked seven attractive miniature challot and seven skinny unattractive challot, symbolizing the seven years of feast and seven years of famine. My fellow students enjoy the anticipation of seeing my interpretations, and I am enriched by the extra Torah study needed to find a challah connection!

Stephen H. Olson, San Francisco, CA

When I was diagnosed as being gluten intolerant, friends said, "So the whole year is like Pesach for you." The reality is that yes, it was, except that during Pesach I really couldn't eat anything. The hardest part was the feeling of not participating in the holiday with its traditional foods. Ditto for Shabbat. In the intervening years, I've been able to replicate favorite foods in a gluten-free version. I now look forward to the gluten-free challah I make every Shabbat as well as a plethora of foods throughout our holiday cycles.

Nancy Israel, Dallas, TX

Food is information. Like a computer, the quality of the input determines the results. If I eat junk food, I become someone different than if I were to eat wholesome food. What is true physically is true spiritually. When I am conscious that my food comes from God and that it is part of a holy cycle of life, it shapes me. When I offer thanks for the gifts of food, it shapes me. My personal food choices affect me in spiritual ways, as surely as they influence my health and my shape.

Rabbi Louis Rieser, Derry, NH

While today I am a vegetarian, I stopped eating veal when I was a teenager after learning why the calf meat was so tender. A few years later, I was surprised when I ate at a kosher restaurant and was told the pink meat inside the wonton was not pork, but rather veal. Why is this kosher? Years later, my father and stepmother, helping me plan my wedding, suggested veal as the main course. They didn't understand my strong ethical challenge, which caused a pre-wedding disagreement. No veal was served. And the Viennese dessert table was amazing.

Rabbi Faith Joy Dantowitz, Milburn, NJ

Eggs as metaphor: A friend shared recently that her grandfather "candled eggs" by using candle silhouetting to make sure that the egg has not been fertilized. This inspection is also done by breaking an egg and checking for blood. The humble egg becomes a metaphor for life. Both at Pesach and at times of mourning, eggs symbolize the circular nature and the fragility of *life*. Therefore, using free-range eggs (versus eggs that have been born behind bars) reflects our willingness to look for kinder ways to celebrate life.

Rabbi Judith Edelman-Green, Kfar Saba, Israel

The smell of roasting chicken fills the house each Friday. The aroma brings us back to our shtetl ancestors who honored Shabbat with the best meat they could buy—chicken. Shabbat deserves a wonderful meal. It is a time when we are given a glimpse of the messianic age, which will look, tradition suggests, just like the Garden of Eden. However, in Eden, Adam and Eve lived as vegetarians. Only after they left the Garden did they eat meat. So, the ideal Shabbat meal should be a vegetarian dinner. We should switch the chicken for chickpeas and the brisket for broccoli to gain a true "taste" of the world-to-come.

Rabbi Amy Schwartzman, Falls Church, VA

From an early age we taught our children that keeping kosher is our way to bring God, Judaism, and ethics into our kitchen. The limitations we embraced made our lives more special and sacred. When our daughter developed serious food allergies, our limitations grew. While nuts are not on her allergy list, so many children face this life-threatening allergy that we decided to add that to our list of *t'reif* items. For our family's food choices are no longer only about *k'dushah* (holiness), they are also about *pikuach nefesh* (saving life)—two mitzvot for the price of one.

Kevin Moss, Falls Church, VA

There are many ways to keep kosher. Choosing my personal variant is one way to define "my kind of Jews"—those with which I can share a meal without anyone going out of his way to accommodate the other. It turns out that I rarely find "my kind of Jews" around here—most of those I meet do not keep kosher and the few who do probably doubt my kashrut. As an Israeli living in America, it is easy to forget that I came here to sojourn, not to settle. Keeping kosher is a constant reminder that I am an alien and this is not my place.

Raziel Haimi-Cohen, Westfield, NJ

A home economics major in college, I decided that when I married I would keep a kosher home, because I wanted to have my future children grow up in an environment where they knew they were Jewish long before they started attending Hebrew school. Why keep kosher in the twenty-first century? According to Maimonides, it keeps God in our daily lives. Today, we are no longer segregated for our identity. Yet, perusing packages for a *hechsher*, nonkosher ingredients, or dairy components when making a meat meal reminds me daily that I am a Jew and that God is being sanctified in my home.

Tina Wasserman, Dallas, TX

I grew up in an active Reform household, yet until I was twelve I had no knowledge of kashrut. One week my family went to a friend's house for a Shabbat meal. After a delicious chicken dinner, I asked for a glass of milk. "I'm sorry. No milk," said the hostess. A few moments later I went to the kitchen and happened to notice there was milk in the fridge. I was jubilant—I ran into the dining room, shouting gleefully, "Guess what? There *is* milk after all!" It was an embarrassing way to learn about a central Jewish tradition. As a rabbinic student, I vowed that my students would understand the history, practice, and meaning behind kashrut, whether or not they chose to practice it as individuals.

Rabbi Laurie Katz Braun, New York, NY

My initial reaction to the "Let's keep kosher" suggestion from my partner was that it was a ploy to have more beautiful dishes in the cabinet. Our initial rationale: observe mitzvot and *feel* more Jewish and be able to welcome *all* Jewish friends to dine. Here are the parameters: Organics rule over kosher seals of approval. *T'reif* is ordered in and happens on reusable plasticware. Glass, Pyrex, Corningware, and hardy takeout containers are "*kashered*" in the dishwashing machine without looking back. So, I do feel more Jewish in my kitchen. The uninitiated are intrigued by our loyalty, creativity, and marital agreement in creating a "Reformadox" teaching kitchen. Alas, for our *shomer kashrut* friends, we order in their favored seals of approval!

Chaim Lieberman, RJE, Miami, FL

Growing up as a rabbi's daughter, I was acutely aware of the excitement and heightened tumult as Shabbat approached. We were all attuned to the fact that my father needed to have dinner precisely at a certain hour in order for him to have a few moments to prepare his last-minute thoughts and be at synagogue on time for services. However, it was not until I became a mother myself did I gain a deepened appreciation of the magnitude of my mother's role in making it all happen like clockwork. The table was set with exquisite attention to detail, the meal was always cooked to perfection, and the three children were clean and ready to get to synagogue on time.

Amy Rubin Schottland, South Orange, NJ

God commanded Adam and Eve to be vegetarians. That was what God wanted for our dietary practices. God commanded Noah to eat whatever he wanted, as long as it was dead. That is what humans want for our own dietary practices—unrestrained omnivorism. In ultimate wisdom, God offered a compromise: God commanded Moses concerning prohibited and permitted meats and forbade boiling a kid in its mother's milk. These were developed and evolved by the Rabbis of the Talmud into the dietary laws called kashrut. If we are able to live by this compromise, that is wonderful. If we are able to live closer to what God wants and go vegetarian, even better.

Rabbi David N. Young, based on the teaching
of Bob Sugarman, North Miami Beach, FL

When I set up my own first kitchen with its limited space, I thought long and hard about how keeping kosher could work for me. Avoiding mixing milk and meat was beyond my culinary skills, and stocking two sets of dishes while teaching the revolving door of housemates the complexities of kashrut seemed unlikely. So, I chose the path of most control. I opted to be kosher by buying kosher. Like taking the SATs on Sunday, not Saturday, I felt I was championing the people who didn't have the choice and, in so doing, supporting an industry, a community, a family.

Marci Wiseman, Miami, Florida

My imperfect Reform kashrut: I eat no mammals. It all starts at Genesis 1: the vegan diet is God's ideal. Yet, humans have an insatiable appetite for meat; thus the post-Flood compromise: we may eat animals but must kill them first. In Leviticus, a more restrictive compromise: only certain animals may be eaten. The ideal remains unchanged: lions to lie down with the lambs, not eat them. In this unredeemed world, striving for holiness, neither prepared for a vegan diet nor giving in wholly to meat craving, I pray that my attempt at a dietary mitzvah is pleasing.

Rabbi Barry H. D. Block, San Antonio, Texas

I get up in the morning to children shouting from their cribs, and I don't stop moving and doing and running until eighteen or twenty hours have passed. It is nonstop. I don't have time, for the slow-food movement, for slow-anything. Yet, every night that we eat as a family, we say a blessing. After my husband or I throw dinner together and get the kids' hands washed and sit them down and take a breath, we give thanks. Thanks to God for giving us this food and these bodies, which allow us to eat and taste. Thanks to the people who harvested our plants and fruits. Thanks to the geniuses who invented frozen pizza. And thanks for each other. Our boys chime in with "Amen." And we eat. It's a just moment, but it is filled with holiness, and it changes everything.

Rabbi Annie Belford, Houston, Texas

I am a Reform rabbi. My husband is a recovering Lubavitcher Jew, whose primary attachments to his Orthodox past are observance of Shabbat and kashrut. He will eat out only in kosher or purely vegetarian establishments, while I will eat a vegetarian meal in a non-kosher restaurant. Until we bought a vacation home in the Berkshires, this made vacationing miserable for me. Since we do not generally move in observant circles, this has also made social relationships challenging: not everyone is comfortable with a guest who will only eat celery sticks at the table. Ours is an intermarriage of a different kind.

Rabbi Pamela Wax, North White Plains, NY

One of my secret pleasures is to dine out in fancy restaurants where the wine flows freely and the food melts in your mouth. At these moments, thinking solely with my stomach, I'm reminded of the words of Isaac Luria, "Do not imagine that God wants you to eat for mere pleasure or to fill your belly. No, the purpose is mending. . . . By saying a blessing before you enjoy something, your soul partakes spiritually. This is food for your soul" (a *kavanah* by Isaac Luria, translation by Daniel Matt in *The Essential Kabbalah* [HarperOne, 1996], 149). Isaac Luria teaches that we can mend the cosmos even while eating, by bringing God to our table. By reciting the *Motzi* before the meal, the food that nourishes our body can also be the catalyst to heal our world.

Rabbi Andy Gordon, Scarsdale, NY

Perspective: History and Trends of Jewish Dietary Practices within Reform Judaism

While a book dedicated to Reform kashrut may be ground-breaking, discussions within the Reform Movement concerning kashrut are nothing new. Part 1 explores our Reform history with kashrut and perspectives on the place of kashrut in today's Reform Judaism. The diversity of opinions presented here reflects the strength of the Reform Movement. We foster educated choice and the resulting variety of practice and belief.

Synthesizing Reform Judaism's history with kashrut, Carole B. Balin ("Making Every Forkful Count: Reform Jews, Kashrut, and Mindful Eating, 1840–2010") demonstrates to us that "a survey of culinary history thus provides a window into our fundamental beliefs as Reform Jews." Lance J. Sussman's "The Myth of the *T'reifah* Banquet: American Culinary Culture and the Radicalization of Food Policy in American Reform Judaism" provides an in-depth examination of this iconic moment in Reform memory. Their chapters are complemented by Aaron Gross's "Continuity and Change in Reform Views of Kashrut 1883–2002," in part 4. In 1979 Simeon J. Maslin's *Gates of Mitzvah* opened the world of ritual mitzvot to the Reform Movement. Reprinted from this volume, "Kashrut: A Reform Point of View" provides a timeless overview of kashrut and the reasons why Reform Jews may want to embrace its rituals. Building on this foundation, Rachel S. Mikva ("Adventures in Eating: An Emerging Model for Kashrut") and Richard N. Levy ("Kashrut: A New Freedom for Reform Jews") share their passion and visions for Reform kashrut. Providing a *d'var acher*, a different point of view, Seth M. Limmer ("On Kashrut") offers some surprising suggestions, along with a strong criticism of kashrut. Alan Henkin ("Kashrut and Autonomy") applies Kantian thought to kashrut to create an argument in favor of Reform kashrut. Illustrating the trend toward increased observance of dietary laws among Reform Jews, Richard N. Levy and Marc Gertz share their results of the 2005 Union for Reform Judaism Biennial Survey in the piece "Is Dietary Practice Now in the Reform Mainstream? A Survey of Attendees at the 2005 Houston Biennial." Part 1 ends with a "Real Life / Real Food" vignette shared by Eugene B. Borowitz in his often quoted "A Holy Moment at McDonald's." The scene described exemplifies the balance between the holy and the secular that the Reform Jew seeks.

1

MAKING EVERY FORKFUL COUNT

Reform Jews, Kashrut, and Mindful Eating, 1840–2010

CAROLE B. BALIN

Introduction[1]

Everything about food—how we acquire it, who prepares it, what we consume, and with whom we eat—matters. The particulars of gastronomy reveal a world of behaviors and beliefs that communicates far more than ingredients or nutrition.

Take, for example, the culinary annals of modern Jewish history. In more ways than one, Emancipation hit Western Jewry in the *kishkes* (gut). At least in theory, release from age-old communal strictures freed Jews from dietary restrictions and empowered them to partake freely of formerly forbidden foods. As the stranglehold of rabbinic authority loosened, many Jews turned their palates into laboratories for experimentation, while others sealed their lips against such assimilation. What historian Hasia Diner maintains for American Jewry is equally true for modern Jews in general: reality "shattered the orderliness of Jewish consumption, which [had been] based on a relatively broad consensus over kashrut."[2] As is well-known, except for a minority of traditionalists, Jews slowly left the confines of their kosher kitchens and entered the *t'reif* (unkosher) domains of their gentile neighbors and local eating establishments. In due time, they would even come to stock their own pantries with nonkosher items as their ties to the traditional Jewish world unraveled and they became more engaged with society around them. To this day, a Jew's dietary intake may reveal as much about that person's Jewish identity as his or her relationship to the world at large.

For nearly two centuries, Reform Jews have rejected, adapted, resuscitated, embraced, and even invented Jewish dietary law. Their changing view of kashrut results from an understanding of and belief in the elasticity of Judaism and its traditions, and the inevitable and necessary influence of historical circumstances upon them. A survey of culinary history thus provides a window onto our fundamental beliefs as Reform Jews.

T'reif and the Reform Jew, 1883 and 1976

T'reif plays a pivotal role in the canonized narrative of the Reform Jewish past. Students of Reform Jewish history know well about the shock waves that spread across the lavish banquet hall of the Highland Hotel in Cincinnati on July 11, 1883, when waiters placed the first of a nine-course meal before two hundred honored guests gathered to celebrate the first rabbinical ordination in the United States. "Terrific excitement ensued" and "two rabbis rose from their seats and rushed from the room" to protest the littleneck clams arrayed on their plates.[3] Historians christened the meal the "t'reifah banquet," and at least one scholar has claimed that it led to the "radicalization of food policy in Reform Judaism,"[4] as well as a thunderstorm of protest that may well have catapulted Conservative Judaism to prominence in America.[5] Whether one interprets it as a badge of honor or a scandal of immeasurable ignominy, the banquet has achieved iconic status in the history of Reform Judaism.

This conspicuous consumption of t'reif in 1883 is neither the first nor the last in the annals of Reform Jewish history. Four decades earlier, in 1841, two hundred Jewish men and women of Germany's upper crust gathered in a sumptuous hotel dining room and supped on a feast of crabs, oysters, and a pig's head. The dinner commemorated the twenty-fifth anniversary of the *Freischule*, the free school for impoverished boys established two years prior to the founding of the famed liberal Hamburg Temple in 1818. Not all of the guests ate *t'reif*, and the students themselves consumed a festive meal the following day that adhered to dietary strictures.[6] Yet, for the first time, liberal Jews had exhibited their rejection of fundamental aspects of the dietary laws beyond the privacy of their own homes.[7]

In the twentieth century, too, *t'reif* made a noteworthy comeback at an important gathering of Reform Jewish leaders and other notables. Along with Edward H. Levi—the U.S. attorney general under Ford and the son and grandson of rabbis who had served Reform congregations in Chicago—supporters of HUC-JIR met for a weekend at the culmination of a year of activities designed to celebrate the school's centennial.[8] Festivities were held at the historic landmark Netherland Plaza Hotel in downtown Cincinnati. When its doors opened in 1931, the hotel was said to have "challenged the splendor of Solomon's Temple" with its rare Brazilian rosewood paneling, German nickel-silver lighting fixtures, and soaring ceiling murals in the style of French art deco.[9] On Sunday, March 28, 1976, after awarding an honorary degree to Isaac Mayer Wise's granddaughter Iphigene Ochs Sulzberger, President Alfred Gottschalk hosted a luncheon in her honor. In due time, waiters appeared with the first course, the hotel's signature salad, a mix of vegetables topped with ham. Just as the distinguished historian Jacob Rader Marcus pronounced, "There's *t'reif on* this plate," the waiters snatched up the salads and replaced them with new salads, *sans* pork, within a matter of minutes.

The "*t'reifah* banquet" and the "ham jam" (as I have coined it) are reflective of two distinct periods in American social history. The former occurred at the height of the Gilded Age when the fancy dinner party was a fixture of middle-class life. As the United States developed a modern industrial economy, its per capita income came to lead the world. For better or worse, Reform Judaism, with its ethos of civility and aesthetics, became a natural religious home for Jews seeking to climb the social ladder. By the 1970s when the ham jam occurred, the social order in America had realigned in response to demands by women, minorities, and gays for full legal equality. General concerns about race and ethnicity led Jews to turn inward to discuss what it meant to be Jewish in America. Some lamented a lost Jewish identity, claiming that the process of Americanization had imperiled their heritage and risked the loss of their uniqueness. Reform Jews of the 1970s were largely done proving themselves to gentile society.

In more ways than one, the varying historical contexts of 1883 and 1976 would dictate Reform Jews' responses to the serving of *t'reif* at an official meal of HUC-JIR. In the late nineteenth century, the president of HUC neither condemned nor denounced the food faux pas. Rather than apologizing, Wise went on the offensive against traditionalists who had pointed an accusatory finger at the coordinators of the event. In the pages of his weekly newspaper the *American Israelite*, he lambasted such detractors as persnickety eaters who mistakenly concerned themselves with outdated food regulations. As he admonished his readers:

> No one has appointed those very orthodox critics overseers of the kitchen or taskmaster of the stomach. It is about time to stop that noise over the culinary department of Judaism. The American Hebrew's religion centers not in kitchen and stomach.[10]

Although Wise himself did not consume "pork, ham, ba[con] [and] lobster . . . either [at] home in College Hill or Mound St[reet] Temple," he made an exception for oysters.[11] Moreover, he kept a pair of pigs on his farm to consume leftovers; one he called "Kosher," the other "Treyf."[12] Those particulars notwithstanding, as leader of the Reform Movement, Wise maintained that the dietary laws should not be followed as a matter of religious course. Rather, they should be evaluated on the basis of their rationality, humanitarian concern for animals, and hygienic merit. Biblical rather than Rabbinic sources of legitimation were to be consulted to determine kashrut's appropriateness to modern life.

Within two years of the *t'reifah* banquet, Reform rabbis officially codified this position when they jettisoned specifically "Mosaic and Rabbinical laws as regulate diet" in their legendary Pittsburgh Platform. By rejecting a ritual requirement that set Jews apart from the mainstream, they were keeping with the "spirit of broad humanity of [the] age" and calling on Jews to "extend the hand of fellowship to all who cooperate . . . in the establishment of . . . truth and righteousness among men."[13] Culinary freedom would allow Jews to break bread with their Christian neighbors, a prerequisite to the utopian messianism that had captured their theological imagination. As Peter Knobel put it, the framers of the Pittsburgh Platform "did not desire to escape Judaism but to fulfill it."[14]

At the turn of the nineteenth century and well into the twentieth, temple sisterhoods provided Reform Jewish homemakers with cookbooks full of recipes, both traditional and not. The ingredients reveal how Jewish identity was being newly constructed in the kitchen through patent rejection of dietary laws and enthusiastic acceptance of gastronomic diversity.[15] Take for instance the "Olympia Salad" of Mrs. S. Aronson of Seattle, which appears in the *Famous Cook Book* of the Ladies Auxiliary to Temple de Hirsch:

> On a bed of shredded lettuce, put a slice of tomato, heart of artichoke, put on crab legs, shrimps, or lobster. Over all pour Thousand Island dressing. Garnish with riced egg.[16]

Although it called for crustaceans, Mrs. Aronson's fanciful salad contained no pork products. Some forms of *t'reif* were deemed acceptable; others remained repulsive. While culinary eclecticism was the order of the day, pigs were decidedly beyond the pale.[17] Like their leader Wise, Reform Jews by and large rejected pig on the basis of some remnant of internalized religious taboo. As scholar Barbara Kirshenblatt-Gimblett expressed about this era in American Jewish history, "culturally formed thresholds of disgust" were not crossed.[18]

Even into the late twentieth century, there was a limit as to how far Reform Jews would publicly flaunt their rejection of the dietary laws, as illustrated by events following the ham jam. As documents testify, President Gottshalk would not stomach the mistake made by the Netherland Plaza Hotel at the final dinner commemorating HUC-JIR's centennial. John F. Power, the director of catering, accepted blame for the blunder and sent letters of apology to the president and every guest at the luncheon, stating:

> I am writing this letter to apologize for my negligence for the luncheon on Sunday, March 28, 1976. I accept complete responsibility for the serving of our Netherland salad with ham for your luncheon. . . . I humbly apologize, and realize, that because of my error, you were caused many embarrassing situations.[19]

In response, Gottschalk wrote privately to Power, "Indeed, the luncheon did cause us *serious embarrassment* since the dietary restrictions were very clearly delineated to you beforehand [emphasis added]."[20] According to Vera Sanker, HUC-JIR's national coordinator of the centennial, she had instructed the hotel caterer that the salad should under no circumstances be served with ham. Chicken and cheese toppings were, however, deemed "kosher" and could be served to the assembled guests.[21]

Like Wise, Gottschalk would not abide pork; however, his immediate reaction to the flagrant violation of kashrut of his day was one of sensitivity rather than Wise's dismissive remarks. Gottschalk well knew his constituency, for over the course of the twentieth century, Reform Jews in increasing numbers evinced greater adherence to ritual practice, including adoption of certain aspects of the dietary laws. Whereas surveys of Reform Jewish practice taken in 1928 and 1930 did not even ask about kashrut, presuming it had been rejected altogether, by the mid-twentieth century close to a quarter of surveyed Reform Jews kept kashrut to some degree.[22] In fact, three years after the ham jam, the

Central Conference of American Rabbis published its first full-scale guide to Jewish observance, *Gates of Mitzvah*, which had this to say about the "tradition of kashrut":

> Many Reform Jews observe certain traditional dietary disciplines as a part of their attempt to establish a Jewish home and life style. For some, traditional kashrut will enhance the sanctity of the home and be observed as a mitzvah; for some, a degree of kashrut (e.g., the avoidance of pork products and/or shellfish) may be meaningful; and still others may find nothing of value in kashrut. However, *the fact that kashrut was an essential feature of Jewish life for so many centuries should motivate the Jewish family to study it and to consider whether or not it may enhance the sanctity of their home* [emphasis added].[23]

Remarkably, with these words, Reform rabbis were essentially over-turning their century-long indifference toward longevity in Jewish life as a raison d'être for retaining particular Jewish practices. That is to say, until the 1970s, official documents of the Reform Movement did not consider the tenacity with which Jews of the past clung to kashrut as a factor in determining its relevance for contemporary Reform Jewry. For this generation, however, that fact in and of itself (i.e., "the fact that kashrut was an essential feature of Jewish life for so many centuries") became justification "to study it and to consider [it]."

At the same time, Reform Jews' questions on kashrut submitted to the CCAR Responsa Committee show a serious and growing interest in the topic.[24] Responsum 49, "*Kashrut* in Reform Judaism," a lengthy document issued in the same year as *Gates of Mitzvah* (whose text is actually cited in the responsum), explains why Reform Jews "observe the dietary laws, totally or in part."[25] In responding to the questions, "What is the Reform attitude toward kashrut? What should be done for those who observe kashrut in wartime or during other emergencies?" the Committee acknowledged the movement's rejection of kashrut as official policy but asserted as well that individuals were never prevented "from adopting certain of the dietary laws for a variety of reasons," including

a. add[ing] to their personal expression of Judaism; the daily meals serve as reminders of Jewish ideals; . . . some form of dietary observance may be carried out as a daily reminder of Judaism; the form may be left to the individual or congregation;

b. provid[ing] an additional link with other Jews and a link to history; it enables Jews of all groups to eat in their home or their synagogue;

c. encourag[ing] ethical discipline; a large number of Reform Jews observe a modified form of the dietary laws by abstaining from pork products, animals specifically prohibited, seafood, and the mixing of meat and milk.

This catalog of reasons shows that Reform Jews who observe the dietary laws were teetering toward particularistic aspirations, in contrast to the wholesale universalism of a bygone era.[26] Adopting aspects of kashrut could translate into deeper commitment to the unique traditions of the Jewish past, strengthening group solidarity (i.e., *K'lal Yisrael*), or honing a discipline particular to Jewish forebears. Every forkful, it seems, could be an opportunity to assert one's Jewish identity. Or, as Morris Allen, a rabbi at the forefront of changing how Conservative Jewry thinks about kashrut, quips: we can all "chew by choice."[27]

As a final observation on the topic, the CCAR Responsa Committee quoted verbatim from Simeon Maslin's *Gates of Mitzvah* when it noted that "one might opt to eat only kosher meat or even to adopt some form of vegetarianism so as to avoid the necessity of taking life." These words would prove prescient as the next generation of Reform Jews turned its sights toward creating ever more ways of keeping kosher, including the greening of Jewish dietary practice.[28]

Reform Kashrut, 1980s and Beyond

No longer an oxymoron, "Reform kashrut" has entered the Jewish lexicon, though there is no consensus on what this means exactly. Numbers of Reform Jews have adopted one or more aspects of the traditional Jewish dietary restrictions (e.g., abstaining from eating shellfish, separating milk from meat, eating only kosher meat). Others—in keeping with the Reform Movement's characteristic concentration on ethics—are holding traditional kashrut to moral standards distilled from values intrinsic to Jewish texts but not, in some cases, applied heretofore to diet (e.g., *k'dushah, sh'mirat haguf, bal tashchit, oshek, tzaar baalei chayim*).[29] Finally, a small group of Reform Jews is embracing food practices that have nothing whatsoever to do with traditional notions of kashrut. Rather, their diet is derived from aspirations to create a healthier and more sustainable global community as well as justice in food industry practices—all of which is interpreted as expressing Jewish values (e.g., limiting intake of red meat, becoming a vegan, eating free-range pork raised by workers who are fairly compensated).[30] URJ president Eric Yoffie seems to be taking his cues from the latter.

Yoffie's initiative "*Shulchan Yarok, Shulchan Tzedek* [Green Table, Righteous Table]," which he launched at the 2009 Biennial in Toronto, calls on synagogue leaders to "carefully, thoughtfully, Jewishly" formulate new eating guidelines for their communities.[31] Significantly, Yoffie argues:

> This [initiative] is not about kashrut. . . . We—as a Movement—have put kashrut aside. . . . We do not accept the authority of the kashrut establishment, and its problems are for others to resolve.

Instead, he recommends that Reform Jews adopt "our own definition of what is proper and fit to eat." According to Yoffie, in contrast to a century ago, his constituency understands that "Jewish eating has a profoundly ethical dimension" and that "God cares what [they] eat, and that eating can be an entrance to holiness."

Yoffie is correct. Reform Jews today are expanding the definition of kosher beyond kashrut to encompass all food-related activities undertaken for religious reasons. In so doing, they are taking back the hold on Jewish tradition(s) otherwise abdicated to halachic Jews. At the same time, they are raising all sorts of exciting possibilities for reaching the goal articulated in the Pittsburgh Platform of "extending a hand to all who cooperate . . . in the establishment of . . . truth and righteousness among [humankind]."

Thus, this culinary history of Reform Judaism comes to a close with a description of a weekly meal served in Baltimore, which shows how one segment among many North American Reform Jews is practicing the very best of Reform kashrut.

Every Thursday since 2008, a long line of hungry people leads to the door of St. Gregory the Great, a local Catholic parish in Baltimore founded in 1884. They wait for lunch at this African American church known for its vibrant liturgy, gospel choir, and weekly soup kitchen. The produce served to the guests is not grown at a farm but at *Gan Chiae* (Garden of Life), which is located on the grounds of Temple Oheb Shalom, a Reform congregation whose members engage in planting and harvesting its community garden. This project yields not only four thousand pounds of fresh produce per year, but also meaningful relationships between local Christians and Jews, who understand perfectly what kosher, in all its dimensions, can mean.[32]

NOTES

1. I wish to acknowledge Kevin Proffitt and Camille Servizzi of the American Jewish Archives for their generous help in securing relevant documents, as well as Tina Weiss of the library of HUC-JIR, NY, for her kind assistance. I'm grateful to Karen Perolman and Ariana Silverman for inspiring me to consider alternative ways of keeping kosher.

2. Hasia Diner, *Hungering for America: Italian, Irish, and Jewish Foodways in the Age of Migration* (Cambridge, MA: Harvard University Press, 2001), 178.

3. David Philipson, *My Life as an American Jew* (Cincinnati: J.G. Kidd & Son, 1941), 23. Philipson described the first course as shrimp, but extant menus show it was littleneck clams. See the full menu of the *t'reifah* banquet in Ronald Isaacs and Kerry Olitzky, eds., *Critical Documents of Jewish History: A Sourcebook* (Northvale, NJ: Jason Aronson, 1995), 60–61.

4. See Lance J. Sussman's excellent analysis of the historical implications of the *t'reifah* banquet, "The Myth of the Trefa Banquet: American Culinary Culture and

the Radicalization of Food Policy in American Reform Judaism," *AJA Journal* 57, no. 1–2 (2005): 29–52.

5. Joan Nathan, "A Social History of Jewish Food in America," and Jenna Weissman Joselit, "Food Fight: The Americanization of Kashrut in Twentieth-Century America," in *Food and Judaism*, Studies in Jewish Civilization, vol. 15, ed. Leonard J. Greenspoon, Ronald A. Simkins, and Gerald Shapiro (Omaha, NE: Creighton University Press, 2005); and John J. Appel, "The Trefa Banquet," *Commentary* 41, no. 2 (February 1966): 75–78.

6. Michael A. Meyer, *A Response to Modernity* (Detroit: Wayne State University Press, 1988), 114, 421n51.

7. For more on early German Reformers' attitudes toward kashrut, in addition to Meyer, see "Resolutions Passed at the Third Conference of German Rabbis held at Breslau from July 13 to July 24, 1846," *CCAR Yearbook*, 1890–91, p. 99; Leopold Stein, #12-15,"*Torat Hayim*," and "Dietary Laws," in *The Rise of Reform Judaism*, ed. W. Gunther Plaut (New York: CCAR Press, 1963), 261–62 and 212ff.

8. Vera Sanker (national coordinator of the centennial celebration), "Recollections from the HUC Centennial," privately transmitted to the author, June 2010.

9. http://www.associatedcontent.com/article/386508/haunted_hotel_hilton_cincinnati_ohio.html?cat=37; http://www.ashe2010.org/HCNP%20Walking%20Tour%20History.pdf. Alas, by 1976, the art deco décor had largely been covered over with vinyl wall panels, plywood, and utilitarian carpet. The hotel was renovated and brought back to its original splendor in 1981.

10. *American Israelite*, August 3, 1883.

11. Correspondence between Jacob Rader Marcus and Wise's daughter, Mrs. Albert J. May, February 16, 1966, American Jewish Archives.

12. The information about oysters and the anecdote about the pigs appear in "The First Ordination and the Terefa Banquet," *AJA Journal* 26, no. 2 (November 1974): 128.

13. All quotations are excerpted from the Pittsburgh Platform (1885).

14. For a brief historical survey of Reform Judaism's attitude toward kashrut, see Peter S. Knobel, "Reform Judaism and Kashrut," *Judaism* 39, no. 4 (1990): 488–93.

15. See Barbara Kirshenblatt-Gimblett, "The Moral Sublime: The Temple Emanuel Fair and Its Cookbook, Denver, 1888," in *Recipes for Reading: The Community Cookbook and Its Stories*, ed. Anne L. Bower (Amherst: University of Massachusetts Press, 1997), 136–59, and "Kitchen Judaism," in *Getting Comfortable in New York: The American Jewish Home, 1880–1950*, ed. Susan L. Braunstein and Jenna Weissman Joselit (New York: The Jewish Museum, 1990), 77–105; Ruth Ann Abusch-Magder, "Kashrut: The Possibility and Limits of Women's Domestic Power," in *Food and Judaism*, 169–92; and correspondence between Elizabeth S. Plaut and Jacob Rader Marcus concerning the influence of the writer's aunt, Fanny Greenbaum Schoenfeld, on the famed *The Settlement Cookbook*, October 13, 1977, American Jewish Archives.

16. *Famous Cook Book* by the Ladies Auxiliary to Temple de Hirsch (Seattle, 1925), at "Feeding America: The Historic American Cookbook Project," Michigan State University, http://digital.lib.msu.edu/projects/cookbooks/.

17. During the period, pork was viewed as unhygienic, difficult to digest, and unhealthy. See Kirshenblatt-Gimblett, "Kitchen Judaism," 103n18.

18. Ibid., 80.

19. John F. Power to Alfred Gottschalk, March 30, 1976, Alfred Gottschalk Correspondence, American Jewish Archives.

20. Alfred Gottschalk to John F. Power, April 7, 1976, Alfred Gottschalk Correspondence, American Jewish Archives.

21. Sanker, "Recollections from the HUC Centennial."

22. Meyer, *Response to Modernity*, 322, 375.

23. Simeon J. Maslin, ed., *Gates of Mitzvah: A Guide to the Jewish Life Cycle* (New-York: CCAR Press, 1979), 40.

24. According to Mark Washofsky, chair of the CCAR Responsa Committee, there is only a handful of responsa on this subject, as verified by the index of Reform Responsa on the CCAR website, which lists only four. One deals with consuming fish in the shape of shrimp! (E-mail correspondence with Washofsky, June 17, 2010.)

25. See Responsa 49, "*Kashrut* in Reform Judaism," in *American Reform Responsa* (New York: CCAR Press, 1983), 128 and "Kashrut: A Reform Point of View," in *Gates of Mitzvah*, 130–33. See Chapter 2, this volume.

26. Aaron Gross emphasizes this point in "Continuity and Change in Reform Views of Kashrut 1883–2002: From the *Treifah* Banquet to Eco-Kashrut," *CCAR Journal*, Winter 2004, 6–28. See Chapter 20, this volume.

27. Rachel Barenblat, "Rethinking Kashrut: An Interview with Rabbi Morris Allen," *Zeek*, November 2007, http://www.zeek.net/711kashrut/.

28. Maslin et al add that some may avoid certain foods or limit their appetite because of the growing scarcity of foods in parts of the world (*Gates of Mitzvah*, 132).

29. Ariana Silverman calls this "values based decision making" in "Green Table, Just Table and Ethical Eating in the Reform Movement," rabbinical thesis, HUC-JIR, 2010. See her appendix for a thought-provoking approach to making food choices.

30. See Karen R. Perolman's contribution to this volume (chap. 22), along with her "Beyond Flesh and Blood: Jewish Law and Ethics of Meat Consumption," rabbinical thesis, HUC-JIR, 2010.

31. See the full text of Eric Yoffie's Shabbat morning sermon delivered at Biennial 2009 at http://blogs.rj.org/reform/2009/11/president-yoffies-shabbat-serm.html.

32. For information on this joint venture, see Jennifer Williams, "City's St. Gregory Begins 'A New Day,'" *The Catholic Review*, December 17, 2009, 10, at www.catholicreview.org; and Becca Fuchs, "Gan Chiae Community Garden Temple," *Tzedek v'shalom, The Justice and Peace Newsletter of the Commission on Social Action of Reform Judaism*, Summer 2005, 4, at http://archive.urj.net/_kd/Items/actions.cfm?action=Show&item_id=7772&destination=ShowItem.

2

THE MYTH OF THE T'REIFAH BANQUET

American Culinary Culture and the Radicalization of Food Policy in American Reform Judaism[*]

LANCE J. SUSSMAN

O n July 11, 1883, one of the great landmark events in the history of Judaism in the United States took place at Cincinnati's Highland House overlooking the Ohio River.[1] The "t'reifah banquet" or "Highland House affair" is, perhaps, Reform Judaism's most widely known faux pas but also one of its least-studied occurrences.[2] Often invoked against classical Reform Judaism both from within and from outside the Reform Movement, the t'reifah banquet can also be understood both as a cautionary tale and an object lesson for Judaism's most liberal religious movement.[3] By exploring the t'reifah banquet more thoroughly, placing it into its historical context, and reexamining the chain of events that followed it, we can also learn a great deal about Judaism in America, then and now.[4]

Viewed from the perspective of its own time, the well-known Cincinnati repast of July 1883 was closely patterned after the grand banquet style of American culinary culture in an age of excess. Within the

Adapted with permission from Lance J. Sussman, "The Myth of the Trefa Banquet: American Culinary Culture and the Radicalization of Food Policy in American Reform Judaism," *The American Jewish Archives Journal*, vol. 57, 29–52.

continuum of Reform Jewish history, the *t'reifah* banquet's pork-free menu reflected a broader culinary pattern of select kashrut—that is, Jewish religious dietary pratice—among nineteenth-century American Jews. It also represented a midpoint between the general compliance with traditional kashrut at public events that characterized American Reform Judaism until the 1870s and a radical break with kashrut that increasingly characterized mainstream Reform beginning in the early 1880s. The radicalization of Reform food policy was occasioned by general trends in American culinary culture, upward socioeconomic mobility among American Reform Jews, and the influence of religious modernism on the Reform Movement. Remarkably, Reform food policy largely remained radicalized until the end of the twentieth century when, for the first time in more than a century, the possibility of returning to select traditional dietary practices was brought up for serious discussion and review.

As is well known, the radicalization of Reform food policy in the 1880s also served as an accelerant in the formation of the nascent Conservative Movement. At the same time, kashrut issues among newly arrived East European Jews resulted in their establishing numerous social service institutions to regulate kashrut. Ironically and sadly, a celebration in honor of the first ordination class of the Hebrew Union College (HUC), which was supposed to signal a new era of intrafaith cooperation among American Jews, instead proved to be a call to arms and contributed to the permanent factionalization of American Jewish religious life.

Historiography: The Myth of the *T'reifah* Banquet

For many years following the Highland House affair, the memory of the *t'reifah* banquet apparently remained alive at the grassroots level but did not attract scholarly attention. In his 1941 autobiography, *My Life as an American Jew*, David Philipson, a member of the first HUC ordination class and an eyewitness to the banquet, published an account of the dinner that was replete with misinformation and strong personal opinion. However, Philipson's "memory" of the dinner became the codified text on what had occurred nearly sixty years earlier. In Philipson's account, "terrific excitement ensued when two rabbis rose from their seats and rushed from the room. Shrimp had been placed before them as the opening course of the elaborate menu."[5] In fact, contemporaneous reports of the dinner do not fully substantiate that the dinner had been dramatically disrupted. For sure, shrimp was not served as the first course; rather, it was littleneck clams!

Philipson also appended a historical thesis of his own. "This incident," he opined, "furnished the opening to the movement that culminated in the establishment of a rabbinical seminary of a Conservative birth."[6] While perhaps slightly overstated, Philipson's observation helped nurture a rich historiographical tradition in American Jewish history that, in particular, looked at the founding of the first Jewish Theological Seminary (JTS) in New York and the rise of the largest Jewish denomination in the United States for most of the twentieth century.

While Philipson's facts were slightly revised by memory and, perhaps, a little embellished, his thesis concerning the place of the *t'reifah* banquet in American Jewish history eventually attracted serious scholarly attention. In 1966, Professor John J. Appel published a historical analysis of the *t'reifah* banquet in *Commentary* magazine. Appel concluded that the inclusion of shrimp, crab, and clams on the menu of the *t'reifah* banquet was not a caterer's error but reflected the "ambivalent, sometimes contradictory attitude" of Rabbi Isaac Mayer Wise toward kashrut and, more significantly, "was deliberately arranged by some Cincinnati businessmen." In fact, the determination of the final menu was probably more benign and lacked any intention to antagonize the guests of HUC and the Union of American Hebrew Congregations (UAHC), whose tenth anniversary was combined purposefully with the college's first ordination service. Like Philipson, Appel also argued that the *t'reifah* banquet played a role in the series of events that ultimately led to the formation of the Conservative movement in American Judaism.[7]

Appel's investigative work and brief reflections on the *t'reifah* banquet, now nearly forty years old, serve as the logical point of departure for an expanded discussion of the banquet. While Appel succeeded in doing much of the historical spade work on the events of July 11, 1883, and the subsequent fallout in the national Jewish community, he did not fully address the wider context in which the *t'reifah* banquet took place. A review of the relevant primary literature clearly demonstrates that the menu was typical for its time and place with respect to general culture of American and American Jewish banquets of the 1880s. Moreover, Appel did not address the significant "pork-free" aspect of the dinner and its contemporaneous medical justification, which was also applied to reevaluate the "fitness" of oysters for Jewish consumption.

With respect to the denominational consequences of the dinner, again, Appel's research was narrow in its scope. The reaction of the traditionalists to the *t'reifah* banquet was not only confined to the founding of the first JTS and the subsequent emergence of a Conservative Movement but also involved a wider splintering of American Judaism into three principal groupings early in the twentieth century. Indeed, heightened concern about kashrut among East European Jews in America early in the 1880s might explain the heated reaction of several traditional East Coast Jewish journalists. Ironically, the *t'reifah* banquet was also significant within the history of the Reform Movement, whose views of the traditional dietary laws were in tremendous flux in 1883. As will be seen, the Cincinnati dinner was also part of a larger radicalizing trend that was to reposition the Reform Movement as a whole on the issue of kashrut.

The Highland House Affair

The basic facts surrounding the *t'reifah* banquet are generally not well known and have remained embedded in the primary literature of the Highland House affair. Three groups within the American Jewish community converged in Cincinnati in July 1883 for a series of meetings and celebrations. As stated, HUC's first ordination service was combined with the UAHC's tenth anniversary; Cincinnati was also host to a meeting of the Rabbinical Literary Association, a forerunner of the Central Conference of American Rabbis (CCAR).[8] The triple linkage guaranteed excellent representation from many of the most elite circles in American Jewish life during the Gilded Age.

HUC had been established in 1875 by Wise with the help of the UAHC. It was representative of a new type of rabbinical school pioneered earlier in the nineteenth century in Italy and Germany. Several attempts at opening rabbinical schools, or at least preparatory schools, had already failed in the United States by the time Wise founded HUC (although Maimonides College, established in Philadelphia in 1867 by Isaac Leeser, had ordained a class of four rabbis before closing in 1869). Wise was determined not only to keep his school open but to develop it into an important, respectable institution. To its president, commencement exercises for the first class at HUC were nothing less than a personal victory and the fulfillment of a lifelong dream.[9]

Wise, born in Steingrub, Bohemia, in 1819, had arrived in the United States in 1846. Although he had a limited Jewish education, he quickly emerged as a leading and highly controversial Jewish voice in America. After serving two pulpits in Albany, New York, he settled in Cincinnati in 1854, where he launched both an English- and German-language Jewish newspaper, the *Israelite* and *Die Deborah*, and published his own prayer book, *Minhag America*. He believed that he had the capacity to articulate a Judaism that would unify the vast majority of American Jews under a single organizational umbrella. After a number of false starts and seemingly endless disputes within the national Jewish community, he finally helped launch the UAHC in 1873 and HUC in 1875. Now, eight years after the founding of HUC, he was about to witness and participate in the culmination of years of hard work in America.[10]

At 2:30 in the afternoon of July 11, all three groups converged at the Plum Street Temple in downtown Cincinnati for commencement exercises for the college. The Moorish synagogue's altar was lavishly adorned with flowers. In addition to a number of speeches by rabbis, including both traditionalists like Benjamin Szold and radicals like Kaufman Kohler, lay leaders of HUC and the UAHC also were invited to speak. A choir made up of five women and three men offered "excellent music." Two students, representing their class of four, spoke as well. "At the conclusion," the July 12, 1883 edition of the *Cincinnati Enquirer* reports, "Dr. Wise pronounced them duly ordained rabbis."[11]

At the request of a special ad hoc committee headed by Julius Freiberg (1823–1905) representing Cincinnati's leading Jewish families, some 215 guests were invited to continue the celebration of the first class of ordainees at a grand banquet at the Highland House, a restaurant and resort on Cincinnati's Mt. Adams. Freiberg, a wealthy businessman who had founded the distilling firm of Freiberg and Workum that introduced bourbon whiskey to the world, was active in a broad range of civic and Jewish organizations, including Cincinnati's Chamber of Commerce, B'nai B'rith, the Jewish Hospital of Cincinnati, the UAHC (president, 1889–1903), and HUC.[12]

Arrangements were made to transport the guests on the Eden Park streetcars from Fifth and Walnut in downtown Cincinnati to the Highland House. A dinner orchestra and menu greeted the two hundred guests who rode cable cars to the top of Mt. Adams. A beautiful printed menu adorned with a colored feather informed the guests, including a number of Christian clergy and professors from the University of Cincinnati, that an elegant French cuisine dinner composed of nine courses and five alcoholic drinks would be served.

The caterer for the evening was well known in the Cincinnati Jewish community. Gustave Lindeman (d. 1928) was the food manager of the Jewish Allemenia Club in Cincinnati and, subsequently, a swanky non-Jewish club in Dayton after a flood destroyed a restaurant he operated in the Queen City. Lindeman, who lived most of his life in Dayton, viewed himself as "just Jewish" and steered clear of denominational labels. He married Henrietta Oaks on May 10, 1868. Rabbi Wise officiated.[13]

Nearly a hundred years after the *t'reifah* banquet took place, a granddaughter of Gustave Lindeman, Edith Lindeman Calisch of

Richmond, Virginia, maintained in a private correspondence that "Gus Lindeman evidently was given carte blanche when it came to the menu for the banquet and this menu was accepted by Rabbi Wise and members of the committee." In her unverified apologium, Calisch added that "my grandfather, though Jewish, had no knowledge of whom the guests were to be and had merely followed instructions to provide 'an elegant and sumptuous meal.'"[14]

When first asked for an explanation as to who decided on the menu for the evening, a defensive Wise wrote in his *Israelite* on August 3, 1883, that "said chief cook, himself a Jew wool-dyed, was to place before the guests a kosher meal." "So it was understood," the president of HUC continued, "in Cincinnati all along, and we do not know why he diversified his menu with multipeds and bivalves."[15] Two weeks later, in his German-language *Die Deborah*, where Wise generally disclosed his own viewpoint more fully, the bilingual editor admitted that "the Cincinnati Banquet Committee allowed a few dishes to be served which are forbidden according to Jewish ritual law."[16] Subsequently, however, when pushed to explain the actions of the committee, Wise went on the offensive and further embroiled himself in controversy.

By any standard, the party Lindeman provided HUC and UAHC on July 11, 1883, was lavish, even in an age of excess. For sure, the dinner was extremely costly. Some mistakes in the French spelling on the menu and the inclusion of cheese at the end of the menu suggests that the hosts and their food provider were not fully tutored in fine cuisine and were stretching to impress their East Coast guests. The celebration, including its food, decorations, music, and toasts, reflected the excessive banquet culture of its era and is part of a larger historical continuum of banquets, from the dining and drinking excesses of the biblical King Ahasuerus to contemporary American bar and bat mitzvah receptions and Israeli wedding receptions.[17]

The *Cincinnati Enquirer* covered the event in great detail and called the banquet a "Jewish Jollification." According to the *Enquirer*, "The banquet at the Highland House was the most brilliant event of the session of the council. [T]he arrangements were complete in every detail, providing every possible comfort for the large gathering of ladies and gentlemen."[18] The complete menu was also reported in the daily paper as a seemingly noncontroversial matter of public record.

A number of original texts of the menu have survived over the years and are in collections of the American Jewish Archives in Cincinnati. The first course was littleneck clams and a sherry followed by a consommé and Sauternes, a Bordeaux wine. The third course was large and included beef tenderloins with mushrooms, soft-shell crabs, a shrimp salad, potatoes in lobster bisque sauce, and another selection of Bordeaux wine. The entrée was sweetbreads accompanied with peas. The fifth course featured frog legs in cream sauce, breaded chicken and asparagus, followed by pigeon and squab embedded in pastry, salads, and G. H. Mumm extra-dry champagne. Of course, there were plenty of desserts, including ice cream and assorted cakes. Indeed, almost every violation of kashrut was in evidence—seafood, *t'reif* meat, mixing milk and meat—with the one exception of pork.[19] It is very possible that the sponsors of the dinner sincerely believed, from the perspective of "moderate Reform," that this one exception rendered the banquet religiously acceptable to Jewish traditionalists at the repast, particularly in a city that sported the nickname "Porkopolis." They could not have been more wrong.

Unlike the non-Jewish reporter at the *Enquirer*, an anonymous Jewish reporter filed a story with the *New York Herald* strongly professing that *not* everyone was impressed with the UAHC convention or comfortable with the menu. Probably written by a member of the distinguished Mendes family, the New York–based story began by stating that "a candid review of the work [of the Cincinnati Council] does not call forth special praise." It ended with a brief comment that "a painful episode was the banquet, on the menu of which, were dishes forbidden by Jewish law. Yet rabbis and laymen assembled for Jewish interests, instead of rising in a body and leaving the hall, sat down and participated."[20]

Five days later, on July 27, an article appeared in New York's *Jewish Messenger*. Twenty-two-year-old Henrietta Szold, who had accompanied her father, Rabbi Benjamin Szold, to the Cincinnati convocation, had served as an anonymous correspondent for the paper. Her numerous abilities were recognized by the paper's editor, who offered her a column under a nom de plume, Shulamith.[21] As Shulamith, Szold wrote on a broad range of contemporary topics, particularly anti-Semitism and her experiences with the rapidly expanding East European immigrant community in Baltimore, where she lived.[22] "I eat, drink and sleep Russians," she once told her sister, Rachel.[23] Personally anchored in and respectful of the Jewish tradition and mindful of her journalistic responsibilities, Szold was stunned by the fare served at the Highland House, which stood in stark contrast to her own daily experience and what she observed in her home city.

"I would be outraging my own feelings were I to omit recording the indignation which was felt by a surprisingly small minority at the manner in which the banquet was served," Szold wrote. "There was no regard paid to our dietary laws," she continued, "and consequently two rabbis left the table without having touched the dishes, and I am happy to state that I know of at least three more who ate nothing and were indignant but signified their disapproval in a less demonstrative manner."[24]

On the other hand, the mere presence of Szold and other women at the banquet was somewhat revolutionary in and of itself. According to food historian John F. Mariani, "[W]omen were not admitted to all dining rooms, and until the 1870s separate rooms were provided for them to take their meals at eastern hotels."[25] Mixed seating was first introduced to the American Reform synagogue in 1851 in Albany, New York, and remains a significant issue in modern Judaism in the United States and globally.[26]

Word of the *t'reifah* banquet spread quickly throughout the Jewish press, with East Coast critics of Wise pressing the attack, demanding both an explanation and an apology. Wise, who in his own publications depicted the banquet along the same positive lines as suggested by the *Cincinnati Enquirer*, was soon placed on the defensive. However, instead of apologizing, Wise stonewalled and then retaliated with charges of hypocrisy, pointing to the dismissal of several leading Orthodox rabbis in the United States and Europe on the grounds that they had eaten forbidden foods.[27] Wise also offered arguments defending the inclusion of seafood on the menu and, at one point in the discussion, even referred to oysters as "ocean vegetables."[28]

A number of Wise's loyal readers sent letters of support to his publications and labeled his critics "ignorant fanatics."[29] Wise's "new Judaism," a Chicago correspondent wrote, "has a right to assert itself and in the very publicity of such occasions, we want to show our faces."[30] A rabbi from Pittsburgh wrote that "[i]f Wise's critics could see the hypocritical, self-indulgent though secret violations of kashrut by the European rabbinate, they would stop complaining about Rabbi Wise's attitude."[31] A Denver-based pro-Wise rabbi remarked that the Cincinnati dinner was the proper occasion to relegate "kitchen Judaism to the antique cabinet where it belongs."[32]

The charge of "kitchen Judaism" was not unusual at that time for radical reformers to employ against their opponents in the Jewish community. Wise himself had written as early as 1865 that he didn't "worry about the kitchen."[33] Later, in 1893, he attacked Orthodox Jews in England for their "kitchen and stomach" religion.[34] Although only speculation, it is possible that "kitchen Judaism" is not only a pejorative term for an unthinking folk religion but is inherently misogynistic as well.[35] Banquets and the principles of "the new Judaism" were the work of men. Modern women, though tempted by culture and its culinary delights, were still tethered to the kitchen in the eyes of Wise and his so-called progressive supporters.

Meanwhile, the board of Rodeph Sholom Congregation in Philadelphia, led by its scholarly anti-Wise rabbi, Marcus Jastrow, voted to censure Wise in April 1884, accusing him of undignified behavior and questioning his academic credentials.[36] Subsequently, the UAHC appointed a special committee of five distinguished leaders to look into the matter. Not surprisingly, they acquitted Wise of all charges. The traditional Jewish press in the East, led by the Mendes family and Phillip Cowen (1853–1943), founder and publisher of the *American*

Hebrew, immediately protested that the UAHC's findings were a white-wash. Facetiously, Cowan remarked that not only did Wise not know the laws of kashrut, but he was equally unfamiliar with the American practice "of eating oysters only in months with an 'R' in them."[37] Wise, of course, claimed that the crusade against him had ended with his complete exoneration.[38]

Curiously, the continued controversy had little effect on the size and composition of the UAHC, which actually grew from 99 congregations in 1883 to 102 in 1884 before dropping to 98 in 1885. By contrast, the affair had a devastating but not fatal effect on HUC. In 1884, the year after the Highland House debacle, five students were ordained, including Ludwig Grossman, Max Heller, Isaac Rubenstein, Joseph Silverman, and Joseph Stolz. However, no one was ordained in 1886 and only one in 1887. Wise himself blamed the drop in the graduation rate to the controversy that lingered for several years after the great Highland House faux pas.[39]

Contextualizing the *T'reifah* Banquet

In its own controversial and unintended way, the Highland House affair actually confirmed the centrality of food practices in traditional Jewish life, a social/historical dimension of the Jewish experience increasingly interesting to scholars of ancient Israel and Rabbinic Judaism. Viewed broadly, kashrut is part of an essentially universal phenomenon in religious life in which food is imbued with extraordinary symbolic and social value. "Food in religious life," writes James E. Latham, "is a subject of immense proportions."[40] Conversely, abrogating religiously sanctioned food customs is equally laden with value for rebels, reformers, and schismatics who not only violate old norms but may seek to superimpose new symbolic foods of their own.

In his unpublished article on the *t'reifah* banquet, Appel astutely compared it to "a gastronomic incident which inaugurated the Swiss Protestant Reformation in 1522."[41] Ulrich Zwingli (1484–1531), a dissident priest, publicly defended the eating of meat during Lent that year. Although Zwingli himself followed traditional Catholic culinary practice in preparation for Easter, he defended the right of others to break with church tradition, especially when the reforms did not contradict scripture. Conflict with the Catholic Church quickly escalated, and in response, Zwingli wrote his first major reformatory treatise, *Archeteles*, questioning the whole ceremonial structure of the Roman Church.

In comparing the two *"t'reifah* banquets," Catholic and Jewish, it is interesting to note that both Wise and Zwingli were not themselves thoroughly radicalized in their eating habits. Moreover, the Swiss controversy ultimately resulted in a schism in the Swiss Church, a process that Zwingli, much like Martin Luther, led.[42] In the case of Reform Judaism, it was the increasingly attenuated ties of ethnicity and family as well as the external realities of anti-Semitism that prevented a true schism from occurring within the nineteenth-century Jewish community.

The enormous symbolic value ascribed to food in religious life certainly applies to Jewish tradition, stretching all the way back to the earliest days of ancient Israel. A contemporary Israeli archeologist, Israel Finkelstein, has even come to the conclusion based on his own extensive field work that "half a millennium *before* the composition of the biblical text, with its detailed laws and dietary regulations, the Israelites chose, for reasons that are not entirely clear, not to eat pork. Monotheism and the traditions of the Exodus and covenant apparently come much later."[43] Similarly, contemporary anthropologists including Mary Douglas and Jean Soler, who offer structuralist approaches to the study of food norms in ancient Israel, as well as Marvin Harris, who follows an ecological approach, all place dietary laws at the center of the Israelite religious experience.[44] Samuel Krauss and Max Grunwald, both of Vienna, researched and published pioneering critical works in the early decades of the twentieth century on *"Juedischen Volkskueche,"* documenting the importance of the culinary in traditional postbiblical Jewish life.[45] More recently, Barbara Kirshenblatt-Gimblett has written a number of monographs on Jewish cooking in the United States and Canada; and English scholar John Cooper published a book-length study in 1993 titled *Eat and Be Satisfied: A Social History of Jewish Food*, which offers a comprehensive look at Jewish food customs as well as the halachah of kashrut.[46]

By contrast, the larger history of the food culture of American Jews is still largely unknown. Although Jacob R. Marcus, doyen of the study of the American Jew, characterized the religion of early American Jews as an "orthodoxy of salutary neglect," it is abundantly clear that kashrut was never entirely absent among American Jews and, as the case of the *t'reifah* banquet demonstrates, was often at the epicenter of their religious life. By the middle decades of the nineteenth century, at least three distinct positions vis-à-vis the dietary laws had developed among American Jews: ritually observant, pork-free, and nonobservant.[47] For the most part, however, serving kosher food at public Jewish occasions and in Jewish communal institutions through the Civil War and Reconstruction was the norm. It was not until the early 1880s that the radicalized nonkosher position fully rooted in public Judaism in the United States.

Keeping kosher in America in the middle decades of the nineteenth century was problematic at best. Two major issues, *sh'chitah* (ritual kosher slaughter) and the production of Passover matzah, faced the Jewish community, which grew rapidly from a few thousand individuals in 1820 to 150,000 people on the eve of the American Civil War. The responsibility for both kosher meat and matzah initially belonged primarily to individual synagogues. However, the American principle of the separation of church and state meant that no outside regulatory power was available to help enforce standards, and the Jewish community itself, particularly in the larger cities, was highly resistant to creating pan-communal structures to supervise kashrut. The widespread employment of Judaically unknowledgeable gentile assistants to the Jewish butchers further complicated the issue of obtaining legitimately kosher meat. In New York during the 1850s, independent unions of kosher butchers and matzah bakers were formed, reflective of the rise of independent kosher food operators in the community. With an increase in the rate of Jewish immigration toward the end of the nineteenth century, the problems of the American kosher food industry became even more acute.[48]

A survey of food policies of Jewish hospitals in the United States prior to the Civil War reveals that keeping kosher was the norm. An advertisement for a ball to benefit Mt. Sinai Hospital in New York in 1852 assured prospective patrons that the event would be kosher.[49] Similarly, New Orleans's new Jewish hospital announced in 1855 that it would provide its patients with kosher food,[50] as did Philadelphia's Jewish Hospital nine years later.[51]

On the other hand, a large number of American Jews in their private lives practiced a selective kashrut that by its very nature was more subjective and uneven than systematic in actual practice. The debate over selective kashrut centered on two issues: pork and oysters. While most American Jews seemed to refrain from eating pork, it was a different story with seafood. A leading exemplar of the pork-free approach was Mordecai Manuel Noah (1785–1851). "Noah," his biographer Jonathan D. Sarna writes, "was vitally concerned that food brought into his home not contain lard, a swine product."[52] He even helped develop a chemical test that could detect the presence of lard in olive oil. While Noah also refrained from eating pork in public, he openly violated other dietary restrictions including the eating of turtles and oysters.[53]

A widespread opinion developed on medical grounds among nineteenth-century Jews justifying the "no pork, yes oyster" viewpoint. Pork was correctly held to be highly susceptible to contamination. Similarly, many American Jewish apologists, including Wise, argued that Jewish slaughter practices were more medically fit than alternative methods. When the German government adopted the Jewish mode of slaughtering animals as a health measure for food served to its military in 1894, Wise loudly applauded the action.[54] The American military also investigated serving kosher food during the Spanish-American War for health reasons. Moreover, almost immediately after the Civil War, the consumption of beef in the United States began to increase rapidly, aided by a number of technological advances including refrigerated rail cars (1871) and barbed wire (1875). Not surprisingly, pork consumption began to recede.[55]

Oysters were not only widely viewed as healthy but also as being an aphrodisiac. In general, Americans consumed millions of oysters during the nineteenth century. So many oysters were transported between the Atlantic coast and Cincinnati that the stagecoach route was referred to as the "Oyster Line."[56] Thereafter, the oysters were transported by canal barge and rail. Oyster houses, oyster saloons, and oyster bars were found in American cities in every region. Special oyster dishes and even an oyster cracker were developed. Before they began to deplete in the 1880s, the oyster beds in the Chesapeake Bay produced fifteen billion bushels of oysters per year. Charles Dickens once commented on the American passion for seafood that he saw "at every supper at least two mighty bowls of hot stewed oysters."[57] By analogy, it might be said that oysters were for nineteenth-century American Jews what Chinese food became for their twentieth-century descendants.[58]

Determining Wise's personal food policy is not easy. Frequently inconsistent, he readily changed or revised his views for opportunistic purposes. He was openly hostile to "kitchen Judaism," yet he clearly refrained from eating swine. On the other hand, as stated previously, Wise frequently argued that oysters were kosher and, it can be assumed, he ate them. "There can be no doubt," Wise wrote in the *American Israelite* in 1895, "that the oyster shell is the same to all intents and purposes as the scales to the clean fish, protecting against certain gases in the water."[59] At various times, he wrote against the washing and salting of meat, the prohibition of mixing milk and meat, and the special food restrictions during Passover. "Those who waste their religious and moral sentiments in small and insignificant observances which make them neither better nor more useful," Wise wrote, "diminish and impair their religious and moral capacity."[60]

While changing patterns in American Jewish food culture affected Jewish men, it was Jewish women, as food consumers, cooks, and the principal stewards of "kitchen Judaism," who were profoundly affected by the new culinary climate of the post–Civil War era. According to Kirshenblatt-Gimblett, the first Jewish cookbook to appear in America, Esther Levy's 1871 *Jewish Cookery Book*, was primarily written to promote both traditional women's domesticity and kashrut among American Jewish women. In Levy's own words, "[W]ithout violating the precepts of our religion, a table can be spread, which will satisfy the appetites of the most fastidious." Similarly, as early as 1863, the *Jewish Messenger* condemned "tables with forbidden viands for which many young Jewesses betray a singular relish."[61]

To a great extent, the interest in cuisine, referred to in the *American Israelite* as an "anomalous monster," was class based. "Contributors to the *Israelite* and *Die Deborah*," according to Maria T. Baader, "repeatedly reminded their readers that neither housework nor children's education could be fully delegated to servants without serious damage to home and family." Baader added that children's manners, "especially table manners, also required the close supervision of the mother."[62]

However, Levy and others were swimming against the cultural tide in the nontraditional and rapidly acculturating sector of the 1870s American Jewish community. Not only was culinary accommodation waxing in the post–Civil War American Jewish community, but the gastronomic accommodationists found theoretical support among both moderate pork-free reformers like Wise and, especially, the more radical German Reform rabbis in the years following the Civil War who advocated the complete abolition of the dietary laws.

Initially, American Reform Judaism was of a more conservative bent with respect to its dietary practices. Several of the first Reform congregations in the United States officially kept the dietary laws. According to historian Leon A. Jick, even radical congregations like Har Sinai of Baltimore (founded in 1842) and Emanu-El of New York (founded in 1843) "remained substantially traditional in their ritual practice. Men and women were seated separately, heads were covered, and the Sabbath and dietary laws were 'strictly observed.'"[63] Writing in 1859, Chicago-based Reform Rabbi Bernard Felsenthal (1822–1908) asserted that "it would be irresponsible and reprehensible to advocate the total disregard of the dietary laws."[64] However, with only a few exceptions, culinary traditionalists were unable to hold the line in the antebellum Reform Movement.[65]

The debate over the dietary laws in the early Reform Movement in central Europe was more nuanced than the discussion in the United States but not particularly passionate. In 1833, Michael Creizenach (1789–1842), a teacher at Frankfurt's liberal Jewish Philanthropin School, suggested that "the laws of Torah regarding forbidden foods and the laws regarding the separation of milk and meat be strictly observed, but that the rules relating to the slaughter and preparation of meat by non-Jews are abandoned."[66] A moderate Reform rabbi, Leopold Stein (1810–1843), who was appointed to a pulpit in the Frankfurt community in 1843, wrote in his guide for Jewish life, *Torat Hakim,* that only the Torah's laws regarding forbidden foods and the "prohibition of the eating of blood" be observed and that "he who does not observe these encumbering [Rabbinic] ordinances has not only not transgressed the holy law, but has contributed in a conscientious and salutary manner to the restoration of the law in its purity, as well as to the possibility of living it in the present."[67] In 1847, Hungarian reformer Moses Bruck (1812–1849) argued that Reform Jews observe none of the "dietary regulations at all except that matzoth along with leavened bread would be eaten on Passover."[68] However, none of these positions proved compelling to the rank and file of the Reform movement.

In 1846, the issue of kashrut was scheduled to be discussed in Breslau at the third of three major Reform rabbinic conferences. Collectively, these conferences significantly shaped the religious program of the German Reform Movement. However, unlike many of the other issues debated, the question of kashrut failed to generate much controversy. Rabbi David Einhorn (1809–1879), who was later brought to the United States in 1855 to serve Har Sinai Congregation in Baltimore, Maryland, had been a member of the committee at the 1846 convention charged with making recommendations on how the dietary laws should be viewed by Reform Judaism. According to Reform historian Michael A. Meyer, the conference did not have time to take up the issue while in session.[69] Subsequently, according to British historian Harry Rabinowitz, Einhorn published the findings of the committee in his journal, *Sinai*, and argued that "dietary laws, with the exception of the prohibition to consume blood and animals that died an unnatural death, were directly related to the levitical laws of purity and priestly laws of sacrifice and were, therefore, of a mere temporary ceremonial character and not essentially religious or moral."[70]

If Wise was the principal builder of the Reform Movement in America, its leading theologian and liturgist was the radical Einhorn. Born in Dispeck, Germany, Einhorn received a traditional yeshivah education before studying for his doctorate in the German university system. Radicalized both by his education and his conflicts with the Orthodox community, Einhorn developed a theological system he termed "Mosaism." A Reform ideological purist, he believed in a spiritualized "mission of Israel" shed of its priestly and medieval trappings, including the observance of the dietary laws. He articulated his views in German to his American followers in *Sinai* and was the driving force behind the first conference of Reform rabbis in the United States, held in Philadelphia in November 1869.[71]

Although it is always risky to argue from silence, it seems the Philadelphia conference, convened fourteen years after Einhorn's arrival in the United States, also, like the Breslau conference, did not take up the question of kashrut because the rabbis felt the issue had already been resolved, theoretically and practically, in favor of nonobservance.[72] If so, a split had developed between the moderate reformers who organized the UAHC in 1873 and who, following the prevailing American Reform custom, still maintained something of kashrut and did not eat pork; and the East Coast radicals, like Einhorn and Samuel Hirsch, who called for the abrogation of the dietary laws.

In his remarks of October 10, 1872, calling for the establishment of a union of American synagogues, Moritz Loth (1832–1913), a successful businessman, community activitist, prolific author of fictional works, and president of Wise's Reform congregation Bene Jeshurun in Cincinnati, asserted that the dietary laws and *sh'chitah* "shall *not* be disregarded, but *commended* as *preserving health* and prolonging life." Religious unity, Loth correctly understood, included a public and official commitment to kashrut, a commitment bolstered by medical and statistical proof.[73] According to Marcus, when the UAHC met in New York City in 1879, almost a decade later, "to celebrate its marriage with the Board of Delegates of American Israelite" with a "great feast at Delmonicos," the banquet was kosher.[74]

So what happened? Why just a few years later did the moderate lay leadership of the Reform Movement, and perhaps even Wise himself, come to the conclusion that abstinence from pork alone constituted compliance with the dietary demands of the Jewish tradition? The answer is complex. American Jewish food folk customs, German Jewish affluence and class identification, general American banquet and culinary culture, and the ascent of "modern religion" in the 1870s and 1880s in the United States, which greatly bolstered and radicalized Reform Judaism nationally, all figure in the historical equation that resulted in the decision (or lack of a decision) to serve *t'reif* at the grand celebration at the Highland House in July 1883.

Without question, the long-term general dietary pattern in a large sector of the American Jewish community was to refrain from eating pork and other swine products while ignoring other traditional restrictions. This "no-pork" position comfortably combined Jewish tradition, contemporary culture, and modern science. Furthermore, the immense popularity of seafood in the United States in the nineteenth century, a belief in its extranutritional benefits, and rationalizations about its food classification resulted in the broad rejection of levitical restrictions on seafood among American Jews. But there was still more to the story.

Rationalizing away the dietary restrictions of traditional Judaism was not only based on science, culture, and class but also on a specifically religious argument, first introduced by the radical German reformers but then broadened and popularized by Protestant religious modernists in the United States. In his landmark 1992 study, *The Modernist Impulse in American Protestantism*, Harvard professor William R. Hutchison suggests that 1883 was the high-water mark of a

"New Theology" of religious modernism as represented in the writings of Washington Gladden, Henry Ward Beecher, Theodore Munger, Charles A. Briggs, and Newman Smyth. Thereafter, "the incidence of hostility to liberalism increased" and, within a short time, denominational- and seminary-based heresy trials created headlines across the United States that would last for years.[75]

The New Theology, according to Hutchison, "refused to recognize any fundamental antagonism between the kingdoms of faith and of natural law."[76] "The dominating theme of the New Theology," Hutchison emphasizes repeatedly, is "God's presence in the world and in human culture."[77] Smyth, one of the advocates of religious modernism, summed up his view in 1887 by stating that "the church is rapidly learning that many of the social and secular conditions of the present time are providential arrangements in the use of which the kingdom of God can be advanced."[78] For Reform Jews in the 1880s, the New Theology of culture and their own movement's belief in progressive revelation and the mediation of God's will in contemporary culture dovetailed perfectly—or so they thought.

In essence, Freiberg, Loth, and Wise were embedded in a kind of cultural and religious cocoon in Cincinnati. Given the culinary culture of the country, the ascent of religious liberalism, and the pervasiveness of *t'reif* in uptown American Jewish homes and social clubs, it is not altogether inexplicable why they allowed, or even ordered, Lindeman to serve clam, crab, and shrimp to their guests at the Highland House on July 11, 1883. They were unable to see the complete landscape of American Jewish life and, even more significantly, wrongly assumed that they were the engine pulling the train of American Judaism. Their faulty thinking was to have repercussions for years to come.

Denominational Consequences of the Highland House Affair

Reflecting in his memoirs about the Highland House affair, the aging Philipson was correct in linking the *t'reifah* banquet to the founding of the first JTS in December 1886 and the subsequent denominational developments in both the Orthodox and Conservative streams in American Judaism. For two years after the *t'reifah* banquet, the debate over the culinary offense and its ideological underpinnings continued to rage until a group of Reform rabbis under the leadership of Kaufman Kohler (1843–1926), Einhorn's son-in-law and one of the banquet's speakers, promulgated the 1885 "Pittsburgh Platform." The codification of radical Reform, including, as will be shown, the complete rejection of the dietary laws, convinced a coalition of traditionalists under the leadership of Sabato Morias (1823–1897), *chazan* of Mikveh Israel Congregation in Philadelphia, to found a rabbinical seminary parallel to HUC for "the preservation in America of the knowledge and practice of historical Judaism."[79]

Founded in 1886, the JTS, with Morais serving as its first president, was thoroughly Orthodox in its intent and practice, even though it modeled its name after the Conservative Juedisch-Theologisches Seminar in Breslau, Germany. Morias himself talked of an "Orthodox Seminary," as did one of its earliest Hebrew and Bible instructors, Bernard Drachman (1861–1945), who later helped shape modern Orthodoxy and served as president of the Union of Orthodox Jewish Congregations from 1908 to 1920.

Kashrut was one of a cluster of interrelated issues that first caused a broad coalition of American Jewish traditionalists to withdraw from the Reform Movement. Subsequently, questions of kosher supervision also played a role in the further subdivision of the traditionalists into Conservative, modern Orthodox, and fervently Orthodox camps. Newly arrived East European rabbis generally questioned the *hashgachah* (rabbinic kosher supervision) of the American Jewish communal institutions, especially the hospitals and orphanages that preceded their arrival in the United States, and determined to set up their own social service operations.[80]

As early as 1879, four years before the *t'reifah* banquet, Congregation Beth Midrash Hagadol "endorsed a movement to unite the religious Jewry of New York under a chief rabbi" with responsibilities to supervise and regulate the city's growing kosher food trade.[81] In June 1887, several congregations formed the Association of American Orthodox Hebrew Congregations to recruit a chief rabbi for New York whose responsibilities would include the supervision of the *shochtim* (ritual slaughterers).[82] "So great is the scandal in this great holy city," Rabbi Moses Weinberger wrote that year in his Hebrew language book, *Jews and Judaism in New York*, "that thousands of honest families who fear and tremble at the thought of their straying into one tiny prohibition or sin never realize or suspect that they are eating all sorts of unkosher meat, carcasses trodden underfoot."[83]

On July 7, 1888, a rabbi from Vilna, Jacob Joseph (1848–1902), arrived in New York to become the chief rabbi of the city's growing Orthodox population. Known as a good public speaker and Zionist, Joseph attempted to impose a kosher meat tax and immediately became embroiled in controversy with nearly every sector of "downtown" Jewry. Debilitated by illness, Rabbi Joseph survived as an invalid from 1895 to 1902.[84] A subsequent attempt by the organized Jewish community, Kehillah (1908–1922), to regulate kosher meat also ended in failure.[85]

Ironically, Cincinnati, though smaller in every respect than New York, was destined to become a major center of the kosher food industry in the United States. Just three years after the *t'reifah* banquet took place, Isaac Oscherwitz, a recently arrived German Jewish immigrant, established a kosher meat business in Cincinnati under the family name that quickly emerged as one of the leading suppliers of kosher meat in the United States.[86] That same year, 1886, Rabbi Dov Behr Manischewitz also arrived in Cincinnati and two years later founded his matzah and kosher food supply company, which not only revolutionized the production of matzah but also played a significant role in Jewish philanthropy, the yeshivah world, and American tax law.[87] By the end of the 1880s, the Oscherwitz and Manischewitz companies were operating successfully, in sharp contrast to the chaos of New York's kosher food industry. At the same time, the increasingly radical Reform Movement continued to move away from the dietary law observance after the heat of the Highland House affair had simmered down in the larger American Jewish community.

Reform Judaism and Kashrut Since 1885

The controversy following the *t'reifah* banquet, its denominational consequences, and the deepening problems in the U.S. kosher food industry in the 1880s probably neither slowed nor accelerated the pace of radicalization within the Reform Movement. On October 28, 1883, two members of HUC's first ordination class, Rabbi Joseph Krauskopf and Rabbi Henry Berkowitz, married their wives in a double ceremony in Coshocton, Ohio. A "no-pork" dinner was served, including fried and scalloped oysters, lobster salad, and cold buffalo tongue, to mention but a few of the many courses provided.[88] The following year, the *t'reifah* banquet's caterer, Gustave Lindeman, was contracted to cater a banquet for a Jewish fraternal order in Cincinnati and, again, oysters were served as an appetizer. Even an 1891 cookbook published by the Bloch Publishing and Printing Company of Cincinnati, complete with a six-pointed Star of David on the title page, includes numerous recipes for oysters and soft-shell crabs.[89]

Within two years of the *t'reifah* banquet, Kohler, who had succeeded his father-in-law, David Einhorn, at New York's Beth El Congregation in 1879, convened a group of rabbis in Pittsburgh to craft an authoritative platform for Reform Judaism in America. It was at this convention that the rabbis rejected even the "no-pork" *minhag* (custom). Kohler had been a student of Rabbi Samson Raphael Hirsch, the architect of modern Orthodox Judaism in Germany. While studying for his doctorate at the University of Erlangen, Kohler left Orthodoxy and embraced a radical philosophy of Reform Judaism. In 1885, in the wake of the *t'reifah* banquet, he gave a series of lectures defending Reform against attacks from one of New York's leading conservative rabbis, Alexander Kohut, who in the heat of the exchange had declared that "Reform is a Deformity."[90] From his exchanges with Kohut, Kohler concluded the time had arrived for a platform to be promulgated for the Reform Movement in America. He even recruited Wise to serve as the head of the ad hoc conference.

Interestingly, the text of the Pittsburgh Platform of 1885 is less a defense of Reform against attacks from traditional Judaism as it is an apologium for Reform Judaism against criticisms leveled by Felix Adler and the Ethical Culture movement. Although a radical document from the perspective of "historical Judaism," the Pittsburgh Platform also represents a midpoint between traditional Jewish theism and ethnicity on the one hand and Adler's deracinated secular ethicism on the other. Sharply attacked from outside the Movement from the left and the right, the Pittsburgh Platform quickly became both the ideological standard as well as a textual symbol of Reform Judaism in America.[91]

Animated by a rational, optimistic faith, the Pittsburgh Platform of 1885 was clearly a Judaic parallel to the New Theology of the Protestant modernists. As such, it viewed culture—at least the part of contemporary culture it favored—as providential. Apparently, that culture had no place in it for traditional Jewish dietary practices and, in the fourth plank of the platform, the last vestige of kashrut was officially abrogated by the assembled rabbis:

> We hold that all such Mosaic and Rabbinical laws as regulate diet, priestly purity and dress originated in ages and under the influence of ideas altogether foreign to our present mental and spiritual state. They fail to impress the modern Jew with a spirit of priestly holiness; their observance in our days is apt rather to obstruct than to further modern spiritual elevation.[92]

By stating that "all such Mosaic and Rabbinical laws as regulate diet," Kohler and his supporters had effectively pushed the Reform Movement beyond its "moderate" no-pork position and into a borderless gastronomic antinomianism. Reform culinary culture now had no limits. Synagogue banquets and Sisterhood cookbooks alike were soon to include not only seafood but pork dishes as well. Viewed historically, the Reform Movement had institutionalized a truly radical vision of Judaism.

The situation was particularly pronounced in—although not limited to—the South. For example, Steven Hertzberg reports that in Atlanta, Georgia, "by the midnineties, forbidden foods like ham, game, and shellfish were unabashedly consumed in public. Oyster pâté à la Baltimore was served to Rabbi Reich and the leading members of the Temple at the Concordia Hall dedication banquet in 1893, and two years later delegates to the regional B'nai B'rith convention in Atlanta dined on fresh lobster washed down with 'Palestine Punch.'"[93] As late as 1935, at the Triennial Conference of the National Council of Jewish Women in New Orleans, the entrées for the Sabbath dinner were "Baked ham aux légumes or Swiss and Bacon."[94]

Approximately half a century later, the Pittsburgh Platform was superseded by the 1937 Columbus Platform and that by the 1987 San Francisco Bicentennial Statement. While both of these documents included significant, even monumental, changes in the ideology and practice of American Reform Judaism, the movement's official views of kashrut have remained virtually unchanged for nearly a hundred years. As late as 1979, the Responsa Committee of the CCAR retrospectively concluded that "although dietary laws were discussed at length during the last century and early in this century, they ceased to be a matter of primary concern for Reform Jews. This is also clearly indicated by the lack of questions regarding dietary laws addressed to the Responsa Committee through the decades."[95]

However, other forces were already at work within American Reform Judaism, and by the end of the twentieth century, the Reform movement, led by neo-traditionalist members of the CCAR, began to rethink its official view of the dietary laws.[96] In 1979, the same year the Responsa Committee essentially reaffirmed Kohler's understanding of Reform Judaism, another CCAR publication, *Gates of Mitzvah*, declared that "the range of options available to the Reform Jew is from full observance of the biblical and Rabbinic regulations to total nonobservance." This new and emerging viewpoint suggested that "Reform Judaism does not take an 'all or nothing' approach."[97] In 1999, a second Pittsburgh Platform directly countered Kohler's original

Pittsburgh Platform and maintained that some of the commandments not historically observed by Reform Jews "demand renewed attention as the result of the unique context of our own times."[98]

Defining "the unique context of our times" now becomes the task of the contemporary Reform Movement both in terms of its foundational ideas as well as in determining the mandated religious practices of Reform Judaism. The issue of kashrut has become particularly complex for contemporary Reform Judaism; it involves not only the issue of defining mitzvah in a Reform context but also answering questions about *hashgachah* and the ethics of food production and consumption. Today, as in the past, the Reform Movement continues to negotiate the many tensions and relationships that exist between tradition and innovation, religious resistance and cultural adaptation, as well as the internal needs of the Reform community versus the place of Reform Judaism in the pan-historical faith and global people called Israel. In the deepest sense of the terms, the Reform Movement needs to decide yet again what it believes to be kosher (fit) and what it deems to be *t'reif* (unfit).

NOTES

*The original research for this article was done in preparation for the Jacob R. Marcus Memorial Lecture, sponsored by the American Jewish Archives (AJA), at the annual convention of the Central Conference of American Rabbis (CCAR), June 2001, Monterey, California. Special thanks to the AJA's director, Dr. Gary P. Zola, for his support and patience and to Barbara Steinberg, my administrative assistant, for her help.

1. Debra Nussbaum Cohen, "A Menu for Reform," *Wall Street Journal*, July 6, 2001.

2. The only critical research on the *t'reifah* banquet is John J. Appel's "The Trefa Banquet," *Commentary* 41, no. 2 (February 1966): 75–78. Also see his longer, nineteen-page paper, "The Trefa Banquet" unpublished paper, n.d., AJA SC-5978, which was presented at the 63rd Annual Meeting of the American Jewish Historical Society in Cincinnati in March 1965.

3. According to Appel, general historians of the American Jewish experience as well as "conservative" historians generally skirted or "tactfully avoided the issue" of the *t'reifah* banquet up to the 1960s. John J. Appel, "The Trefa Banquet," unpublished paper, n.d., AJA, SC-5978, pp. 2–3. However, after the publication of his

article in *Commentary*, the banquet assumed a more central, and sometimes more polemical, history in the historiography of the non-Reform movements in American Judaism. For a recent example, see Elliot Dorf, *Conservative Judaism: Our Ancestors to Our Descendants* (New York: United Synagogue of Conservative Judaism, Department of Youth Activities, 1977, 1996), who suggests the serving of nonkosher food may have been a "deliberate attempt by Isaac Mayer Wise to drive the more traditional members out of the Reform camp so that he could more easily form a radical program for the Reform movement" (p. 13). Pro-Reform authors tend to minimize their reporting of the *t'reifah* banquet or not report it at all. For example, see Michael A. Meyer, *Response to Modernity: A History of the Reform Movement in Judaism* (New York: Oxford University Press, 1988), 263, 267, 282. James G. Heller, in his *Isaac M. Wise: His Life, Work and Thought* (New York: Union of American Hebrew Congregations, 1965), refers to the Highland House affair as "trivial and ridiculous" (p. 452). Also see "Chapters in American Jewish History," Chapter 52, 2000, American Jewish Historical Society, http://www.ajhs.org.

4. The scope here is limited to the United States due to a lack of secondary literature on Reform experience in Canada. According to Rabbi Sharon Sobel, the Canadian regional director of the Union for Reform Judaism (URJ), the current practice "in Greater Toronto is that most of the Reform congregations are kosher style. Some use kosher meat but only have one set of dishes. There are one or two strictly kosher congregations" (e-mail correspondence with the author, August 12, 2005). More broadly, see Gerald J.J. Tulchinsky, *Taking Root: The Origins of the Canadian Jewish Community* (Hanover, NH: University Press of New England, 1993); and his *Branching Out: The Transformation of the Canadian Jewish Community* (New York: Stoddart, 1998).

5. David Philipson, *My Life as an American Jew* (Cincinnati: Kidd, 1941), 23. For another example of the development of myth as reality in American Jewish history, see the "Rebecca Gratz legend" in Dianne Ashton, *Rebecca Gratz: Women and Judaism in Antebellum America* (Detroit: Wayne State University Press, 1997).

6. Philipson, *My Life*, 23.

7. Appel, "The Trefa Banquet," 75–78. Also see Daniel Jeremy Silver, "The Trefa Banquet Story or a Study in Causation," unpublished, typescript, n.d., AJA, Box 511.

8. The Rabbinical Literary Association, 1880–1882, was founded by Rabbi Max Lilienthal. See Sidney Regner, "The History of the Conference," in *Retrospect and Prospect: Essays in Commemoration of the Seventy-Fifth Anniversary of the Founding of the Central Conference of American Rabbis*, ed. Bertram Wallace Korn (New York: Central Conference of American Rabbis, 1965), 2.

9. Heller, *Wise*, 444.

10. A considerable literature exists on the life of Isaac M. Wise. Most recently, see Sefton D. Temkin, *Isaac Mayer Wise: Shaping American Judaism* (Oxford: Oxford University Press, 1992). Heller's *Wise* (see note 3) is a massive, though less critical, study.

11. *Cincinnati Enquirer*, July 12, 1883, p. 4.

12. "Julius Freiberg," in *Reform Judaism in America: A Biographical Dictionary and Sourcebook*, ed. Kerry M. Olitzky, Lance J. Sussman, and Malcolm H. Stern (Westport, CT: Greenwood Press, 1993), 64–65.

13. Based on correspondences from and to Edith Lindeman Calisch, a granddaughter of Gustave Lindeman, on file at the American Jewish Archives: Calisch to Norman Podhoretz, May 1, 1966; Calisch to J. Appel, May 21, 1966; Calisch to J. Appel, June 18, 1966; Calisch to Jacob R. Marcus, March 14, 1975 and April 25, 1977. All found in AJA, SC-456. Country clubs founded by German Jews in America generally continue to eschew traditional Jewish dietary restrictions.

14. Calisch to Marcus, March 14, 1975, SC-12418.

15. *American Israelite*, August 3, 1883, p. 4.

16. *Die Deborah*, August 17, 1883. Author's translation.

17. The "Menu Collection of The New York Public Library"—especially the Buttolph Collection, which covers the years 1890–1910—contains more than 25,000 menus including banquet menus. For general histories of food in America, see endnote 56.

18. *Cincinnati Enquirer*, July 12, 1883, p. 4.

19. Mark Bauer, a chef and instructor at the French Culinary Institute of New York City, reviewed the menu with the author (e-mail correspondence, July 24, 2000).

20. *New York Herald*, July 22, 1883. Photocopy available at AJA. The article was probably filed either by Henry Pereira Mendes (1852–1937), rabbi of Shearith Israel congregation in New York City and a founder both of the JTS and the Union of Orthodox Jewish Congregations of America; or his older brother, Frederic de Sola Mendes (1850–1927), rabbi of Congregation Shaaray Tefila in New York City, who worked within the Reform Movement and later became a member of the CCAR.

21 Joan Dash, *Summoned to Jerusalem: The Life of Henrietta Szold, Founder of Hadassah* (New York: Harper & Row, 1979), 25.

22. "Shulamith," *Jewish Messenger*, July 27, 1883.

23. Dash, *Summoned*, 25. For Wise's reaction to the arrival of increasing numbers of Russian Jews in America, see *American Israelite*, May 21, 1886, p. 6, where he suggests that "no immigrant student over the age of fourteen be sent to the College as after that age it is difficult to change their manners or speech to the purely American." Initially, he was more welcoming.

24. *Jewish Messenger*, July 27, 1883, p. 6. A humorous account of a private dinner at Wise's home during the Szolds' visit was reported by Bertha Szold, a younger sister of Henrietta, who accompanied her and her father to Cincinnati. About the dinner at the Wises', Bertha wrote, "There were fifteen or twenty rabbies [sic] there. At dinner when we were going to eat the turkey, some more rabbies came in, then everybody got up from the table to talk to the rabbies that came in, then the rabbies that came in took the other people's places and began to eat, and then went off. Not long after dinner we had ice cream and cake, and then we went home." Quoted in Alexandra Lee Levin, *The Szolds of Lombard Street: A Baltimore Family, 1859–1909* (Philadelphia: Jewish Publication Society, 1960), 159.

25. John F. Mariani, "Restaurant," in *The Encyclopedia of American Food & Drink* (New York: Lebhar-Friedman Books, 1999), 269.

26. Jonathan D. Sarna, "The Debate over Mixed Seating in the American Synagogue," in *The American Synagogue: A Sanctuary Transformed*, ed. Jack Wertheimer (New York: Cambridge University Press, 1987), 363–94.

27. In 1869, Wise had reported on the dismissal of Rev. Dr. Bernard Illowy because he did not adhere strictly to the regulations of the milk and meat laws (*American Israelite*, September 24, 1869). Isaac Leeser (1806–1869), the leading voice of antebellum Jewish traditionalism, left his position at Mikveh Israel in Philadelphia in a storm of controversy, in part because of a suspicion that he did not strictly adhere to the dietary laws. On Leeser, see Lance J. Sussman, *Isaac Leeser and the Making of American Judaism* (Detroit: Wayne State University Press, 1995), 175.

28. *American Israelite*, April 4, 1895, p. 4. The notion of oysters as sea vegetables was suggested to the author by Jonathan D. Sarna in a private correspondence (April 4, 2000) and is based on Professor Sarna's reading of Louis Finkelstein's Hebrew introduction to his father's (Simon Finkelstein) prayer book. S. Finkelstein, *Seder Tefilah* (Jerusalem, 1968), 10 [in Hebrew]. For Wise's complex views on oysters, see Dena Wilansky, *Sinai to Cincinnati* (New York, 1937), 237–40.

29. Reactions by Wise's supporters are reported in Appel, "The Trefa Banquet," typescript, pp. 10–11.

30. *American Israelite*, March 7, 1884, p. 6.

31. *Die Deborah*, July 18, 1884.

32. *Die Deborah*, August 10, 1883.

33. *Die Deborah*, vol. 11, p. 34.

34. *American Israelite*, November 9, 1893.

35. On women and kashrut in nineteenth-century America, see endnote 61.

36. *American Israelite*, May 9, 1884, p. 4; May 23, p. 4.

37. *American Hebrew*, July 25, 1883. Cowen's autobiography, *Memories of an American Jew*, was published in 1932. He published the work of numerous American Jewish luminaries, including Henry P. Mendes, Emma Lazarus, Mary Antin, and Alexander Kohut.

38. *American Hebrew*, July 18, 1884.

39. Wise reported that there were no graduates from HUC in 1885 because of opposition to the college. See *American Israelite*, April 3, 1885, p. 4.

40. James E. Latham, "Food," in *The Encyclopedia of Religion*, vol. 5, ed. Mircea Eliade (New York: Simon & Schuster Macmillan, 1995), 387–93.

41. John J. Appel, "The Trefa Banquet," unpublished paper, n.d., AJA, SC-5978, p. 19.

42. For more on Zwingli, see W. P. Stephens, *Zwingli: An Introduction to His Thought* (Oxford: Clarendon Press, 1992).

43. Israel Finkelstein and Neil Asher Silberman, *The Bible Unearthed: Archeology's New Vision of Ancient Israel and the Origin of Its Sacred Texts* (New York: The Free Press, 2001), 120.

44. Mary Douglas, *Purity and Danger: An Analysis of the Concepts of Pollution and Taboo* (New York: Routledge, 1966, 1984); Jean Soler, "The Semiotics of Food in the Bible," in *Food and Drink in History: Selections from the Annales*, vol. 5 (Baltimore: Johns Hopkins Press, 1979), 126–38; Marvin Harris, *Cannibals and Kings: The Origins of Culture* (London: Fontana Collins, 1977).

45. John Cooper, *Eat and Be Satisfied: A Social History of Jewish Food* (Northvale, NJ: Jason Aronson, 1993), xiii.

46. Also see Erich Isaac, *Commentary* 41, no. 1 (January 1966): 36–41.

47. In recent times, other positions have developed within the Reform Movement including levitical (no pork, no seafood), eco-kashrut, and ethical kashrut. For a recent discussion of kashrut in American Reform Judaism, see "The Civilized Diet: A Conversation with Rabbi Simeon Maslin," *Reform Judaism*, Summer 2007, pp. 38, 41, 50.

48. Harold P. Gastwirt, *Fraud, Corruption and Holiness: The Controversy over the Supervision of Jewish Dietary Practice in New York City, 1881–1940* (Port Washington, NY: National University Publications, 1974), 18–26.

49. Allon Schoener, *The American Jewish Album: 1654 to the Present* (New York: Rizzoli, 1983), 93.

50. Jacob R. Marcus, *Memoirs of American Jews, 1775–1865*, vol. 2 (Philadelphia: Jewish Publication Society of America, 1955), 87.

51. Schoener, *American Jewish Album*, 94.

52. Jonathan D. Sarna, *Jacksonian Jew: The Two Worlds of Mordecai Manuel Noah* (New York: Holmes & Meier, 1980), 141.

53. Ibid.

54. Dena Wilansky, *Sinai to Cincinnati* (New York: Renaissance Book Company, 1937), 247.

55. Mariani, "Restaurant," in *Encyclopedia*, 269.

56. Mariani, "Oysters," in *Encyclopedia*, 226. For more on the history of food and eating in America, see Donna R. Gabaccia, *We Are What We Eat: Ethnic Food and the Making of Americans* (Cambridge, MA: Harvard University Press, 1997); and Harvey A. Levenstein, *The Paradox of Plenty: A Social History of Eating in Modern America* (New York: Oxford University Press, 1994). For a comparative perspective, see Hasia R. Diner, *Hungering for America: Italian, Irish and Jewish Foodways in the Age of Migration* (Cambridge, MA: Harvard University Press, 2001).

57. Mariani, "Restaurant," in *Encyclopedia*, 269.

58. Numerous theories, none definitive, exist on American Jews' attraction to Chinese food. See Gaye Tuchman and Harry G. Levine, "New York Jews and Chinese Food: The Social Construction of an Ethnic Pattern," *Contemporary Ethnography* 22, no. 3, (1992): 382–407; Mimi Sheraton, "A Jewish Yen for Chinese," *New York Times Magazine*, September 23, 1990, p. 71; and Jenna Weissman Joselit, *The Wonders of America: Reinventing Jewish Culture, 1880–1950* (New York: Hill and Wang, 1994).

59. Quote in Joan Nathan, *Jewish Cooking in America* (New York: Alfred A. Knopf, 1994), 14.

60. Quoted in Wilansky, *Sinai*, 246.

61. Both Levy's and the *Messenger*'s quotes are reported in Barbara Kirshenblatt-Gimblett, "The Kosher Gourmet in the Nineteenth Century Kitchen: Three Jewish Cookbooks in Historical Perspective," *Journal of Gastronomy* 2, no. 4 (Winter 1986/1987): 63.

62. Maria T. Baader, "From 'The Priestess of the Home' to 'The Rabbi's Brilliant Daughter'": Concepts of Jewish Womanhood and Progressive Germanness in *Die Deborah* and *The American Israelite*, 1854–1900," in *Leo Baeck Institute Year Book* 43, 1998, p. 67.

63. Leon A. Jick, "The Reform Synagogue," in *The American Synagogue*, 86. Also see Kevin Proffitt, "A Kashrut Challenge in Nineteenth Century American

Judaism," *10 Minutes of Torah*, August 2, 2005. Accessed at http://tmt.urj.net/archives/2socialaction/080205.htm.

64. Quoted in W. Gunther Plaut, *The Growth of Reform Judaism: American and European Sources until 1948* (New York: World Union for Progressive Judaism, 1965), 265–66.

65. For example, Leeser reports in *The Occident* (vol. 16, 1858, p. 360) that Har Sinai congregation in Baltimore abolished kashrut.

66. Plaut, *The Growth of Reform Judaism*, 212–13; Meyer, *Response to Modernity*, 119–21.

67. Plaut, *The Rise of Reform Judaism: A Sourcebook of Its European Origins* (New York: World Union for Progressive Judaism, 1963), 260–65.

68. Meyer, *Response*, 160.

69. Meyer, *Response*, 150.

70. Harry Rabinowitz, "Dietary Laws," in *Encyclopaedia Judaica* (Jerusalem: Keter, 1971), vol. 5, column 44.

71. A full, critical biography of David Einhorn is a major desideratum. See Kaufman Kohler's eulogistic essay in the *Yearbook of the Central Conference of American Rabbis* (Cincinnati: CCAR, 1909), 215–70.

72. Sefton D. Temkin, *The New World of Reform* (London: Leo Baeck College, 1971), 111–12.

73. *Proceedings of the Union of American Hebrew Congregations* (Cincinnati: Bloch and Company, 1879), vol. 1, p. i. On Loth, see "Moritz Loth," in *Reform Judaism in America*, ed. Kerry M. Olitzky, 132–33.

74. Jacob Rader Marcus, *United States Jewry, 1776–1985*, vol. 3 (Detroit: Wayne State University Press, 1993), 108. Delmonico's, established in 1827 by two Swiss brothers, was the first "public restaurant" to open in the United States and was known for its lavish meals and excessive portions.

75. William R. Hutchison, *The Modernist Impulse in American Protestantism* (Durham: Duke University Press, 1992), 105.

76. Ibid, 97.

77. Ibid, 79.

78. Ibid, 102.

79. Alvin Kass, "Jewish Theological Seminary of America," in *Encylopaedia Judaica* (Jerusalem: Keter, 1971), vol. 10, column 96.

80. In St. Louis, neither the Jewish hospital nor the orphanage provided kosher food. See Walter Ehrlich, *Zion in the Valley: The Jewish Community of St. Louis*, vol. 1 (Columbia, MO: University of Missouri Press, 1997), 390–91.

81. Harold P. Gastwirt, *Fraud, Corruption and Holiness: The Controversy over the Supervision of Jewish Dietary Practice in New York City, 1881–1940* (Port Washington, NY: Kennikat Press, 1974), 55–73.

82. Ibid.

83. Jonathan D. Sarna, *People Walk on Their Heads: Moses Weinberger's Jews and Judaism in New York* (New York: Homes and Meier, 1982), 50.

84. Abraham J. Karp, "New York Chooses a Chief Rabbi," *Publications of the American Jewish Historical Society* 44, 1955, pp. 129–98.

85. Arthur A. Goren, *New York Jews and the Quest for Community: The Kehillah Experiment, 1908–1922* (New York: Columbia University Press, 1970), 76–85. For a

discussion of the subsequent history of the kosher food industry in the United States, see Saul Bernstein, *The Orthodox Union Story: A Centenary Portrayal* (Northvale, NJ: Jason Aronson, 1997).

86. A 1998 film documentary directed by Bill Chayes, *Divine Food: 100 Years in the Kosher Delicatessen Tradition*, focuses on the Oscherwitz family.

87. Jonathan D. Sarna, "Manischewitz Matzah and the Rabbis of the Holy Land: A Study in the Interrelationship of Business, Charity and Faith" [in Hebrew], *Gesher* 140, Winter 1999, pp. 41–49. Also see Ari Y. Greenspan and Ari Z. Zivotofsky, "Hand or Machine: Two Roads to Fulfilling the Mitzva of Matza," in *Jewish Observer*, April 2004, pp. 20–33.

88. A handwritten invitation to the Berkowitz-Krauskopf wedding (October 28, 1883) and a fragment of a newspaper clipping reporting on the ceremony and dinner are on file at the AJA.

89. *Aunt Babette's Cook Book. Foreign and Domestic Receipts for the Household. A Valuable Collection of Receipts and Hints for the Housewife, Many of Which Are Not to Be Found Elsewhere* (Cincinnati: Bloch, 1891).

90. Hasia R. Diner, *The Jews of the United States* (Berkeley, CA: University of California Press, 2004), 120.

91. Benny Kraut, *From Reform Judaism to Ethical Culture: The Religious Evolution of Felix Adler* (Cincinnati: Hebrew Union College Press, 1979); Sefton D. Temkin, "The Pittsburgh Platform: A Centenary Assessment," *Journal of Reform Judaism* 32, Fall 1985, pp. 1–12.

92. Meyer, *Response*, 388. A complete text of the Pittsburgh Platform (1885) is also available online at http://ccarnet.org/documentsandpositions/platforms.

93. Steven Hertzberg, *Strangers Within the Gate City: The Jews of Atlanta, 1845–1915* (Philadelphia: Jewish Publication Society, 1978), 68.

94. Faith Rogow, *Gone to Another Meeting: The National Council of Jewish Women, 1893–1993* (Tuscaloosa, AL: University of Alabama Press, 1993), 127. Currently, food service at many "Jewish" country clubs continues to include both swine and seafood (author's observation).

95. "Responsum 49: *Kashrut* in Reform Judaism (1979)," *American Reform Responsa: Collected Responsa of the Central Conference of American Rabbis*, ed. Walter Jacob (New York: Central Conference of American Rabbis, 1979), 128–31.

96. Arnold Jacob Wolf, "The Need to Be Commanded (1967)," in *The Reform Judaism Reader: North American Documents*, ed. Michael A. Meyer and W. Gunther Plaut (New York: UAHC Press, 2001).

97. *Gates of Mitzvah: A Guide to the Jewish Life Cycle*, ed. Simeon J. Maslin (New York: Central Conference of American Rabbis, 1979), 40, 130–32. The Union of Reform Judaism's Canadian summer camp, Camp George, founded in 1999, is under the supervision of the Kashruth Council of Canada.

98. Meyer and Plaut, *Reader*, 210.

3

KASHRUT

A Reform Point of View

Simeon J. Maslin, ed.

> Many Reform Jews observe certain traditional dietary disci-
> plines as a part of their attempt to establish a Jewish home and
> life style. For some, traditional kashrut will enhance the sanctity
> of the home and be observed as a mitzvah; for some, a degree of
> kashrut . . . may be meaningful; and still others will find noth-
> ing of value in kashrut.
>
> *Gates of Mitzvah, "Marriage and the Jewish Home," E-6*

No guide for Jewish living would be complete if it failed to address the issue of kashrut, i.e., the fitness of certain foods according to Jewish tradition. Kashrut has been a basic part of Judaism for too long to be ignored; its role in the life of the Jew and in Jewish history ought not to be underestimated. The home in Jewish tradition is the *mikdash m'at* (small sanctuary) and the table is the *mizbei-ach* (altar);[1] it is reasonable, therefore, to ask the Reform Jew to study and consider kashrut so as to develop a valid personal position.

Judaism has always recognized a religious dimension to the consumption of food. Being a gift of God, food was never to be taken for granted. And if this was true of food generally, it was especially true

Adapted from Simeon J. Maslin, ed., *Gates of Mitzvah: A Guide to the Jewish Life Cycle* (New York: CCAR Press, 1979), 130–33.

of meat, fish, and fowl, which involve the taking of life. And so it is not surprising to find literally scores of passages in the Torah[2] and the later Rabbinic literature specifying which foods are permitted, which forbidden, and how they are to be prepared.

Kashrut—generally translated as "the dietary laws"—involves a whole series of food disciplines that range from the avoidance of pork and shellfish to the eating of matzah on Pesach. (It should be noted that there is a wide gamut of Jewish dietary observance that is unrelated to kashrut, from the major prohibition against eating on Yom Kippur to such minor customs as eating blintzes on Shavuot, hamantaschen on Purim, and latkes on Chanukah.) Jewish tradition considered kashrut to be an especially important part of the code that set Israel apart as a "holy people." Maimonides viewed kashrut as a discipline. "It accustoms us to restrain both the growth of desire and the disposition to consider the pleasure of eating and drinking as the end of man's existence." For many centuries it was kashrut which most conspicuously separated the Jew from the Diaspora society in which he/she lived.

The Reform Movement has, for the most part, ignored the question of the relevance of the dietary laws. W. Gunther Plaut writes of kashrut: "The almost total silence of Reform literature on this subject is witness to the fact that it no longer was of real concern to the liberal leadership."[3] The Reform position was set out in the Pittsburgh Platform of 1885: "We hold that all such Mosaic and Rabbinical laws as regulate diet, priestly purity, and dress originated in ages and under the influence of ideas altogether foreign to our present mental and spiritual state. They fail to impress the modern Jew with a spirit of priestly holiness; their observance in our days is apt rather to obstruct than to further modern spiritual elevation." Although this blanket rejection of the dietary laws as outmoded represented the "official" position of the Reform Movement through most of a century, it did not prevent individual Reform Jews and Reform congregations from adopting certain of the dietary laws for a variety of reasons, including the desire not to offend traditional relatives or guests.

The basic features of the traditional dietary laws are: (1) all fruits and vegetables are permitted and may be eaten with either dairy or meat dishes; (2) any type of fish that has fins and scales is permitted; (3) domestic fowl are permitted but birds of prey are prohibited; (4) all domestic animals which have both a split hoof and chew their cud are permitted; (5) meat and milk may not be eaten together, and the utensils used to prepare and serve meat or milk foods must be kept separate; and (6) fowl and animals which are permitted must be slaughtered and prepared for eating according to ritual law.

In attempting to evolve a personal position on kashrut, the Reform Jew or the Reform Jewish family should understand that there are several options, e.g., abstention from pork products and/or shellfish, or perhaps adding to this abstention the separation of milk and meat; these practices might be observed in the home and not when eating out, or they might be observed all the time. Or one might opt to eat only kosher meat or even to adopt some form of vegetarianism so as to avoid the necessity of taking a life. (This would be in consonance with the principle of *tzaar baalei chayim*—prevention of pain or cruelty to animals.) The range of options available to the Reform Jew is from full observance of the biblical and Rabbinic regulations to total nonobservance. Reform Judaism does not take an "all or nothing" approach.

In the Torah (Lev. 11:44 and Deut. 14:21) the Jewish people is commanded to observe the dietary laws as a means of making it *kadosh*—holy. Holiness has the dual sense of inner hallowing and outer separateness. The idea of sanctifying and imposing discipline on the most basic and unavoidable act of human behavior, eating, is one of the reasons that may lead a person to adopt some form of kashrut. Among the other reasons that one may find compelling are: (1) identification and solidarity with the worldwide Jewish community, (2) the ethical discipline of avoiding certain foods or limiting one's appetite because of the growing scarcity of food in parts of the world, (3) the avoidance of certain foods that are traditionally obnoxious to Jews, e.g., pork, which may provide a sense of identification with past generations and their struggle to remain Jews, (4) the authority of ancient biblical and

Rabbinic injunctions, and (5) the desire to have a home in which any Jew might feel free to eat.

One or more of these reasons as well as others might influence certain Reform Jews to adopt some of the dietary regulations as a mitzvah, while others may remain satisfied with the position articulated in the Pittsburgh Platform. However, the fact that kashrut was for so many centuries an essential part of Judaism, and that so many Jews gave their lives for it, should move Reform Jews to study it and to consider carefully whether or not it would add *k'dushah* (holiness) to their homes and their lives.

NOTES

1. See *Gates of Mitzvah*, "Marriage and the Jewish Home," E-1 and E-7.

2. The basic biblical passages on kashrut are Leviticus 11 and Deuteronomy 14.

3. W. Gunther Plaut, *The Growth of Reform Judaism* (New York: World Union for Progressive Judaism, 1965), 265.

4

ADVENTURES IN EATING

An Emerging Model for Kashrut

RACHEL S. MIKVA

Maaseh shehayah—There was a young family in America whose parents had no use for kashrut. The three children grew up eating fine *t'reif* of all sorts, never knowing what they weren't missing. In 1969, however, they spent a week eating only what they could afford to buy with the value of food stamps budgeted for a family of five. It was a week of powdered milk and canned food, learning to empathize with those struggling in poverty. Beginning in 1970, they honored the grape boycott organized by Cesar Chavez to call attention to the plight of migrant farmworkers in California. When the youngest of these children grew to become a rabbi, she reflected on these early adventures in eating as a fundamental education in kashrut.

Now she proposes an emerging model for contemporary liberal observance of kashrut. After a brief review of the evolution of the Reform Movement's thinking on the place of mitzvot in general and kashrut in particular, this article presents a "meta-halachic" structure that examines traditional explanations for the rules of keeping kosher and discusses possible modern applications or extensions of the commandments.

Adapted with permission from Rachel S. Mikva, "Adventures in Eating: An Emerging Model for Kashrut," *CCAR Journal*, Winter 2004, 55–66.

Historical Background

Still influenced by the working assumptions of classical Reform Judaism, the family's practice certainly upheld the original (1885) Pittsburgh Platform's rejection of traditional kashrut.

> Today we accept as binding only the moral laws, and maintain only such ceremonies as elevate and sanctify our lives, but reject all such as are not adapted to the views and habits of modern civilization. We hold that all such Mosaic and Rabbinical laws as regulate diet, priestly purity and dress originated in ages and under the influence of ideas altogether foreign to our present mental and spiritual state. They fail to impress the modern Jew with a spirit of priestly holiness; their observance in our day is apt rather to obstruct than to further modern spiritual elevation.[1]

Yet the family's "adventures in eating" also embraced principles articulated by the movement at its 1999 Pittsburgh Conference:

> We are committed to the ongoing study of the whole array of mitzvot and to the fulfillment of those that address us as individuals and as a community. Some of these mitzvot, sacred obligations, have long been observed by Reform Jews; others, both ancient and modern, demand renewed attention as the result of the unique context of our own times.[2]

Our *maaseh* is, in fact, anecdotal evidence for how the two radically different Reform statements are connected. Reform Jews still reject rituals altogether foreign to our present mental and spiritual state: *shlogen kapores* (swinging a chicken above one's head symbolically transferring sin, and then slaughtering it as vicarious atonement) and *sheitl* (the wig worn by ultra-Orthodox married women who shave their heads so as not to tempt other men with their lovely locks) are two examples. At the same time, we have always sought out acts that elevate and sanctify our lives. The food-stamp diet and the grape boycott were new "mitzvot" decades before we regularly used that appellation; they were sacred disciplines that transformed eating into ethical instruction, a mundane activity into a gateway to holiness.

An earlier draft of the 1999 platform, then called "Ten Principles for Reform Judaism" (circulated in August 1998), has a statement even more on point:

> In the presence of God we may each feel called to respond in different ways: some by offering traditional or spontaneous blessings, others by covering our heads, still others by wearing the tallit or *t'fillin* for prayer. Some will look for ways to reveal holiness in our encounters with the world around us, others to transform our homes into a *mikdash m'at*, a holy place in miniature. Some of us may observe practices of kashrut, to extend the sense of *k'dushah* into the acts surrounding food and into a *concern for the way food is raised and brought to our tables* [emphasis added].[3]

The 1998–99 documents acknowledge that our mental and spiritual states are not eternally fixed; they are in motion. The observances that are apt to further modern spiritual elevation are different, not only between generations and among individual Jews, but also for one person over the course of a lifetime.

The later statements also acknowledge more wholeheartedly the value of turning to the sources of Jewish tradition for guidance in our daily lives, and the possibility that *k'dushah* is specifically located in investing the minute actions that fill our days with religious purpose and meaning.

These disparities are reflective of the transition from early modern thinking to later or postmodern thought. Our 1885 Platform was heavily influenced by a dominant Protestant theory of ritual. Arnold Eisen describes the impact in *Rethinking Modern Judaism*,[4] and made the same point more succinctly in his address to the 1999 CCAR Convention:

> The model has a theory of ritual for what counts as religious practice. And the model does not have room for anything that is even vaguely law-governed, and nothing that governs everyday activity like what you eat and what you wear and who you have sex with.

> Ritual is something you do in a peak experience that is wholly
> other, on a Sunday morning, set apart from the rest of life, when
> you contact the *mysterium tremendum*. That is ritual.[5]

It did not leave much room for Jewish practice. As indicated by the
subsequent platforms of Reform Judaism, however, theories of ritual
evolved, including our own. Certainty of a singular truth has given way
to the multivocality more conducive to Jewish life. Mitzvah again has
the potential to be commandment, and "everyday" rituals have reen-
tered our religious repertoire.

The resulting reconsideration of kashrut, among other mitzvot,
has been significant. Reform synagogues, synods, and summer camps
have examined kosher options. Individual Reform Jews have found
that rituals related to diet do, indeed, command their souls or open
valuable gateways to holiness and community. The movement has
recognized that its own ethical impulses related to production and
distribution of food products are connected to the long-standing
teachings of kashrut. In recent decades, the liberal Jewish world has
frequently used the term "eco-kosher" to identify this extension of
the dietary laws. Today, a serious Reform exploration of kashrut requires consideration of the traditional restrictions, as well as these
"modern mitzvot," that should perhaps be attached to our religious
instruction on eating.

A concomitant development has been Reform Judaism's attitude
toward the application of ancient sources.

> We believe in a *torat chayim*, a living Torah. Though the literary
> sources of our tradition were written long ago in a very different
> time and place, we affirm that these texts, through proper and
> prayerful interpretation, address us as well, yielding teachings that
> have direct bearing upon our own day and our own lives.[6]

In order to explore an emerging model of kashrut, then, we turn to
Torah and to commentary from the ages to shape our path. As when
the Rabbis of old tried to preserve the *values* laid out in Torah, even as

the *laws* evolved,[7] so too should our dietary guidelines build upon the Jewish traditions we have inherited.

An Emerging Model for Kashrut

While Torah gives extensive instruction[8] regarding clean and unclean animals, indicates parts of the creatures that one is forbidden to eat, and repeats several times the injunction not to boil a kid in its mother's milk, the text is relatively silent on the reasons for such restrictions. It frequently contextualizes these mitzvot within the pursuit of holiness and consecration to God, but commentators have found a host of additional reasons for these unique laws. Even *m'farshim* who are generally loathe to offer such rationales[9] add their perspectives on the justification of kashrut.

Using the five categories of purpose identified by *The Torah: A Modern Commentary*,[10] this article will discuss their interpretive foundations and possible modern applications.

To Separate Ourselves from Our Pagan Neighbors

Much attention—both positive and negative—has focused on how kashrut still has the potential to separate Jews from their non-Jewish neighbors, even though classical paganism is passé. Some view the issues that arise as fertile ground for exploring the tension between assimilation and segregation, for asserting our particular identity within a universalist ethic. Others, Jewish and non-Jewish, have been quite critical of the potentially isolating effects of the practice for a Jew in modern life. Most liberal Jews who keep kosher make some accommodation to minimize this effect, at least eating off anyone's dishes. In a society that has been sensitized to the growing number of vegetarians and others with their own dietary restrictions, this is generally sufficient to bridge the gap.

The tradition supports an alternative focus, however: to separate ourselves from paga*nism*, rather than from the pagans themselves. Boiling a kid in its mother's milk, for instance, was thought to be a pagan rite. In refusing to do it, the Israelites could reject idolatry by the very way they cooked their food. Maimonides surmises as much in his *Guide of the Perplexed:*

> Perhaps such food was eaten at one of the ceremonies of their cult or at one of their festivals. A confirmation of this may, in my opinion, be found in the fact that the prohibition against eating meat [boiled] in milk, when it is mentioned for the first two times [Exod. 23:19, 34:26], occurs near the commandment concerning pilgrimage. . . . It is as if it said: When you go on pilgrimage and enter the house of the Lord your God, do not cook there in the way they used to do.[11]

Idolatry today is frequently associated with the materialism that pervades every aspect of our society; in this incarnation, it is a worship of money. There are no magical fertility rites, but this contemporary paganism still makes of ultimate importance that which *we* create and acquire. It enshrines profit above people; it bows to corporate pressures and stock markets instead of to God. And, just as in ancient times, it touches the very food we eat.

There are countless examples. Florida farm workers are paid 1.2 cents per pound for picking tomatoes. To earn $25 a day, one worker must pick two thousand pounds of tomatoes! Some growers have been cited for slave conditions: armed guards force laborers to work ten to twelve hours per day, six days a week. Chocolate, coffee, and other foods are similarly "tainted" by horrendous labor practices pursued in the name of the almighty dollar.[12]

Genetically modified crops can be seen as technologically advanced versions of the same temptations. They are more resistant to pests or drought, increasing productivity and profit. Agricultural companies will tout the potential to help subsistence farmers, but these altered foods have also been linked to severe allergic reactions, increased soil erosion, and breeding of resistant pests. Dumping of the products in some markets has led to the invasion of species and a weakening of biodiversity. Several corporations are pursuing "terminator" technology—sterile seeds that would guarantee annual seed purchases, ruining small farmers that cannot afford them, and potentially devastating the food production chain.[13] A Reform kashrut should resist these forms of paganism as well. Torah speaks repeatedly of the significance that God created living organisms with the seed of creation inside them. In addition, many of these modifications violate even a liberal interpretation of restrictions against *kilayim*, mixing seeds (Lev. 19:19). While these concerns are not classical elements of kashrut, the biblical instructions at their core link them to Jewish dietary laws.

Reform Jews will rightly insist on continuing to eat with their neighbors, even their pagan ones. Yet they can separate themselves from the idolatrous practices that pervade the food industry. Traditional kashrut sets up a fence for some of them, but the CCAR could be very instrumental in informing the community about current concerns, thereby shaping contemporary practice to live by the highest values of Torah.

To Promote Human Hygiene

The suggestion that one rationale for kashrut is to promote human health and hygiene has caused much debate over the centuries. Rambam,[14] Rashbam,[15] and Ramban[16] all hold it to be true, but others, like Abarbanel[17] and the author of *Akeidat Yitzchak*,[18] vociferously reject the idea. Torah is more than a minor medical treatise. Why are there plenty of healthy pork eaters? Why doesn't Torah teach about poisonous plants? Why does it use the language of abomination and detestation instead of unhealthy or hard to digest? The profundity of its purpose, they argue, is greater than the promotion of human hygiene. Nevertheless, it remains one of the more commonly assumed bases for the dietary laws.

A translation of these principles to modern times requires little imagination. New proclamations about the positive and negative effects of various foods are issued every day. In following the dictates of Torah, we are commanded to choose life. This is keeping kosher. While sorting out the surfeit of information may be challenging, we can assert as a movement that an element of kashrut is the command to eat healthfully.

To Develop a Discipline by Which Israel Can Consecrate Itself to God

Some of the commentators who reject the health-food explanation focus instead on the discipline of following God's command. The *Sifra* makes the point in a rather amusing way: Don't say that you hate pork. Say that you'd love to eat pork, but your Father in heaven has forbidden it, so you have no choice. In this way, you will keep far from transgression and accept upon yourself the rule of heaven.[19]

This rationale may seem to defy extension; "because I said so" is almost always the end of a conversation. Yet serving God even while eating turns our table into an altar. God is the focus not only for the blessings that come out of our mouth, but also for the food that goes in. For many Reform Jews who keep kosher, the ability to serve God with one of our most basic animal instincts is a compelling dimension of the dietary laws. Nothing is consumed without stopping to think what the Most High might have to say about it. And with a living Torah, God never shuts up.

So when our parents told us to clear our plates because there were children starving in India (or Africa, depending on your age), that was keeping kosher. We might have been tempted to send our leftover green beans, but every time we ate, we stopped to think about the world God created with the potential to feed us all . . . except that we cannot find a kosher way to share it.

What would God think about the juice box that does not biodegrade? Is a thermos a more "kosher" alternative? Soaps and cleaning supplies have to be kosher too, even though we do not eat them.

Would God prefer alternative cleansers, without bleach and unnecessary chemicals? Such questions have no end. The principle of obeisance may extend kashrut most of all.

To Identify with the Feelings of Animals and Inspire Hesitation about Eating Meat

Rav Kook teaches with great passion that the rules of kashrut should inspire in us a sort of guilt about eating meat. Before the Great Flood, humanity is vegetarian. Permission to eat meat is understood by our tradition to be a sort of concession to our violent appetites, which become all too evident by the time of Noah.

> The commandments came to regulate the eating of meat, in steps that will take us to the higher purpose. . . . These actions will bear fruit and ultimately educate mankind. The mute protest will, when the time is ripe, be transformed into a mighty shout and succeed in its aim. The very nature of the principles of ritual slaughter, with their specific rules and regulations designed to reduce pain, create the atmosphere that you are not dealing with things outside the law, that they are not automatons devoid of life, but living beings.[20]

The concept is not new: Rambam, too, speaks of *tzaar baalei chayim*, understanding the pain of all living creatures. We are instructed not to slaughter an animal and its young on the same day (Lev. 22:28), "for in these cases animals feel very great pain, there being no difference regarding this pain between man and the other animals. For the love and the tenderness of a mother for her child is not consequent upon reason, but upon the activity of the imaginative faculty, which is found in most animals just as it is found in man."[21]

Ibn Ezra argues that this prohibition, along with the warning not to take a mother bird and her eggs, teach sensitivity to life. Although he insists that the complete reasons for kashrut are concealed, it is clear that boiling a kid in its mother's milk would be cruel.[22]

Sensitivity, it seems, comes in several gradations. While the vegetarian movement continues apace, Rav Kook describes that practice as messianic, to be achieved after we have mastered more basic objectives, such as world peace. Torah offers a gradualness for those whose carnivorous drives cannot be fully subdued. Kook folklore tells that the *rav* himself ate meat once a week, chicken on Erev Shabbat, as a sign that we had not yet arrived. En route, however, there are choices we can make that extend our sensitivity to animal life: we can refuse to eat veal—baby calves with their feet chained to the side of a stall their entire lives so they will not stand up or wander around and spoil that tender flesh. We can buy nest eggs, so that chickens do not have to live their lives in tiny cages just so we can have scrambled eggs in the morning. We can seek out milk from cows that have not been given growth hormones, which cause increased infection and discomfort for the animals.

Traditional kashrut certainly limits the amount of meat we consume, since we do not eat meat "out" except in kosher restaurants. The separation of meat and milk can prompt us to be conscious of the sources of our food, and the price paid to bring it to our table. Contemporary expansion of the principles would further advance our appreciation of *tzaar baalei chayim*.

To Develop a Life of Holiness and Wholeness

The midrash asks quite boldly: What does God care whether we kill an animal this way or that? The purpose of the law is to refine humanity.[23] Kashrut enables an aspect of holiness and wholeness. You are what you eat. The spiritual is expressed in material ways and vice versa. Also, the ritual and the ethical are intimately connected, each dependent on the other. Ritual acts take on significance when they are understood as signposts on the road toward healing our broken world; and ethical impulses are in constant need of symbolic reminders, reinforcements—a rhythm and a schedule lest we get too busy or distracted to think about what God may require of us.

Philo, anxious to demonstrate to the Greco-Roman world how enlightened Jewish dietary practices are, interprets them to be controls on our bodily appetites. The restriction against pork (the "most delicious" of meats) keeps us from becoming self-indulgent. We do not eat carnivorous animals in order to train us in the ways of gentleness and kindness. Focusing on animals that chew their cud inspires us to grow in wisdom as we "chew" over what we have studied, and so forth.[24] Similarly, the letter of Aristeas[25] claims the dietary laws are ethical in intent, and he points to a verse from Ezekiel (33:25) that equates the consumption of blood with the sins of idolatry and murder. Thus, our aversion to the blood of an animal is to tame our violent instincts, and we do not eat birds of prey in order not to prey on others.

It is precisely through such mundane concerns that we approach the holy. Checking ingredients becomes a sacred activity. What we eat and how it got to our table matter. This embrace of mitzvot in shaping a life of *k'dushah* is, perhaps, most appealing to Reform Jews; it is the essential *taam* for our reconsideration of many commandments. If the purpose of the law is to refine humanity, if the act of eating is a gateway to learning, to spiritual growth, and to ethical striving—then we must also incorporate contemporary concerns. Our capacity for compassion and commitment to justice can extend to all the "animals" involved in food production, including human labor. Philo's "chewing" over the words of Torah prompts us to invest the time and effort to grow wise in the ways of the food industry in the modern world. *Shopping for a Better World*[26] and *Silent Spring*[27] can become holy books. Institutes that educate us in regard to sustainable farming and grocery stores that promote organic and other "eco-kosher" products are holy communities.

An additional motivation for some liberal Jews to keep kosher has been *K'lal Yisrael,* a desire to connect with the extended community of Israel. In some cases, it is the principle, every Jew should be able to eat in my home; for others, it is simply a powerful chain of tradition linking us through time and space. Just as the rationales for traditional kashrut are not mutually exclusive (Rambam cites them all!), so too can we contemplate contemporary extension of the values combined with standard definitions of kashrut. Contrary to the original Pittsburgh

Platform, the dietary laws do still "sanctify our lives" and "further modern spiritual elevation."

There are some instances, however, in which we may need to challenge the standards directly, not merely add to the regulations. If there is a more humane way to slaughter animals, we should pursue it—advocating within the Jewish community, and approving meat plants that use it, if traditional kosher slaughterhouses will not. If the process of a *hechsher* becomes perverted by politics and money, we must try to reform it or even establish our own. The idea that wine needs to be boiled to protect it from the "taint" of non-Jews handling it is deeply offensive. It is not necessarily sufficient to transform the message into a positive value: kosher wine was crafted from the very beginning by Jews who seek to create a wine for sanctification. The concept of kosher wine may need to be struck from the Reform standard.

If one reads any generic explanation of movement positions, the Reform Movement is still described as dismissing the value of kashrut, and indeed, most of our members do not observe the dietary laws in any significant measure. A serious revival in the community would require an enormous commitment to education and a rabbinic body devoted to the ongoing development of guidelines. Kashrut would need to be revitalized with modern extensions of its sacred purposes, and our *k'hilot* acclimated to new "adventures in eating."

Is it worth it? Rabbi John Rayner was quoted a generation ago stating, "After all, religion is not primarily concerned with eating habits. To create the impression that this is one of Judaism's chief preoccupations is to debase it in the eyes of Jews and non-Jews."[28]

Nonetheless, kashrut has taken on a strange centrality in Jewish identity. Non-Jews who know very little about our faith have heard something about "kosher." Liberal Jews trying to describe their level of observance are often heard to say: I don't keep kosher or anything like that, but we observe the holidays, and so forth.

Would we, could we, be so known by this new kashrut? The one that demonstrates—by where we shop, how we cook, what we eat—that we value each person, all of us created in the image of God; that we are committed to preserve the earth and its animals entrusted to our care; that our most basic animal need, to eat, is transformed, and becomes an entrance to holiness.

NOTES

1. "Declaration of Principles," 1885 CCAR Conference in Pittsburgh, items 3 and 4.

2. "A Statement of Principles for Reform Judaism," adopted at the 1999 CCAR Convention in Pittsburgh, in the section on Torah.

3. "Ten Principles of Reform Judaism," Sixth: We Are Open to Expanding the Mitzvot of Reform Jewish Practice. Third Draft, August 1998.

4. Arnold M. Eisen, *Rethinking Modern Judaism: Ritual, Commandment, Community* (Chicago: University of Chicago Press, 1998), part 1.

5. Arnold M. Eisen, 1999 CCAR Convention, Pittsburgh, "A Program of Reflection."

6. Mark Washofsky, CCAR Responsa Committee, "5762.8, Preventive War," p. 1.

7. Consider, for example, the profound transformation of *lex talionis*. While the Talmud lays out intricate arguments for why "an eye for an eye," etc., mandates compensation rather than retaliation, it quite consciously moves away from the *p'shat* in shaping the law. Still, it seeks to sustain the underlying values of equal, measured, and direct justice. See Babylonian Talmud, *Bava Kama* 83b–84a.

8. See especially Leviticus 11 and Deuteronomy 14, Lev. 7:22–27, Exod. 23:19.

9. Their concern focuses on the danger of *taamei hamitzvot*, rationales for the commandments, somehow lessening their divine authority. If "because God said so" is not sufficient, and the logical basis fails to persuade, it could lead to abandonment of the mitzvah.

10. W. Gunther Plaut, ed., *The Torah: A Modern Commentary* (New York: UAHC Press, 1981), commentary on Deuteronomy 14, p. 1444.

11. Maimonides, *Guide of the Perplexed*, trans. Shlomo Pines (Chicago: University of Chicago Press, 1963), 3:48. Sforno makes a similar comment on Exod. 23:19. While the evidence for such practices is somewhat speculative, Theodor Gaster and other modern "scientific" approaches echo the concept. See *Myth, Legend and Custom in the Old Testament* (New York: Harper and Row, 1817), citing a Ugaritic "Poem of the Gracious Gods," which mentions seething a kid in milk as part of a ritual celebration, and a Karaite letter that claims there was an ancient custom among the heathen using the kid-milk mixture to sprinkle on trees, crops, etc., for a fruitful year.

12. Internet sites such as CorpWatch.org offer up-to-date information on these issues.

13. CorpWatch.org, agresearch.cri.nz, mercola.com.

14. Maimonides, *Guide*, 3:48. "Among all those forbidden to us, only pork and fat may be imagined not to be harmful. But this is not so, for pork is more humid than is proper and contains much superfluous matter. . . . The fat of the intestines [*cheilev*], too, makes us full, spoils the digestion, and produces cold and thick blood."

15. Commentary to Lev. 11:3. "All the cattle, creatures, fowl and fish . . . that the Holy One of Blessing has forbidden to Israel are vile. They damage and overheat the body; therefore they are termed unclean. Even expert doctors will so attest."

16. E.g., Commentary to Lev. 11:9. The fish without fins and scales live in lower waters, breed in musty swamps, and can be injurious to health.

17. *Sh'mini*; key word: *Vay'dabeir Adonai el Moshe.*

18. Isaac b. Moses Arama, *Sh'mini, Shaar Shishim* (chap. 60). He suggests instead that they have a deleterious effect on our intellectual powers and ethical sensibilities.

19. *Sifra, K'doshim* 9:12.

20. Abraham Isaac Kook, "Fragments of Light: A View as to the Reasons for the Commandments," cited in *Abraham Isaac Kook*, trans. Ben Zion Bokser (New York: Paulist Press, 1978), 318–19 (translation is not followed in its entirety).

21. Maimonides, *Guide* 3:48.

22. Exod. 23:19, Deut. 22:6.

23. *B'reishit Rabbah* 44:1, *Vayikra Rabbah* 13:3.

24. Philo, *The Special Laws*, 4:97ff.

25. An otherwise unknown Egyptian Jew of the first century B.C.E.

26. Council on Economic Priorities, 2000.

27. Rachel Carson (New York: Houghton Mifflin, 2002; originally published in 1962).

28. *Liberal Judaism*, 1968, as cited in *Encyclopaedia Judaica*, "Dietary Laws," 45.

5

KASHRUT

A New Freedom for Reform Jews

RICHARD N. LEVY

In May 1999 in Pittsburgh, the CCAR passed a statement that read in part:

> We are committed to the ongoing study of the whole array of mitz-
> vot and to the fulfillment of those that address us as individuals and
> as a community. Some of these mitzvot have long been observed by
> Reform Jews; others, both ancient and modern, demand renewed
> attention as the result of the unique context of our own times.

For several of the members of the task force that drafted the Principles, part of the intention of that paragraph was to rescind publicly a state-ment passed in Pittsburgh 114 years before, which rejected "all such Mosaic and Rabbinical laws as regulate diet, priestly purity, and dress." The prevailing view of Reform Judaism until the end of the twentieth century was that Reform was opposed to kashrut. Despite positive com-ments in *Gates of Mitzvah* (1979), by 1999 the Conference was still not ready to name kashrut specifically as one of these "ancient mitzvot"— there had been too loud an outcry when it appeared in a draft of the

An earlier version of this essay originally appeared in *CCAR Journal*, Winter 2004, 45–54.

Ten Principles in the Fall 1998 issue of *Reform Judaism* magazine. Why this continued reticence when "the unique context of our times" has seen the once homogeneously omnivorous North American diet dissolve into a stew of antibiotic-free, vegetarian, vegan, low-cholesterol, low-sodium, macrobiotic, lactose- and sugar-free regimens that enable people to express their beliefs through the food they eat?

The reticence about embracing kashrut has many sources. For some Reform Jews, kashrut was permanently tainted by their own or their parents' unpleasant experiences with it growing up. For one hundred years many Reform Jews who might have considered observing kashrut felt inhibited by the atmosphere of hostility to the practice inspired by the Pittsburgh 1885 rejection, despite the two platforms (Columbus in 1937 and the Centenary Perspective in 1976) that were intended to weaken its influence. Individual inhibitions were strengthened by some rabbinic colleagues who have felt uncomfortable discussing dietary mitzvot, either out of a theological conviction that they are inappropriate or because they themselves may not observe them. Rabbis may have similar objections to some aspects of Shabbat and Festivals that the CCAR's classic *Gates*[1] series recommends, but we do not withhold these books from our members' shelves. Even if our personal response to the Torah's dietary calls is "No," we restrict our people's freedom to make choices if we do not provide information that allows every Reform Jew to respond according to his or her own religious values.

Pittsburgh 1999 created a framework to free us from the rejectionism of Pittsburgh 1885, finally giving us permission to adopt a diet that can increase the holiness of our lives. The time has come to make it explicit that kashrut is no longer out of bounds for Reform Jews—that Reform Jews are free to observe the dietary mitzvot. Reform Jews deserve to be liberated from their historic inhibitions, so they may enter this dialogue with Torah and with God to explore what their response to those mitzvot can be in the twenty-first century.

Through that dialogue, Reform Jews will come to understand their freedom to keep kosher in a greatly expanded sense—to see it as a "new freedom," different from what it meant for Jews a century ago. The time has come to demonstrate how broad the dietary possibilities might be for those Reform Jews who want to deepen the spiritual content of their lives by transforming the act of eating into a celebration of the presence of God in their homes, an advancement of social justice in the fields and agricultural factories, and a contribution to the health of individuals and the planet itself.

Just as we have set forth models of Shabbat observance for our people, so we can create models of dietary practice, and just as they are free to follow our Shabbat examples, reject them, or find models of their own, so, of course, are they free to do the same with kashrut.

Some Jews argue that the only proper observance of God's desired diet is to become a vegetarian. I believe that while vegetarianism in some ways advocates an impressively high standard of dietary discipline, it also has the effect of cutting us off from a number of the Torah's dietary mitzvot, again restricting our observance. Vegetarianism thus reflects a flawed understanding of the nuanced dietary program in the Bible.

The Torah makes it clear that God did not create a world of fruits and vegetables and animals just for the fun of it. As Genesis 1 describes the steps in the Creation, Genesis 2 describes their purpose: trees and grasses were to provide food for human beings, and the earth and animals were to provide a purpose for human existence—to care for the earth, to serve the earth, and to nurture its creatures. Not until after the Flood, when the earth, as Genesis 6 tells us, was destroying itself, did God reveal another purpose for the creation of animals—to sublimate the violent nature of earth-bound creatures. The only creatures punished in the Flood are those that had helped destroy the earth—humans and animals. To strengthen human dominion over the animal realm, God allowed large creatures to eat smaller ones, and human beings were allowed to eat them all. Some people think that the permission to eat meat after the Flood was a compromise of the Edenic ideal of a vegetarian existence, which was to be reinstated in the messianic time when, in Isaiah's vision, the lion would eat straw like the ox (Isaiah 65:25).

I don't know whether I believe that God doesn't want us to eat animals—the Torah seems to support both sides of that argument.

Before the Flood, God does not indicate any purpose for animals in the scheme of the Creation. In Genesis 1, only birds and sea creatures and human beings are blessed. In Leviticus 11:40, the Torah makes it clear that there is no intrinsic value to an animal dying a natural death. Such a creature is called *n'veilah*, and we are forbidden to eat it. In the description of the High Priest's Yom Kippur ritual (Leviticus 16), the fortunate animal is not the goat that is kept alive, doomed to wander sin-laden through the wilds of Azazel, but the one whose death comes in a *korban*, as part of a ritual sacrifice. All animals, like all humans, must die. The question is, does an animal's death fulfill a purpose? The Torah seems to say—whether you agree with its reasoning or not—that the animal's purpose is to nurture bigger animals and human beings. Human beings, after all, also nurture the earth when we die and are buried.

Although God seems to see nurturing other creatures as one of the purposes for the existence of animals, God clearly wants human beings to think about the lives they are taking. Consider the long lists of creatures permitted and forbidden, the near-death struggle in *Parashat Vayishlach* from which Jacob emerges wounded in his loins, the source of the prohibition against sirloin and tenderloin and porterhouse. Consider the statement in Genesis 9:4 that blood represents the life that belongs to God and not to us, and the Rabbis' tortured extensions of the simple command to avoid boiling a kid in its mother's milk. Taking an animal's life may be permitted, but we are to empathize with the animal's pain, with *tzaar baalei chayim*. If the ideal is the reinstatement of the Edenic condition, then to confront the realities of consuming animals with every meal we buy, prepare, and consume not only builds our Jewish identities, but also makes us aware many times each day of God's mitzvot—and reminds us of our failure to create societies free from violence and lustful appetite. The encounter with the realities of taking the lives of living creatures reminds us of our own creatureliness as human beings, even as the dietary section in Deuteronomy 14:21 reminds us that our destiny is to be an *am kadosh*, a holy people to Adonai our God. We are creatures, whom God commanded to consume other creatures to live—but we can also be holy, striving to climb out of creatureliness into godliness. It is a struggle: Jacob's frail body versus the spirit; *k'doshim tihyu*, Leviticus 19:2 tells us—we are *becoming* holy; we have not yet reached the goal.

We learn in the third chapter of Leviticus about the *zevach sh'lamim*, the "whole offering," which, Baruch Levine notes in *The JPS Torah Commentary*, is described in I Samuel 9 as a meal shared by priests and laypeople.[2] This is the origin of the idea that every meal is like a sacrifice to God, a *korban*, a word stemming from the Hebrew *kareiv*, that which brings us near to God. With the Temple destroyed, our table has become the altar, and the food we consume on it should assist our march to holiness. What we would not offer on the Temple altar, the Torah tells us, we should not offer on our dining room table.

Confronting the mitzvot of eating, Reform Jews cannot be content to look only at the mitzvot considered part of dietary practice in the past. We need to look at all the things the Torah says about eating. Reform Judaism has long held that new times reveal new aspects of God's will—the Pittsburgh Principles define Torah as "God's ongoing revelation to our people and the record of our people's ongoing relationship with God." If *tzaar baalei chayim*, compassion toward animals, is a value—is indeed, one of the seven mitzvot commanded to all human beings (see *B'reishit Rabbah* 16:6)—we need to investigate the methods by which animals are slaughtered and be assured that our meat comes from the most humane possible practices of slaughter. When we know that some animals are fed and penned in destructive ways, like geese for pâté de foie gras and calves for veal, we should deal with them the same way the Torah deals with pork and shellfish. When the Torah prohibits us from participating in *oshek*, the oppression of laborers (Lev. 19:13), I believe it means we need to refrain from eating the foods produced by oppressive labor—like fruits or vegetables sold under labels of growers who refuse to offer their workers minimum wage and decent conditions in the fields and factories, and who insist upon spraying their products with pesticides that harm workers and consumers. The value of *bal tashchit*, the avoidance of practices destructive of nature (based on Deut. 20:19–20), should lead us to build aspects of conservation into our observance as well.

How Do All These Principles Fit into a Coherent Whole?

The permission to eat meat and the prohibition against eating blood were part of the *b'rit*, the covenant God made with the children of Noah after the Flood. The Rabbis believed that the prohibition of *tzaar baalei chayim* was part of the Noachide covenant as well. The prohibition against eating certain kinds of meat, fish, and fowl and the prohibitions against *oshek* and *bal tashchit* were part of the covenant made at Sinai. *As circumcision is a sign of the covenant in the male body, so the dietary laws—all of them—imprint the covenant in the bodies of all Jews.* The nature of our skin, our weight and height, our physical condition, are formed in part by the dietary choices we make. The foods we eat and refrain from eating make their mark on our very bodies, as another aspect of the covenant sealed in the flesh. And because some of these practices trace back to Noah and his descendants, they tie us to God's will not only as Jews, but as part of all humanity.

Observance of the principle of *bal tashchit* connects us to our purpose as human beings in guarding the earth as we till it. A Reform understanding of the food laws even ties us to the principle behind so many mitzvot, the reminder that we were strangers in the land of Egypt—as so many of the men and women who harvest our food in the sweltering fields are strangers on the land, traveling from field to field in search of some of the hardest, most backbreaking work human beings can perform in this technological age. A Reform expansion of dietary practice through these additional mitzvot not only assists us in our climb to holiness, it is a fulfillment of the very covenant God made with humanity and the Jewish people.

How can we carry out this covenant? Won't such expansive standards make Reform dietary practice seem more stringent than the Orthodox?

And with so few Reform Jews seemingly committed to kashrut, can there be infrastructure to support Reform dietary practice?

I would propose that we establish a Reform Kashrut Board to make recommendations for individuals and synagogues, recognizing that even though a minority of Reform Jews in a synagogue may keep kosher, the synagogue community can help its members understand what kashrut is in a Reform context and offer them models for personal observance if they feel called to it. After all, synagogues observe Shabbat as a community even though many of its individual members do not, and the synagogue provides models for Shabbat observance that its members may or may not follow. How can we provide the tools to aid the average Reform Jew in making new decisions about the mitzvot of Jewish dietary practice if they cannot recognize what that practice looks like? Once some guidelines are developed, we can explore whether we want to train our own *shochtim* and *mashgichim*—kosher slaughterers and supervisors—or whether we wish to contract with some more liberal members of those professions who have indicated they might like to work with us. As for keeping track of the changing practices of growers regarding their farm workers, there is already a precedent for keeping Reform kosher consumers posted. Just as Orthodox organizations supervising kashrut issue periodic advisories about products that have acquired or lost a *hechsher*, a Reform Kashrut Board could issue advisories notifying Reform Jews of certain brands of mushrooms or berries they should avoid and encouraging them to buy other brands. *We can work out a structure for Reform practice.* We need to persuade each other that it is worth doing so and show by our own example how our lives and the lives of our families and communities, as well as everyone involved in the process of raising and marketing food, will benefit.

Maimonides argues that one of the original reasons for kashrut was to separate the Israelites from the idolatrous practices in which many forbidden animals figured. We are more wary than we were a century ago of the seductive excesses of conspicuous consumption that are the idolatries of our own time. Kashrut offers discipline that can help us resist those seductions. Still, Reform has classically favored integration into society, not separation from it. If we keep kosher, does that not bar us from sharing meals with non-Jews? And today, does it not bar us from sharing meals with Jews who do not keep kosher? I think in twenty-first-century America it need not do either. With dietary diversity proliferating across North America, most party hosts routinely ask their guests whether they have dietary restrictions and happily accommodate them. Paradoxically, the problem is often greater for Jews who do not keep kosher than it is for non-Jews. Intelligent Jewish hosts suddenly become paranoid at the thought of inviting a kosher friend for dinner. Will they eat vegetables? Will they drink coffee? And rather than ask about their practice, the fear of seeming ignorant sometimes leads the would-be host to decide just not to invite them.

But this is hardly an argument against keeping kosher—it is rather an argument that we should involve our friends in celebrating the changes we have brought to our homes. Synagogues might create Home Consecration Committees, developing and enacting a ritual (complete with new music) to accompany the disposal of nonkosher utensils and food (or delivering it to a local food bank), the *kashering* of a stove, the inauguration of new dishes—turning what can be a wearying procedure into a community mini-festival, with plenty of people present to help (and learn how to do it). When our kitchen is in order, we might invite our friends over to explain our new rituals and show them which foods or combinations we will not eat, what we will, and why. If the meals we serve are tasty, we may even encourage our friends to start considering aspects of kashrut themselves.

Finally, how about the argument that "so few Reform Jews keep kosher—why should the Movement even pay attention to it?" My very unscientific research has led me to doubt this old assumption. Yes, if you ask most Reform Jews, "Do you keep kosher?" they will reply in the negative. But if you ask them, "Do you eat pork?" a surprising number will say, "No." If you ask them, "Do you eat shrimp or oysters?" a smaller number, but still a number, will also say, "No." If you ask them, "Do you mix milk and meat?" some others will shake their heads as well. Our assumption that few Reform Jews keep kosher has been based on an all-or-nothing proposition. A survey of several hundred respondents among the regional URJ leaders attending the 2005 Biennial in Houston confirmed my feeling that there are many Reform Jews who keep some form of kashrut (see chapter 8).

Is it legitimate to keep only some aspects of kashrut? Of course it is. Kashrut comprises a number of discrete mitzvot, and we may feel called by some of them but not necessarily by all of them. If we are to include *oshek* and *tzaar baalei chayim* in our definition, there are non-Reform Jews who according to our standards will also not keep all the mitzvot of kashrut. Such a situation would be a reminder that, for all Jews, kashrut is, as my erstwhile Hillel colleague Rabbi David Berner taught me, a continuum, on which a large number of Jews find themselves and on which many religious decisions remain before one takes all of the steps. It is a reminder, too, that Leviticus 19:2, *K'doshim tihyu*, "You shall become holy," is a lifelong process.

In the unique context of our own time, kashrut can be a "natural" for Reform Jews. It nurtures our yearning to deepen our spiritual lives; it responds to our classic imperatives for social justice; it brings us into closer contact with our godly role as guardians of Creation; it opens new opportunities to mingle with today's diverse population of Jews and non-Jews; it offers a variety of disciplines that can keep us from sliding into the maw of North American materialism. Freed from the restrictive bonds of the past, Reform Jews have a remarkable opportunity to let kashrut flourish once again as a way to strengthen the nurturing bonds of the covenant between the Jewish people and the Creator of all life.

NOTES

1. The series includes *Gates of Mitzvah* (1979), *Gates of Shabbat* (1996), and *Gates of the Seasons* (1983).

2. Baruch A. Levine, *The JPS Torah Commentary: Leviticus* (Philadelphia: Jewish Publication Society, 1989), 15.

6

ON KASHRUT

Seth M. Limmer

The *CCAR Journal* has called for articles in order to produce a volume that might reflect the current status of the laws of kashrut in the thought and practice of Reform rabbis.[1] This paper is intended to add one more voice to the discussion, to advance a point of view on the subject I feel has yet to be brought to the forefront. I will attempt to demonstrate that there is a principled Jewish position rejecting the organized system of kashrut as it exists in our time.[2] However, even as my reasoning takes me beyond the kashrut system, it does not remove from me the onus of approaching diet in religious terms; necessarily, it calls me to understand the implications of my rejection for the future of any eating that might be called "Jewish." Hence a new understanding of a constructive Jewish approach to eating is my ultimate conclusion.[3]

Biblical and Rabbinic Kashrut

In the history of Jewish cultural anthropology, the two most visceral taboos remain pork and the uncircumcised penis. A cursory comparison of the biblical etiology of these two traditions makes clear that while

---

Adapted with permission from Seth M. Limmer, "On Kashrut," *CCAR Journal*, Winter 2006, 59–77.

the latter is derived from the covenantal acts of Abraham, the origins of the former are more difficult to discern; the Torah itself teaches that it is no crime for a human being to eat prohibited foodstuffs.[4] Current archaeology argues that disdain for the pig is rooted in ancient Israelite society as deeply as artifacts in the Judean hills.[5] Yet the apodictic lists of Leviticus fail to offer us any insight into the rationale that created such a heavily cleft divide between the foodstuffs our biblical ancestors were able to enjoy and those that remained prohibited.[6]

Likewise, subsequent Jewish history has failed to create a solitary explanation for the totality of dietary laws that might provide a creedal rationale other than "this is simply how Jews have eaten for millennia."[7] The Rabbis, however, further categorized Jewish eating into a more detailed taxonomy, and created the standard appellation for all food deemed religiously "fit," literally, kosher.[8] But these Rabbis, despite their various offered rationales for eating only kosher foods, mostly reinforced a system of Israelite eating that preceded them both historically and logically.[9] In anthropological terms, these Rabbis built a fence not around the Torah, but around a previously existing and deeply ingrained cultural behavior. Taboo foods remained taboo.

These taboos did not operate in a vacuum of Jewish life. Alongside the restrictive food prescriptions rested the Jewish inclination to enjoy the wonders and experiences of our senses.[10] Our tradition repeatedly reminds us that we are flesh-and-blood incarnations of the divine image who are created to participate in, protect, and partake of God's creation. This entirely human aspect and potential Daniel Boyarin has labeled "carnal"; he concludes that we are a people for whom the pleasures of the flesh are never necessarily denied.[11] The subtlety of this carnality is the recognition that, while abstinence and asceticism have not come to define our people, likewise orgies and *Saturnalia* have also not entered into our religious practice:[12] Judaism seeks a nuanced lifestyle that allows us to enjoy the pleasures of our world so long as we do so in a constructive fashion that strives to maintain human dignity.[13] Obviously, it is the subtle nuances of precisely this balance that are at the heart of this and other religious debates. For while it is clear that illicit sexual relationships such as incest clearly violate fundamentals of human dignity, it is far more difficult to discern how the consumption of prohibited foods *a priori* devalues human worth.[14] The conjoining of created beings to partake fully and constructively in the Creation is a compelling Jewish principle that leads us to celebrate our life cycles with bountiful feasts, to savor the passage of our seasons with appropriate species, and even to imagine the menu of messianic meals. Hence with kashrut two powerful streams of our religion's consciousness are in conflict: constructive carnality and dietary taboo. We Jews are meant to enjoy the wonders of creation, yet certain legitimate aspects of that benefit have been proscribed (not for humanity, but only for Jews). At the heart of this issue, there needs to be a resolution of the tension within a tradition that has constantly affirmed finding joy in life, yet has also long maintained a set of proscriptions that appear to prohibit enjoyment that does not seem to harm any person.[15]

Before we examine that tension, we need to remember that, for our Rabbis, religious eating was not solely a matter of prohibiting the consumption of certain foods and food combinations. Moving beyond the biblical text, our Sages addressed not only what Jews ate, but how they ate as well. To begin with, their system of kashrut included a method for slaughtering those animals deemed fit to eat.[16] If our Rabbis were unable to formulate a unifying rationale for prohibiting certain foods, they were far more successful in deriving principles of slaughtering that have stood the tests of both time and logic. By intertwining the biblical precept that prohibits eating "the blood of any kind of flesh"[17] with the verse that associates blood with life's essence, our Sages discover a religious principle behind the laws of proper slaughter.[18] They teach that out of respect for all the sacred life that God has created, we must ritually recall that divine creation prior to taking advantage of it for our own gustatory purposes. While we might be entitled to slaughter an animal in order to satiate our own hunger, our religion reminds us that we nonetheless need to remember our secondary role in the transcendent order of the universe; by returning to God the blood representing the divine life that inhabits all, we remember God's primacy in the order of our universe.

Affixing this reminder of transcendence to the chain of events leading to eating was hardly the only spiritual innovation our Rabbis either discovered or created relating to the Jewish manner of food consumption. In the spirit of the laws of proper slaughter, the Rabbis promulgated specific blessings to be recited immediately before and after eating.[19] Among the purposes of these ritual rehearsals were the expression of gratitude before the God whose beneficence allows humankind to eat and the reminder of human humility in the face of the One who provides for all. Specifically, the blessing before meals is designed to remind the person about to eat that it is ultimately God, and not humanity, who is responsible for all the food we are fortunate enough to eat. Likewise, the blessing following the meal moves the community to participate in a universal drama, to pray to the God who sustains not just one specific set of people eating, but the entire world. To take seriously the recitation of these two blessings on a repeated daily basis is to understand that our Rabbis, who created these prayers, approached the table with a tremendous sense of gratitude and humility.

Gratitude and humility were not all our Rabbis expected our ancestors to bring with them to their tables. In the wake of the world-altering event that was the destruction of the Second Temple, our Sages sought to relocate throughout the world the holiness that was previously considered to exist exclusively in the Holy of Holies in Jerusalem. Part of this religious reconstruction included a redefinition of the sacred sacrificial altar: no longer residing atop Mount Zion, the altar was now seen as residing in every home where Jews approached eating with proper piety. The table around which Jews gathered to dine in proper fashion was labeled a "small altar"; the very act of eating was likened to the sacrifices that brought God the enjoyment of sweet savor.[20] Through this powerful reconstruction, eating in proper religious fashion was lifted to the highest level of human piety; to adopt a sincere sense of humility and gratitude, to dine in sacred community, elevated each Jew to the vaunted status of priest.

All this, of course, only captures the proverbial tip of the iceberg of Rabbinic thinking, innovation, and legislation regarding eating. Volumes have been written trying to understand what I have briefly summarized in a few paragraphs; entire aspects of the kashrut system have not been mentioned in this paper. The topics I cover in this section, as will be seen below, are those that for me play the most forceful roles in determining my personal Jewish beliefs about proper religious consumption. It is because my purpose here is to present one person's approach to the subject that I feel at all comfortable omitting such a tremendous amount of material. It is through the Rabbinic understanding of taboo, separation, carnality, and sanctity that my views on contemporary kashrut are forged.

Contemporary Kashrut

Any current position on kashrut would be incomplete if it took into account only the traditional teachings of our Bible and Talmuds; living in a cosmopolitan society, participating in a Jewish world consisting of varied approaches to our inherited tradition, we know that it cannot be only the realities of Rabbinic antiquity that inform our contemporary discussion of kashrut. Although many consider (at least) our Orthodox coreligionists as maintaining a kashrut that is Rabbinic, we understand that such claims to "traditional" practice often cloak a chasm of difference between our Sages' praxis and our own. Modern systems of food service and delivery, innovations in science and technology, and the globalization of commerce and of Judaism make it impossible for any twenty-first-century kashrut to resemble precisely the eating practices of our ancestors. While myriad commonalities remain—foremost among them the continuance of ancient taboo—the organized system of contemporary kashrut is much more influenced and guided by Rabbinic tradition than it is properly "traditional."

Modern Orthodox variations from, and expansions of, Rabbinic dietary practice are as important to understand as are the vast differences in our society from not only Temple times, but medieval ones as well. While Talmudic legislation remains a primary source for the origins of many contemporary kashrut observances, the entire system of the mainstream dietary laws in America remains a product of the Jewish communities of Europe. Ghettos both pre- and post-Emancipation, whether externally imposed or internally enforced, allowed the creation of exclusive and total Jewish societies. In such closed communities, food practices and taboos grew in strength as the solitary way of Jewish living became defined more clearly. The only butchers were kosher ones; every grocer and shop observed the practices of kashrut. Dietary laws were as natural a part of life as any small-town custom; with little to no outside influence, with no basis for comparison with other traditions, kashrut's hold on the Jewish diet strengthened.

Emancipation brought with it the demise of the cultural incubus known as the externally imposed ghetto. With the perspective of centuries, we are able to see that among the many outcomes of this historical event is the weakening power of our ancient food taboos. Jews have been exposed, for quite some time now, to people who eat on but one set of plates, who slaughter animals in nonkosher fashion, who bless only before meals, and who dine on all varieties of biblically prohibited foods. Over time, at least in America, this has led to a major change in the Jewish community: the erosion if not eradication of once insuperable food taboos.[21] This can be seen in the evidence that a significant portion, if not the majority, of American Jews no longer define the boundaries of their diet by the principles of our ancestors.[22] This is important not because the majority of Jews should be able to determine proper Jewish practice, but instead because of the anthropological data it unearths: foods once banned by ancient taboo are now socially as licit as chopped liver, latkes, and lox.[23]

The weakening of once-omnipotent taboo is not the only contemporary change to the kashrut system. Globalization, organization, and commerce have left their mark as well. There is an identifiable kashrut system in America and abroad: in most major metropolitan centers it is as easy to find kosher restaurants as it is to discover kosher labels on bottles of Coca-Cola at the supermarket. *Mashgichim* and *vaadei kashrut* are plentiful in areas of high Jewish population density; these, whose job it is to ensure the observance of Jewish dietary practice, can be found in the phone book. In consideration of their clientele, non-Jewish grocers and major chains create a special section of their stores during the weeks before Passover. Kashrut has left the boundaries of the Jewish community and has entered into the consciousness and finances of the culture at large. Industry is the appropriate term to describe the influence and resources of this intersection of the Jewish and financial worlds.

This kosher industry operates worldwide, almost without exception, under the aegis of various Orthodox and ultra-Orthodox communities. The stated purpose of these various food producers and supervisory societies is to ensure strict adherence to Jewish dietary law in all aspects of food production, storage, preparation, and consumption. Because Jews have spread out over so large a geographical area, and inasmuch as our community represents a large consumer base, major corporations strive to cater to our perceived dietary needs. Almost every major brand of soda not only possesses a certifying stamp, but also wears a special "kosher for Passover" yellow cap come the month of Aviv. Corporate giants such as Nabisco ceased making the wildly popular Oreo cookies with animal fat in order to widen their appeal to the Jewish community. These companies perceive a huge upside to "target" marketing the kosher community; similarly is there money to be made by those Jewish organizations that supervise and authenticate the religious propriety of national and global products.

Unfortunately, in the current state of the certifying and supervising community, many of the organizations that strive to enforce kashrut ultimately are tempted by the incredible potential they possess to reap large financial gains. This can be seen in the almost inexplicable kosher creations of our day: through the wonders of scientific innovation, it is today possible—if religiously inconsistent—to eat crab legs, bacon, and cheeseburgers that are kosher.[24] In these cases, it seems as if in the rush to cash in on the legalization of once-illicit foods, those who certify as kosher even imitations of taboo foods are somehow missing the forest of the prohibitions for the trees. The intent in these cases seems not to be to enforce age-old taboos, but to circumvent them through the marvels of technology. At the very least, this new way of eating seeming *t'reif* that is nonetheless kosher adds a disingenuous air to contemporary kashrut.

But the kosher industry has more serious credibility problems than the legalization of foods that seem to exceed the taboo. A cursory search of reliable news organizations reveals the level of complaints and lawsuits lodged regarding kashrut boards' perceived impropriety or criminal offenses.[25] Many people with whom I discuss this subject share some disheartening anecdote; the sense of "gangsterism" and "corruption" in the kashrut industry has led one author to describe it as "a Jewish Mafia."[26] There are numerous stories of unfortunate families who—whether as grocers, butchers, or caterers—have either been forced into new businesses or had to close their businesses entirely because of local kashrut boards. The certifying societies' concern in these cases has much less to do with kashrut than it does with profit. Anecdotal evidence makes it easy to infer the existence of serious corruption in the kashrut industry.[27] Certifying rabbis and boards have been known to hold up a certification for causes as trivial (and non-halachic) as a shopkeeper refraining from displaying a *pushke* for a particular pet cause.[28] Kashrut has become a big business and, like other business, it at times falls prey to pitfalls of advantage and avarice. Sometimes it unfortunately appears as if the certification of kashrut has far less to do with the preservation of a sacred system than it does with the elevation of mammon.

The system of Jewish dietary observance finds itself under incredible pressure in our day. On the one hand, a majority of modern Jews find themselves less and less affected by the power of aging taboos; conversely, the smaller segment of the Jewish population dedicated to preserving kashrut can find little agreement in defining religiously proper strictures and enforcements of the system.[29] This divide is further complicated by the entrance of corporate America (and its concomitant financial resources) into the realm of kosher food. As often happens, the potential for and competition over large profits cast a shadow of suspicion over an industry that may have subjugated its religious goals to the more powerful bottom line. The entirety of this situation is of serious consequence for discerning a contemporary stance on kashrut.

Kashrut Today

In my personal attempt to understand kashrut, all the above information comes into play. It is likely clear from my presentation that I find powerful and persuasive the elements of humility, gratitude, and sanctity that the Rabbis brought with them literally to their tables. I find it interesting that Jewish food taboos are losing their power in our day, but for me this contains little compelling impact. More influential in my consideration of kashrut is the current state of the kosher industry, which I understand to be in serious conflict with our dietary regulations' religious core. All these realities weigh in the balance of my opinions regarding kashrut. Yet the issue that remains at the center of my thinking about kashrut is the tension between a religion's set of food prohibitions and that same religion's impulse not to prohibit without cause.[30] Here I refer to my understanding of Israel's "carnal" nature: a dedication to enjoy the constructive pleasures of our divinely created world; more specifically, a religious approach that abhors asceticism. It is this principled dedication to affirming life that comes into conflict most directly with that part of kashrut that continues to adhere to ancient food taboos. The resolution of this tension is at the heart of my understanding of kashrut today.

I resolve this tension by acknowledging that while the power of taboo can exceed category, a restriction's influence becomes self-limiting when it fails to justify its continued reinforcement.[31] An inexplicable taboo, therefore, does not carry a particularly authoritative voice in my religious understanding (and, I believe, in the approach of Reform

Judaism as well).[32] Especially when such an enigmatic proscription comes into conflict with another religious principle, the taboo becomes further weakened: in this case, a comprehensive and convincing religious principle (carnality) earns a privileged position over an ancient yet unfathomable taboo (kashrut). My initial response to the issue of kashrut is informed by my fundamental religious commitment: Jewish principle should take precedence over unprincipled practice (no matter how deeply ingrained).[33] Thus the traditional food taboos of our people are for me cut off by this hermeneutical blade: because I find no compelling reason to obey these taboos, I am disinclined to maintain this tradition of which I can make no sense.[34] This disinclination in turn is only strengthened by my commitment to the Jewish principle that urges us to enjoy constructively the delights of God's creation, so long as our enjoyment brings harm to no one.[35] Hence the unjustified Jewish dietary tradition is eliminated not only on the basis of its own inner inexplicability but also because of its conflict with the important religious principle of carnality; in this manner Judaism teaches me to reject kashrut.

Nevertheless, I recognize that doing away with a taboo as powerful as kashrut is not like moving past the rituals of *kaparot*.[36] As I indicated above, I believe there to be valid and worthy pieces of the Jewish dietary experience; the question that remains, then, is whether or not the spiritual arguments added by our Sages are compelling enough to salvage some aspects of the modern system of kashrut. Are the humility, gratitude, and respect for life that parts of the dietary laws attempt to reinforce of sufficient value to preserve even the meritorious pieces of the kashrut system? The answer to this question for me lies not in our inherited practices, but rather in the current state of the kosher world. The aspect of contemporary kashrut that bears heavily on my determination here is the subjugation of Jewish dietary practice to external considerations. Not only do I find troubling what appears to be the frequency with which the kosher industry focuses more on monetary issues than spiritual ones, but I also have grave difficulty supporting an industry that, I suspect, financially sustains causes at direct odds with my Jewish beliefs.[37] Furthermore, as I explained above, a dark cloud of suspicion hangs over the commercial side of contemporary kashrut; like major companies known to prevent union organizing, akin to national chains known for taking advantage of workers, the kashrut industry of today does not seem worthy of the support of religious people.

It is because of these major difficulties—compromised principles, unjustifiable taboos—that I believe the obstacles that are part and parcel of contemporary kashrut make it impossible for me to follow this path of dietary observance even in part. Just as my commitment to the constructively carnal nature of humanity prevents me from following ancient proscriptions, so too does my disdain for religious corruption prevent me from participating in those aspects of kashrut that I otherwise find compelling. Out of a reflective thought process I consider deeply religious and completely Jewish, I must reject kashrut as it is currently formulated; I believe it religiously appropriate not to keep kosher. However, this does not mean that I maintain that the Jewish people should forsake kashrut.

Kashrut Tomorrow

I have arrived at my position on kashrut primarily by adhering to the belief that we as Jews are meant to understand and celebrate our carnal nature. Our physical incarnation is not meant to be experienced without boundaries; parameters of respect and sanctity should—as in every other aspect of Jewish living—be brought to bear here. Therefore the task remaining for me is to restore the sacred fragments of a shattered system of religious diet; this is concomitant with my commitment to carnality, as any belief in the sacred nature of our veritable incarnation must maintain that every physical act should aspire to the heights of holiness.

We in our time should seek to implement those intellectually valid and spiritually uplifting aspects of our Jewish dietary practice that make our eating a sacred, life-affirming act: understanding the family table as a small altar, approaching that table with humility and gratitude, and appreciating the sanctity of the animal life we take in order to eat our meals. Creating a sense of sanctity in our dining communities, using blessings to focus our thoughts on our privilege of eating, and following an ethical system regarding the types of foods we consume are worthy actions many Jews—Reform and otherwise—already incorporate into their own personal cultures of making their diets religiously "fit." The literature and practice that surround the concept of "eco-kashrut" help all of us determine how to ensure our consumption is in keeping with the respect our religion requires. However lofty and laudable these practices are, however, I do not believe they are sufficient for the long term. If we are to move toward a new Jewish way of eating, if we are to fulfill our mandate to keep Judaism living and vibrant for new generations, then a great deal of difficult work lies beyond these worthy advances.

The first step, I believe, is the removal not only of the prefix "eco" from but also of the Orthodox monopoly on the word "kashrut." Although not in keeping with Amram's prayer book, we rightfully refer to our publications as *siddurim*; although we include women, we correctly call our prayer circles *minyanim*. Similarly, we should reclaim the word "kosher" for what it means, and use it to define what we consider to be "fit" Jewish consumption without the self-effacing shame of prefixes. I believe we should do this not only nominally, but institutionally: the CCAR should train rabbis to be Reform *mashgichim* and local boards of rabbis should operate as *vaadei kashrut*. I even believe that we as a movement have the ability to recover the ancient respect for the blood our people considers to be at the heart of life: I for one would buy at a premium meat whose blood was spilled in keeping with respect for animal life by a URJ *shochet*.[38] As the largest collection of Jews in America, we have the ability to shape Jewish diet for years to come, to create an evolving kashrut founded completely upon a liberal perspective of our Jewish faith; instead of returning to a dietary "tradition" that suffocates under others' thumbs, we Reform Jews should instead embrace our religious tradition by taking these serious matters into our own hands.

Until such a comprehensive Reform Jewish system can be brought into place, all of us must operate in the arena of the unfortunate realities of the status quo. It is, finally, on the current state of affairs in the Reform Movement regarding kashrut that I want to focus. So long as we continue to manifest our approaches toward Jewish diet in so many distinct fashions, I believe it to be imperative that we maintain a Judaism that is truly liberal and understanding of all thoughtful determinations on the subject. While we as colleagues often seem tolerant of one another in our words, our actions betray a different undercurrent of thought. For if we truly believe in a Judaism that is liberal, we would recognize that all reflective approaches to religious eating are valid in Reform Judaism; especially regarding those in our community who refrain from the kashrut system for religious reasons, all should understand that such a Jewish decision is neither a vestige of a nineteenth-century assimilationist tactic nor an indisciplined "easy way out."

Such tolerance and liberality require changes in our current dietary praxis. I speak primarily of the decision usually made when large groups of Jews gather together to dine: the religious choices of those who join the modern kashrut system are given preference over those who have chosen religiously to stand outside of the contemporary kosher world. The underlying assumption here is that it is not a difficulty for Jews who reject kashrut to eat kosher food; conversely, it would be deemed improper to serve nonkosher food to those who follow such dietary restrictions. This is an unfair rejection of what I consider a valid religious position; pragmatically, it leaves many without religiously acceptable food to dine on when the only meal is certified by an ethos and an industry that Judaism causes them to reject. It clearly seems far less than liberal when the religious convictions of those of us who reject kashrut are accorded little value by the institutions created to carry forward liberal Judaism.

If we are truly to be a Reform Judaism with regard to diet, then we need to create a system for gatherings, conventions, and *kallot* that allows those who maintain kashrut and vegetarian diets to eat according to their religious convictions while simultaneously affording those who religiously choose to refrain from these systems the opportunity to dine in keeping with their understanding of our Jewish faith. A liberal Judaism should have no problem when a vegetarian dines next to a person who keeps kosher while a third person eats pork across the table; if each of the three eats in accordance with deeply held religious beliefs, it becomes a testament to the power of our reflective community and the depth of respect we bear for each other's religious choices. Instead of worrying about what sits on a neighbor's plate, we should be involved in movement-wide advocacy for holy approaches to eating: not exclusively of one system, but rather in favor of bringing humility, gratitude, and sanctity to all our dining experiences.

In sum, I believe there exists a principled Jewish position that rejects the current system of kashrut as organized in our time, even as it simultaneously advances a religious revisioning of kashrut for the future. I believe it is possible and worthwhile—without forsaking the sacred intent our tradition has always sought in approaching the table—to remove from contemporary religious expression many of the particular practices our people has promulgated throughout its history. Our most ancient taboos teach us that matters of the body are most important, be it how we mark our flesh or how we consume the flesh of an animal. From these visceral cultural markers of our people, we need not merely to focus on millennia-old practices, but rather to understand the equally ancient principles from which they develop: as divinity incarnated in flesh, we possess a sacred responsibility toward our own carnality. It is that attempt to understand what it means to celebrate deeply humanity's flesh-and-blood existence that compels me to revision "fit" Jewish eating in ways that I can truly consider kosher.

NOTES

1. I regret the fact that I was not able to produce this paper in a fashion timely enough for that important issue. Not wanting to take unfair advantage of my

tardiness, I have written this article in response to the general call and not to any individual's (already printed) work.

2. I have always held fast to the tenet that serious-minded and well-informed liberal Jews could reach distinct conclusions on the same subject yet simultaneously co-exist as congregants and colleagues. Therefore, when I claim that there exists a valid Reform position that maintains that kashrut is no longer a religiously appropriate system, I make this proposal for myself and those who agree with me only; I intend no disrespect for those who disagree with my approach (as I, in turn, disagree with theirs).

3. This seems to be the appropriate time to note that the structure and approach of this paper are necessarily idiosyncratic, personal, and sometimes anecdotal. It is because I make no claim to the creation of any categorical imperative for all Jewry that I feel comfortable with this approach; because the best religious choices are the ones to which we are most deeply committed, I feel it is most fitting for me to draft this article in the voice of the first person. Furthermore, because I see this essay only as a personal, and not as a wholesale, rejection of kashrut, I believe it is neither necessary nor beneficial to rehearse the reasons people possess for keeping kosher.

4. Deuteronomy 14:21 allows forbidden foods to be given to non-Jews and makes licit their consumption.

5. I. Finkelstein and N. A. Silberman, *The Bible Unearthed* (New York: Free Press, 2001), 119.

6. My understanding here of Leviticus 11 is that the potential "explanations" for refraining from eating the listed animals are in fact the laws themselves. Like the Rabbis, I see the real proscriptive principles here as "You shall not eat of those that chew the cud, or of those that divide the hoof" (11:4) and "All that do not have fins and scales . . . you shall not eat of their flesh" (11:10–11). Obviously, no such totalizing principle is offered for birds (and subsequent tradition has likewise failed to create a convincingly complete taxonomy). (It should be noted that here, as throughout the paper, biblical translations are my own, and citations are from the Masoretic text.)

7. Here my intention is hardly to ignore the variegated spectrum of thinkers who have attempted to make logical and religious sense out of the dietary laws they inherited. Maimonides called forbidden foods "unwholesome"; Abarbanel considered the taboos "medicinal" in nature. Modern thinkers, as well, have entered into the realm of justifying ancient prohibitions: Isaac Klein considers kashrut a "discipline in holiness," while Samuel Dressner maintains they teach us lessons for "respect of life." (For an overview of these and other thinkers, see I. Klein, *A Guide to Jewish Religious Practice* [New York: Jewish Theological Seminary, 1992], 302–4. See also an authoritative article in the *Encyclopaedia Judaica*.) Contemporary anthropology would teach us that such taboos intend arbitrarily to impose order on a universe understood itself as arbitrary (M. Douglas, *Purity and Danger* (London: Routledge, 1984]).

Despite these many proffered rationales for the taboos of the kashrut system, the fact that so many major (Jewish and non-Jewish) thinkers disagree so widely on this issue indicates to me one truth: any reason other than "This is just how Jews have always eaten" is not fathomable. Nonetheless, there is one particular aspect of kashrut for which our Rabbis were able to make a determination that has held the test of both time and logic: the rationale for proper draining of blood from a slaughtered animal. This will be discussed below.

8. The orthographical root of kashrut, *k-sh-r*, appears only six times in the Bible. Not only is it never used to describe foodstuffs, but the root is employed only in the later courtly books of *K'tuvim* (Writings): Esther (8:5) and Ecclesiastes (2:21, 4:4, 5:10, 10:10, and 11:6).

9. Although this would need to be the thesis of another essay, it is likely that the biblical authors were similarly engaged not in creating laws regarding foods, but rather in using their legislative power to enforce a dietary practice already in place for countless generations.

10. That this appreciation of the natural world was important to the Rabbis can be seen in the lengthy list of blessings they created to mark the "miracles that happen every day," a list that includes but is not limited to rainbows, rulers, the seven species, and spices.

11. See not only the entire content of his work on the subject, but most fittingly his conclusion, which states, "The Rabbis insisted on the corporeality of human essence and on the centrality of physical filiation and concrete historical memory as supreme values" (D. Soyarin, *Carnal Israel* [Berkeley: University of California Press, 1993], 325). This corporeality Boyarin links to our creation in the divine image in his claim that "the acceptance of fleshiness in its most material and lower body forms [was understood by our Rabbis] as the embodiment of God's wisdom" (Boyarin, 34). The consistent thesis of *Carnal Israel* is that our Rabbis, despite serious ambivalence, nonetheless remained committed to the principle that the constructive fulfillment of our literal incarnation was of positive value. Of course, it is over the proper definition of "constructive" that there was continued Rabbinic (and subsequent) argument. Incidentally, although embracing Augustine's definition of Judaism as "carnal," Boyarin nonetheless argues against Augustine's intended derogation.

12. See Boyarin, 35, and his chapter "Engendering Desire" (107ff.), which attempts to detail the balance our Sages sought between proper sexual expression and an unhealthy overstimulation of carnal desire.

13. Laws of kashrut regulate types of permissible foods, not amounts; laws of sexuality prohibit certain relationships, not particular acts. Of course, in the promulgations regarding both eating and sexuality, there are provisions that seek to prevent "gluttony." Boyarin weighs in on this matter, suggesting that balances need to be found in sexual activity (Boyarin, chaps. 4 and 5). I would argue that similar nuances of appropriate behavior should be applied to the realm of eating. My ultimate disagreement with the Rabbis is therefore not formal, but rather a matter of particulars.

14. See n. 4 above for the Torah's direct provision on this subject. For further evidence, infer from the fact that non-Jews are allowed (by the Noachide covenant) to eat these foods, that there is no violation of human dignity involved. This is especially made clear in comparison to the illicit sexual unions, which are proscribed for non-Jews as well as Jews. (For the Rabbis' perceived connection in type between sexual and food taboos, see Babylonian Talmud, *Makot* 23b.)

15. I recognize that this argument is most likely the novelty of my work; this tension I describe was evidently not experienced by the Sages of our Rabbinic tradition. Whether or not this tension was felt by those Jews in the non-scholarly class of antiquity is both undiscoverable and immaterial; what is clear is that this disconnect within a tradition that is both life-affirming and behavior-curtailing

is experienced in our time. This is attested to foremost in the arena of diet: not only do contemporary Jews disagree as to what should properly be called kosher, they also disagree as to whether or not anyone should continue to heed the laws of kashrut. For a portion of modern Jewry, the power of dietary taboo seems to have significantly weakened; for another segment of the population, the taboo is far more localized to small communities. The impact of this situation will be examined later in this paper.

16. Derived in part from the priestly sacrificial descriptions, the rules of proper slaughter and "fit" slaughterers are enumerated in Babylonian Talmud, *Chulin* 9a.

17. Lev. 17:14. See also Lev. 3:17, 7:26, 19:26; Deut. 12:16ff.; I Sam. 14:34; Ezek. 33:25, 39:17ff. It should be noted that the context in Leviticus 17 (as well as in Deuteronomy 15) makes specific provision for pouring the blood out on the ground. Most interestingly, Gen. 9:4 also relates this legal precept to Noah and his sons; intrinsically, it seems as if the laws respecting life-blood were intended to hold for all humanity (as R. Chanania b. Gamliel intuits in Babylonian Talmud, *Sanhedrin* 59a).

18. On the appositive association of "life" and "blood," see the interpretation of Gen. 9:4 offered by R. Chanania b. Gamliel in Babylonian Talmud, *Sanhedrin* 59a.

19. *Mishnah B'rachot* 6 and 7.

20. Babylonian Talmud, *B'rachot* 54b.

21. While it might seem as if the ancient taboos have been completely erased, I do not think this is the case for *all* contemporary Jews who do not feel bound by them. While I am familiar with many Jews who eat biblically prohibited foods, they fall into (at least) two categories: those who do so with some underlying sense of impropriety and those who have no idea they are violating any sort of biblical or Rabbinic principle. Both types are instructive here: the child who tells a rabbi that his favorite food is a bacon cheeseburger evidences a taboo that has completely disappeared; the congregant who eats prohibited foods on a regular basis but becomes embarrassed when seen doing so by a rabbi demonstrates that even a taboo that has lost its regulatory power is nonetheless somehow compelling.

22. I believe, without delving too deeply into sociological surveys, that Reform, Conservative, and unaffiliated Jews constitute the vast majority of American Jewry. I would also hazard, from anecdotal evidence and purely non-scientific sampling, that the majority of Jews in each of these groups do not adhere to the totality of the kashrut system.

23. Interestingly, it is by these last three—and not the kashrut system—that many people today define "Jewish" eating.

24. I have seen all these items for sale at various markets: the crab legs were artificial; the bacon was made from turkey; the cheeseburger was a combination of a veggie burger and soy-based cheese.

25. One brief web search resulted in ten articles on the subject from reputable news sources such as *The Forward, Jewish Week,* and *Legal Affairs.* This count of articles includes neither the tremendous amount of material in print regarding the recent New York State ruling regarding kashrut nor notorious cases of violation (such as the Empire Chicken scandal in Chicago) that preceded temporally the establishment of many newspapers' online archives.

26. These quotations are from Samuel E. Freedman, *The Book of Kashruth:* A *Treasury of Kosher Facts and Frauds* (New York: Bloch, 1970), 167–68. In discussing

the lack of integrity many intuit regarding the kashrut industry, my intent is not to condemn every individual *mashgiach* or *vaad kashrut*; however, I find this information pertinent because it does seem to me that a segment of the industry surrounding kashrut has become corrupt.

27. In addition to the material in Freedman, I have heard many such stories in my lifetime, and have experienced one personally that seems most appropriate to share here. I recall one spring in high school when I went shopping with my mother at the local supermarket to buy food to eat during the week of Passover. I asked my mother what we could get for dinner, and her response was, "Anything, so long as it's kosher for Pesach." It was much to her surprise that I returned to the shopping cart and placed two packets of pork chops in the top basket. Just as my mother became infuriated with my insouciance, I pointed out to her a rather startling peculiarity: the pork chops were stamped with a "Kosher for Passover" seal. The two of us went to inquire of the manager just how it was possible that pork chops became certified for Jewish consumption. His response was that the rabbis from the kashrut board came into the supermarket as they do every spring, charged a certain amount of money per roll of kosher stickers, and reminded him not to put them on anything containing bread. He apologized for not knowing about the pork prohibition, and promised to have all the stickers removed immediately.

28. Furthermore, the granting of a kashrut certificate, both in Israel and America, has to do not only with the nature of food, but also with the setting in which it is offered. The Israeli Religious Action Center has described the "kashrut certificate club" wielded by Israeli authorities: kosher food is often denied a certification if the place serving it commits some ancillary act of purported "impropriety," be it selling that kosher food on Shabbat, or serving it at a wedding officiated at by a Reform rabbi (Y. Meir, "Kashrut Certificate Club Used Again," www.irac.org).

29. While many of these more conservative Jews wholeheartedly share almost a wholesale commitment to the biblical and Talmudic rules of kashrut, they nonetheless remain so divided that—while agreeing about taboo, slaughter, and a variety of other issues—they often refuse to recognize the *hechsher* of rival groups.

30. I understand that in the span of Jewish thought and practice, the traditions of kashrut have carried far more weight than thoughts of our "carnal" nature (whose very definition remains for some the subject of academic debate), and I know that historical practice is not on my side here. Nevertheless, as a Reform Jew I feel not only entitled but obligated to seek the essence of our religion's values that for centuries nourished (even from behind invisible curtains) our people's souls. That this has been the stance of the Reform Movement in its correct reconstruction of the roles of women and homosexuals—achieved through weighing the principle of being created in the divine image over centuries of unjustifiable exclusionary practice—makes me feel even more comfortable about employing here the definition of our Jewish nature as carnal to reexamine how we approach our consumption of flesh.

31. Jews have long held fast to our taboo against iconography; the non-placement of certain kinds of art in our sacred spaces remains a part of widespread Jewish practice today because we understand the prohibition to be rooted in both our disdain for idolatry and our yearning to imagine a God beyond depiction. Our dietary taboos differ from our iconic ones insofar as, at least for me, they contain no such compelling religious principle at their core. On this latter issue, see n. 7 above, where I try to make

clear that although Judaism has long sought to offer a rationale for kashrut, no solitary definition has ever emerged as the clear reason. More importantly, of the many reasons for maintaining Jewish dietary laws that I have studied, I have found none that are convincing to me. It is precisely because I recognize that many of our historical reasons for kashrut are experienced as compelling by others in our community that I consider my position on kashrut as but one of many religiously valid approaches.

32. That Reform Judaism hears the voice of taboo as less authoritative is probably best seen through Reform Judaism's rightful upheaval of perhaps Judaism's most deeply ingrained taboo, namely that which separated women from the religious sphere dominated by men. The depth to which our Reform violation of this age-old taboo is felt can be seen in other Jews' visceral and vituperative reactions to female leaders, congregational presidents, educators, seminary professors, cantors, and—of course—rabbis. Regardless, neither the taboo nor others' reaction to our violation of it stands in the way of our knowing we have made the proper Jewish decision and have paved the most appropriate Jewish roads.

33. Here I remain unabashedly pre-postmodern in my dedication to the tenet that it is possible to live a vibrant Jewish life that is consistent with our rational, emotional, and spiritual selves.

34. The indefinable term "tradition" has carried tremendous authority throughout Jewish history; I believe that in place of blindly inheriting "tradition," we need instead to ensure that the traditions we carry forward as Jews remain essentially connected to the core of our faith. The hermeneutic I employ in such situations is my version of Ockham's razor: to evaluate a traditional Jewish practice whose rationale is difficult to locate, I ask myself if the "tradition" carries within it the potential to undermine the central values of our faith. We see religions all over the world justifying horrifying practices—ranging from under-education of children to the submission of women up through the call for holy war—under the banner of "traditional" practice. (It is important to note that all these violations—to this day—continue to be committed in the name of Judaism as well.) We as liberal religionists need to be especially careful never to march under such a flag, even if for a seemingly harmless stroll through the "traditional" park; it is our religious burden to investigate tradition thoroughly and thoughtfully. For when religion begins to sublimate and subjugate positive and harmless experiences in our societies, when tradition tramples needlessly on the potential delights of our world, then we have lost Judaism's life-affirming rudder that steers us to create holiness out of the raw material of God's creation. When we so allow the name of religion to be sullied, not only will our congregants rightfully be suspicious, but the concept of a constructive sacred tradition will continue to be denigrated in the court of public opinion; of this, we as religious leaders necessarily need to be on guard.

35. I realize here that one might counter by saying that my refusal, especially as a rabbi, could be harmful (or at least offensive) to other Jews who believe maintenance of the system is important. It is not this type of harm, namely the harm of valid intellectual disagreement, of which I am wary. Again, I find instructive here the cases of women's religious rights: our movement did not shy away from complete inclusion because it would offend Jews who disagreed. Ultimately, a liberal religion needs to live up to its name and remain committed to staunch disagreement among colleagues and within communities. For me, that is the definition of a vibrant Judaism.

36. I think it is safe to say that our dietary laws have been far more definitional for our people—from within and without—than the practice of slaughtering a chicken on the morning before Yom Kippur and then circling it around our heads to atone for our sins. It is because I understand how central kashrut has been to Judaism that I think its rejection demands a higher standard of argument.

37. Those people who receive money for enforcing the current kashrut system are usually the same ones who in turn denounce Reform Judaism and support non-liberal approaches to religion. It is in this subtle fashion that the kashrut industry tends further to undermine not only those holy aspects of Jewish eating, but also the fundamental commitments of my religious expression. An example of this can be seen through the case of money spent to ensure proper slaughter: the romantic notion of concern for the sacred lifeblood of an animal is obliterated by the practical knowledge that the money spent to spill a cow's blood with religious respect often ultimately supports organizations unfortunately lacking in respect for the human blood that flows in the veins of the women and homosexuals they religiously repress.

38. Not only would this represent Reform Judaism putting its proverbial money where its mouth is, but it would ensure that the money flowing into the kosher industry from liberal Jews would go to support liberal causes.

7

KASHRUT AND AUTONOMY

Alan Henkin

Autonomy has been the battle cry of Reform Judaism since the inception of our movement, for a good reason: it is the philosophical tool we used to relieve ourselves of the traditional understanding of a binding, obligatory mitzvah system, many of whose components were uncongenial to modern living. Autonomy as an important modern moral category is usually ascribed to the German philosopher Immanuel Kant (1724–1804). His locus classicus on the subject is his short but eloquent *Groundwork for the Metaphysic of Morals*, published in 1785.

According to Kant, any system of right or wrong imposed on an individual from the outside cannot be deemed moral or ethical because freedom must be a condition of morality.[1] Moreover, in order for a duty to truly obligate a moral agent, that person must think through the duty to the point of willing it to be a universal obligation.[2] Kant formulated all this in his famous categorical imperative: "Act only on that maxim through which you can at the same time will that it should become a universal law."[3] Nowadays this is known as the principle of universalizability.[4] Moral principles and rules must be knowable in theory universally. To be sure, autonomy can have many different

Adapted with permission from Alan Henkin, "Kashrut and Autonomy," *CCAR Journal*, Fall 1999, 1–6.

meanings, such as self-governance, spontaneity, authenticity, and rational obedience.[5] For the purpose of this essay I will follow Kenneth Seeskin's view of autonomy because it stays close to Kant's: "An action is autonomous if the maxim one imposes on oneself conforms to an objective, universal law."[6]

Revealed morality, by definition, is not universally knowable. Only the recipient of the revelation, like the Israelites at Sinai, knows the content of revealed morality; therefore it cannot be universalizable, and cannot be moral on Kantian terms. Any heteronomous system, that is, any behavior system whose origin is outside the moral agent, like the mitzvah system, is *ipso facto* non-moral. It may be legal, constitutional, conventional, but not moral. The issue of autonomy cuts to the heart of the mitzvah system: either we do mitzvot because God commands them in some way (in which case the mitzvot cannot be moral by Kant's definition) or we do mitzvot because they are morally right (in which case their divine origin is irrelevant to their rightness). This is the dilemma Kant's theory of autonomy presented and continues to present to Judaism.

Kant exercised considerable influence on eighteenth- and nineteenth-century liberal German Jews through such thinkers as Solomon Maimon, Lazarus Bendavid, and Solomon Steinheim. Kant's impact on liberal Judaism was magnified by the late nineteenth-century neo-Kantian revival of Hermann Cohen and Ernst Cassirer. Thus the founders of Reform Judaism in the early and mid-nineteenth century operated in an environment saturated with Kantian philosophical thought. They appreciated his understanding of religion as, essentially, a system of ethics.

The early Reformers began to apply the principle of autonomy to Judaism. If the individual Jew cannot accept a mitzvah as right, that is, cannot self-appropriate or self-legislate a mitzvah as right for him or her, then it must be rejected as non-moral, if not immoral, and not obligatory. Sometimes autonomy was discussed in terms of individual conscience, but it all came down to the same thing: tradition cannot command a Jew; only a Jew can freely command himself or herself.

Thus autonomy provided a very powerful intellectual tool, coincident with Jews' emancipation into the modern world.

Radical reformer Samuel Holdheim (1806–1860) illustrated the embrace of autonomy in the extreme. Michael Meyer has argued that Holdheim's intellectual career may be characterized as a search for religious authority.[7] "Authority lay not in the texts at all, but in reason and conscience."[8] In 1847 Holdheim wrote, "Conscience is that indubitable revelation of religion to which Judaism attaches its teaching. . . . Every revelation must be verified by the inner voice of conscience. Reason not only has a weighty say in [individual] matters of religion, rather it is the most certain touchstone of everything that is taught in the name of religion."[9] While few Reformers went so far as Holdheim in his assertion of Kantian autonomy, Kant's ethic of self-legislation has permeated the early movement.

In recent years, among Reform Jewish thinkers, Eugene Borowitz has devoted the most energy to the issue of autonomy. Chairing the CCAR's Centenary Perspective Committee, Borowitz helped to shape the San Francisco Platform of 1976 to emphasize the role of autonomy in Reform Jewish life:

> Reform Jews respond to change in various ways according to the Reform principle of the autonomy of the individual. . . . Within each area of Jewish observance Reform Jews are called upon to confront the claims of Jewish tradition, however differently perceived, and to exercise their individual autonomy, choosing and creating on the basis of commitment and knowledge.[10]

In such writings as "The Autonomous Jewish Self,"[11] "Autonomy and Community,"[12] and *Renewing the Covenant*,[13] he has argued for a highly nuanced understanding of autonomy, in which the freedom of the individual Jew is balanced against the demands of covenant and community. Drawing largely upon Buberian categories, Borowitz holds that the self must be conceived as both individual and social at the same time. Thus he writes, "[K]nowing that my selfhood is indissolubly involved with God and the Jewish people means that my sense of Jewish duty now comes with God's presence behind it and as part of what I must do as part of the people covenanted to God, albeit interpreted through my specific individuality."[14]

We in the 1900s are postmodernists, whether we like it or not. Partly that means that we are acutely aware of our own historical situatedness, as well as the historical situatedness of all people and all thought systems. It is ironic to note that at the same time that Kant was writing, the areas of central and western Europe were experiencing the diminution of royalty, the emergence of bourgeois culture, and the rise of early capitalism. In other words, politically, economically, and socially the individual emerged as the focus of cultural power, at the same time that Kant was creating a philosophical system of morality that also located all power in the individual over and against the church and the state. In other words, this thing we call autonomy is a piece of ideology, not philosophy. It is a thought system in defense of a particular social order. Autonomy is not an absolute truth, contrary to what most of modern philosophy has said.[15]

And if you don't believe that the ethic of autonomy is suspect on these grounds of intellectual history, take a lesson from analytic philosophy. In analytic philosophy, any time a proposition creates linguistic problems, there must also be logical and ontological problems as well. Take this proposition: "Chaim ought to be autonomous." That is a paradox: I am placing a heteronomous judgment on Chaim. Theoretically; only Chaim can say, "Chaim ought to be autonomous." For me to say, "Chaim ought to be autonomous," is a self-contradiction. In imposing autonomy on Chaim, I am violating his autonomy.[16]

Or take this proposition: "Chaim chooses not to be autonomous." This catches us in another paradox: in choosing not to be autonomous, Chaim is exercising his autonomy. All of this is to demonstrate that this simple philosophical truth of autonomy, upon which Reform Judaism has staked so much, isn't so straightforwardly truthful after all.[17]

Many other difficulties are embedded in this notion of autonomy. Let me focus on one more as it pertains to kashrut. Let's say I make this statement: "I promise to meet Chaim tomorrow for lunch." In so saying, I sacrifice my autonomy. I give up my freedom in order to meet Chaim for lunch tomorrow. I am no longer free to do what I want at lunchtime tomorrow. Indeed, most of our lives are made up of commitments, loyalties, communities, and traditions, and they necessarily restrict our freedom. That is, autonomy is inconsistent with very important acts of human living. Really, were we to insist on autonomy now and always, we would strip ourselves of the most basic, fulfilling, and important facets of our lives—our marriages and friendships, our jobs and our affiliations, our beliefs and our communities.[18]

This brings us to kashrut and Reform Judaism. People are not born into nothing. "Nobody begins everything anew; each generation relies on what has been accumulated, in theory as well as in practice, by former generations."[19] We are born into a family, a community, a culture, and a tradition. These inheritances of ours do a lot of good work for us before we get here. They give us holidays, modes of behavior, and ways even to eat. These are not bad things. Thank God no new child has to reinvent culture. We are spared having to repeat mistakes of our ancestors, and we are given the building blocks of creating new forms. Even subscription to the notion of autonomy can take place only within the context of a tradition. In philosophical circles, autonomy can occur only within a philosophical tradition that teaches the rightness of autonomy; in other words, the truth of autonomy is partially heteronomous. Community—philosophical, religious, political—always constitutes obstacles to autonomy, or, more exactly, community provides the boundaries in which autonomy can be selectively exercised.

Here is the dilemma in terms of kashrut and autonomy. In choosing between keeping kashrut and not keeping kashrut the individual Jew is not choosing between Jewish dietary rules and his or her own freely invented rules. Rather, the Jew is choosing between competing heteronomous systems of eating. If an individual Jew decides not to keep kashrut, then whose system of eating rules will he or she follow? In American society we enjoy a variety of systems to choose among, but they all share common, baseline rules that are codified in public health regulations. These include, for example, prohibitions on the meat of dogs, horses, rats, and human beings. Ultimately a person's selection of eating systems is not freely chosen. These decisions are shaped by a complex matrix of heteronomous, social rules about eating.

In other words, to my way of thinking, the claim that calling upon Reform Jews to keep kashrut is a violation of their autonomy is foolish. When it comes to eating, we are choosing within competing rule systems about food. Autonomy is irrelevant. The proper question is: Which community's rules about eating do you wish to accept?

NOTES

1. Immanuel Kant, *Groundwork for the Metaphysic of Morals*, trans. H. J. Paton (New York: Harper and Row, 1964), 99–100.

2. Ibid., 98–99.

3. Ibid., 88.

4. William Frankena, *Ethics* (Englewood Cliffs, NJ: Prentice-Hall, 1973), 25.

5. Kenneth Seeskin, "Autonomy and Jewish Thought," in *Autonomy and Judaism*, ed. Daniel Frank (Albany, NY: State University of New York, 1992), 21. See also Gerald Dworkin, *The Theory and Practice of Autonomy* (Cambridge: Cambridge University Press, 1988), 34–47.

6. Ibid.

7. Michael Meyer, *Response to Modernity: A History of the Reform Movement in Judaism* (New York: Oxford University Press, 1988), 81.

8. Ibid.

9. Quoted in Meyer, *Response to Modernity*, 413n70.

10. Meyer, *Response to Modernity*, 392–93.

11. Eugene Borowitz, "The Autonomous Jewish Self," *Modern Judaism* 4 (1984): 39–55.

12. Eugene Borowitz, "Autonomy and Community," in *Autonomy and Judaism*, ed. Daniel Frank (Albany, NY: State University of New York, 1992), 9–20.

13. Eugene Borowitz, *Renewing the Covenant* (Philadelphia: Jewish Publication Society, 1991), especially chap. 12, "The Social Side of Selfhood," 170–81.

14. Borowitz, "Autonomy and Community," 20.

15. Postmodern ethics has as its hallmark "post-autonomy." See Susan E. Shapiro's rumination on Emmanuel Levinas's ethical category of the heteronomous Other in her "Toward a Postmodern Judaism: A Response," in *Reason after Revelation: Dialogues in Postmodern Jewish Philosophy*, ed. Steven Kepnes, Peter Ochs, and Robert Gibbs (Boulder, CO: Westview Press, 1998), 85–86.

16. Dworkin, *Theory and Practice of Autonomy*, 39.

17. Ibid.

18. Ibid., 21–33.

19. Ze'ev Levy, "Tradition, Heritage and Autonomy in Modern Jewish Thought," in *Autonomy and Judaism*, ed. Daniel Frank (Albany, NY: State University of New York, 1992), 41.

8

IS DIETARY PRACTICE NOW IN THE REFORM MAINSTREAM?

A Survey of Attendees at the 2005 Houston Biennial

RICHARD N. LEVY AND MARC GERTZ

To take the pulse of attitudes toward religious practice in the Reform Movement, the professional staff of the Union for Reform Judaism, headed by Rabbi Eric Yoffie, its president, has periodically commissioned surveys of the practices of clergy and laypeople attending the Union's Biennial Convention, who constitute "the national leadership of the Reform Movement at the local level." These surveys, which have included only Biennial attendees and not the Movement as a whole, have generally inquired into such issues as worship, Shabbat and Festival practice, and study. In 2005, at the urging of the Joint Commission on Worship, Music and Religious Living, whose director at the time was Rabbi Sue Ann Wasserman, the survey was broadened to include a number of questions on dietary practice. This marked the first time that such questions had been asked. This innovation reflected a desire on the part of the Kashrut Task Force of the Commission to test the widely held perception that kashrut was of marginal interest to Reform Jews because very few Reform Jews kept kosher. Many classical Reform Jews have believed that little has changed since the rejection of dietary restrictions in the 1885 Pittsburgh Platform.

It was widely believed that when one asks most Reform Jews, "Do you keep kosher?" the chances are great that they will say, "No!" However, the theory that we wanted to test was, how will Reform Jews respond if you ask specific dietary questions, like "Do you eat pork?," "Do you eat shellfish?," "Do you mix milk and meat?," and, especially given the social justice commitments of the Movement, "Do you take ethical concerns into account in your diet?" And so, Dr. Marc Gertz of Florida State University, who had conducted these surveys in previous years, added a number of questions on specific dietary practices to the Biennial query. Of the 526 attendees at the 2005 Biennial in Houston who responded, some surprising results emerged: *Practices of kashrut are now at the top of the observance ladder among many leaders, clergy and lay, in the Reform Movement.*

About as many respondents said they refrain from pork as light candles on Friday night, and more refrain from eating shellfish than attend Shabbat morning services. Based on this survey, we can no longer say that kashrut is a marginal issue for Reform Jews.

To many people, that seems an incredible statement. When the new Pittsburgh Principles were being debated in 1998, an outcry ensued among many Reform Jews when a draft of the document asserted, "Some of us may observe practices of kashrut, to extend the sense of *k'dushah* into the acts surrounding food and into a concern for the way food is raised and brought to our tables." Despite the cautionary words "some of us" and "may," readers (including some rabbis) of the draft in *Reform Judaism* saw in these statements evidence that the CCAR rabbis were trying to lead the Movement into an area that had long been considered out of bounds for Reform Jews.

At least among the self-selected clergy, educators, and laypeople who attended the Houston Biennial, the animus toward Jewish dietary practices that has been around since at least 1885 in general no longer holds true. Of these respondents, 62 percent refrain from eating pork at home (51 percent refrain in restaurants), and 46 percent refrain from eating shellfish at home (34 percent in restaurants); whereas 58 percent of the respondents light Shabbat candles always or usually, 79 percent go to Shabbat evening services weekly or most Friday nights, and 37 percent go to Shabbat morning services weekly or most Saturday mornings.

Other forms of dietary restrictions are less widely practiced: 35 percent of the respondents refrain from mixing milk and meat at home (29 percent in restaurants), and 28 percent eat vegetarian at home (38 percent in restaurants, perhaps to avoid kosher dilemmas while eating out).

Yet, if we wish to paint a full picture of Reform dietary practices, the survey indicates that we need to expand the definition of "dietary practice," as 43 percent of the respondents refrain from eating foods they regard as ethically questionable.

However, as Reform Jews, should we not also expand the "dietary" definition to holiday eating practices? Here the numbers are often staggering: 100 percent of those surveyed eat matzah on Pesach (98 percent lead or attend a seder), 80 percent refrain from *chameitz* (leavened products) throughout the week of Pesach, and 94 percent eat apples and honey on Rosh HaShanah.

The survey also inquired about the saying of *Motzi* at meals. Only 13 percent of all respondents say it at most meals, 29 percent say it at some meals (a total of 42 percent), and 10 percent do not say it at all; 48 percent say *Motzi* only on Shabbat. Of those who eat pork, only 6 percent say *Motzi* at most meals, 26 percent say it at some meals, but 55 percent say it on Shabbat. This is one of the most intriguing findings of the survey, because it suggests that a remarkable percentage of those who ignore the most well-known of the dietary restrictions want to infuse some religious consciousness into their meals. Here, too, we should understand Reform dietary practice as a way to turn mealtime into a spiritual occasion, whether through refraining from biblically prohibited foods, using mealtime to alleviate harm to the environment or to workers in the fields and factories, imbibing of foods that help one sense the spiritual nature of a holiday, or saying blessings at the dining table. Local leaders of the Reform Movement have succeeded in turning the dining room into a sanctuary, as the table has traditionally been seen as a reflection of the altar in the Temple.

Which Reform Jews Observe These Practices and Why

As might be expected, the highest percentage (38 percent) of respondents who refrain from pork, shellfish, and the mixing of milk and meat (Jews we have classified as having "high dietary restriction") are clergy—rabbis or cantors. But the second highest group of those refraining (27 percent) are members of congregational boards of trustees—higher than the percentage of educators (24 percent) and much higher than congregational officers (17 percent). In this area, the officers lag behind the board members, perhaps because they are of a different generation. Of those who observed several dietary restrictions, 56 percent of board members were between the ages of forty-one and sixty; 76 percent of board officers were in that age range, as were 42 percent of educators and 51 percent of clergy. Of the clergy, a significant percentage were younger: 46 percent were between twenty-five and forty.

If one adds the percentages of officers (17 percent) and board members (27 percent) who have "high dietary restriction," the number (44 percent) *exceeds* the percentage of clergy who have these restrictions (38 percent).

What are their motivations? Of board members who keep many dietary practices, 71 percent do so because it "helps them feel Jewish"; 46 percent because it is "what they grew up with"; 32 percent because they are Reform Jews; 29 percent, a significant number, because they believe "God wants them to." Of rabbis and cantors, 85 percent say it "helps them feel Jewish"; 54 percent because they are Reform Jews; very few because it is what they grew up with; 28 percent because they believe it is "what God wants them to do." Among educators, 92 percent say it "helps them feel Jewish"; 46 percent say it is because they are Reform Jews; and 38 percent say it is because they feel it is "what God wants them to do." How far have we come from the 1885 Pittsburgh

Platform—and even from the ambivalence on dietary issues reflected in the lead up to the 1999 Principles!

Other insights emerge in analyzing those who show "high dietary restrictions." Among board members, 79 percent are married to Jews, 25 percent were raised in Reform households, 39 percent were raised in Conservative households, 14 percent were raised in Orthodox households, 14 percent are Jews-by-choice, and 7 percent were raised secular. In addition, 64 percent have been to Israel, 46 percent had a bar or bat mitzvah as a teenager, and 43 percent had a bar or bat mitzvah as an adult. Similar percentages prevail for board members who observe a large number of other ritual matters included in the survey.

Of rabbis and cantors who observe "high dietary restrictions," 77 percent were raised in Reform households, 15 percent in Conservative households, and only 3 percent in Orthodox households; 85 percent had a bar or bat mitzvah as a teenager, 67 percent went to Jewish summer camp, and 62 percent participated in Hillel. Here, too, similar percentages prevailed for clergy who were "highly ritualistic."

So while the percentage of clergy and lay leaders who have a high level of dietary restrictions is roughly similar, there is a considerable discrepancy between their motives for doing so. More clergy grew up in Reform homes than these lay leaders and were clearly influenced in their practice by their Reform upbringing, by summer camps, and by Hillel. This also contributes to the finding that dietary practice has become an accepted part of Reform Jewish practice in the early twenty-first century. Also remarkable is that 28 percent of these dietary-observant clergy believe such practice is "what God wants them to do." For over a quarter of them, this is not merely an ethnic act, not merely an act consistent with Reform Jewish belief, but a spiritual act—an act that aligns them with the will of God.

"Born Reform Jews" and Jews-by-Choice

Another comparison made in the survey was between dietary and other ritual practices of Jews raised in Reform homes and those of Jews-by-choice. Because the number of Jews-by-choice in the sample was small (forty-seven), the most significant comparisons were where the gap was between 15 and 20 percent or higher. Thus, in the area of eating pork, 77 percent of Jews-by-choice surveyed refrain from eating pork at home, while 60 percent of respondents raised as Reform Jews refrain from eating pork at home, a gap of 17 percent. More Jews-by-choice (55 percent) refrain from eating shellfish at home than do raised Reform Jews (43 percent), a gap of 12 percent; and while 42 percent of raised Reform Jews eat dairy on Shavuot, 55 percent of Jews-by-choice do so, a difference of 13 percent. In other dietary areas, the numbers are statistically equal. Two insights appear from these statistics: one, they would seem to dispel the notion that if Reform were to emphasize issues of diet, it would alienate Jews-by-choice; second, that in the area of pork and perhaps shellfish, a significant percentage of Jews-by-choice may feel that dietary practice can strengthen the religious decision they have made to become Jewish, extending their awareness of their new identity into the details of their diet. Indeed, as part of its 2001 "*Divrei Giyur*: Guidelines for Rabbis Working with Prospective *Gerim* [Converts]," the CCAR has urged that prospective Jews-by-choice be encouraged to bring aspects of Jewish dietary practice into their lives.

What Are the Implications of This Survey for the Reform Movement?

First, the survey suggests that the Movement needs to widen its definition of Jewish dietary practice to include not only biblically forbidden foods and mixtures, but also "ethically questionable" foods, the product of cruel practices involving farmworkers or animals; foods typically associated with holidays; and the sanctifying of meals by the saying of *Motzi*. Educational materials issued by the Movement should discuss all of these as different means to bring *k'dushah* to the table, acknowledging that some are easier to introduce than others, but that any of them can provide an entry point for the process of turning one's table into an altar before God.

Second, if, as it appears from this survey, dietary practice holds a place among such widely practiced rites as candle lighting and Shabbat service attendance, it is important that the Movement begin to devote as much educational attention to the various aspects of Jewish diets as it does to issues of prayer and Shabbat observance. This would be a bold step, since observance of kashrut still evokes much more controversy among some Reform Jews than does prayer or Shabbat observance, whatever the percentage of actual practice may be. And as we expand the dimensions of dietary practice to include ethical and holiday issues, we should not turn away from the "more traditional" elements like biblically forbidden foods, which clearly have grasped the imagination of a significant number of our congregational leaders in local communities. If a third of such laypeople and over half of the surveyed clergy who observe dietary practice do so "because they are Reform Jews," it is incumbent upon us to share that finding with the whole Movement and to discuss the Reform significance of less observed areas like mixing milk and meat, eating kosher meat, and vegetarianism as well. When we do this, we will, of course, do so in the Reform spirit that recognizes and encourages individual decisions. To emphasize this can fortify us against those who still see any discussion of dietary practice in the Reform Movement as an infringement on individual choice and as contrary to Reform ideology.

To affirm the growing place of dietary practice within the Reform Movement will also strengthen us in advocating for certain practices in the Jewish world at large. If concerns about treatment of food workers and animals are a part of the Movement's dietary commitments, we can take a much more effective role in urging Jews in other movements and the food industry as a whole to take these concerns seriously and to begin to effect new policies.

This survey of attendees at the 2005 Houston Biennial is a limited survey, but it is also a window into a growing area of Reform practice and concern. If we take it as a signal to increase our educational offerings regarding the value of dietary practice in deepening the religious life of Reform Jews, if we take it as an invitation to become involved in improving the lot of humans and animals on whom we depend for our food, this survey can have implications and impact far beyond the number of respondents. If we see it as a wake-up call to address a significant new area of Reform practice, we will pay further honor to those of our Movement who see their attendance at national Biennials as a way to lead the Movement in important directions as this century unfolds.

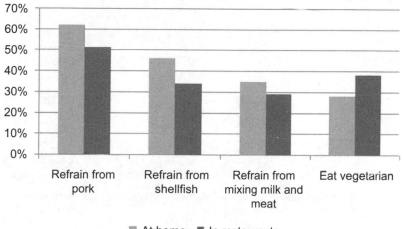

Jewish Dietary Practices

Legend: At home, In restaurants

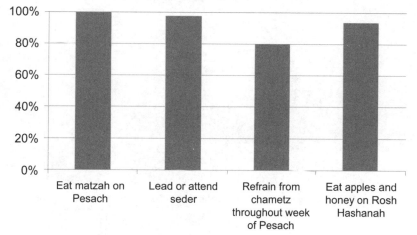

Holiday Eating Practices

Saying Motzi at Meals

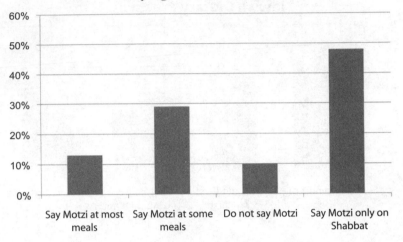

High Dietary Restrictions

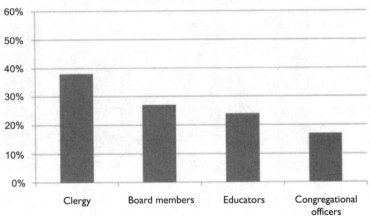

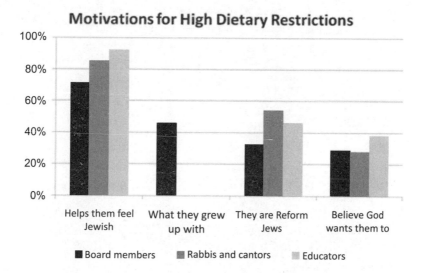

Motivations for High Dietary Restrictions

Legend: Board members, Rabbis and cantors, Educators

Categories: Helps them feel Jewish, What they grew up with, They are Reform Jews, Believe God wants them to

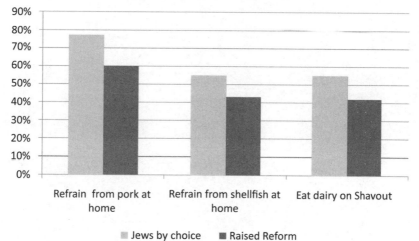

Differences in Dietary Practices

Legend: Jews by choice, Raised Reform

Categories: Refrain from pork at home, Refrain from shellfish at home, Eat dairy on Shavout

9

REAL LIFE / REAL FOOD
A Holy Moment at McDonald's

EUGENE B. BOROWITZ

I dash out between classes to grab a fried-fish sandwich at McDonald's. As I find a seat in the crowded, semi-greasy table area, I am quite preoccupied. I have to get back to class early because someone wants to see me and I'm troubled because I'm not sure I prepared adequately for the meeting I will be leading later. As I hastily unwrap the sandwich I remember—this time—my Jewish duty to say a *Motzi* before I eat. Something inhibits me from doing that in McDonald's . . . if I say the *b'rachah* out loud, other people will feel uncomfortable. So, not wishing to be a public nuisance or because of my inhibitions, I say it to myself silently—which, because of the tumult, isn't always easy. If I let all this overwhelm me, I know that saying the *Motzi* will not be very meaningful. So, hoping to let its spiritual purpose work, I must become dead still, taking control of my frazzled self, center my soul for a precious minute, and only then say the *b'rachah*.

If I am to find the Transcendent even in McDonald's, I must do my part in seeking it—in this case by fighting cultural norms and my personal drive to get on with my work. Yet if I ignored my Jewish duty,

Adapted with permission from Eugene B. Borowitz, *Renewing the Covenant* (Philadelphia: Jewish Publication Society, 1991), 111–12.

I would come to most meals mired in the muck of using and being used. I make no claim that every time I follow this ritual I encounter the Transcendent.

Judaism rejects automatic means of summoning up God, as in magical religion, but that it does not happen every time does not mean it never happens. Although I have no special gift for spirituality, something does occasionally happen. Saying my *Motzi* amid the city rush, I sometimes again fleetingly but truly touch the Ultimate, reaffirming in this instant what I believe and must yet do. For all that these slight, intangible experiences pass quickly, few things are as precious, for they momentarily restore to me everything the metropolis seems organized to take from me.

· Part Two ·

Buffet of Educated Choices:
Jewish Ritual Law

The Sacred Table explores the many facets of Reform dietary practice, providing a rich buffet from which liberal Jews can shape their personal kashrut. Of course, any discussion of kashrut must begin with the ritual laws. "An Overview of Ritual Kashrut" seeks to provide the basic laws and sources that define kashrut. When possible, the development of the law will be referenced. However, this is not a comprehensive discussion of ritual kashrut, its minutia, its historical and legal development, its spiritual meanings, or its most stringent levels of implementation, as that would require its own book. Rather, this chapter seeks to provide a convenient overview of ritual kashrut and to give its readers the tools to evaluate for themselves the value of adding such observances to their lives. It is designed to be used in conjunction with the totality of this book. While the following guide presents a detailed overview of kashrut, it is expected that individuals will adapt this knowledge according to their own needs and interests. Rather than setting an expectation of observance, this chapter is to facilitate informed choice. Interestingly, *The Sacred Table* represents the first time that the ritual laws of kashrut are spelled out for an official Reform publication.

In the "To Learn More" section at the back of this book, a number of guides that focus on ritual kashrut are listed for further study. They reflect a broad range of approaches from liberal to strictly traditional. In using these resources, take into account the particular religious view of their authors. As with all Jewish matters, there is a great range of practice in the kashrut world. This mini-guide seeks to document a standard definition of ritual kashrut and its normative variations. For support on specific questions concerning understanding and implementing ritual kashrut, consult your rabbi and community.

Passover has its own additions to the kosher laws along with its own challenges to the Reform approach to dietary laws. In "Passover Kashrut: A Reform Approach" a general overview to Passover kashrut is presented. This includes an approach to these observances for those who do not usually keep kosher or those who are in particular unfamiliar with Passover kashrut. This section can especially be used as a resource for teaching and counseling. The CCAR responsum "Pesach Kashrut and Reform Judaism" guides us through several interesting Pesach issues posed by Lawrence Englander and answered by Mark Washofsky and the CCAR Respona Committee: What should be the standards of Pesach kashrut for Reform Jews? What foods should be prohibited? What is our position regarding rice and legumes (*kitniyot*)? How do we deal with the requirement of *biur chameitz*? Do we destroy our *chameitz*, sell it, or put it away?

Part 2 concludes with a "Real Life / Real Food" essay by Ellen Weinberg Dreyfus ("Kashrut: A Family History"), in which she explores the various approaches to ritual kashrut across the different generations of her family. It reflects the generational shift that many Reform Jews feel in their own families and communities.

10

AN OVERVIEW OF RITUAL KASHRUT

Mary L. Zamore

The foundation of the laws of kashrut are found in the Torah, with a majority of the laws presented in the Book of Leviticus and then repeated with minor variations in the Book of Deuteronomy. That foundation is argued, clarified, commented upon, and greatly expanded throughout the generations of Jewish sacred texts that follow the Torah. In fact, many of the laws of kashrut continue to be in flux through the sixteenth century.[1] Some liberal Jews feel it is most accessible, and even more authentic, to follow just the biblically based laws. As Jeff Brown asks in "Creating a Reform Communal Dietary Policy" (chapter 49):

> What are we Reform Jews to make of the fact that parts of kashrut were established so late in Jewish history? How (if at all) should these realizations affect the way we think about our sense of obligation to Jewish law? Are we more apt to be swayed by the call of an ancient practice or a more modern one?

The answers are clearly up to the individual Jew. However, it is important to remember that little in Judaism is strictly biblical. When we implement biblical commandments, we must interpret the text in order to live its words. This leap between text and action is interpretative. On the other hand, moving beyond the biblical laws to consider the Rabbinic additions to halachah opens the door to seemingly endless layers of laws. These come out of the Rabbinic impulse "to build a fence" (*s'yag*), meaning to hedge against any possible violations against initial laws by creating secondary laws. As Brown implies in his questions, it is innate to Reform Judaism to simplify the laws and to remove fences when they are deemed unnecessary.

It should be noted that most often the Torah gives the commandments but does not explain the reasons behind the dietary laws. The motivation is gleaned from the context of the law or interpreted. The laws outlined here will be the basis of the discussions found in the rest of this volume. The meaning of the laws will be fleshed out in this way.

An Overview of the Taxonomy

One way to view kashrut is that all food is divided into two categories: *kasher* (kosher[2] or fit) and *t'reif* (unfit). Appearing in the Bible, the word *kasher* is not used for food laws; rather food sources are described as *t'horah/tahor*, meaning "clean," or *tamei/tumah*, meaning "unclean." While words with the Hebrew root *k-sh-r* appear in the Bible three times, in the book of Esther, the word *kasher* is used to mean "proper" or "appropriate." This is close to its post-Biblical use in which *kasher* refers to both food and non-food related matters, meaning "ritually fit." Used in the Torah, the Hebrew *t'reifah* literally means "torn" or "damaged," referring to animals. When *t'reifah* appears in its colloquial Yiddish form *t'reif*, it means "unkosher." An extended discussion of *t'reifah* is found below.

Another way to view the taxonomy is to see that kashrut divides permissible foods into three categories: meat (*basar* in Hebrew, *fleishig* in Yiddish), dairy (*chalav, milchig*), and neutral (*stam, pareve*). Several chapters in *The Sacred Table* explore the tension between the Jewish view of meat eating and vegetarianism. However, this overview of ritual kashrut begins with the assumption that meat eating is a native part of our dietary laws.

Milk and meat cannot be eaten together; neutral foods can be eaten with either. This division is based on the commandment "You shall not boil a kid [young goat] in its mother's milk" (Exod. 23:19, 34:26; Deut. 14:21). The details and expansion of this law will be discussed later. In Western culture, meat can include land animals, birds, and sometimes fish, yet kashrut puts them into different categories. Kashrut today groups land animals and birds as meat, while fish is considered pareve.[3] Coming from kosher birds, unfertilized eggs are also considered to be pareve. Fruits, vegetables, and grains are pareve, as long as they are prepared without contact with meat or milk. Therefore, rice cooked in chicken stock is categorized as meat.

Meat

The Torah prohibits eating meat that is from a torn animal or from a carcass (animal that is dead before ritual slaughtering). Using the word *t'reifah*, Exodus 22:30 commands, "You shall not eat flesh of an animal that was torn in the field." The Rabbis interpreted "torn" to mean that the animal was injured before it died. In a related category, Deuteronomy 14:21 states, "You shall not eat of any carcass." Here *n'veilah* is translated as "carcass" or "corpse." The Rabbis interpreted this to mean that the animal died before it could be slaughtered according to Jewish law. This could include animals that die naturally or are not slaughtered by a kosher method. In Deuteronomy 12:21 we are told, "You may slaughter [*zavach*] from your cattle and your flocks that *Adonai* has given you, as I have commanded you." Since the laws for kosher slaughtering do not appear in the Bible, this phrase is traditionally interpreted as pointing to the laws that are described by the Rabbinic laws. A biblical word (Lev. 1:5) using the Hebrew root *sh-ch-t*, *sh'chitah*, meaning "slaughter" or "kill," is the term used to refer to ritual kosher slaughter.

The Torah is very clear about which animals may be eaten, providing both a list of abhorrent animals and permitted animals, as well as guidelines to apply in general. Clearly, the Torah can only address the animals known in biblical times. Therefore, the general guidelines were important as Jews spread out across the world and encountered new species. For example, bison are kosher even though they are not mentioned directly in the Torah. It should be noted that these guidelines are also helpful because there are animals mentioned in the Bible that we cannot definitively identify today. This identification problem is particularly difficult when we discuss kosher birds (see below).

Many liberal Jews eat non-*shechted* meat but avoid those animals prohibited by the Torah; others will only eat *shechted* meat.[4] In Leviticus 11:2–3, we are provided with the general guidelines as to which types of mammals we may eat. These animals must have both cloven hoofs and chew their cud:

> These are the creatures that you may eat from among all the land animals: any animal that has true hoofs, with clefts through the hoofs, and that chews the cud—such you may eat.
>
> (Lev. 11:2–3)

The text continues with specific examples of animals that are forbidden:

> The following, however, of those that either chew the cud or have true hoofs, you shall not eat: the camel—although it chews the cud, it has no true hoofs: it is impure for you; the daman—although it chews the cud, it has no true hoofs: it is impure for you; the hare—although it chews the cud, it has no true hoofs: it is impure for you; and the swine—although it has true hoofs, with the hoofs cleft through, it does not chew the cud: it is impure for you. You shall not eat of their flesh nor touch their carcasses; they are impure for you.
>
> (Lev. 11:4–8)

Deuteronomy adds this list of permitted animals:

> You shall not eat anything abhorrent. These are the animals that you may eat: the ox, the sheep, and the goat; the deer, the gazelle, the roebuck, the wild goat, the ibex, the antelope, the mountain sheep.
>
> (Deut. 14:3–5)

Meat, but Not the Whole Animal

Later in this book, the "eat meat or be vegetarian" debate is thoroughly explored. The following verses are frequently emphasized by those who believe Jews should eat meat. After the Flood, God tells Noah and his sons:

> And let the awe and dread of you be upon all the land animals, and all the birds of the sky, and all that creep on the ground, and all the fish of the sea: they are given into your hands. Any small animal that is alive shall be food for you, like green grasses—I give you [them] all. But flesh whose lifeblood is [still] in it you may not eat.
>
> (Gen. 9:2–4)

These verses precede the covenant between God and Abraham; therefore God is addressing all humanity in what is known today as the Noachide covenant, the seven laws given to humanity. While humanity is permitted by these verses to eat meat, we are not allowed to ingest blood. This commandment (Gen. 9:4) leads to two laws in kashrut. The first, *eiver min hachai*, literally meaning "flesh torn from a living body," prohibits eating flesh or limbs from a live animal—clearly not a huge issue today, but pertinent to biblical times. Equally as appetizing, the second law prohibits drinking blood from a live animal. This prohibition is repeated many times throughout the Torah, including in Leviticus:

> And if any Israelite or any stranger who resides among them hunts down an animal or a bird that may be eaten, that person shall pour

out its blood and cover it with earth. For the life of all flesh—its blood is its life. Therefore I say to the Israelite people: You shall not partake of the blood of any flesh, for the life of all flesh is its blood.

(Lev. 17:13–14)

Transgressing this commandment leads to the severe punishment of "being cut off" from the community (Lev. 17:14). It should be noted that hunting is not permitted by the laws of kashrut. The restrictions on ingesting blood led to very detailed instructions on how to slaughter permitted land animals and birds and how to prepare them for cooking. Belonging to the pareve category, fish do not have a ritualized slaughter, and their blood is not prohibited.

In addition to the blood, a specific type of fat is also prohibited for consumption. This commandment appears in a section of the Torah in which God is giving Moses many commandments concerning the sacrifices:

You shall eat no fat of ox or sheep or goat. Fat from animals that died or were torn by beasts may be put to any use, but you must not eat it. If anyone eats the fat of animals from which offerings by fire may be made to the Eternal, the person who eats it shall be cut off from kin.

(Lev. 7:23–25)

The type of fat, *cheilev*, referred to here is suet, a hard, course fat.[5] There is a second type of fat, *shuman*, which is permitted.[6]

Another part of the land animal that is forbidden is the *gid hanasheh*, sinew of the thigh muscle. This commandment links every generation of Jews to the transformative moment in Jacob's life. The night before meeting his long-estranged brother Esau, Jacob encounters a mysterious stranger, and they fight. When the stranger cannot win, "he struck Jacob's hip-socket, so that Jacob's hip-socket was wrenched as [the man] wrestled with him" (Gen. 32:26). At the end of this episode, we receive this commandment: "To this day that is why the people of Israel do not eat the sinew of the thigh muscle that is in the socket of the hip, because he struck Jacob at the sinew of the thigh muscle" (Gen. 32:33). The implementation of this commandment, however, varies among Jewish communities throughout the world. Some Jewish communities believe that you can remove the sinew of the thigh muscle, meaning the sciatic nerve, and the *cheilev*, the forbidden fat, and then the thigh meat is permitted. This type of process requires a high level of training and a great deal of time to execute. Avoiding these issues, most communities prohibit the entire thigh muscle entirely and, therefore, forego the filet mignon and sirloin cuts. These types of regional differences will also be discussed in chapter 11 in regard to Passover. The unused parts of the animal, along with animals that did not pass the entire kosher inspection, are sold on the secondary market.

The laws outlined above lead to the development of Jewish ritual slaughter known as *sh'chitah*. The one who does the kosher slaughtering is referred to as a *shochet*. A full view of *sh'chitah* is seen through the account of Josh Whinston and Gersh Lazarow (chapter 23, "Blood, Sweat, and Tears: The Making of a Reform *Shochet*"), who outline the laws and values that guide ritual slaughter. As they explain, the primary goal is to carry out a quick slaughter; the second goal is to drain the blood from the animal, collecting it and covering it with dust as commanded (Lev. 17:13; *Shulchan Aruch, Yoreh Dei-ah* 28:1, 28:5). Next, the animal must be checked by a *shochet*, who inspects for abnormalities that may render the animal *t'reif*. These may include broken limbs or a perforation of the brain or its membranes.[7]

Glatt

At this point in the slaughtering process, there may be an additional level of inspection that looks at the lungs to see if there are certain kinds of adhesions. If there are none, the animal can be labeled *glatt* kosher. *Glatt* means "smooth" in Yiddish (*chalak* in Hebrew), a reference to the lungs being smooth. If minor adhesions are found, they must be further inspected to see if they are in the range of permissible. If they are, the meat can be labeled kosher, but not *glatt* kosher. For several hundred years, there has been a requirement among Sephardic Jewry that the lungs of all kosher mammals be *glatt*. Among Ashkenazic Jews, *glatt* kosher has been a special level of stringency, but there is a growing trend in the contemporary Orthodox community to accept only *glatt* kosher meat. As a result of this higher level of stringency, the phrase "*glatt* kosher" is sometimes applied (imprecisely) to all circumstances in which a more stringent interpretation of kosher is being applied. The more precise term to use in such circumstances is the Hebrew term *m'hadrin*, literally meaning "beautified or embellished." When a food is labeled *l'mehadrin*, it means it is following an ultra-Orthodox interpretation of kashrut.

Salt

After the blood draining and inspection, the meat is then *kashered*, processed to remove all blood. Performed within seventy-two hours of the slaughter, this process can be done by soaking and salting or by broiling. Today almost all kosher meat is sold pre-*kashered*; in the old days you had to do it at home. Soaking and salting are used for most cuts of meat; broiling is used for liver, for example.

Birds

As discussed above, birds are considered to be meat. Rather than list the traits of kosher or forbidden birds, the Torah merely lists the forbidden birds in Leviticus and Deuteronomy. Listing twenty forbidden birds, Leviticus commands:

> The following you shall abominate among the birds—they shall not be eaten, they are an abomination: the eagle, the vulture, and the black vulture; the kite, falcons of every variety; all varieties of raven; the ostrich, the nighthawk, the sea gull; hawks of every variety; the little owl, the cormorant, and the great owl; the white

owl, the pelican, and the bustard; the stork; herons of every variety; the hoopoe, and the bat.

(Lev. 11:13–19)

Deuteronomy states, "Every clean bird you may eat" (Deut. 14:11), and then lists twenty-one forbidden birds (Deut. 14:12–18). Since some of the birds are listed with the modifying phrase "after its kind," the finite list has room for interpretation. The other opportunity for interpretation is that it is not always clear which bird is which when translating the ancient Hebrew. For example, it was debated whether ostrich is forbidden. Today, the normative interpretation of forbidden birds follows a list of twenty-four forbidden birds, including ostrich. As Jews encountered new species of birds, the Rabbis extrapolated guidelines from these lists. Therefore, birds of prey are forbidden. Then, there are four physical characteristics that all the permissible birds have in common. Kosher birds do not seize their prey, and they do have a crop, a gizzard that can be peeled, and an extra toe. Ultimately, most of the permitted birds are allowed because a tradition, *mesorah*, of eating them exists, as the the Talmud states, "R. Yitzchak said: A kosher bird is eaten on the basis of a tradition" (*Chulin* 83b).

Swarming Bugs and Creepy Crawlies

While they may not be your first choice for dinner, there are some types of bugs that are permitted. Otherwise, the Torah is quite clear concerning which bugs and reptiles are forbidden. They are referred to as *sheretz*, "swarming things." As Leviticus commands:

> All winged swarming things that walk on fours shall be an abomination for you. But these you may eat among all the winged swarming things that walk on fours: all that have, above their feet, jointed legs to leap with on the ground—of these you may eat the following: locusts of every variety; all varieties of bald locust; crickets of every variety; and all varieties of grasshopper.

(Lev. 11:20–22)

While the text refers to four legs, the Rabbis put all insects (which have six legs) into the same category of forbidden food. While many authorities think it is impossible to identify and, therefore, eat the exact correct bugs referred to in Leviticus, there are others who feel that they preserve an important tradition by eating certain grasshoppers (*chagavim*). There are Yemenite and Moroccan communities who enjoy them.[8]

The other swarming things, like rodents, snakes, worms, and so on, are forbidden in the continuation of the Leviticus 11 text:

> The following shall be impure for you from among the things that swarm on the earth: the mole, the mouse, and great lizards of every variety; the gecko, the land crocodile, the lizard, the sand lizard, and the chameleon.
>
> (Lev. 11:29–30)

> You shall not eat, among all things that swarm upon the earth, anything that crawls on its belly, or anything that walks on fours, or anything that has many legs; for they are an abomination. You shall not draw abomination upon yourselves through anything that swarms; you shall not make yourselves impure therewith and thus become impure. For I the Eternal am your God: you shall sanctify yourselves and be holy, for I am holy. You shall not make yourselves impure through any swarming thing that moves upon the earth.
>
> (Lev. 11:42–44)

Fish and Seafood

The Torah provides guidelines for those creatures from the water that are permissible to eat:

> These you may eat of all that live in water: anything in water, whether in the seas or in the streams, that has fins and scales— these you may eat. But anything in the seas or in the streams that has no fins and scales, among all the swarming things of the water and among all the other living creatures that are in the water—they are an abomination for you and an abomination for you they shall

remain: you shall not eat of their flesh and you shall abominate their carcasses. Everything in water that has no fins and scales shall be an abomination for you.

(Lev. 11:9–12)

These laws, which are repeated in Deuteronomy 14:9–10, command that permitted fish must have fins and scales. This excludes shellfish, octopus, eel, skate, and catfish, for example. The definition of scales sometimes affects the kosher status of fish. Therefore, the status of certain fish, like sturgeon and swordfish, has been hotly debated. The Conservative Movement holds that these are kosher.[9] The eggs (roe or caviar) of a kosher fish are kosher.

Dairy

From a liberal point of view, milk and milk products are a simple matter. Milk that comes from a kosher animal is kosher. Milk products are kosher, barring any unkosher additives. There is a lot of debate about cheese, since rennet and lipase are frequently used in the cheese-making process. Aiding the production of hard cheeses, rennet is a natural enzyme derived from the lining of a calf's stomach; lipase, an enzyme added to some cheeses to help create the desired flavor, is from animal tongue. Both can be produced to be kosher for cheese making (Babylonian Talmud, *Chulin* 116b), but almost all cheeses that are certified kosher use a non-animal-derived rennet, also known as microbial enzymes. There are strictly vegetarian cheeses (many are also certified kosher) that use the same approach. Most liberal Jews follow the Conservative opinion written by Rabbi Isaac Klein that nonkosher rennet does not affect the kashrut of cheese.[10]

Prohibition against Mixing Milk and Meat

Three times the Torah commands, "You shall not boil a kid [young goat] in its mother's milk" (Exod. 23:19, 34:26; Deut. 14:21). Over the development of kashrut, this commandment has been applied narrowly, as well as broadly. Later in this volume, animal rights, inspired by this verse and other texts, will be discussed. Today, a normative understanding of the separation of milk and meat is that we do not cook or eat milk and meat products together. Some liberal Jews use a visual understanding of this law, meaning that they do not worry about the unrecognizable ingredients; for example, they might not eat cheeseburgers but might not worry about the broth used in the rice casserole. Others inspect all ingredients in order to keep milk and meat completely separate and not mixed in the same meal.

A stricter level of application of this law calls for the milk and meat ingredients to be completely separate *and* everything that touches these products to be separate. Therefore, it is common in kosher kitchens to have two sets of all cooking and serving implements. This obviously entails a financial investment in plates, pots, utensils, and so on, as well as a physical/mental investment in keeping them all separate. There are extensive laws addressing the different materials used in making these implements, the different ways they are used in cooking, and the different ways they can be made unkosher by mixing milk and meat on them. When food is mixed, it becomes unkosher, and usually that status cannot be reversed. When cooking implements are rendered unkosher either by having *t'reif* or by having both milk and meat touch them, they can usually be brought back to a neutral state (sometimes easily, sometimes not). These details will not be reviewed here.

Waiting

If one is eating milk and meat separately, the question then becomes when she can shift between them. For instance, if one is eating a meat dinner, when can he have ice cream for dessert? Many people wait a set period of time (see below) in between eating milk and meat, or more correctly meat and milk. It is stated that way because traditionally the Rabbis point to the narrative in which Abraham welcomed the three messengers from God. The three came to announce that Sarah will have a son by Abraham. Demonstrating the value of hospitality, Abraham set his household to welcome the strangers by offering them food and drink. He served his guests: "He took sour milk and [sweet] milk and the calf he had prepared and set [it all] before them" (Gen. 18:8). Notably, Abraham served milk and meat. The Rabbis point out that he served milk, then meat. The time for waiting between consuming milk and meat is much shorter than that for meat followed by milk. This not only reenacts Abraham's hospitality, but also it reflects an ancient view of digestion that meat would take longer to digest. It was also observed that meat leaves a greasy residue in the throat and particles in between the teeth, and therefore more time is needed to allow this residual meat to be cleansed away.

Therefore, to delineate meat and milk meals, there are set waiting periods between these two types of food. When switching from milk to meat, there is no waiting, as the Talmud teaches, "How long must one wait between cheese and meat? And he said to him, 'Not at all'" (*Chulin* 105a). Most people change table settings, rinse the mouth, or eat a piece of bread before continuing on to meat (*Chulin* 104b–105a). There are many opinions on this topic.

Switching from meat to milk involves another set of laws with lots of regional variations. Throughout the world there are different traditions as to how long to wait. They range from Ashkenazic practice, which calls for six hours of waiting; to German practice, three hours; to Dutch Sephardic practice, seventy-two minutes. If one did not grow up waiting and want to take on this practice, he can pick a tradition that connects to his family history or pick the one that feels right. The spirit of the law is to think before switching between milk and meat.

Conclusion

There are a myriad of other kashrut laws. They have not been included in this guide for several reasons. Some of the laws do not easily mesh with Reform Judaism's worldview. For example, there is a set of laws, *bishul akum* (pagan cooking), that address the preparation and handling of food by non-Jews. These laws draw a division between Jews and non-Jews, which is not supported by Reform Judaism's value of inclusivity and the reality of intermarried families. A discussion of some of these laws can be found in chapter 32.

There are hundreds of other laws related to minute details in specific situations. These are not raised here partly because of space considerations. However, there is a more important reason for excluding these laws. Ritual kashrut can quickly become laborious when too much emphasis is put on the endless minutiae. This guide has tried to find a balance between providing solid information and going on endlessly. Casting aside empty ritual, the early Reformers cut out the repetitions in our prayer services. While the current generation of Reform Jews embraces ritual, they still are the inheritors of this practical aesthetic. For those who want to incorporate ritual practices into their personal kashrut, the goal is to find a balance between meaningful ritual and burden. Clearly, this is a task for each individual.

NOTES

1. For example, issues surrounding the separation milk and meat, including the use of separate dishes.

2. Sometime the term "kosher-style" is used. This is a misnomer that has little concern with actual ritual law. While some of the foods described as kosher-style may or may not be ritually kosher, this title really refers to Jewish soul food, reminiscent of the food lovingly cooked by one's Ashkenazi grandmother, if you had one (who cooked).

3. It should be noted that during the tannaitic era (the first and second centuries C.E.), there was a difference of opinion on whether fowl should be classified as meat or as pareve (see Babylonian Talmud, *Chulin* 104b).

4. English-speaking Jews tend to use the colloquial verb *shechted* to refer to kosher slaughter.

5. W. Gunther Plaut, ed., *The Torah: A Modern Commentary*, rev. ed. (New York: CCAR Press, 2005), 692, comm. 23.

6. Lisë Stern, *How to Keep Kosher* (New York: William Morrow, 2004), 29.

7. Ibid., 35.

8. Stern, *How to Keep Kosher*, 28.

9. Isaac Klein, *A Guide to Jewish Religious Practice* (New York: The Jewish Theological Seminary of America, 1979), 305.

10. Samuel H. Desner, *Keeping Kosher: A Diet for the Soul* (New York: The United Synagogue of Conservative Judaism, 2000), 77.

11

PASSOVER KASHRUT
A Reform Approach

Mary L. Zamore

Set Yourself Up for Success

Many liberal Jews mark Passover by adjusting their regular eating habits, yet they claim no connection to regular kashrut. This book demonstrates that Reform kashrut is not an all-or-nothing matter. Jews who sanctify Passover through the eating of matzah and refrain from eating *chameitz* should proudly embrace these rituals, even if they eschew regular kashrut. (The same attitude should be held by those who keep kosher in their homes but do not restrict their diets outside.)

At the same time, Jewish leaders must make Passover kashrut accessible by educating their communities and helping them plan in advance for the holiday. Clarifying the laws and providing easy solutions to logistical barriers help families to keep and enjoy Passover kashrut. Many Jews become overwhelmed and, despite good intentions, give up in the middle of the holiday. Often they have not prepared their kitchens in a way that makes Passover easier to keep; they have not taken the time to excite their children about the holiday. Therefore, they start the holiday at a handicap. The processes discussed in chapters 48 and 49 can help individuals, families, or communities clarify their expectations for Passover eating.

For all dietary practice, but especially for Passover, it is important to know that one mistake does not signal the end of the ritual. Rather, mistakes are an invitation to evaluate what went wrong and to correct expectations or logistics for the future.

The Laws

A gastronomic reminder of the Exodus from Egypt, the foundation of Passover kashrut, is found in the following verses:

> This day shall be to you one of remembrance: you shall celebrate it as a festival to the Eternal throughout the ages; you shall celebrate it as an institution for all time. Seven days you shall eat unleavened bread; on the very first day you shall remove leaven from your houses, for whoever eats leavened bread from the first day to the seventh day, that person shall be cut off from Israel.
>
> You shall celebrate a sacred occasion on the first day, and a sacred occasion on the seventh day; no work at all shall be done on them; only what every person is to eat, that alone may be prepared for you. You shall observe the [Feast of] Unleavened Bread, for on this very day I brought your ranks out of the land of Egypt; you shall observe this day throughout the ages as an institution for all time. In the first month, from the fourteenth day of the month at evening, you shall eat unleavened bread until the twenty-first day of the month at evening. No leaven shall be found in your houses for seven days. For whoever eats what is leavened, that person— whether a stranger or a citizen of the country—shall be cut off from the community of Israel. You shall eat nothing leavened; in all your settlements you shall eat unleavened bread.
>
> (Exod. 12:14–20)

These verses establish the holiday of Passover and command that we should eat matzah and refrain from eating *chameitz*, leavened bread, during the seven days. The Rabbis define *chameitz* as five grains— wheat, barley, spelt, rye, and oats (Babylonian Talmud, *P'sachim*

35a)—that are exposed to water for more than eighteen minutes. This time frame is counted from the minute the water touches the flour to the time it is fully baked. Although the time frame was debated through the development of this law, eighteen minutes is considered the boundary between matzah and *chameitz* (Babylonian Talmud, P'sachim 46a; *Shulchan Aruch, Orach Chayim* 459). Therefore, matzah is produced from start to finish in under eighteen minutes. Kosher-for-Passover foods that contain these grains (e.g., cookies, cakes, crackers, pasta) are usually made from matzah meal (finely ground matzah) rather than flour to ensure that there is no *chameitz* in the product.

In the strictest observance of Passover, the entire household is thoroughly cleaned. All dishes, pots, and utensils are switched to sets reserved for Passover use. All food products containing any morsel of *chameitz* are used up before the holiday or are removed from use and stored away. Then, these forbidden foods are symbolically sold (see CCAR Responsum 5756.9, below). All food brought into the cleaned home must be certified kosher for Passover. This level of observance may be overwhelming to Jews who did not grow up with these practices; it may seem unnecessary to others.

Therefore, the following approach is for those who are just beginning to keep Passover and those seeking a simpler way to keep Passover. It can also be used as a paradigm as to how to teach Passover kashrut within the liberal community. Clearly, this can be adjusted to incorporate more or fewer observances; it can be adjusted according to the age and knowledge levels of the students.

A Simple Model for Keeping Passover Kashrut

Clean your kitchen and eating areas to remove crumbs, etc. (If you eat in your car, you may want to vacuum it out.)

1. Go through your pantries, refrigerator, and freezer, removing all obvious *chameitz*. (*Kitniyot* are discussed below in the CCAR

responsum.) Children love to sort things; engage their help. It will help them learn the laws of Passover and excite them about the holiday.

2. Store away nonperishable foods in closed bags, boxes, or cabinets, so they are not a temptation. Many people mistakenly believe that Jews must throw out all of their unused food before Passover. This is not true and would be wasteful. However, if you can afford it, Passover cleaning provides a wonderful opportunity to donate unused food to a local food pantry. It is also a good time to support your local kosher food pantry so that other Jews can celebrate Passover.

3. If you have an extra refrigerator and/or freezer, put perishable foods in it and tape it shut. If you only have one refrigerator/freezer, designate a particular drawer or shelf for *chameitz*. Place *chameitz* in black plastic bags and then place in the refrigerator/freezer. It is easier to keep the holiday if you are not looking at *chameitz*.

4. Go shopping, buying lots of delicious foods. If you are short on time, consider what is easy to prepare. You do not need to limit yourself to the Passover aisle. There are plenty of foods found throughout the store that are good for the holiday. You can either buy foods that are certified for Passover or read labels to stay away from the five grains. Consider allowing a few treats like sugary Passover cereal if that helps motivate your family. Also, remember that fresh fruits and vegetables are all kosher for Passover, making Passover a great time to return to a back-to-basics diet, avoiding commercially processed foods.

As you feel comfortable with your level of observance, you can evaluate and adjust your practices, adding more rituals as you see fit.

CCAR Responsum 5756.9: Pesach Kashrut and Reform Judaism

Sh'eilah

What should be the standards of Pesach kashrut for Reform Jews? What foods should be prohibited? What is our position regarding rice and legumes (*kitniyot*)? How do we deal with the requirement of *biur chameitz*? Do we destroy our *chameitz*, sell it, or put it away? (Rabbi Lawrence Englander, Mississauga, Ontario)

T'shuvah

These questions are dealt with in brief in *Gates of the Seasons*, one of a series of volumes published in recent decades that testify to a renewed interest in ritual observance among Reform Jews in North America.[1] For many years, questions of ritual observance were deemed to be matters of personal choice and did not rank high at all on the communal agenda of the Reform Movement. That situation, of course, has changed. Today, we acknowledge that an authentically Jewish way of life requires ritual as well as ethical expression. Reform Judaism perceives ritual practice as a mitzvah, a matter of central religious importance. Much pioneering work has been done, particularly in the published works mentioned above, in describing and setting forth the principles and details of Reform observance. The task of this *t'shuvah* on Pesach observance is therefore not so much to issue a ruling as it is

Reprinted from Mark Washofsky, ed., *Reform Responsa for the Twenty-First Century: Sh'eilot Ut'shuvot*, vol. 1, *1996–1999/5756–5759* (New York: CCAR Press, 2010).

to supply the background and discussion necessary for an understanding of the practice of Pesach kashrut in our movement.

1. *Chameitz*, Rice, and Legumes

"It is a mitzvah to abstain from eating leaven [*chameitz*] during the entire seven days of Pesach."[2] By *chameitz*, the tradition means those grains from which matzah may be baked: wheat, barley, oats, rye, and spelt.[3] No other foodstuffs are regarded as *chameitz*. In this, the halachah rejects the opinion of R. Yochanan ben Nuri, who forbids the eating of rice and millet during Pesach because they "resemble *chameitz*."[4] Talmudic law, rather, forbids the use of rice and legumes (*kitniyot*) as flour for the baking of matzah and therefore permits us to eat them during the Festival.[5]

According to long-standing Ashkenazic custom, however, rice and legumes are forbidden for Passover consumption. This prohibition is first mentioned[6] in the thirteenth century by two French authorities, R. Yitzchak of Corbeil[7] and R. Manoach of Narbonne.[8] R. Yitzchak writes that "our teachers observe the custom" of not eating rice and legumes during the Festival, though he adds that this custom is not universally accepted and that "great sages" disregard it. Among these was his own teacher and father-in-law, the great tosafist R. Yechiel of Paris, who argued that since the Talmud ruled that these foodstuffs are not *chameitz*, there is no reason to prohibit them today. R. Yitzchak, reluctant "to permit something that for so long has been widely regarded as forbidden," feels the need to justify the custom. He does so not on the grounds that rice and legumes are *chameitz* ("since not even a beginning Talmud student would make that mistake"), but because these foodstuffs resemble *chameitz* in that they are cooked in the same fashion. Since this resemblance can lead to confusion—people might mistake a *chameitz* mixture for one of rice or legumes—the rabbis issued a decree forbidding the latter.[9] R. Manoach, for his part, suggests that the prohibition originates in a widespread—but mistaken—belief that rice and legumes are forms of *chameitz.* Unlike R. Yitzchak, however, R. Manoach does not attempt to defend this "errant" custom, and he suggests a Talmudic basis for dismantling the prohibition altogether.

These sources tell us a great deal about both the history and the halachic status of the custom to abstain from rice and legumes during Pesach. We learn that while the prohibition was well-known in France by the thirteenth century,[10] some leading rabbis of those communities rejected it on clear halachic grounds. We know that the custom did not spread beyond Ashkenazic Jewry; rabbis in Spain and elsewhere did not hesitate to express their astonishment against it.[11] And although the prohibition did gain wide acceptance among the Ashkenazim,[12] some leading Ashkenazic authorities, including R. Yaakov Emden, were still criticizing it as late as the eighteenth century.[13]

The early Reformers in Europe, convinced that this observance was both unnecessary and burdensome, abolished it altogether.[14] The Orthodox opponents of the new movement responded to this decision in much the same way as they responded to virtually all the innovations that the Reformers introduced into Jewish religious life, namely by insisting upon the sanctity of the entire received tradition. They defended the prohibition of rice and legumes despite its halachic weakness and despite all the criticisms that had been leveled against it over the centuries. Few of them, to be sure, attempted to justify the *minhag* (custom) on the grounds of its original purpose.[15] They argued, rather, that the very existence of the *minhag* is proof that it must be retained. They noted, for example, that a Rabbinic decree that prohibits something in order to establish a "fence around the Torah" has the full force of law; we are not permitted to rescind it.[16] Some claimed that once a *minhag* is widely accepted by a community, it acquires the status of a vow, which is valid under the law of the Torah.[17] While this prohibition, as a *minhag*, does not enjoy the same status as that of *chameitz*,[18] under normal circumstances Orthodox rabbis continue to insist upon its observance.

Reform practice, following the standard of the Talmud, permits the eating of rice and legumes during Pesach. We do not take this stand because we disparage custom and tradition. On the contrary: our "rediscovery" of the centrality of ritual observance to Jewish life, described at the outset of this *t'shuvah*, demonstrates that we take the claims of tradition with the utmost seriousness. This Committee, in particular, in its approach to the answering of the *sh'eilot* submitted to it, has tended to uphold the standards of traditional practice except in those cases where good and sufficient cause exists to depart from them. And our movement has recognized for nearly two centuries that the prohibition of rice and legumes is just such a case. Yet as we have seen, this observance, which presents a significant burden upon Jews during Pesach, has no halachic justification: the Talmud clearly rejects the suggestion that rice and legumes are *chameitz*. And the likelihood that our people will confuse legume dishes with *chameitz* dishes is too remote to be taken into serious consideration.

We do not accept the Orthodox argument that a customary observance, once widely adopted, can never be annulled. This notion is questionable, in general, as a matter of halachah,[19] especially when the observance is based upon a mistaken interpretation of the law.[20] In our specific case, moreover, there is absolutely no evidence that this customary prohibition was ever ratified by rabbinic decree or accepted as binding in the form of a vow. Had a decree or a vow existed, after all, those authorities who criticized the practice down to the eighteenth century would never have spoken so bluntly against it. We think, rather, that some rabbis resort to these arguments in order to support practices and customs whose original purpose—if there ever was a legitimate original purpose—no longer holds. When a religious practice has outlived its purpose, when its retention is perceived by the community as unnecessary and burdensome, Reform Judaism affirms the right of the observant community to alter or annul that practice in favor of a new standard that better expresses our understanding of Torah and tradition and the religious sensibilities of our age.

Our position does not, of course, prevent Reform Jews from adopting the traditional prohibition as a matter of choice. On the contrary: *Gates of the Seasons* notes that "Ashkenazi custom" adds rice and legumes to the list of prohibited foods on Pesach, implying that observance of this custom is a valid option for Reform Jews.[21] The mere fact that a traditional practice is not "obligatory" does not imply that we should not follow it or that we should discontinue it. Jewish religious practice draws its strength from many sources. Chief among these, to be sure, is the "logic of the law," the nature of our observances as these are defined in the classic sacred texts. Also important, and in many ways no less important than the texts, however, is the "living law" as it has developed in the life of the religious community. *Minhag* is the concrete expression of the religious consciousness of the people, their way of expanding upon and adding texture to the more abstract principles derived from the texts. For many people who take religious living with all seriousness, the abstention from rice and legumes is an integral feature of Pesach observance precisely because this is the way the holiday has been observed for many centuries within their religious community. We do not urge them to abandon that practice; indeed, a number of members of this Committee observe it as well. We say rather that, as a matter of Reform communal practice, our "standards of Pesach kashrut" allow the observant Reform Jew to eat rice and legumes during the Festival.

2. The Removal of *Chameitz*

"It is a mitzvah to remove leaven from one's home prior to the beginning of Pesach."[22] This mitzvah is based on the biblical injunction in Exodus 12:15: "on the very first day[23] you shall remove [*tashbitu*] leaven from your house." The precise manner of this removal is the subject of a controversy that stretches back to Talmudic times. Some early Rabbinic authorities interpret the word *tashbitu* as "nullification," an act by which the householder mentally renounces all ownership of the *chameitz*.[24] The Talmud, too, declares that "according to Torah law, a simple act of nullification suffices" to remove *chameitz*.[25]

According to this view, the practices of *b'dikat chameitz*, the search for leaven conducted on the night before the seder, and *biur chameitz*, the burning or other physical destruction of the leaven the next morning, are requirements of Rabbinic law,[26] instituted perhaps in order to prevent against the possibility that one might accidentally eat some of the *chameitz* stored in one's home during the holiday.[27] Other commentators disagree. In their opinion, the Torah requires *biur*, the physical removal of *chameitz*, as well as its nullification. Indeed, they hold, the requirement of *tashbitu* is fulfilled primarily through *biur*. If, as the Talmud says, "nullification suffices," this may refer to *chameitz* in one's possession that one does not know about and therefore cannot burn or scatter.[28] A third interpretation is that the Torah itself permits the "removal" of *chameitz* in either manner, through nullification or through physical destruction; the Rabbis, however, instituted the requirement that both procedures be performed.[29]

The traditional practice observes both *biur* and *bitul* (nullification). The "search" for *chameitz* takes place on the night before the seder (or two nights before, on 13 Nisan, when Pesach begins on Sunday and when it is forbidden to burn the *chameitz* on Shabbat). Following both the search and the destruction of the *chameitz*, one recites the formula of *bitul*, found in traditional Haggadot, which declares that "all *chameitz* in my possession . . . shall be as though it does not exist and as the dust of the earth."[30] Thus, even if *chameitz* inadvertently remains in one's possession, the process of renunciation succeeds in "removing" it in accordance with the Torah's requirement.

To destroy one's *chameitz* becomes impractical and burdensome if one owns a large amount of leaven. The custom therefore arose for a Jew to sell his *chameitz* to a gentile before Pesach and to buy it back from him at the holiday's conclusion. The roots of this practice extend back to tannaitic times. We learn in the *Tosefta* that "when a Jew and a Gentile are travelling on board ship, and the Jew has *chameitz* in his possession, he may sell it to the Gentile and buy it back after Pesach, provided that the sale is a full and unencumbered transfer (*matanah gemurah*)."[31] The development of this law, which apparently deals with a special case, into a regular and normal transaction is a long story that cannot be recounted here. We can simply point to the *Shulchan Aruch* and its commentaries, which accept as a matter of course that a Jew may sell *chameitz* to a gentile "even though the Jew knows the gentile and knows that the latter will guard the *chameitz* and return it to him after Pesach."[32] This custom is now universally practiced in traditional communities. In its most common form, all the Jews in a particular locale or congregation consign their *chameitz* to the rabbi or other notable, who then sells it all to a single gentile.[33]

This device of *m'chirat* (sale of) *chameitz* is effective because it is "full and unencumbered." Although the leaven remains physically within the Jew's property, its ownership is legally transferred to the gentile buyer in a transaction that meets all the formal halachic requirements of an act of sale. As such, it allows the householder to fulfill the mitzvah of the "removal" of *chameitz*, not necessarily under the terms of Exodus 12:15, which as we have seen may demand the physical removal of leaven, but under Exodus 13:7, which is understood to permit one to "see" *chameitz* that belongs to a non-Jew even though it remains within one's property.[34] Therefore, traditionally observant Jews hold that this form of sale is a perfectly valid means of discharging the Toraitic obligation to remove *chameitz*.

Reform Jews, of course, might well object to the fictitious aspect of this device. The sale may be fully "legal," but it is not serious: neither the Jew nor the gentile intend that the *chameitz* be transferred to the latter's permanent ownership. We might also ask whether the "sale" of *chameitz* is a better and more serious means of fulfilling the mitzvah than the process of *bitul*, nullification, described above. As is the case with sale, *chameitz* that is "nullified" remains within one's physical—though not one's legal—possession. Many authorities hold that the renunciation of *chameitz* fully meets the requirements of Exodus 12:15 and/or 13:7.[35]

The traditional halachah, it is true, does draw a distinction: while a Jew may make full use of *chameitz* "bought back" from a gentile after Pesach, leaven that is "renounced" is forbidden for use.[36] The logic of this distinction, however, escapes us. The objection to *bitul*, say the authorities,[37] is that one might declare falsely that "I annulled my *chameitz* before Pesach" when in fact one did not do so; therefore, although renouncing *chameitz* fulfills the Toraitic requirement, the Rabbis impose this penalty to forestall the possibility that one might evade the law. Yet what is *bitul* but a formal legal act that effects the legal—but not the physical—removal of *chameitz* from our possession? Is the "sale" of *chameitz* any different in its purpose and substance? It may be true that some Jews do not seriously intend to "renounce" their *chameitz*; it is certainly true, however, that none of them seriously intend to "sell" it.

We might also object to the sale of *chameitz* on the grounds that it requires the participation of a non-Jew in order that we can fulfill our own religious requirements. While Jews have for centuries relied upon gentiles to serve in such a capacity (the institution of the "Shabbos goy" comes readily to mind), the practice is inelegant at best and demeaning at worst. We prefer to fulfill our mitzvot on our own, especially in this case, when most authorities agree that the method of *bitul* allows us to meet the Torah's demand that we remove our *chameitz* without incurring severe financial loss.

Therefore, "Reform Jews rarely resort" to the sale of *chameitz*; rather, they "make leaven inaccessible in their homes."[38] This is our way of renouncing our possession of *chameitz*, and we believe that we can do so with full seriousness and sincerity. While Reform Jews may wish to sell their *chameitz*, perhaps, again, out of solidarity with traditional Jewish practice, the standards of Reform Jewish observance do not require that they do so.

NOTES

1. Peter S. Knobel, ed., *Gates of the Seasons* (New York: CCAR Press, 1983). The other volumes, all published by the CCAR Press, are W. Gunther Plaut, *A Shabbat Manual* (1972), Simeon J. Maslin, ed., *Gates of Mitzvah* (1979), and Mark Dov Shapiro, *Gates of Shabbat* (1991).

2. *Gates of the Seasons*, 68. According to tradition, the prohibition against eating *chameitz* begins at midday on 14 Nisan (Babylonian Talmud, *P'sachim* 28b, from a midrash on Deut. 16:3). The Rabbis extended the starting point of this prohibition to an earlier hour as a "fence around the law" (cf. *M. Avot* 1:1; *Yad, Chameitz Umatzah* 1:8–9).

3. Babylonian Talmud, *P'sachim* 35a, again based upon Deut. 16:3, which mentions both the words *chameitz* and *matzot*. By the midrashic principle of *hekeish* (comparison), the Rabbis deduce that only those grains that are *chameitz*—that undergo fermentation (*chimutz*)—may be used for matzah.

4. See, however, David Halivni, *Mekorot Umesorot, Pesachim* (Jerusalem: Jewish Theological Seminary of America, 1982), 371–72, who argues that in the original version of his statement (see *Tosefta Challah* 1:1 and JT *P'sachim* 2:4, 29b) R. Yochanan b. Nuri refers in this context not to rice and millet but to *karmit*, another type of grain altogether. If so, then one could argue that no known Talmudic sage ever ruled that rice and *kitniyot* are leaven.

5. Babylonian Talmud *P'sachim* 35a; *Yad, Chameitz Umatzah* 5:1; *Shulchan Aruch, Orach Chayim* 453:1.

6. By the time of its "first mention," the custom is spoken of as a long-standing practice. On its (possible) historical origin, see Yisrael Ta-Shema, *Minhag Ashkenaz Hakadmon* (Jerusalem: Magnes, 1995), 271–82.

7. *Sefer Mitzvot Katan*, chap. 222. See also *Sefer HaMordechai, P'sachim*, chap. 588, which cites the same ruling in the name of R. Yitzchak of Corbeil.

8. In his commentary to *Yad, Chameitz Umatzah* 5:1.

9. The *Tur, Orach Chayim* 453, offers a different explanation for the custom: the possibility that kernels of *chameitz* grain are often found mixed in sacks of *kitniyot*.

10. Just how long it was known there, however, is unclear. For example, the twelfth century *Sefer HaPardes* (ed. Ehrenreich, 46–47), emanating from the "school of Rashi," permits rice and legumes and mentions no custom that prohibits them.

11. See R. Yosef Karo, *Beit Yosef, Orach Chayim* 453: "Nobody pays attention to this matter except for the Ashkenazim"; his *Shulchan Aruch* (*Orach Chayim* 453:1), an authoritative guide to Sephardic practice, permits the consumption of rice and legumes. The *Tur* (who, though writing in Spain, was of Ashkenazic descent) dismissed the prohibition as a superfluous stringency (*chumra yeteirah*) that is not widely observed (*v'lo nahagu kein*; *Orach Chayim* 453).

R. Yerucham b. Meshulam (fourteenth-century Provence and Spain) declared it a "senseless custom" (*minhag sh'tut*; *Toldot Adam V'Chava*, netiv 4, part 3).

12. Isserles, *Orach Chayim* 453:1.

13. *Mor Uk'tziah*, 453. Emden speaks of his own efforts and those of his father, R. Zvi Ashkenazi (the "Chacham Zvi"), to "annul" the "erroneous custom" (*minhag ta-ut*).

14. The decision was issued on January 18, 1810, by the Royal Westphalian Jewish Consistory under the signature of its president, Israel Jacobson. The Consistory noted that the prohibition created a hardship for Jewish soldiers stationed in far-flung wartime outposts who could not obtain sufficient quantities of matzah for the holiday. (A similar hardship argument was raised by Emden, *Mor Uk'tziah*, 453.) See B. H. Auerbach, *Geschichte der Israelitischen Gemeinde Halberstadt* (Halberstadt, 1866), 215–16.

15. An exception is *Aruch HaShulchan, Orach Chayim* 453:5. Even he, though, puts most of his emphasis upon the very existence of the *minhag* as an a priori standard of Jewish observance: "Those who are lenient in this regard testify thereby that they lack the fear of heaven and the fear of sin" (453:4).

16. See *Shaarei T'shuvah* and *Biur HaGra* to *Orach Chayim* 453:1. This subject has a long halachic history, starting with the interpretation of Deut. 17:11. See *M. Eduyot* 1:5; Babylonian Talmud *Beitzah* 5a–b; *Yad, Mamrim* 2:2 and the commentaries thereto. One of the first authorities to apply this principle to the prohibition against rice and *kitniyot* is R. Yaakov Molin (fifteenth-century Germany), *Sefer Maharil, Hil. Maachalot Asurot BaPesach*, no. 16.

17. The most notable is the great opponent of Reform, R. Moshe Sofer; see *Resp. Chatam Sofer, Yoreh Dei-ah* 107, and especially *Orach Chayim* 122, where he applies this theory to the present issue.

18. For example, the Rabbis allow the consumption of rice and legumes during years of drought when its observance would bring great hardship upon the people. See *Chayei Adam* 127:1; *Mishnah B'rurah* 453:6, and *Shaar HaTziyun* ad loc.

19. Though we cannot undertake an extensive analysis of the subject here, we would point to citations in halachic literature that suggest that once the reason for a Rabbinic decree has disappeared, the decree itself may be annulled. See *Tosafot, Beitzah* 6a, s.v. *ha-idena*, and Rabad, *hasagah* to *Yad, Mamrim* 2:2. For a more extensive analysis, see *Reform Responsa for the Twenty-First Century*, no. 5759.7, section 2 (vol. 1, pp. 53–56).

20. When a matter that is permitted is mistakenly regarded as forbidden, the Sages are empowered to rule it permissible (i.e., no vow exists that would reinforce the prohibition on its own). See Babylonian Talmud, *Chulin* 6b; Jerusalem Talmud, *Taanit* 1:6, 59c; *Tosafot, P'sachim* 51a, s.v. *'i atah rasha'i; Shulchan Aruch, Yoreh Dei-ah* 214:1.

21. *Gates of the Seasons*, 67 (B-2).

22. *Gates of the Seasons*, 67.

23. In Babylonian Talmud, *P'sachim* 5a, the Rabbis argue by various means that "the very first day" must refer to 14 Nisan, the day before Pesach, and not to 15 Nisan, the first day of the Festival itself. See *Yad, Chameitz Umatzah* 2:1.

24. Thus Onkelos, in his *Targum* to Exod. 12:15, renders *tashbitu* as *tevatlun*, "you shall nullify."

25. Babylonian Talmud. *P'sachim* 4b. Rashi, s.v. *bevitul be`alma*, explains this rule on the grounds that the Torah does not say *tevaaru*, "burn the *chameitz*," but rather "remove" (*tashbitu*) it, which may be done by "removing" it from our consciousness. *Tosafot, P'sachim* 4b, s.v. *mid'oraita*, disagrees, on the basis of Talmudic evidence that *tashbitu* is understood as physical destruction. Nonetheless, "nullification" is sufficient under the terms of Exod. 13:7: you may not "see" your own *chameitz*, but you are permitted to see *chameitz* that belongs to others and that is ownerless (Babylonian Talmud, *P'sachim* 5b).

26. *Yad, Chameitz Umatzah* 2:2–3, in the printed texts and in the manuscripts (see R. David Kafi ch's edition of the *Mishneh Torah* [Jerusalem, 1986], ad loc.); *Tur, Orach Chayim* 331.

27. *Tosafot, P'sachim* 2a, s.v. *or*. Others explain the requirement of *biur* as a precaution against the possibility that one's renunciation of *chameitz* is not entirely done with full sincerity, in the absence of which the *chameitz* is not annulled and one would retain ownership of it during Pesach (R. Nissim Gerondi to Alfasi, *P'sachim* fol. 1a).

28. *Yad, Chameitz Umatzah* 2:2, according to the reading preserved in *Kesef Mishneh* ad loc.; R. Menachem HaMeiri to *M. P'sachim* 1:1.

29. *Chidushei HaRamban, P'sachim* 2a (although he asserts that *biur* is the preferable method); *Chidushei HaRitva, P'sachim* 2a; R. Nissim Gerondi to Alfasi, *P'sachim* fol. 1a.

30. Babylonian Talmud, *P'sachim* 6b: one who searches out the *chameitz* must still nullify it afterwards; *Yad, Chameitz Umatzah* 3:7.

31. *Tosefta P'sachim* 2:6 (p. 146, Lieberman ed.). See also *M. P'sachim* 2:1.

32. *Shulchan Aruch, Orach Chayim* 448:3; see especially the *Shaarei T'shuvah*, whose long note indicates the extensive discussion this subject receives in the responsa literature.

33. The first authority to institute this practice, apparently, was R. Shneur Zalman of Liady, in his *Shulchan Aruch, Hil. M'chirat Chameitz*. See also *Aruch HaShulchan, Orach Chayim* 448: 27. The "consignment" is effected by means of a *sh'tar harshaah*, a document that appoints a second party as one's agent in the selling of one's *chameitz*.

34. Babylonian Talmud, *P'sachim* 5b; *Yad, Chameitz Umatzah* 4:1ff.

35. See above at notes 24 and 25.

36. *Shulchan Aruch, Orach Chayim* 448:3, 448:5.

37. *Magen Avraham* 8; *Mishnah B'rurah* 25.

38. *Gates of the Seasons*, 128 n. 144.

12

REAL LIFE / REAL FOOD
Kashrut—A Family History

ELLEN WEINBERG DREYFUS

When I was little, I used to mix up the dish towels at my grandparents' house. I knew that there were red striped towels and blue striped towels, but no one ever explained that the red ones were for meat dishes, and the blue ones for dairy. In fact, no one explained the categories of meat and dairy to me. I remember using the gray dishes for lunch at my grandparents' cottage in Michigan, and the green ones with the pictures for dinner, but the difference to me seemed to have more to do with time of day than with what was on the plates. My mother's explanation of her in-laws' observance of kashrut was that these were ancient laws, originally created for hygiene and health reasons. "Now," she told us, "we know that we should cook the pork thoroughly." So we ate everything. A favorite treat was "Francheesies"—slit a hot dog lengthwise, stuff it with cheese, wrap bacon around it, and broil. Can you think of anything less kosher?

When my grandfather moved in with us my junior year of high school, we stopped having pork in the house. As I became more involved with youth group, camp, and NFTY and learned more about Judaism, I started thinking about food from a Jewish point of view. By the time I left for college, I no longer ate pork, although shellfish was still on the menu. I recall asking in the college dining hall if there were bacon bits in the clam chowder, which would put it off-limits. Within a couple of years, I gave up shellfish, and soon after, cheeseburgers. Midway through my HUC year in Israel, just in time for Pesach, I decided that I wanted to keep kosher, at home and away. That has been my practice for the past thirty-five years. That decision was based on several factors: (1) it brought discipline into my life and eating habits; (2) it brought a measure of *k'dushah* (sacredness) to a mundane physical need; (3) it made me feel more Jewish; and (4) I thought that having a kosher home would be valuable for me as a rabbi, so that any Jew could feel welcome eating in my home.

My father's parents, William and Ann Weinberg, children of Polish and Lithuanian Jewish immigrants, kept a kosher home. My mother's parents, Manfred and Sophie Sichel, both of whom died before I was born, emigrated from Germany in 1936. My mother, who was nine years old when she left Stuttgart, thinks they had a kosher home in Germany, but that was given up when they came to America.

In 1977, I married James N. Dreyfus, the son of Marianne and Rabbi A. Stanley Dreyfus *z´l*. The Dreyfus home followed what they referred to as "biblical kashrut"—no forbidden foods, but no separation of milk and meat. This practice conformed to that of their parents. Stanley's father, Marcel, the son of a *chazan* in Alsace, grew up in an observant home and came to America by himself in 1903. When Marcel and Isabella, an Ohio native, made their home in Youngstown, Ohio, they avoided pork but did not keep kosher.

In his article in the Winter 2004 issue of the *CCAR Journal*, "*Qedushah* in Diet: A Symposium on *Kashrut* in Reform Judaism," Rabbi Dreyfus wrote:

> My wife and I do not deliberately eat pork nor serve it at our table. We avoid shellfish. We abstain from such exotic dishes as rabbit, frog legs, whale cutlets, or the prohibited species enumerated in the eleventh chapter of Leviticus. On the other hand, we eat bread and other products of non-Jewish bakeries. We abstain from pork out of our awareness that historically Jews have been mocked,

maligned, and even martyred for their steadfast rejection of the flesh of swine, and that has become a sign of Jewish allegiance, although we insist that *k'dushah* in diet can be pursued quite independently of adherence to the strictures imposed by *halachah* for the slaughter of animals, for the inspection of the carcasses, for the washing and salting of meat, for the separation of meat and milk, and the utensils in which they are prepared and served."[1]

Marianne, Jim's mother, recalls that her parents' home in Berlin and later in London followed the same basic practice. Her grandfather Rabbi Leo Baeck and his wife, Natalie, probably had a kosher kitchen, but Marianne only remembers the extensive changing of dishes and utensils in preparation for Passover. Needless to say, in Theresienstadt, Rabbi Baeck ate whatever meager rations were available. After the war, he lived in London and traveled frequently to the United States to speak and teach. When he first came to Cincinnati to teach at Hebrew Union College, his hosts there assumed that his level of kashrut was above that of the college dining room, so they regularly served him kosher salami, a readily available source of meat. Marianne recounts that her grandfather disliked salami but was too polite to tell them that the regular meals would suffice. When she accompanied him on his second visit, she helped clear up the confusion and provided him with a more varied, if not strictly kosher, diet. She also met there a young Rabbi Dreyfus, then a PhD student at the college.

Marianne recently unearthed a letter that Stanley wrote to his mother in March 1949, informing her that Dr. Baeck would be her honored guest for dinner. He wrote, "A minimum of preparation is desirable. He is a charming old gentleman who is much unimpressed by fuss. He eats everything except non-Kosher meat[2]; but doesn't worry about the dishes. He likes fish. (Of course, he doesn't mix meat and milk.)" In the same letter, he mentions, "His granddaughter is at present touring in the East, and I suggested that she return via Youngstown, so that the three of us might return to Cincinnati together."[3] Thus, this special visit introduced Stanley's parents to their future daughter-in-law, as well as her revered grandfather.

Today, despite the heritage of the Francheesies, three out of four of Norman and Eve Weinberg's children keep kosher homes. As of this writing, two of my children are married, and both have kosher homes. My eldest son's wife is vegetarian, so their kitchen is kosher, dairy only, but he will eat kosher meat elsewhere. My youngest son is presently an unrestricted omnivore. My children's dietary concerns also involve environmental consciousness and sophisticated palates. These lead them to seek out fresh and local food, to read labels carefully, to avoid chemical additives, and generally to eat in a way that keeps them healthy. They know how to cook and understand the importance of food in social and familial interaction. It makes their mother proud.

Gathering at the table for special meals is a cherished tradition. We share recipes handed down through the generations that signify who we are as a family. Recently, my son Ben declared that members of his generation need to learn to make all the old family recipes so that the tradition continues into the future. Time will tell whether the kitchens of future generations adhere to the laws of kashrut, but I pray that the food prepared there will be ample, delicious, and served with love.

NOTES

1. Adapted from A. Stanley Dreyfus, "*Qedushah* in Diet: A Symposium on *Kashrut* in Reform Judaism," *CCAR Journal*, Winter 2004, 34.

2. I assume that by "non-Kosher meat," ASD was referring to forbidden species, rather than beef or poultry that had been obtained from a non-kosher butcher.

3. Private communication, collection of Marianne C. Dreyfus.

Part Three

Environmental Ethics:
Bal Tashchit

With this section of the book, we begin to explore the incorporation of new values into the traditional ritual approach to kashrut. As I explain in the introduction to this volume, I do not separate ritual kashrut from ethically motivated kashrut by referring to the latter as eco-kashrut or ethical kashrut. At the beginning of our need to broaden the definition of kashrut beyond ritual, these terms served the liberal community well. In the 1970s Zalman Schachter-Shalomi coined the term eco-kashrut, and by the 1980s Arthur Waskow and his Shalom Center had popularized its use.[1] While I recognize the great influence these two leaders have had on the modern definition of Jewish environmentalism and kashrut, I hold that it is time to reintegrate eco-kashrut back into kashrut. Then, the message is clear that ritual and ethics are intertwined. All these values—ethical, ritual, or other—sit side by side on the same buffet from which we select our Reform dietary practice. It is best to approach the metaphoric buffet like a real collation, making sure you select from all the food groups. While it is natural to favor one sub-stream of dietary practice over another (e.g., health over ritual, ritual over animal rights, workers' rights over animal rights), it is important to push ourselves beyond our natural passions, interests, and inclinations.

As you read *The Sacred Table*, consider selecting personal dietary practices from every section for a well-balanced diet.

Renewed concern for our environment and our health has brought *bal tashchit* (do not wantonly waste) issues to the forefront of kashrut. As Kevin M. Kleinman explores the breadth of our tradition, he defines the term *bal tashchit* in "Curb Your Consumerism: Developing a *Bal Tashchit* Food Ethic for Today." He demonstrates that *bal tashchit* extends beyond being *shomrei adamah*, "guardians of the earth," to think about the sustainability of the earth and its inhabitants. At their best, *bal tashchit*–driven policies should protect the environment and provide good-quality nutrition for the maximum number of people. Batsheva Appel ("Connecting Locally: Jumping Off the Production Line") expands our understanding of *bal tashchit* in a discussion of connecting to local food and encouraging biodiversity. Taking a multifaceted approach to genetically modified organisms, Mark Washofsky presents a *t'shuvah* (responsum) "On High-Tech Science and Our Food: Three Questions." Tackling a growing concern in the food world, Joel Mosbacher reveals the complexities of industrialized fishing in "Fish: A Complex Issue." Like many subjects in *The Sacred Table*, this chapter easily could be placed under more than one value heading. "Fish: A Complex Issue" helps us see the impact of industrial fishing not only on the environment, but also on fish. Mosbacher also reveals the highly wasteful practices common in industrialized fishing. Barbara Lerman-Golomb explores the importance and possibilities of gardens for our communities in "Getting Back to the Garden." Finally, Joseph Aaron Skloot ("Let Your Table Be to You a Temple") shares an experience that has shaped his view, and will challenge ours, of bananas.

NOTE

1. David A. Teutsch, *A Guide to Jewish Practice: Kashrut* (Wyncote, PA: Reconstructionist Rabbinical College Press, 2003), 33.

13

CURB YOUR CONSUMERISM

Developing a *Bal Tashchit* Food Ethic for Today

Kevin M. Kleinman

> When the Holy Blessed One created the first human, God took Adam and led him around all the trees of the Garden of Eden. And God said to Adam, "See My works, how good and praiseworthy they are! And all I have created, I made for you. [But,] be mindful then that you do not spoil and destroy My world. For if you spoil it, there is no one after you to repair it.
>
> *(Kohelet Rabbah 7:13)*

The message embedded in this midrash acknowledges and praises God as the creator of the earth and then charges the human race with the task of using our planet's precious resources wisely.[1] The last line in this text is a forewarning: we must be responsible caretakers of the planet's resources, to use only what it is necessary, and to be conscious of the negative impact that human beings can have on the ecosystems of the earth if we are not careful. God reminds Adam, the first human, that there is only one world to provide for the needs of human beings, plants, and animals. Then, God leaves the fate of the world in our hands. Throughout history, human beings have depended on balance in the natural world: everything necessary for survival comes from the earth. Food, raw materials for clothing and shelter, and energy sources are all grown on and extracted from the land. Our ancestors knew that they had to treat the earth with care, lest they go without these necessities of life, putting into question their own fate.

For the past few hundred years, though, this wisdom in this midrash has been overshadowed by the human tendency to accumulate more than what is necessary for survival. Beginning with the Industrial Revolution, our society has been able to produce and distribute more food and goods at a lower cost than ever before. We have been trained to eat things and buy things without thinking about the resources needed to produce and ship them all over the world, without thought of the human labor required to grow and harvest food and assemble products.

It is time to return to the wisdom of our ancient texts and traditions; time to examine our patterns of consumption and disposal of food, energy, and material goods; time to cultivate a different ethic. This paradigm shift will allow us to recognize our species' unnecessary waste and wanton destruction of the planet's finite resources and ultimately give us opportunities to live truly in partnership with God. It will also give us guidance for ways that we can allow the earth to heal and, as a result, create a healthier society, since what is good for the earth is ultimately good for humanity.

Guiding these ethics are the prohibitions of *bal tashchit*, the biblical and Rabbinic laws forbidding unnecessary waste and reckless destruction of resources that are beneficial to human beings. The laws of *bal tashchit* originate in Deuteronomy 20:19–20: "When in your war against a city you have to besiege it a long time in order to capture it, you must not destroy its trees, wielding the ax against them. You may eat of them, but you must not cut them down." This chapter will illustrate how they are expanded in Talmudic literature to prevent wasting all other food resources, energy sources, and material goods. In the Middle Ages, the author of *Sefer HaChinuch* refined the guidelines of *bal tashchit* to forbid wasting any edible food sources, down to even the tiniest of morsels of food. Rambam made the equitable distribution of resources a social justice issue under the category of the laws of *bal tashchit* in the *Mishneh Torah*.[2] Finally, we must continue to cultivate a *bal tashchit* ethic for today, standing firmly on the shoulders of our ancestors, and fulfilling our responsibility to guard and protect our world, especially when it comes to choosing the types of food we eat and understanding the impact those choices make on our own health and the health of our planet. In the following pages, we will explore a sampling of texts that define the development of these laws.

Biblical Origins of *Bal Tashchit*

> When in your war against a city you have to besiege it a long time in order to capture it, you must not destroy its trees, wielding the ax against them. You may eat of them, but you must not cut them down. Are trees of the field human to withdraw before you into the besieged city? Only trees that you know do not yield food may be destroyed; you may cut them down for constructing siegeworks against the city that is waging war on you, until it has been reduced.
>
> (Deut. 20:19–20)

Chapter 20 of the Book of Deuteronomy contains the biblical origins for the Rabbinic category of *bal tashchit*. It should be noted that Deuteronomy uses the term *lo tashchit* (do not destroy), while the Rabbinic texts use the synonymous term *bal tashchit*. Verses 19–20 prohibit cutting down the fruit trees that surround a besieged city during a time of war, while allowing non-fruit-bearing trees to be cut down and made into instruments of war. The Israelites were allowed to eat the fruit, but they were not permitted to cut them down in order to gain an advantage during combat.

Deuteronomy 20 creates a distinction between trees that produce fruit and trees that do not. According to the medieval biblical commentator Abraham ibn Ezra from eleventh-century Spain, the former is a source of life and the latter is not. For him, there is an implicit relationship between fruit trees and human beings, the fate of one being bound to the fate of the other. Stressing the sacred relationship between fruit trees and human beings, Ibn Ezra writes that the trees of the field are not to be cut down because "the life of man depends on the trees of the field."[3] Ibn Ezra's comment implies that the fate of human beings is intimately linked to that of the trees of the field. If humans cut down the fruit trees while besieging a city, then they would essentially be abusing themselves as the beneficiary of the fruit from those trees.

Fruit trees are vital to human beings' existence in times of peace and, all the more so, in times of war. Inherent in Deuteronomy 20:19–20 is the notion that human beings must treat the environment with special care all the time. The implication is that the destruction of trees leads to the loss of food sources and, therefore, the loss of human life that is dependent on this sustenance.

Expansion of *Bal Tashchit* in the Talmud

In certain key passages, the Talmud expands the notion of what is included for protection under the laws of *bal tashchit* to prohibit the waste and destruction of anything beneficial to human beings. The discussions in these passages can be divided into three categories: unnecessary waste of food, oil, and commercial goods. By expanding the legal category of *bal tashchit*, the Rabbis in the Talmud advanced their religious and ethical understanding that all resources have sacred origins and should be used to their maximum potential with extreme care. They affirmed that one should endeavor not to waste anything useful, either accidentally or intentionally.

In the following example from the Babylonian Talmud, Rav Chisda and Rav Papa (fourth-century-C.E. Babylonian sages) discuss the imperative to eat food and consume beverages that are produced locally and to take fewer resources over those that must travel further from their point of origin to the consumer and are more resource intensive to produce:

> Rav Chisda said: When one can eat barley bread but instead eats wheaten bread, he transgresses the sin of *bal tashchit*. Rav Papa said: When one can drink beer but instead drinks wine, he transgresses

the sin of *bal tashchit*. But there is actually no problem (in doing so, for seeking to avoid transgressing the sin of) *bal tashchit* with regard to one's body is a greater (consideration).

(Babylonian Talmud, *Shabbat* 140b)

The intentional use of *bal tashchit* by Rav Chisda and Rav Papa projects an ethic of protecting resources that go into the production of food and beverages. These three statements contain several inter-related concepts regarding a person's wealth, the accessibility and affordability of food resources, and human health. Rav Chisda makes a general prohibition against eating wheat bread when barley bread is available. What then is the difference between these kinds of bread, and why does Rav Chisda make such a strong statement, calling a person a sinner for choosing wheat bread when barley bread is available? These questions also apply to Rav Papa's restriction on drinking wine when beer is available.

Barley was one of the first grains domesticated by human beings. By the Talmudic period of Jewish history (third to seventh centuries C.E.), barley bread was considered food for poorer people, though it was once the staple of all classes. In an article about the role of barley in the ancient world, C. W. Newman and R. K. Newman discuss the nutritional differences of barley and wheat breads during this time period:

> In ancient Rome, bread made from wheat was considered more nourishing, more digestible, and in every way superior to barley bread. As in later cultures, barley bread was consumed predominantly by slaves and the poor. After the fall of the Roman Empire, barley bread was considered inferior to rye and wheat breads.[4]

It was common practice to make beer from readily available barley supplies. While beer was a common beverage at this time, wine was a luxury item, as it was more expensive and took more resources to produce and distribute. Beer could be made at any time of year from the available grains. Grapes grow in only certain geographical climates and are harvested only once a year. Thus, during the time the Talmud was written, barley bread and beer were stigmatized as food and drink for the lower classes.

It is now possible to view Rav Chisda's and Rav Papa's statements in terms of their contribution to the expansion of *bal tashchit*. Rav Chisda considers it unnecessarily wasteful to eat wheat bread when barley bread is also available. Regarding the use of common resources, it can be inferred from this that common foods cost less money and use fewer resources to produce than fancy, gourmet, or luxury foods. According to Rav Chisda, when given a choice, one is religiously and ethically obligated to consume foodstuffs that require fewer resources to produce and are less expensive. Rav Chisda and Rav Papa expand *bal tashchit* to consider social, environmental, and economic factors when determining what type of food to eat and beverage to drink. They deem it inappropriately wasteful to eat a product that is superfluously expensive and requires more resources to produce.

Expansion of *Bal Tashchit* in the Middle Ages

Medieval sages picked up on the Rabbinic expansion of the legal category of *bal tashchit*. Rabbi Aaron HaLevi from Barcelona wrote *Sefer HaChinuch* around the year 1300. This source is a commentary on each of the 613 commandments as systematized by Maimonides's *Sefer HaMitzvot*. *Sefer HaChinuch* comments on *bal tashchit* in the following, where it is explained as having religious and ethical roots:

> The purpose of this mitzvah [*bal tashchit*] is to teach us to love that which is good and worthwhile and to cling to it, so that good becomes a part of us and we will avoid all that is evil and destructive. This is the way of the righteous and those who improve society . . . that nothing, not even a grain of mustard, should be lost to the world, that they should regret any loss or destruction that they see, and if possible they will prevent any destruction that they can. Not so are the wicked, who are like demons, who rejoice in destruction of the world, and they are destroying themselves.
> (*Sefer HaChinuch, mitzvah* 529)

According to *Sefer HaChinuch*, people who follow the laws of *bal tashchit* are righteous, and each positive action is considered a religious act, a way to become closer to God. This passage goes on to credit the righteous with creating a better society. The author defines waste in very small terms, even as little as one mustard seed. This understanding of *bal tashchit* expands the Rabbinic notion of how far one must go to avoid unnecessarily destroying food. Finally, the author of *Sefer HaChinuch* understands the connection between the destruction of the planet and the destruction of the self. The conclusion of his comments foreshadows the doom for those who have no concern for how their actions impact the ecosystem.

Developing a *Bal Tashchit* Food Ethic for Today

The Industrial Revolution (late eighteenth and early nineteenth centuries) brought many changes to civilizations throughout the world. People moved to cities en masse from the countryside. Technologies were developed to increase the production of food and the manufacturing and distribution of goods. These changes transformed how people acquired things. They were no longer solely dependent on subsisting on their land and making their own goods. Factory farms and production centers were able to mass-produce almost everything, driving down their costs. Rapid industrialization and advancements in science and technology solved many problems and enhanced the quality of human life.

At the same time, however, there are unintended environmental consequences, endangering the health of both the planet and human beings. The earth's resources are becoming depleted at an alarming rate, causing species extinction, soil erosion, and famine that displaces millions of people worldwide. Factories are polluting the air, land, and water. The wide use of pesticides is changing the makeup of the soil in a way that is detrimental to human health. All of this combined, plus supplying enough energy for transportation, heating and cooling, and other individual household needs and desires, is changing the climate of our planet.

The Reform Jewish community is beginning to respond to these environmental problems with a belief that we have a religious mandate to act as stewards of creation. Individuals and organizations have begun to use a Jewish vocabulary to accompany their environmental work, giving it a spiritual and religious context. Our synagogues and camps have taken this message to heart and are greening our facilities, including the way we approach food service. This is an important step in reducing the amount of harm to our bodies and to our land. We must examine the types of foods that we eat and pay attention to the distance they travel to get to our plates.

Using the laws of *bal tashchit* as a guide, we can reduce the impact that our food choices have on the earth. By eating food that is not treated with harsh chemicals as they are grown and foods that are grown closer to the places that we live, we fulfill the dictums of our tradition not to destroy the land or waste food. The laws of *bal tashchit* have been expanded throughout history to meet the changing needs of Jewish communities. With each development, the prohibitions against destroying resources and wasting food have been made meaningful and relevant for the societal complexities of their time period. From protecting fruit trees in times of war, to saving water and land from pollution; from prohibiting the unnecessary destruction of clothing, utensils, and food to encouraging greater consumer consciousness and simple living, the prohibitions that fall under the rubric of *bal tashchit* have been influential in protecting the planet and bringing people closer to God.

We need to continue to learn from the wisdom of our ancestors in developing a *bal tashchit* food ethic for today. For thousands of years the Jewish community has done our part to ensure that the world will be left intact for future generations. We should strive to adhere to God's warning to Adam. The world is full of many beautiful and useful resources. We must, however, remember to use them wisely, to guard and protect them, to ensure that the planet will continue to flourish for many years to come.

NOTES

1. Modern Jewish environmental teachings use the term *shomrei adamah*, "guardians of the earth," to emphasize our responsibility as the earth's caretakers. This phrase comes from the Hebrew in Genesis 2:15 in which God commands human beings to "work [*l'ovdah*]" the earth and "keep [*ul'shomrah*]" the earth.

2. *Mishneh Torah, Hilchot Eivel* 14:24.

3. Ibn Ezra on Deuteronomy 20:19–20.

4. C. W. Newman and R. K. Newman, "A Brief History of Barley Foods," *Cereal Foods World* 51, no. 1 (2006): 5.

14

CONNECTING LOCALLY
Jumping Off the Production Line

BATSHEVA APPEL

Surrounded by an endless variety of edible plant life (Gen. 1:29–30), Adam and Eve were placed in the Garden of Eden by God, to till and to tend (Gen. 2:15), to work in the Garden, and to be *shomrei adamah*, "guardians of the earth." Life was easy in Eden, for everywhere they looked food was readily at hand, every tree pleasing to the sight and good for food (Gen. 2:9). Today, however, how ironic it is that we too are surrounded by food, but we have lost our sense of *kesher*, our connection to the food, to the land, and to our Creator.

We are immersed in a culture of endless eating opportunities. Even in stores unrelated to food, we are tempted to eat. We go shopping for hardware or office supplies, and there are snacks and drinks near the checkout. All of this food is at hand before we even consider the plethora of restaurants and fast-food establishments in our communities. In many cases we don't have to leave the car to eat. Especially in communities that are considered food deserts,[1] areas where there is extremely limited access to affordable, nutritious foods, there is plenty of low-nutrition, high-calorie food available at fast-food restaurants and convenience stores. Some, like Michael Pollan, might decry these choices in such venues as not real food,[2] but this is what is marketed to us as food. Therefore, it is what most of us consider to be food.

Yet with all of this food at hand, we are farther than ever from a sense of *kesher* to our sources of sustenance. Even when we think about healthy eating, we reduce food to proteins and carbohydrates, vitamins and minerals, fiber and fat. We label our food as good or bad. Food is more than a combination of chemicals that taken in the right doses keeps us alive. Food, in and of itself, is neither good nor bad. The food we eat sustains us, nourishes us, and connects us to each other, to the earth, and to the Creator of the earth. Food is to be enjoyed and savored.

If we have no *kesher* to our food, we are even farther from a sense of *kesher* to the land. We do not know the sources of our food, how our food is grown, where it is grown, how it is harvested or the ramifications of those choices. We do not understand that the cultivation of what we eat can actually be destructive to the fertility and the sustainability of the land. This destruction of essential resources is an unnecessary waste that the biblical and rabbinical literature would call *bal tashchit* (explored further by Kevin M. Kleinman in chapter 13). Ignoring or, even worse, ruining the land is counter to God's expectation that we will be *shomrei adamah*.

In the last decade there has been a developing movement to reconnect with our food and with the land by emphasizing the eating of locally grown foods. A person who adopts this approach to eating is called a "locavore."[3] In this chapter, I will suggest how this is a very Jewish impulse, as well as a delicious one. I will also suggest a variety of ways to reconnect, including purchasing local foods at groceries, as well as at farm stands and farmers' markets. Other ways to reconnect include participating in community supported agriculture (CSA), in home, community, or synagogue gardening, or in the urban farming movement.

Why Do We Eat Locally and Why Is It Jewish?

Rabbi Yosei [of the school of] Rabbi Bun said: It is even forbidden to live in a city that doesn't have a source of fresh produce. Rabbi Hezekiah the priest in the name of Rav said: In the future a person will have to give an accounting for everything that his eyes saw, but he did not eat.

(Jerusalem Talmud, Kiddushin 48b)

Here in the Jerusalem Talmud, we are given two important Jewish reasons to eat locally: the preservation of green spaces in towns and cities for the health of the residents, and the enjoyment of eating food. Eating locally grown food preserves farms in and around cities and towns. Without a viable market for the food that is produced, it is difficult for farmers to keep farmland for agricultural use and not turn it over to residential or commercial use. Agricultural land use is more easily sustainable than homes or businesses, depending on how the land is farmed.

The statement that we are expected to enjoy the things that we see is not a call to gluttony, but a reinforcement that we are to enjoy the pleasures of this world, particularly food. For those who live in the East, there is nothing to compare to the taste of the first of the season's local strawberries in the spring, or really fresh tomatoes or sweet corn in the summer, or the new apples in the autumn. Locally grown, picked in season fruits and vegetables taste fresher and better, because they do not have to be harvested under-ripe in order to endure the long shipping period. We get to enjoy them in their prime. When we search out locally grown food in its season, we reinforce our connection to how the food is grown and to the land itself, because we witness that different foods have their seasons and recognize when those seasons shift.

Another reason to eat locally is that it preserves the diversity of what is grown.

> The Rabbis said: Even though you may think them superfluous in this world, creatures such as flies, bugs, and gnats have their allotted task in the scheme of creation, as it says, "And God saw everything that God had made, and behold, it was very good" (Gen. 1:31).

(B'reishit Rabbah 10:7)

This midrash reinforces how everything has a purpose in creation, even the things that we might think we would be better off without. When we require our food to be shipped long distances, we reduce the number of varieties that are grown, thereby reducing the biodiversity. The varieties of tomato that "travel well"—in other words, the tomatoes that can be shipped with minimal loss—become the predominant varieties of tomato that are grown. When the characteristics of disease and pest resistance or adaptability to climate are added in, the number of choices represented in the supermarket can become even fewer. Eventually this push to market eliminates the varieties of tomato that are available. We lose more than taste as we limit the number of varieties of tomato or strawberry or corn or anything else that is grown for our consumption. When we diminish biodiversity, our agricultural industry becomes vulnerable to one disease or pest that can threaten an entire crop. The gains that we achieve in developing a tomato that is more marketable makes the tomato plant more vulnerable. As Wendell Berry writes in his essay "The Pleasure of Eating," "But as scale increases, diversity declines; as diversity declines, so does health; as health declines, the dependence on drugs and chemicals necessarily increases."[4] With the increasing demand for locally grown food, there is an increasing interest in "heirloom" varieties of tomatoes, as well as other types of produce. These older varieties are more fragile and less disease resistant, but have amazing colors, flavors, and taste.

How Do We Eat Locally?

As more people have been exploring the localism movement, it is becoming easier and easier to be a locavore.

Groceries and Markets

There are more signs labeling foods that are produced or grown locally every time we go shopping. Even those big-box stores that sell food are offering more locally grown produce. It is now required by law[5] that the origins of fruits and vegetables be posted, which makes it much easier to shop with buying local in mind.

Farmers' Markets

LocalHarvest (www.localharvest.org) lists over five thousand farmers' markets, where farmers can bring in their produce and sell it directly to the consumer. Some areas have permanent markets that are open year-round, like the famous Pike Place Market in Seattle. In some places the farmers' market is seasonal and is open only one or two days a week. In all instances, it pays to shop carefully, asking where the produce is from, as some markets permit sellers to offer fruits and vegetables that they have purchased rather than only things that they have grown.

Get to know the sellers and farmers at your farmers' market. Not only can they can give you a window into how the food is farmed, they let you know what items to expect in the coming weeks or how to prepare different things. In addition, it is helpful for them to hear what their customers want.

Other tips for shopping farmers' markets include the following:

- Arrive early in the day, when the produce and the selection are at their best.
- When you first arrive at the market, do a quick circuit to see what is available at the market that day and determine what you might want to purchase. Many farmers' markets now offer a variety of things beyond fruits and vegetables, including meat, cheeses, eggs, and honey.
- Have a list, but be prepared to be flexible. What is in the market depends on what is available in the field. The sweet corn and the tomatoes have their own schedule; they don't care if you are prepping for a dinner party.
- Bring cash in case the sellers don't take credit cards.
- Bring your own bags to carry everything home.

If you are uncertain whether there is a farmers' market near you in the United States, check LocalHarvest, do a web search, or inquire in your local department of agriculture.

Farm Stands and Pick-Your-Own

Farm stands, as their name implies, are located on or near farms in exurban or rural areas. They are seasonal and usually have only a limited selection of choices. In some cases, there will be someone to help with your selections. In other cases, everything will be sold by the honor system—leave your money as you take your produce. Farm stands can be a wonderful way to get fresh produce in season.

The pick-your-own option gives you the chance to be involved in the harvesting of different fruits and vegetables, such as strawberries, raspberries, blueberries, apples, or pumpkins. The different crops are farmed, and everything is set up for people to come and harvest as much or as little as they want. Generally one pays by the flat or by the pound. Make sure you understand the pricing before you start picking. To find local pick-your-own farms, look for advertisements in the newspaper and ask around.

CSA (Community Supported Agriculture)

The last two decades have seen the development of CSAs around the country until there are more than thirty-five hundred CSAs listed on www.localharvest.org, a website that can help you to locate a CSA near you. A farmer with a CSA sells shares of the coming harvest to a number of people before the season begins. With the improved cash flow, the farmer can plan for the coming season and, as the growing season starts, concentrate on farming. Throughout the season each of the shareholders receives a weekly share of whatever is produced by the farm that week. If all of the brussels sprouts are eaten by pests, then there are no brussels sprouts in this week's share and possibly for the entire season. If the tomato plants have a bountiful week, then there will be pounds of tomatoes in that week's share.

CSAs benefit the farmers by letting them get to know the people who eat the food that they grow, as well as guaranteeing that they will be able to sell all that they produce. The shareholders benefit by having a steady stream of fresh produce all summer. They also get to know the farmer who grows their food as well as the ups and downs of farming, learning more about how the food comes to the table. Some CSAs are organic; many are not. Some emphasize education and getting to know the farm; others do not. Also, there are specifically Jewish CSAs, which can be found through www.hazon.org.

January is the best time to begin looking, as many CSAs sell out of shares by spring. If you are just beginning, consider getting a half-share or splitting a full share with someone else. Sometimes you might have the option of getting a share that lasts for only a few weeks. You should know that a CSA box can contain lots of unfamiliar vegetables in large quantities. Some CSAs post or distribute recipes. Most CSAs drop off boxes to specific locations for pick up by the shareholders. Some have the option of picking up your share directly from the farm, and sometimes you can pick some of the produce yourself. Generally there is a system for swapping with other members the produce that might not interest you. Undistributed produce is often donated to local hunger relief organizations.

Home, Community, and Synagogue Gardens

Of course, the freshest tomato is the one that you have grown yourself. In chapter 17, Barbara Lerman-Golomb speaks to the many benefits of gardening at home or in a community garden. The food can be enjoyed by you, your family, and friends or can be shared with soup kitchens and food pantries. Ample Harvest (www.ampleharvest.org) has a program to match home gardeners who have extra produce with food pantries in order to share the bounty.

Urban Farming

Urban Farming is the latest innovation in growing more food locally. There are any number of cities (Milwaukee, Chicago, Washington,

D.C., Los Angeles) that are far removed from rural areas and agriculture. Yet there is farming happening within the city limits on plots of land that are compact but nevertheless produce large amounts of food. These projects differ from community gardens in that they are run as a single farm rather than different plots of lands where many different people raise different things. The impetus behind urban farming is to use the land in a sustainable manner, to bring fresh produce to areas where there might be little or no access to affordable fruits and vegetables, and to help people reconnect with the sources of their food.

All of these aspects of being a locavore foster a sense of *kesher*. When we eat foods in their seasons, we remind ourselves of the agricultural seasons. When we can see the farms and orchards where our food is grown, we develop a sense of the land around us. When we speak with the people who grow the food, we remember that food does not just show up on our table, but there is a great deal of real effort to bring us the food that we eat. When we develop all of these connections, we place ourselves within creation instead of outside of it. Berry speaks of this connection:

> A significant part of the pleasure of eating is one's accurate consciousness of the lives and world from which food comes. . . . In this pleasure we experience and celebrate our dependence and our gratitude, for we are living from mystery, from creatures we did not make and powers we cannot comprehend.[6]

The Jewish way of celebrating "our dependence and our gratitude" is to recite the blessings for the food we eat, before and after eating. When we say that God "brings forth bread from the earth" in the *Motzi*, we are not speaking of bread that just appears ready for us to eat; rather we remind ourselves of the partnership between God, Creator, and humanity, farmer and baker. The less we know about the steps it takes to produce the food that we eat, the farther away we are from the connections to the sources of our sustenance, to the land, and to God. By eating locally, we connect to each of the steps that it takes to put food on our table. Then when we say the *Motzi*, we know that it is through our partnership with the Creator of the earth that bread is brought forth from the earth.

NOTES

1. *Access to Affordable and Nutritious Food—Measuring and Understanding Food Deserts and Their Consequences: Report to Congress*, http://www.ers.usda.gov/Publications/AP/AP036/.

2. Michael Pollan, In *Defense of Food: An Eater's Manifesto* (New York: Penguin Books, 2008).

3. Sometimes local food is also referred to as "farm to table" cuisine. A more structured segment of the local food movement, Slow Food is an international movement founded by Carlo Petrini in 1986. It emphasizes traditional and regional cuisine by promoting the farming of plants, seeds, and livestock characteristic of the local ecosystem.

4. Wendell Berry, "The Pleasures of Eating," in *Bringing It to the Table: On Farming and Food* (Berkeley, CA: Counterpoint Press, 2009), p. 231.

5. http://www.ams.usda.gov/AMSv1.0/cool.

6. Berry, "The Pleasures of Eating," p. 234.

15

ON HIGH-TECH SCIENCE AND OUR FOOD
Three Questions

MARK WASHOFSKY

Are GMOs (genetically modified organisms) a Jewish issue? The steadily increasing presence of genetically modified foodstuffs on our supermarket shelves raises a number of important and difficult questions, and at least three of them are questions of specifically Jewish concern. A satisfactory answer may not be possible, but these questions are most definitely worth asking, because they touch upon some of the most central elements of our relationship as religious Jews to our tradition and to the natural world around us.

1. Are We Playing God?

Does genetic modification of existing species of plants and animals constitute an improper interference with the order of the universe (*sidrei b'reishit*)? By engaging in these procedures, do we usurp the authority of God or of nature, arrogating too much power for ourselves? This is the sort of question that any religious tradition might ask, and ours is no exception. We find a classic expression of this view in the commentary of Nachmanides (Rabbi Moshe ben Nachman, or Ramban) on the Torah's prohibition of *kilayim*: "You shall not let your cattle mate with a different kind [*kilayim*]; you shall not sow your field with two kinds of seed" (Lev. 19:19). This commandment teaches us, he writes, that God's creation is perfect and that we deny this perfection when we engage in the mixing of the distinct animal and plant species.[1] One could rely upon this insight concerning our relationship to the natural world in order to prohibit the new technologies of genetic engineering that blur the lines between existing species and that create new ones. Yet Jewish tradition, in the main, does not take that step. Most contemporary rabbinical authorities read the *kilayim* texts strictly. In their view, the mitzvah forbids only the actual physical mating of animals and the sowing of seeds, and it does *not* cover the sort of "mixing" that takes place in a laboratory and that we call genetic engineering or genetic modification.[2]

This more restrictive reading of the text coheres with another traditional Jewish understanding of our relationship to nature. That understanding is classically exemplified by none other than Nachmanides himself, in his commentary to Genesis 1:28, a verse in which God grants dominion over the earth to humans. Nachmanides explains this "dominion" as the right of humans "to do as they wish" with the animals, "to build up, to tear down," and to exploit the resources of the physical world. His comment reflects an *instrumental* conception of the world—that is, that we are entitled to make use of nature and bend it to our purposes. Such a conception is of pivotal importance in the history of our culture, for if we did not view the world in an instrumental manner, we humans might never have felt entitled to pursue science and technology, activities that suggest a sense of mastery over nature. With respect to our particular concern here, we should note that some contemporary authorities cite this latter comment of Nachmanides as evidence that Jewish tradition would permit us to engage in the processes of genetic modification.

These two conflicting viewpoints present us with an interpretive dilemma. Does Nachmanides to Leviticus 19:19 contradict Nachmanides to Genesis 1:28? Is there a way to accommodate both points of view in our Judaism, or does consistency demand that we choose one approach and reject the other? However we resolve this conflict, its existence indicates at the very least that Jewish thought does not obviously prohibit genetic engineering. There may be other reasons to worry about these technologies (see below). Perhaps, even if we are entitled to manipulate the natural world for our own purposes, it is a good thing to do so in a spirit of humility, remembering at all times that it is God's universe that we are manipulating. Nonetheless, there is no convincing proof that our tradition rejects the genetic modification of existing species as an unwarranted transgression of the line that separates human action and divine prerogative.

2. Is It Kosher?

As a Reform Jew who observes kashrut, this question is of practical importance to me. It isn't just food for thought (sorry). Does genetic modification of a species affect its status under the traditional dietary laws? Would a pig be kosher if it were genetically engineered so that it chews a cud? In reverse, would a cow still be kosher if it were modified so that it no longer chews its cud or has split hoofs? Does a tomato spliced with genetic materials taken from animals become *fleishig* or *b'sari* (meat) rather than pareve? And what if the animals that provide those materials are of nonkosher species? One way of addressing these questions is to define genetically modified species of plants and animals as "mixtures" of different characteristics. The traditional rules concerning kashrut have a great deal to say about such mixtures (e.g., forbidden substances that accidentally mix with permitted ones, or milk that accidentally falls into a pot containing meat), and these rules may aid us in defining the status of genetically modified foods. The problem, of course, is that genetically modified foods may not really be "mixtures" in the classic sense of that term. Moreover, there is nothing accidental in their creation. Another approach involves the theory advanced by some scholars that the Torah does not apply its ritual categories and prohibitions to phenomena that we cannot see with the naked eye. This theory, which on one level is very helpful,[3] would suggest that Jewish tradition is neutral when it comes to the microscopic realm of genes, chromosomes, and DNA. That conclusion would be unfortunate: these very small things carry potentially enormous consequences, and we would not want to think that Torah has nothing to say about them.

Perhaps we should acknowledge that the details and technicalities of traditional kashrut law do not truly speak to this very new and dramatically different reality. Perhaps it would be better to begin our thinking from a more basic, theoretical starting point: the new genetic modification technologies, that is, challenge us to reconsider just what we mean by the word "species." Do we classify an animal or a plant as a member of a particular species according to its outward signs (the Hebrew term is *simanim*)? If so, then an animal that chews its cud and has split hooves is kosher regardless of changes introduced to its genetic structure. Or do we conclude that those changes produce a different animal or plant that can no longer be classified on the basis of its outward appearance? In that case, we cannot be sure that something is a pig or a cow or a tomato until we perform the necessary genetic analysis. This raises issues that extend far beyond the realm of kashrut; indeed, they touch upon our most fundamental ways of perceiving and knowing the world around us.

3. Is It Safe?

Our third question is the biggest one of all. Even if traditional Jewish theology and legal thought do not forbid the creation of genetically modified foods, it may still be a bad idea to promote these technologies. To put this another way, while Jewish tradition in general and Reform Judaism in particular are welcoming toward scientific progress, not every product of science is a progressive one. Those who advocate the genetic modification of plants and animals do so for good and understandable reasons: to create new strains of plants that are resistant to drought, pests, and herbicides; to develop animals that are more desirable as food or that are more effective producers of milk or eggs; to improve the nutritional content of foods, and so forth. Yet the introduction of new genetic strains necessarily involves a long list of potential dangers. Some of these are risks to human health, while others may adversely affect the environment. We cannot be sure that newly spliced genes created in the laboratory through recombinant DNA technology will not enter human and wild populations, and there is no way of predicting with certainty that these mutations will not cause harm to people and to the natural world. As Jews we consider these possibilities a call for action, especially given our tradition's concern for human health and environmental responsibility.

A "call for action" does not mean, of course, that we are required to oppose the new genetic technologies as a matter of course. We can hardly be opposed in principle to improvements in crops, livestock, and agricultural production, especially in the face of the challenges posed by world population growth and climate change. We Reform Jews have always affirmed the blessings of modernity and its culture, including its scientific culture. Rejection of technological progress is arguably an "un-Reform" stance; we make very unconvincing Luddites. But neither are we obliged to recite a *b'rachah* over any and every "advance" that issues forth from the laboratory, especially before it has been carefully vetted for dangers it may pose to the world. To be sure, scientists and the governments and corporations that fund them are not likely to desist from developing and employing new technologies merely because Reform Jews protest and sign petitions. Yet that's no excuse for apathy. On the contrary, the most effective sort of control upon unbridled technology may well come from the concerned voices of religious people who understand that the covenant that binds us to God demands that we act as devoted stewards of God's creation.

In short, Judaism is more than the sum total of a particular set of observances and theological doctrines. It is, as the old saw has it, "a way of life," a way of perceiving and relating to the world. When we remember that, we are well on our way to discerning just how the Torah would have us act to safeguard the world. As we consider the brave new world of genetically modified organisms and high-tech food, our best response is perhaps a qualified "yes," a "*yasher koach*, but. . . ." We are cognizant of the blessings afforded by modern science. But we are no less aware of the need to supervise those blessings carefully, mindful of the enormous consequences—positive and otherwise—that techno-logical advances may bequeath to those who come after us.

NOTES

1. Ramban, Commentary to Leviticus 19:19.

2. See the CCAR Responsum no. 5768.3, "On Human Genetic Modification," http://data.ccarnet.org/cgi-bin/respdisp.pl?file=3&year=5768. Note, too, that Rashi, in his commentary to Lev. 19:19, writes that the prohibition of *kilayim* has no dis-cernible rationale (*taam*). Thus, not everyone agrees with Ramban that the prohi-bition has a specific "purpose" that we might use as a basis to oppose the genetic modification of species.

3. R. Yechiel M. Epstein, *Aruch HaShulchan, Yoreh Dei-ah* 84:36. For example, a strictly literal reading of Leviticus 11 and Deuteronomy 14 would forbid us to drink water, since water is teeming with microscopic creatures that by definition are not kosher. The theory described in the text allows observant Jews to drink water, and that's a very good thing!

16

FISH
A Complex Issue

JOEL MOSBACHER

It has been a long and winding road that has led to my writing this article about fish. I grew up a meat eater, but I was always disgusted by fish. My parents could not get me to eat any of the magnificent fish dishes that they prepared. Perhaps it was the Purim goldfish I won each Adar, but I just couldn't get myself to eat things with fins and scales.

It was only as an adult that I came around to try, then like, and then eventually really like fish. As I began to cook for myself, and then as the chief cook in my family, I began to love fish of all sorts. However, one year into our marriage, my wife, Elyssa, became a vegetarian. I kept eating fish in restaurants and in other people's homes, but I didn't begin to prepare fish again until Elyssa decided to reintroduce fish to her diet when she became pregnant with our oldest son in 1998.

In the latest twist, this past year I read Jonathan Safran Foer's *Eating Animals*, and my wife, around the same time, began to add other kinds of meat, in addition to fish, to her diet. I had read the work of Michael Pollan and Mark Bittman; I had read Barbara Kingsolver's *Animal, Vegetable, Miracle*, and had seen the documentary *Food, Inc.* As a result, I had already been seriously rethinking my meat intake. Little that I read in Foer's work surprised me, until I came to the section on fish. Those four pages (pp. 189–93) have challenged me, as a Jew and as a human being, to question the ethics of eating fish. These days, my wife is eating fish, chicken, and turkey, and I am not eating any meat—especially not fish. This has been my dietary journey thus far, but I am not at all convinced that this is where the journey will end.

Foer disturbed and agitated me when he wrote, "Although one can realistically expect that at least some percentage of cows and pigs are slaughtered with speed and care, no fish gets a good death. Not a single one. You never have to wonder if the fish on your plate had to suffer. It did."[1] This was a stunning statement—one that Foer backs up by explaining the realities of both wild-caught and farm-raised fish.

While aquaculture, the industrial farm equivalent for raising sea animals in confinement, was presented as a solution to the overfishing of wild fish, it turns out to have actually increased the demand for wild-caught fish by 27 percent between 1988 and 1997 even as aquaculture expanded exponentially.[2] Aquaculture has thus not reduced the demand for wild-caught salmon.

The realities of aquaculture must make us cringe as Jews, we who are commanded not to cause undue suffering to animals. Farm-raised fish live in water that is so fouled and crowded that it makes it hard for them to breathe, and they cannibalize one another at a high rate. They have nutritional deficiencies that weaken their immune systems, and they are slaughtered in horrible, inhumane ways. Fish raised through aquaculture live in terrible suffering and die the same way.[3] To combat the illnesses—parasitic bacteria, rickettsia, lesions—that farm-raised fish contract, producers introduce chemicals and medications. Millions of other fish destined for sale in the United States are raised with chemicals and drugs not approved for use in this country.[4] Yet, as we have seen with Chilean fish producers, devastating viruses still spread, killing millions of fish each year. When we purchase most farm-raised fish, we are violating the values of both *bal tashchit* and *tzaar baalei chayim* by supporting an industry in which large-scale death rates and animal suffering are inherent in nearly all methods of aquaculture. The first value is drawn from a commandment given to us in Deuteronomy

20 not to wantonly destroy God's creation, and the second value is rooted in the commandment from Exodus 23 to prevent suffering to animals.

Sadly, wild-caught fish are hardly a more humane alternative. While they live freely before they are caught, unfettered by cramped and filthy conditions, the methods of catching the sea animals we crave—trawling, longline fishing, purse seines[5]—also kill millions of sharks, marlins, sea turtles, albatross, dolphins, and whales each year. This kind of "scorched-earth style of 'harvesting' sea animals,"[6] where 80 to 90 percent of what fisheries catch—so-called by-catch—are thrown back, dead, into the ocean, goes against the value of *bal tashchit* in a way that we can no longer ignore as people of faith. This knowing wastefulness is akin to Maimonides's teaching with regard to cutting down fruit trees:

> We do not cut down fruit trees outside the [besieged] city, nor do we take away from them the water channel so that they may dry up, as it says, "Do not destroy its trees" [Deut. 20:19], and anyone who cuts down [such a tree] gets lashes. And [this rule is] not only during a siege, but at all places; anyone who cuts down a fruit tree in a manner of destruction is lashed.[7]

We cannot ignore the parallel between the cutting down of fruit trees in pursuit of a city and the cutting down of innumerable species in pursuit of the one or two most desirable ones. Maimonides makes this extrapolation explicit when he teaches further, "And it is not only trees, but anyone who breaks vessels, tears clothing, tears down a building, plugs a spring, or wastes food in a manner of destruction, transgresses 'Do not destroy.'"[8] When we consume wild-caught salmon or tuna, we are, at the same time, participants in a system that is wantonly destroying the diversity and vibrancy of God's creation.

Furthermore, nearly one-third of wild-caught fish in the world are reduced to fish meal and fed to farmed fish, cattle, and pigs. Using fish meal to feed farm-raised fish is, as Mark Bittman writes, "astonishingly inefficient. Approximately three kilograms of forage fish go to produce one kilogram of farmed salmon; the ratio for cod is five to one; and tuna . . . [the] ratio is 20 to 1."[9] Surely we as Jews, who are commanded not to seethe a calf its mother's milk (Exod. 23:19), we who are commanded to shoo away the mother bird when we take her eggs (Deut. 22:6–7), must learn from these values that to feed a fish with fish meal should violate any holistic sense of kashrut.

These fishing systems are not only ecologically troublesome; they are also cruel in the various methods by which hundreds of different species are crushed together to die slowly over hours. If kosher slaughter of farm animals is meant to help them die quickly and painlessly, the methods of fish slaughter in wild-caught fisheries result in the opposite effect—slow, painful, brutal deaths. Even if Jewish tradition says little or nothing about how fish should be slaughtered, surely we should extrapolate from what it does say about slaughtering land animals to know that fish should not be made to suffer in any of these ways.

So what is a Jew to do? Foer and others advocate that we eat no fish at all, which is certainly a legitimate option, and perhaps the best one. God made Adam and Eve vegetarians, and perhaps this is the Jewish ideal. But what if we seek a middle ground? Like Noah after the Flood, might there be parameters under which we could eat some fish and still be the *shomrei adamah*, the guardians of the earth (Gen. 2:15), that Adam Eve were called to be?

Firstly, not all aquaculture is bad. China accounts for approximately 70 percent of the world's aquaculture, where it is small in scale, focuses on herbivorous fish, and is not only sustainable, but also environmentally sound.[10] This model shows that it is possible to do aquaculture in a humane way—not in the industrialized manner in which it is done in other settings. However, some gourmets worry that if we stay on the track we are currently on, "this wondrously varied component of our diet will go the way of land animals—get simplified, all look the same, and generally become quite boring."[11] Fish produced through aquaculture certainly does not taste as robust and is not as varied as wild fish. Environmentalists, on the other hand, worry about upholding China as a model of sustainable aquaculture, as Chinese food production practices are not always transparent. Bittman and others advocate that if we are to eat fish, we should eat lower in the food chain. If we began to eat more fish such as wild sardines, anchovies, and herring, "we would be less inclined to feed them to salmon raised in fish farms. And we'd be helping to restock the seas with larger species."[12]

There are also efforts afoot in Alaska and other places to create sustainable fishing that limits the catch to what the ocean can produce. There are monitoring systems that can reduce by-catch by as much as 60 percent and regulations that incentivize fishermen to have a stake in protecting the wild resources.[13]

Many extraordinary organizations exist that can help environmentally conscious consumers make ocean-friendly choices. The Marine Stewardship Council has established a system of certification for fisheries that operate in a sustainable manner.[14] The Monterey Bay Aquarium publishes pocket guides to help consumers and businesses make good decisions about what seafood to buy or avoid.[15] These organizations, along with others such as the Seafood Choices Alliance and the Blue Ocean Institute, strive to promote sustainability for our oceans on the one hand and knowledgeable consumers on the other.

The drives to go local, eat organic, and buy fresh have become food mantras for all who are environmentally conscious consumers. But, according to a group of economists and food researchers, it seems that when it comes to eating fish, "if the motivation is to truly make our diets more earth-friendly, then perhaps we need a new mantra: Buy frozen."[16] According to these researchers, fresh salmon has about twice the environmental impact as frozen salmon, because most of us live far from where our fish is caught or farmed. Most fish we eat is fresh and shipped to us by air—the world's most carbon-intensive form of travel. When fish is flown fresh to us from Alaska, British Columbia, Norway, Scotland, or Chile so that we can eat it twenty-four hours after it was caught, the climate burden of the transport of that fish "swamps the potential benefit of organic farming or sustainable fishing."[17] We would be far better off, if we are concerned for the earth, eating fish that is flash frozen at sea and transported by ship, rail, or truck—fish whose quality and taste is practically indistinguishable from fresh.

Sometimes, ignorance is bliss. The question that I have asked myself, and that we all must ask, is, once you know, how will you respond? As Jews, we can have a variety of responses to what we now know about industrialized aquaculture and wild-caught fisheries. We might, as we humans sometimes do, seek to return to a kind of knowing ignorance. We can ignore what we know, letting our desires to eat whatever we feel like eating control us. "I know that this fish suffered in life and/or in death. I know that it might be harmful to the earth and/or to me. But I am going to eat it anyway." But this, I argue, is not a Jewish decision. We are called upon by Shimon ben Zoma in *Pirkei Avot* 4:1 to master our impulses.

If and when we decide to master those impulses—to do whatever we want, to eat whatever we want—we still must consider what our decision will be. We can, as mentioned previously, become vegetarians, choosing to get as far "off the grid" as possible, eating no fish and therefore avoiding the issues raised in this article altogether. This is a legitimate choice—one with which I am currently living and struggling.

There is one more option for us, once we know what we know. We can choose to use that knowledge to make the grid better from within. We can make knowledgeable and righteous consumer choices, using the power of the mighty dollar to help drive consumer demand for better, healthier, more humane options. And we can share what we know with others, inviting them to join us in striving to improve the system, using the power of people and faith to demand change from those with the power to make change. I believe that it is this choice—not to ignore the truth or abstain from the pleasures of the world, but to seek to make change—that *Sefer HaChinuch* calls us to when it teaches:

> The root of this commandment [do not destroy] is known [to be] so that it teaches our souls to love the good and beneficial and cleave to it, and through this good will cleave to us and we will distance from all evil and from all manner of destruction. And this is the manner of the pious and of deed who love shalom and rejoice in the benefit of creatures and drawing them close to Torah and

they do not waste so much as a mustard seed in the world and any waste or destruction that they see troubles them and if they can preserve [an item] they would preserve it from destruction with all their power.

(Sefer HaChinuch, mitzvah 529)

NOTES

1. Jonathan Safran Foer, *Eating Animals* (New York: Little, Brown and Company, 2009), 193.

2. Ibid, 189.

3. Ibid.

4. Alexei Barrionuevo, "Chile Takes Steps to Rehabilitate Its Lucrative Salmon Industry," *New York Times*, February 5, 2009.

5. A large fishing net made to hang vertically in the water by weights at the lower edge and floats at the top. It closes around a school of fish, like an old-fashioned drawstring purse.

6. Foer, *Eating Animals*, 191.

7. Maimonides, *Mishneh Torah, Hilchot M'lachim* 6:8.

8. Ibid., 6:10.

9. Mark Bittman, "A Seafood Snob Ponders the Future of Fish," *New York Times*, November 16, 2008.

10. Ibid.

11. Ibid.

12. Ibid.

13. Ibid.

14. http://www.montereybayaquarium.org/cr/cr_seafoodwatch/sfw_recommendations.aspx.

15. http://www.msc.org/.

16. Astrid Scholz, Ulf Sonesson, and Peter Tyedmers, "Catch of the Freezer," *New York Times*, December 9, 2009.

17. Ibid.

GETTING BACK TO THE GARDEN

Barbara Lerman-Golomb

In the beginning . . . there was a garden.

> When God created the first human beings, God led them around
> the Garden of Eden and said: "Look at my works! See how beauti-
> ful they are—how excellent! For your sake I created them all. See to
> it that you do not spoil and destroy My world; for if you do, there
> will be no one else to repair it."[1]

In the big picture, a garden is a metaphor for planet earth and we are
shomrei adamah, its caretakers. In the small picture, to paraphrase Sigmund Freud, sometimes a garden is just a garden, whether it is in a
back yard or front yard, on a roof, part of a congregation, or a shared
communal garden.

Be they rural, suburban, or urban, gardens provide a way for people
to reconnect with and simply enjoy being in nature. Connecting to
nature through a garden can lead to stewardship in both the small and
big picture. A garden affords us a firsthand opportunity to experience
a miracle. We pop a seed into the soil, supply water, air, and sun, and
voila, we have a small spark of creation.

"Replete is the world with a spiritual radiance, replete with sublime
and marvelous secrets. But a small hand held against the eye hides it

all" (attributed to the Baal Shem Tov).[2] "Too many of us are walking around with blindfolds, unaware, uninspired, aweless, jaded by our natural environment."[3] Abraham Joshua Heschel defined awe as an "intuition for the creaturely dignity of all things and their preciousness to God."[4] Once we stopped seeing miracles, we stopped sensing God's presence in all things.[5]

As metaphor, the garden is symbolic of order out of chaos, in itself, a miracle. It often starts out as a portion of land with various earthly components: dirt, rocks, fallen leaves, insects, random foliage—all intersecting with the four elements. Order is achieved through purposeful, miraculous occurrences—decomposition, pollination, renewal, and regrowth. Yet, our lack of the basic understanding of ecosystems is putting nature at risk. Without the appreciation of everyday miracles, without being humbled by our natural world—the sacred blueprint of Creation—we are rendered incapable of possessing the tools to protect it.[6]

God Is in the Details

To grow a garden is to be godlike. Gardening gives humans one way to emulate the act of Creation. A garden is like a blank canvas awaiting that first dab of color and pattern, filled with possibility and the potential of "Eden." Many people enjoy gardening because they find it therapeutic. But our connection to gardening may be even more basic than that. As children we commonly express an inherent delight in the creative and tactile experience of nature. We build sand castles, mold clay, assemble sticks, collect shells and rocks, and dig in the dirt. We derive pleasure from "getting our hands dirty." Maybe it's in our DNA: gardening puts us in touch with our agrarian ancestral roots as food producers. Dust to dust—dirt to dirt. It also puts us in touch with our most basic beginnings. Our bodies are literally made up of the same six earthly elements as soil: potassium, calcium, magnesium, phosphorous, iron, and manganese. Without soil, there is no vegetation. By cultivating the food that sustains us, we are reminded of our intimate connection to where our food comes from—a daily reminder of the Source of all Life.

In his essay, "A Loaf of Bread," Heschel writes, "We say 'Blessed be Thou, O Eternal our God, Ruler of the Universe, who brings forth bread from the earth.' Empirically speaking, would it not be more correct to give credit to the farmer, the merchant and the baker? [Rather] we bless God who makes possible both nature and civilization."[7] A garden, like the *Sh'ma*, is a wake-up call of interconnectedness, "a reminder not only that we are one with the earth and all of Creation, but that Creation is not a thing of the past, but an on-going process within our lives, and that God daily renews the work of Creation."[8]

Partnership with God

Few things have the ability to bring us closer to God than planting and growing food in a garden. It is the ultimate example of our partnership with God and a manifestation of living Judaism. But in actuality it is a three-way relationship between humans, the earth, and God.

> "The Lord God took the man and placed him in the Garden of Eden to till it and tend it" (Genesis 2:15).
> Let us not underestimate the importance of [this] deceptively simple [verse] . . . God needed human help so that the entire life/ growth process might move forward.
> The early rabbinic commentators jumped on this thought: "The edible fruits of the earth require not only God's gift of rain but also man's cultivation. Man must be a co-worker with God in making this earth a garden" (J. H. Hertz, ed., *Pentateuch Haftorahs*). In other words, paradise was perfect—almost. It was complete—almost. For all its beauty, for all its wonderful design, something was missing. Us! God needed a partner: us.[9]

An example of this interconnection is the special Shavuot wave offering—two loaves of bread, the first products of the spring wheat harvest. As Arthur Waskow explains:

Shavuot celebrates the success of the spring growing season. . . . But there is a special twist in this celebration of growth. The two loaves of bread are unusual—for they are explicitly the products of human labor. Not grain, not sheep or lambs or goats, straight from God's hand—but bread, mixed and kneaded and leavened and baked, is the distinctive offering of Shavuot. So, Shavuot celebrates the partnership of human beings with God in giving food to the world. Having received from God the rain, the seed, the sunshine, we give back to God not just a dividend on the natural growth, but the value we ourselves have added to it.[10]

All I Really Need to Know, I Learned in the Garden

Over the past few years, Jewish educators and community activists have come to value the garden as an empowering teaching tool. A garden is a natural hands-on outdoor classroom for exploring the life sciences and encouraging the adoption of healthy eating habits and sustainable environmental practices. This should not come as a surprise to us. After all, the Garden of Eden was the place where we gained our first sense of knowledge and curiosity about the world around us. The garden, with its fruit-bearing tree, was our first teacher. We learn to emulate the Jewish principal of *bal tashchit*—that the needless destruction of anything that has a purpose is wrong. There is no waste in nature. The *tamar*, date tree, exemplifies this: "The date palm abounds in blessing, for every part can be used, nothing is wasted. The fruit is eaten, the branches are used for blessings on Sukkot, the fibers are used for ropes and the trunk is used for building."[11]

Growing food in a garden, we become more aware of the importance of habitat and diversity for supporting the web of life. *Mah rabu maasecha, Adonai*, "How numerous are Your works, *Adonai!*" (Psalm 104:24). We come to appreciate why it behooves us to give food the dignity and sense of awe it deserves. The garden teaches us responsibility. The better we tend to our garden, whether it is in the small or big picture, the healthier it—and as a result we—will be.

From the garden we learn the cycles of the seasons. "A season is set for everything, a time for every experience under heaven. . . . A time for planting and a time for uprooting the planted" (Eccles. 3:1–2). As we cycle through the seasons, we learn about decay and the fragility of life. This need not be a lesson in death, but a life-affirming lesson; nature recycles itself through composting. Dead plant material that has decomposed is rich in nutrients and breathes new life into a garden.

Community Gardening

Garden projects are a growing trend at congregations and summer camps around the country. At URJ Camp Kalsman in Washington, for example, as part of their *teva* (nature) program, campers participate in building the camp's gardens and orchards and learn about the Jewish commitment to the environment. URJ Greene Family Camp in Texas has a "kibbutz garden" where campers are able to grow a variety of fruits and vegetables. HUC-JIR in Los Angeles, as well, has created a vegetable garden, which is adjacent to the patio of the campus building. Through the garden, HUC students can participate in a grassroots coalition of Jewish organizations called Netiyah (planting). Formed in 2009, this Los Angeles coalition is dedicated to combating hunger through organic gardening and to educating the Jewish community in Los Angeles about food awareness and food justice issues using the relevant values and texts in our tradition.

For congregations in particular, gardens offer a positive and rewarding shared experience. These can range from a garden on synagogue property or piece of land that the synagogue manages, to communal agriculture projects where congregants volunteer in tandem with members of other faith-based institutions or other members of the community. Congregational gardens are a setting for solace and contemplation. The Chasidic rebbe and great-grandson of the Baal Shem Tov, Rabbi Nachman of Bratzlav, prescribed this daily ritual to his followers: "Master of the universe, grant me the ability to be alone;

may it be my custom to go outdoors each day, among the reeds and the grass, among all growing things; and there may I be alone, to enter into prayer, talking to the One to whom I belong."[12] Congregational gardens also provide surroundings of beauty in the tradition of *hidur mitzvah* as a way to realign ourselves with the natural world. "The importance of beauty extends beyond the magnification of ritual practices and is fundamental to an appreciation for the created order and our efforts to sustain it."[13]

Judaism and Food Justice

One element in which most community gardens share is the mitzvah of feeding the hungry. Because the majority of American Jews live in cities and suburbs close to cities, it is logical for them to get involved in urban agriculture projects dedicated to growing produce that is donated to a local emergency food provider such as a food pantry or shelter. Social justice and *tzedakah* are deeply rooted in Jewish agricultural values. These laws are about all members of a community having access to healthy food in a dignified way.[14] There is no better way to show our partnership in *tikkun olam* and to be godlike than to live ethically. In Leviticus we are instructed to conduct the practice of *pei-ah*, to leave the corners of our fields for the poor and the stranger. While most of us are not farmers living an agrarian lifestyle like our ancestors, there are many ways we can bring about the *kavanah* of *pei-ah*, the intention of this mitzvah.

Millions of low-income people in the United States live in areas where the only produce they can get is either frozen or canned, if they are able to get any fruit and vegetables at all. They are living in "food deserts" where affordable, nutritious food is unavailable to them, where fast food and convenience stores selling mostly soda and sweets outnumber fresh food stores. This can lead to unhealthy eating practices and serious health problems;[15] two-thirds of adults in the United States and nearly one in three children are overweight or obese—a condition that increases their risk for diabetes, heart disease, and other chronic illnesses.[16]

A community garden is an efficient way to fight against hunger and malnutrition because it helps feed fresh, healthy food to people who otherwise would not have access; it provides a sense of empowerment with the knowledge and skills to grow your own food; and it helps build community.[17] Urban agriculture programs around the country are training inner-city youth in gardening and other sustainable food production skills, helping to strengthen the local economy and creating healthier, more just communities.

Gardens and Environmental Sustainability

The Rabbis of the Talmud state, "It is forbidden to live in a town that has no garden or greenery" (Jerusalem Talmud, *Kodashim* 4:12). In urban areas in particular, gardens can enhance quality of life, help improve land and air quality, and simply make a city a healthier place to live. A garden uses "land that most people might see as vacant and blighted, and instead sees it as a way to provide healthy food and transform the face of a community by bringing the nature connection to the concrete city."[18] Gardens are key to addressing many of the environmental problems prevalent today, including our most serious threat, global climate change. Community gardens support eating locally, which is critical to conserving energy. Most of the energy consumed by the U.S. industrial food system can be attributed to the use of fossil fuels in the processing, packaging, storing, and transporting of food. A rooftop garden or green roof offers additional benefits. Appropriately, the adage "There's nothing new under the sun" applies to rooftop gardens, which have existed since ancient times. The Hanging Gardens of Babylon, for example, one of the Seven Wonders of the World, used an elaborate irrigation system to create a lush terraced garden built on tiers outside of modern-day Baghdad. On a green roof, soil and vegetation act as a sponge, absorbing and filtering water that would normally plunge down gutters, wash through polluted streets, and overburden sewer systems. Like all foliage, the plants on a rooftop garden remove pollutants, produce oxygen, and provide shade, helping to cool the rooftop surface and the building—critical to urban dwellings that are subject to the Heat Island Effect. This is when metropolitan areas are significantly warmer than surrounding rural areas. A green roof means less air conditioning, less energy consumption, and fewer greenhouse gases going into the atmosphere.

As part of a civic project, the municipality of Jerusalem has inaugurated the first green roof at the Or Torah Stone School in Ramot. The "Green Roof" is a unique ecological project, designed by students of the Bezalel Academy of Arts and Design in Jerusalem, in cooperation with the students of Or Torah and its staff. This is the first step in a project with the broad goal of installing green roofs at schools and other public institutions around Jerusalem—part of the urban objective to develop green areas and create educational institutions that are more environmentally conscious and energy efficient.

Over forty years ago, Joni Mitchell awakened us to the challenge of getting "ourselves back to the Garden."[19] These prophetic words are more relevant and urgent than ever, particularly as we become more concerned with the range and reception of a BlackBerry than with how to grow a blackberry. Caring for a garden, in the small picture, can "serve to reconnect the Jewish spirit to the earth,"[20] supply us with the tools needed to restore and sustain the big picture, our natural world, and rejuvenate Jewish life.

NOTES

1. *Midrash Kohelet Rabbah* 1 on Eccles. 7:13.

2. Abraham Joshua Heschel, *God in Search of Man* (New York: Farrar, Straus and Giroux, 1955, renewed 1983), 85.

3. These ideas were originally developed in Barbara Lerman-Golomb, "Experiential Environmental Education: A Natural Connection," *Coalition for the Advancement of Jewish Education, Jewish Education News, Eco-Judaism* 28 (Summer 2008).

4. Heschel, *God in Search of Man*, 75.

5. David J. Wolpe, *Why Be Jewish?* (New York: Henry Holt and Company, 1995), 66.

6. These ideas were originally developed in Barbara Lerman-Golomb, "Reconnecting with Nature to Sustain Ourselves," in *The Mountains Shall Drip Wine: Jews and the Environment*, ed. Leonard J. Greenspoon, Studies in Jewish Civilization, vol. 20 (Lincoln: University of Nebraska Press, 2009), 66.

7. Heschel, *God in Search of Man*, 63.

8. Lerman-Golomb, "Experiential Environmental Education."

9. Balfour Brickner, *Finding God in the Garden* (Boston: Little, Brown, 2002), 15.

10. Arthur Waskow, *Seasons of Our Joy* (Boston: Beacon Press, 1992), 187.

11. *B'reishit Rabbah* 41.

12. Nachman of Bratzlav, *Magid Sichot*, 48

13. Sandra B. Lubarsky, "Toward a Theology of Beauty: *Hiddur Mitzvah* as an Eco-Theological Imperative," in *The Mountains Shall Drip Wine: Jews and the Environment*, ed. Leonard J, Greenspoon, Studies in Jewish Civilization, vol. 20 (Lincoln: University of Nebraska Press, 2009), 73.

14. These ideas were originally developed in Barbara Lerman-Golomb, "Urban Agriculture: Growing Healthy Food and Growing Communities," *JNF GoNeutral GreenTimes*, Passover 2010.

15. Ibid.

16. U.S. Department of Health and Human Services, *The Surgeon General's Vision for a Healthy and Fit Nation* (Rockville, MD: U.S. Department of Health and Human Services, Office of the Surgeon General, 2010), 1.

17. Lerman-Golomb, "Urban Agriculture."

18. Ibid.

19. Joni Mitchell, "Woodstock," 1969.

20. Nati Passow and Jacob Fine, "Kavanot for Jewish Gardening," *Jewish Farm School, Jewish Gardening Workshop* (Teva Seminar, June 2008): 437.

REAL LIFE / REAL FOOD
Let Your Table Be to You a Temple

JOSEPH AARON SKLOOT

At the edge of the Costa Rican rainforest, a group of American Reform Jewish high school students encountered bags marked "Toxic" and "Flammable" and signs painted "Danger." A stone's throw away, there were one-room ramshackle brick and corrugated metal homes with mud floors and wood fire pits. A few steps to the right, inside a large hanger-like building, were bananas. Heaped in dumpsters, on conveyer belts, piled on the ground—bananas were everywhere.

The students—having chosen to spend their spring break doing mitzvot in Costa Rica—were surprised to learn about the troubling complexity of banana cultivation. Bananas—those ordinary staples of the American breakfast table—don't come cheap. That day, the students learned that bananas are a natural wonder, scarcely found in the wild. To get those sugary, golden-hued fruit to our supermarkets, the U.S.-based companies that control banana cultivation the world over employ a cocktail of toxic fertilizers and pesticides known to harm human beings and animals. They clear acres of virgin forest and replace vibrant tropical ecosystems with banana monocultures. They burn remarkable amounts of fossil fuel to transport their product over vast distances—far more than producers of other crops. They drive down wages by snuffing out competition; they deny their workers health care and education, and they prohibit unionization.[1] The bottom line: transforming this wondrous and rare plant into an everyday breakfast item takes a tremendous ethical and ecological toll.

I love bananas as much as anyone, but the ubiquity of this fruit is an example of a larger trend in American life—the desecration of the nourishing plants and animals God commanded us to "protect and nurture" in the Book of Genesis (2:15). Banana producers have transformed a rare and fragile fruit into an utterly ordinary breakfast staple. They have accomplished this feat through various nefarious technological, political, and economic practices—along the way damaging the earth and the lives of its inhabitants. By contrast, we Jews have an ancient system of mitzvot regulating agriculture, diet, and food preparation. A striking passage in the Babylonian Talmud encapsulates this system in a single sentence: "Rabbi Yochanan and Rabbi Eliezer taught: As long as the Temple stood, its altar atoned for Israel's sins, but now a person's table atones for him" (B'rachot 55a).

For the Rabbis of the Talmud, food—the proper foods cultivated and prepared in the proper manner—could be as holy as the sacrifices offered on the altar of the Temple long ago. After my experience in Costa Rica, it was difficult to imagine how bananas could continue to appear on my home's modern stand-in for the ancient Temple's altar, the kitchen table. The ecological and social harm wrought by banana production has besmirched this fruit's golden reputation; as a consequence, I decided to replace bananas in my diet with other, locally grown, organic fruits. In other words, there may be no better place to start redressing the errors of agribusiness than with those bananas on the breakfast table.

NOTE

1. Organic bananas are certainly an all-around better choice than conventional bananas. Grown without pesticides, they are safer for the agricultural laborers and for

surrounding ecosystems. However, growing them in quantity is difficult and requires the deforestation of virgin forests at high altitudes (where banana-loving diseases are scarce). Moreover, they do little to increase the quality of life of the laborers who grow and harvest them or to decrease quantities of fossil fuel burned in transportation to our markets. See Dan Koeppel's excellent discussion of the topic in *Banana: The Fate of the Fruit That Changed the World* (New York: Plume, 2008), 232–35.

Part Four

Kindness to Animals:

Tzaar Baalei Chayim

Part 4, addressing *tzaar baalei chayim*, the commandment of preventing suffering to animals, provides the tools to navigate through the debates whether or not we should eat meat; how often to eat meat, if we do; and how animals should be raised and slaughtered, if they are to be eaten. In "Kindness to Animals: *Tzaar Baalei Chayim*," Rayna Ellen Gevurtz leads us through the texts addressing this value, exposing us to Jewish tradition's views on kindness to animals. She challenges us to apply these teachings to modern times. We include Mark Sameth's "'I'll Have What She's Having': Jewish Ethical Vegetarianism" as his exploration of vegetarianism adds much to this volume. Aaron Saul Gross ("Continuity and Change in Reform Views of Kashrut 1883–2002") takes a historical perspective on kashrut and, especially, religious vegetarianism. In "Meat Minimalism: Were We Meant to Be Ethical Omnivores?" Karen R. Perolman interweaves concerns for animals, the environment, and human health to propose an ethical omnivorism steeped in Jewish values. Building on issues that Sameth and Perolman raise, the theme of *sh'mirat haguf*, guarding human health, is explored in depth later in this volume.

Two Jews with different opinions on eating meat, Josh Whinston and Gersh Lazarow ("Blood, Sweat, and Tears: The Making of a Reform *Shochet*") recall an extraordinary experience in which they combined study and action to understand fully the Jewish butchering of chickens. Finally, Zoë Klein shares from her blog "A Letter to My Vegetarian Husband," in which she reveals her struggle to follow the dietary practice to which she aspires.

19

KINDNESS TO ANIMALS

Tzaar Baalei Chayim

R A Y N A   E L L E N   G E V U R T Z

When we envision a farm, our minds fill with pictures from childhood songs of animals blissfully grazing in pastures green. Tragically, the reality of today's farms is a different scene entirely: Egg-laying hens are raised in overcrowded cages and debeaked with hot searing knives. Male chicks are "useless," and so they are discarded at birth by being thrown into garbage bags to suffocate or into shredding machines to be turned into food for the other chickens. Calves that are raised for veal are taken from their mothers a day or two after birth and placed in tiny dark cages with their heads chained in place. Beef cattle are overfed, castrated, dehorned, and branded without anesthetics and finally shipped in overcrowded trucks to be slaughtered.

And this is just scratching the surface of the modern industrial reality of mass-produced animal products that lurks behind the plastic-wrapped morsels we find in the supermarket. Today's farms, often termed "factory farms" for their production-line approach to animal rearing, offer a sharp contrast to the Jewish tradition's teaching of *tzaar baalei chayim*, the commandment of preventing suffering to animals.

In the Talmud, the Sages conclude that *tzaar baalei chayim* is a Toraitic obligation. Based on the interpretation of the biblical command to unload a pack animal, "When you see the ass of your enemy lying under its burden and would refrain from raising it, you must nevertheless help raise it" (Exod. 23:5), the Rabbis conclude, "We have learned that *tzaar baalei chayim* [the prevention of suffering to animals] is a biblical obligation" (Babylonian Talmud, *Bava M'tzia* 32a–b). This majority opinion is later supported in the halachic commentaries and codes.[1]

From this point, the Rabbis go on to instruct that *tzaar baalei chayim* is so important that we are permitted to break other mitzvot in order to prevent any suffering to animals, including the laws of Shabbat and *Yom Tov*.[2] That is, the very laws that the Rabbis protected with fences upon fences, must, in certain circumstances, be broken in order to spare an animal from pain.

It is from the core of the halachic body of literature concerning the prevention of suffering of animals that the use of the term *tzaar baalei chayim* has been expanded in recent years to express the more general value placed upon the compassionate treatment of animals scattered throughout our tradition. The Torah and the Rabbinic literature overflow with passages that guide us to be compassionate in our treatment of animals.

Treatment of Animals within the *Tanach*

"God said, 'Let the waters bring forth swarms of *nefesh chayah* [living creatures]'" (Gen. 1:20). From the very beginning, our tradition teaches that God created animals as *nefesh chayah*, as living creatures, or more literally "living souls." This phrase is also used to describe the creation of humankind: "[God] breathed into his nostrils the breath of life, so that the man became a *nefesh chayah*" (Gen. 2:7). The use of the same phrase to describe humans and animals sends a clear message of the commonality that exists between all of God's creatures, human and nonhuman alike.

As we continue forward in the Torah, we note the important role of animals in the lives of our biblical ancestors. The search for a wife for Isaac is one example of such a story. When Abraham's servant is sent to find a wife for Isaac, he prays that the right woman will extend an offer of drink to his camels. And so we read, "When she had let him drink his fill, she said, 'I will draw some for your camels, too, till they are done drinking'" (Gen. 24:19). Rebekah's compassionate act toward the animals helps identify her as suitable to be the next matriarch of the Jewish people.

Our ancestors relied heavily on animals in their agricultural pursuits, and so the Torah provides clear guidance in the treatment of work animals. One such law, "You shall not plow with an ox and an ass together" (Deut. 22:10), teaches that if these two animals were yoked together, one may be injured by the other. Another law asserts the right of an animal to be nourished as it works: "You shall not muzzle an ox while it is threshing" (Deut. 25:4). This prohibition acknowledges that one must not prevent an animal who is threshing the field to follow its basic instinct to eat along the way.

Perhaps the most outstanding example of the Torah's message of compassion for animals is the recognition of an animal's need for rest. This command is deemed so crucial that it is included within the Ten Commandments: "The seventh day is a Sabbath of the Eternal your God: you shall not do any work—you, your son or daughter, your male or female slave, or your cattle" (Exod. 20:10). At a time when our ancestors' livelihood depended upon the physical work that their animals performed, this was a powerful statement of concern for their animals' welfare.

The laws within the Torah also go beyond the treatment of one's own animals, to the laws regarding those within the public domain. One example of this is the obligation to help lift the pack animal of one's enemy if it has fallen under a heavy load (Exod. 23:5), guiding people to put the needs of creatures above human emotion. The Torah also states that we must demonstrate care to animals in the wild. As we read, "If along the road, you chance upon a bird's nest, in any tree or on the ground, with fledglings or eggs and the mother sitting over the fledglings or on the eggs, do not take the mother together with her young. Let the mother go, and take only the young" (Deut. 22:6–7). Maimonides explains that these verses remind us that animals feel emotional pain too: "There is no difference between the pain that a human feels and the pain that these animals feel when they see their young taken away or slaughtered. Like humans, they instinctively care for their young."[3]

Finally, it is important to note that the respect and care that humans are to have for the animal world is modeled by God. As we read, "The Eternal is good to all, and God's compassion is over all God's creatures" (Ps. 145:9). Just as God is praised as having mercy on all the creatures of the world, so too must humans, created in the divine image, behave in a compassionate manner: "A righteous man knows the needs of his animal, but the compassion of the wicked is cruelty" (Prov. 12:10).

Kindness to Animals within the Rabbinic Literature

In addition to the halachic material surrounding the rules of *tzaar baalei chayim*, the Rabbinic literature contains many aggadic tales that underscore the importance of kindness to animals. The following two stories point out that even the wisest people may struggle to learn this value:

> Once a calf en route to slaughter passed before Rabbi Y'hudah HaNasi. It broke away, and hid its head under Rabbi's skirt, and lowed pitifully, as though pleading, "Save me." "Go," said Rabbi HaNasi. "What can I do for you? For this you were created." At that, it was declared in heaven, "Since he showed no pity upon this calf, let us bring suffering upon him." Rabbi was afflicted with a stone in the urinary tract and thrush for thirteen years. One day, his maidservant was sweeping the house. Seeing some weasel pups lying there, she was about to sweep them away. Rabbi said to her, "Let them be, as it is written: 'God's compassion is over

all God's creatures'" (Ps. 145:9). At that moment, it was said in heaven, "Since he is now compassionate, let us be compassionate to him." And he was cured.

(Babylonian Talmud, *Bava M'tzia* 85a)

Within this text, the Rabbis demonstrate that even the learned Y'hudah HaNasi, the very rabbi who is credited with compiling the Mishnah, was punished for his cruel approach to the calf. Even King David struggled to appreciate the inherent value of every one of God's creatures:

Once while seated on the roof of his house, David, king of Israel, saw a wasp eating a spider. David spoke up to the Holy One, "Master of the universe, what benefit is there from these two You created in Your world? The wasp merely despoils the nectar of flowers—there is no benefit from it. Throughout the year, the spider spins but makes no garment." The Holy One replied, "David, you belittle My creatures! The time will come when you shall have need of both of them." Later when fleeing from King Saul, David had taken refuge in a cave. The Holy One sent a spider, which spun a web across the cave's entrance, sealing it. When Saul came and saw the cave's entrance with the web across it, he said, "Surely no man has come in here, for had he come, he would have torn the web in shreds." So Saul went away without going into the cave. And when David went out of the cave and saw the spider, he all but kissed him, saying, "Blessed is your Creator, and blessed are you."[4]

Just as the Torah teaches that Rebekah was chosen to be Isaac's wife because of her care for the camels, so too do we learn that God selected both Moses and later David to lead our people because of their kind acts to animals. As we read:

When Moses our teacher was tending the flocks of Jethro in the wilderness, a lamb scampered off, and Moses ran after it, until it approached a shelter under a rock. As the lamb reached the shelter, it came upon a pool of water and stopped to drink. When Moses caught up with it, he said, "I did not know that you ran away because you were thirsty. Now you must be tired." So, he hoisted the lamb on his shoulder and started walking back with it. The Holy

One then said, "Because you showed such compassion in tending the flock of a mortal, as you live, you shall become shepherd of Israel, the flock that is Mine."

(*Sh'mot Rabbah* 2:2)

How Does *Tzaar Baalei Chayim* Guide Our Food Choices Today?

Looking back through the traditional sources, it is evident that Judaism places a high value on the compassionate treatment of animals. What remains a question is how this value ought to guide us today. Our interactions with animals are vastly different from the small-scale agricultural setting in which our ancestors lived. Today intensive factory farming produces the vast majority of our animal-based food products. As described above, the animals on these industrialized "farms" experience much pain and suffering. It should also be noted that the majority of animals raised for the kosher meat industry are also raised on factory farms. Remarkably, the mainstream kashrut authorities do not consider how an animal lives in bestowing their seal of approval, only how it dies. Therefore, we ask: Do the end products of these intensive farming practices, the foods we consume, justify the pain experienced by the animals? That is, are there times when we are permitted to put aside the rules of compassionate treatment of animals?

Throughout the ages our teachers have attempted to answer this question, starting with the ruling that our tradition does indeed permit the consumption of animals. *Sefer HaChinuch*, a thirteenth-century explanation of the mitzvot, teaches that the Torah allows humans to use animals for sustenance because they are at the top of the "hierarchy of creatures." However, the Torah does not permit humans "to cause them senseless pain" in the process. Thus, many of the laws surrounding *sh'chitah*, ritual slaughter, are intended to cause as little pain as possible during slaughter.[5]

The next piece of text forms the cornerstone in the discussion of under what circumstances we may put aside the rules of *tzaar baalei chayim*. Maimonides rules, "*Tzaar baalei chayim* is waived in cases where the needs of human beings require this."[6] This statement leads to a crucial question for our own time: what is the definition of "human needs" that would permit the suspension of *tzaar baalei chayim*?

Rabbi Moshe Isserles, in his gloss on the *Shulchan Aruch*, attempts to define "human need" as it relates to *tzaar baalei chayim*. He concludes, "Anything that is needed for healing or for similar things do not violate the prohibition of *tzaar baalei chayim*." That is, one can cause a certain amount of pain to animals if necessary for the sake of human health. Isserles then adds financial needs to the category of "human needs" that can suspend *tzaar baalei chayim*, referring to the permission to "pluck feathers from live geese."[7] While he acknowledges that feathers from live geese were an important "human need" for profit, he then overrides this fact by saying it is nonetheless prohibited under the rules of *achzariut*, "cruelty." With this statement, Isserles adds a new dimension to the discussion: cruelty. It seems that "cruelty" is a dimension of pain beyond that of *tzaar baalei chayim*. According to this ruling, even if an act could suspend the rules of *tzaar baalei chayim*, because there is a "human need" for healing or profit, it may be actually forbidden under a broader rubric of "cruelty."

The question of what constitutes enough of a "human need" to suspend the laws of *tzaar baalei chayim* has also been posed in modern-day responsa. Rabbi Moshe Feinstein, one of the preeminent *poskim* of the twentieth century, addresses the manner in which veal is produced: "Each calf is alone in its own very narrow place. There is no room for it even to walk some steps. And they don't feed any appropriate cow food to the calves, and they don't even taste the milk of their mothers. . . . And behold those that do this certainly violate the prohibition of *tzaar baalei chayim*." Rabbi Feinstein then questions whether this business constitutes enough of a financial need to suspend these laws. He answers that the financial need of this industry is nullified, as the business is profiting from the fraudulent representation[8] that pale meat is healthier and tastier than red meat,[9] and therefore the process of raising veal is forbidden.

The question of how to reconcile the value of *tzaar baalei chayim* with modern farming practices was also addressed in the early 1990s by the Conservative Movement of Judaism. Rabbi Professor David Golinkin, chair of the Law Committee of the Rabbinical Assembly, concluded, "We must ensure that veal calves do not spend four to five months in inhumane and intolerable conditions. Jews should join the National Veal Boycott."[10] He then extrapolates to other animals: "This also applies to geese and ducks which have been force-fed in order to enlarge their livers to produce *pate de foie gras*."[11]

Pressing questions regarding the role of *tzaar baalei chayim* and the consumption of animal-based food products remain for us as individuals and as a Jewish community. What constitutes enough of a "human need" to put aside the extensive laws regarding the compassionate treatment of animals? Where is the line between the suffering addressed under the laws of *tzaar baalei chayim* and the added dimension of *achzariut*, "cruelty"? How are our food choices supporting the current practices of the factory farming industry? What changes can we make in our own lives to send a message to improve the lives of the animals raised for food products?

A few solutions have been put forward in an attempt to resolve these issues. Some have proposed that boycotting modern factory farms is the best way to respond to their current practices. While the laws concerning *tzaar baalei chayim* certainly do not demand a vegetarian or vegan lifestyle, some have concluded that this is the best course of action in our current reality. Others have called for the creation and support of new farms on which animals are raised in cruelty-free conditions and that the products from these farms also be authorized by the kashrut organizations.[12] A challenge to this approach is cost. The products from factory farms are cheaper than any small-scale business can deliver. Yet, by promoting such a solution on a community-wide basis, perhaps the supply/demand scales can be tipped in favor of the consumer and the animals. This would take a huge change in purchasing patterns. However, a change is what is necessary. For it is clear that the current situation ought to goad the consciences of all those who take seriously the values of Jewish tradition.

NOTES

1. *Rosh* on *Bava M'tzia* 32 (3:28); *Nimukei Yosef* on *Bava M'tzia* 32 (17B); *Tur, Choshen Mishpat* 272:10–14; *Rema* on *Shulchan Aruch, Choshen Misphat* 272:9; *Aruch HaShulchan, Choshen Mishpat* 272:2.

2. Babylonian Talmud, *Shabbat* 128b; *Rosh* on *Bava M'tzia* 32 (3:28); *Mishneh Torah, Shabbat* 25:26; *Shulchan Aruch, Orach Chayim* 305:19; *Mishnah B'rurah, Orach Chayim* 305 (68, 69).

3. *Moreih N'vuchim* 3:48.

4. *Alphabet of Ben Sira.* The tale goes on to tell the value of a wasp.

5. *Sefer HaChinuch* 451.

6. *Mishneh Torah, Hilchot G'zeilah V'Aveidah* 11.

7. *Shulchan Aruch, Even Ha-Eizer* 5:14.

8. Babylonian Talmud, *Bava M'tzia* 60b.

9. *Igeret Moshe, Even Ha-Eizer* 4:92.

10. Sponsored by the Humane Farming Association. See www.hfa.org/campaigns/boycott.

11. David Golinkin, "Responsa: Is It Permissible for Jews to Purchase and Eat Veal / to Raise Veal Calves?" *Moment*, February 1993, 26–27.

12. Some do currently exist: www.kolfoods.com, www.mitzvahmeat.com, www.lokomeat.com.

20

"I'LL HAVE WHAT SHE'S HAVING"

Jewish Ethical Vegetarianism

MARK SAMETH

In the spring of 1999 my wife and I were at the White Swan Hotel on tiny Shamian Island in Guangzhou, China, finalizing the adoption of our eldest daughter Liana. There were seven families in our adoption group, all in China for the same happy reason. Each night the families would go out to celebrate together at a different restaurant on the island. But one night, after listening to the concierge's recommendations, we just wandered off by ourselves, looking for something a bit more "authentic." We got more than we bargained for *that* night!

A few blocks away from the hotel we found a bustling restaurant, clearly catering to the locals. They had only one copy of their menu in English, which, when the group finally decided to sit down, we passed around the large round table. I say "finally decided to sit down" because it was not immediately agreed that we would. What had given us pause? Inside a metal-fence cage attached to the right wall of the building, the restaurant was showing off its *spécialité de maison*: a sad-eyed donkey, which—according to the sign on the cage—the restaurant would prepare to your liking for a mere thirty-six *yuan*.[1]

Yechh! Were they kidding?

But later I started to think (and is not that always the way?). What is it, I wondered, about unfamiliar food that makes people so uncomfortable? Isn't it, upon reflection, all so irrational? What, I thought, makes cow acceptable to most Americans, but not horse? Pig but not dog?

Our Irrational Diet

I had been a vegetarian for almost ten years the night I found myself standing in the crowd of hungry Americans eye to eye with that Chinese donkey. For one who had previously spent years happily eating bovine meat, my revulsion at the thought of equine meat was not exactly a rational response. But neither had been my decision to become a vegetarian in the first place.

My road to vegetarianism started at an Argentinean restaurant on the Upper West Side of Manhattan. I had found myself there one night and had ordered the mixed grill. But when the waiter placed it in front of me, it suddenly dawned on me that the "sweetbreads" were an animal's *brains*; the liver its *liver*; the heart its *heart*. *Yechh!* It was a "wake-up" experience. That was the last time I tasted red meat.

Under Jewish law, having given up red meat, I could, at that moment, have been considered a vegetarian. Jewish law defines *basar*, "meat," as mammalian flesh; *of*, or "fowl" (which in time I gave up as well), is not, which is why it is technically not subject to the prohibition against mixing milk and meat (although a Rabbinic stringency treats it as if it were); fish is in a category, along with grain, called *pareve*, or "neutral." But even if I was by Jewish standards a vegetarian, how long was I likely to have remained one?

What secured my Jewish vegetarianism was this: I was on a spirituality retreat with my synagogue. Over the course of that retreat I met a woman who would become one of my wife's and my dearest friends. Pamela was a nature lover; a gentle, poetic soul; and—I found out when we sat down to share our first meal together—a vegetarian. There's a Jewish tradition that there are hidden in the world in every generation thirty-six perfectly righteous people for whose sake God allows the world to go on. Everyone who knew Pamela said the same—that she was one of those *lamed-vavniks*. She was our role model. We all wished we could be half as centered, half as calm, half as graceful, and, toward the end (for she died way too young), half as courageous. But one thing we could all emulate, one simple practice of hers that we could all take on, was her vegetarianism. Over the course of that retreat I had more than one opportunity to sit with her, and each time I felt like a *chasid* watching his rebbe. I looked at her and said, in essence, "I'll have what she's having."

I know, I know—not rational. But that's exactly the point from which I wish to begin. I wish to begin by acknowledging that for all of us—meat eaters and vegetarians alike—there are very complicated irrational processes going on in the mind having to do with desire, denial, attraction, and revulsion whenever we sit down to eat food, whenever we simply talk about or think about sitting down to eat food.

Our Irrational Decision Making

I want to argue that vegetarianism is the most rational dietary choice we can make. But I need to begin by saying that I have no illusions about the power of argument alone to change behavior. It was not an argument that made me a vegetarian. I came to vegetarianism as the result of two *experiences*: a negative one (my encounter with offal) and a positive one (my encounter with Pamela). Both were emotional, neither was rational. Cognitive science is today just beginning to identify how significant a role emotions play in human decision making. I just want to acknowledge some of the limits of rational argument before I make mine.

Rational arguments do not prevent us from acting against our own self-interest. A basic assumption held by economists is that we human beings are all capable of making the best decisions for ourselves. But behavioral economist Dan Ariely demonstrates in his book *Predictably Irrational: The Hidden Forces That Shape Our Decisions* how we human beings consistently and predictably act against our own well-being.[2]

Rational arguments do not prevent us from acting against the best inter-est of those about whose well-being we demonstrably care. Psychologist Paul Slovic (of social science think tank Decision Research) has demon-strated how the same people willing to donate money to save a dying child will give *half* as much when asked to save eight dying children. It makes no rational sense, but that's how it is.

What Makes a Diet *Jewish*?

Our ability to reason our way toward good decisions is a limited one. Let's do the best we can. Concerning the question of Jewish diet, two questions present themselves: What makes a diet Jewish? And—if one can venture in our postmodern age to go howsoever tentatively from the descriptive to the prescriptive—what *should* a Jewish diet be?

The basic outline of a traditional Jewish diet comes to us from the Torah. Jews are not permitted to eat blood, flesh torn from a living ani-mal, flesh from an animal that has died a natural death, certain animal fats, or the sciatic nerve. The only animals permissible to eat are those with cloven hooves that chew their cud. Fish are permitted, but only those with both fins and scales. Shellfish are prohibited, as are some birds and most insects. Boiling an animal in the milk of its mother is forbidden. Slaughtering a mother animal and her young on the same day is forbidden. One is required to chase the mother bird away from her nest before taking her eggs.

The Rabbis of the Talmud extended the Torah's dietary laws (known as the laws of kashrut, or "properness") to require compas-sionate slaughter (called *sh'chitah*). The slaughtering knife must be extremely sharp; the animal must be killed quickly. The Rabbis also required householders to maintain separate dishes in order that milk and meat products not contaminate each other.

Beyond the rules laid out in the Torah and Talmud, the local cul-ture of the general community plays a large role in shaping what we think of as Jewish diet. I'm a fourth-generation American. Because so many more of my fellow American Jews are of Ashkenazic (German Jewish) rather than of Sephardic (Spanish Jewish) descent, the Jewish diet here has long been typified by foods such as bagels, blintzes, *kasha varnishkes,* and matzah ball soup, not to mention those famous meat sandwiches of the traditional Jewish delicatessen!

Could there be a food more Jewish than a pastrami sandwich? Piled high between two slices of fresh rye bread, slathered with spicy mustard, full dill and a side of slaw? Is it any wonder there are Jews who consider a pastrami sandwich a religious experience!

But the word "delicatessen" is German. And—believe it or not—the first pastrami sandwich in the United States wasn't served until 1887 (by Sussman Volk[3]), a good ten years after my great-grandparents emigrated here from Eastern Europe, some *two hundred* years after the first Jews to land in America came ashore at Charleston, South Carolina.

My point? The foods that make up a Jewish diet are constantly changing. And we all know what foods American Jews eat today: Japanese, Mexican, Italian, and Chinese.

Now here is where we start to get into arguments. But let me suggest, so that we do not get bogged down, that so long as it violates neither biblical nor Rabbinic dietary rules, any diet made up of food eaten by Jews deserves to be called a "Jewish" diet. In prewar Poland, the "Jewish" diet was essentially halachically prepared Polish peasant food. In modern-day America, it's the "fab four." In India, it's curry. In China, dim sum. In Morocco? Hummus, pita, and shawarma. Ethiopia? *Wot* over *injera.* That, I would argue, is the simple descriptive answer. Jews are a multiethnic people. And so the Jewish diet cannot, by definition, be described ethnically. Ethically, yes.

What *Should* a Jewish Diet Be?

Much more challenging than answering descriptively is trying to answer prescriptively. What, if any, foods *should* define a diet as Jewish? To the Orthodox, as well as to traditionally observant Reform, Conservative, and Reconstructionist Jews, the answer is fairly straightforward. To the traditionally observant, a Jewish diet should consist of foods that get a pass in the Torah and that are then prepared in accordance with the halachah (Rabbinic law) of *sh'chitah* (compassionate slaughter). (It is important to note here that there is nothing contradictory about Reform Jews keeping *kosher*. Isaac Mayer Wise, who founded American Reform Judaism, was passionate about kashrut. And he didn't mince words. He called nonkosher food "poisonous flesh."[4])

But even some Orthodox Jews today are wrestling with the fact that biblical and traditional Rabbinic kashrut is not enough to ensure that so-called compassionate slaughter is compassionate enough. There are Orthodox Jews today who are following a recently established ruling by Rabbi Moshe Feinstein against the consumption of veal. There is, evidently, an evolving understanding in some quarters of the Orthodox community that the cruel conditions under which the calf exists prior to slaughter constitutes an inarguable violation of the prohibition against *tzaar baalei chayim*, against causing needless suffering to an animal.

Other Orthodox authorities—Chief Rabbi of Britain Jonathan Sacks, former Chief Rabbi of Ireland David Rosen, the late Chief Rabbi of Israel Shlomo Goren, and the first Chief Rabbi of pre-state Israel Abraham Kook—all argue, or argued, in favor of vegetarianism. Why should that surprise? The Torah pictures Adam and Eve's Edenic diet as consisting of "all seed-bearing plants on the face of the earth, and every tree that has seed-bearing fruit" (Genesis 1:29). According to our people's sacred myth, animal flesh was not permitted to humans by God until after the Flood; and then, apparently, only as a concession to human frailty (Genesis 9:3).

Vegetarianism is the Torah's ideal. If meat is later allowed, the principle of *tzaar baalei chayim*, of not causing needless suffering to an animal, is yet upheld. Passages in the Torah such as those that require the working animal to rest along with its owner on the Shabbat (Exodus 20:10), prohibit the slaughter of an animal and its young on the same day (Leviticus 22:28), forbid one to eat before one's domestic animals have been fed (Deuteronomy 11:15), prohibit yoking together the larger ox with the smaller donkey (Deuteronomy 22:10), and prohibit the muzzling of one's ox when it is treading grain (Deuteronomy 25:4), all serve to establish *tzaar baalei chayim* as an *ikar g'dolah*, as a major guiding principle.

Now consider: in creating the rules of *sh'chitah*, of "compassionate slaughter," the Rabbis of the Talmud were more stringent about the taking of certain animals' lives than about the taking of others (e.g., fish are not subject to the rules of *sh'chitah*). Why? I am going to guess because of the Rabbis' intuitive understanding that the more developed an animal's consciousness, the more susceptible it is not only to physical but also to psychological suffering.

When Jews consider their diet today, I would argue, it would be reasonable likewise to give added consideration to the effect diet has on the suffering *most especially* of animals of more highly evolved consciousness, to give the highest consideration to those animals that stand to suffer the most.

From this perspective, there is no question that a diet that includes meat means suffering for the one animal on this planet most susceptible to suffering. That animal is the *human* animal. And that's the bottom line of this argument: a meatless diet is the most ethical diet for a human being to follow because it is the diet that causes the least amount of suffering in other human beings.

Effects of Meat Consumption on Human Beings

There are other compelling arguments in favor of vegetarianism. In "Continuity and Change in Reform Views of Kashrut 1883–2002" (chapter 21), Aaron Gross cites Rabbi Barry Schwartz's succinct, four-part argument in favor of a vision of kashrut that (1) mitigates against *bal tashchit*, excessive waste and environmental impact; (2) mitigates against *tzaar baalei chayim*, cruelty to animals; (3) promotes *sh'mirat haguf*, health; and (4) takes into account *oshek*, labor exploitation. I have instead chosen to focus on a fifth—quintessential—issue, *tzaar b'nei adam*, the effect of diet on human suffering.

So here is the short, unhappy take: Over one billion people on the planet are either starving or are chronically undernourished.[5] That's about one-sixth of the entire world's population. Indeed twenty million people—twenty million!—die each year due to hunger.[6] Three out of four of those are children. With the effects of climate change already upon us (unprecedented droughts, the disappearance of lakes and rivers, vast stretches of formerly fertile farmland turning to desert), those already staggering numbers are sure to go up, and dramatically.

Right now in the United States alone, more than half of all water consumed goes to support animal agriculture. Given what climatologists tell us is coming, we will very shortly simply not have enough water to sustain that anymore.[7]

Animal agriculture is inefficient in the extreme. Ever been on a farm? Animals eat a *lot*. You've got to invest eight to twelve pounds of grain for every one pound of edible beef you get back.[8] Unbelievably inefficient. If we gave up our meat-based diets, simply stopped raising animals for food, all of those crops we are now raising to feed those animals would be sufficient to feed every starving man, woman, and child on the planet. Judaism obligates us to address this issue. And with respect to those who are starving to the point of death, our moral obligation to act is, of course, an even higher one: the issue rises to the level of *pikuach nefesh*, the obligation to save human life.

And that is why I find myself so unmoved by (and there is no other way to put it) irrational appeals to Jewish history, culture, tradition, and Rabbinic dicta (and those often taken out of context) used to defend a meat-based diet. *Ein simchah elah b'basar*, "There is no joy without meat" (Babylonian Talmud, *P'sachim* 109a) and all of that. I have great respect for the power and importance of the nonrational. But especially when we consider the pride Reform Judaism takes in its rationalist roots, I would hope—given the short argument posed here and elaborated elsewhere[9]—that Jewish ethical vegetarianism will be formally embraced as the movement's dietary standard.

But What Makes Ethical Vegetarianism *Jewish*?

Now for those who will ask, "But what makes Jewish ethical vegetarianism *Jewish*?" my answer would be this: mindfulness. The Torah requires that we say a *b'rachah* (blessing) of thanks after enjoying a meal. The Rabbis added the practice of saying a *b'rachah* before enjoying a meal, indeed before enjoying any food. The mystics added the practice of saying a *kavanah* (a spiritual intention) before saying the *b'rachah*. More recently I have learned of the tradition of sitting in silence before saying the *kavanah*.

Now I do not always sit in silence, and I often forget to pronounce a *kavanah*, but I always manage at least to say a *b'rachah* before every meal, light snack, piece of fruit, or granola bar (you knew *that* was coming) I may grab throughout the day. I try to be mindful and grateful and aware and in tune. Sometimes it works. Always it makes the moment Jewish.

Of course, being mindful means being mindful, as well, about our choices. The choice to be a vegetarian begins with mindfulness and is reinforced with each food selection. Yet, the much touted "principle of autonomy"—which I support—in no way ensures that we will at all times make the best choices for ourselves or for the world. That is why we are in need not only of compelling, rational arguments worthy of our consideration, but (because our decision making is never the product of purely rational thinking) of negative "wake-up" experiences to catalyze our reevaluation and of positive role models to inspire our emulation.

NOTES

1. Roughly $5.40 (October 2010).
2. Dan Ariely, *Predictably Irrational: The Hidden Forces That Shape Our Decisions* (New York: HarperCollins, 2010).

3. Patricia Volk, *Stuffed: Adventures of a Restaurant Family* (New York: Random House, 2002), 82.

4. James Gunther Heller, *Isaac Mayer Wise: His Life, Work, and Thought* (New York: UAHC Press, 1965), 528.

5. C. G. Scanes and J. A. Miranowski, *Perspectives in World Food and Agriculture* (Iowa: Wiley Blackwell/Iowa State Press, 2004), 53.

6. Wiley-VCH, eds., *Ullams Agrochemicals* (Hoboken, NJ: Wiley-VCH, 2007), 120.

7. UNEP, *Vital Water Graphics: An Overview of the World's Fresh and Marine Waters* (Nairobi, Kenya: UNEP [United Nations Environmental Program], 2008).

8. Richard H. Schwartz, "Jewish Teachings on Resource Conservation," www.Jewishveg.com.

9. Richard H. Schwartz's book *Judaism and Vegetarianism* (New York: Lantern Books, 2001) is a very accessible resource (available online).

21

CONTINUITY AND CHANGE IN REFORM VIEWS OF KASHRUT 1883–2002

From the *T'reifah* Banquet to Eco-Kashrut

AARON SAUL GROSS

The official early Reform stance that kashrut is not useful to the modern Jew and, indeed, potentially harmful, was famously articulated in the Pittsburgh Platform of 1885:

> We hold that all such Mosaic and Rabbinical laws as regulate diet, priestly purity, and dress originated in ages and under the influence of ideas entirely foreign to our present mental and spiritual state. They fail to impress the modern Jew with a spirit of priestly holiness; their observance in our days is apt rather to obstruct than to further modern spiritual elevation.

Although there was a much wider range of opinion on kashrut than this position would imply,[1] the strong anti-kashrut sentiment of the 1885 Pittsburgh Platform (PP) was characteristic of early Reform. However, this early hostility toward kashrut has been reversing along

Adapted with permission from Aaron Gross, "Continuity and Change in Reform Views of Kashrut 1883–2002: From the *T'reifah Banquet* to Eco-Kashrut," *CCAR Journal*, Winter 2004, 6–28.

with broader attitudes toward ritual aspects of Judaism, most notably since the Columbus Platform of 1938.[2] This turn toward ritual was decisively expressed in the 1999 PP, which suggests that certain "sacred obligations . . . demand renewed attention as the result of the unique context of our own times."[3] The last twenty years, particularly, have been marked by a turn to greater interest in kashrut, and it is likely that the Central Conference of American Rabbis' recently formed (2001) Task Force on Kashrut will take up the implicit suggestion of the 1999 PP and further advance this reversal with recommendations for a Reform practice of kashrut within the next few years.

Despite the divergent conclusions the Reform rabbinate reached about kashrut if we compare the 1885 and 1999 PPs, I will argue that a relatively constant nexus of issues related to the status of ritual and ethics in Judaism has been regulating the Reform view of kashrut throughout this period. I aim to explicate the intellectual continuity that has existed alongside the more obvious changes in attitude toward kashrut. I argue that because the practice of kashrut as envisioned in 1885 still remains largely rejected today in Reform Judaism, we find that the particular practice of kashrut to which Reform Judaism is "returning" is quite different from traditional kashrut. The classic Reform valorization of ethics, personal autonomy, and rationality that once helped shape the rejection of kashrut is now reshaping a positive Reform understanding of the dietary laws.

Today, for example, a full range of options for kashrut—from avoidance of pork, to various forms of vegetarianism, to traditional Rabbinic regulations—are presented as valid by the CCAR. I will pay close attention to the suggestion by some that vegetarianism may be a suitable way to practice kashrut: what I will call the "vegetarian-kashrut option."[4] I will identify the particular intellectual-historical background of the vegetarian-kashrut option, and locate it in relation to the broader discussion of kashrut. In exploring this particularity, the complexity of the broader Reform debate around kashrut will be brought into greater clarity.

Two Key Issues Regulating Kashrut

At least two key issues come to bear on the Reform evaluation of kashrut. The first and more obvious is (1) the value accorded to the ceremonial or ritual aspects of Jewish practice, as has been previously highlighted in the excellent article on this topic by Peter Knobel.[5] The second issue is (2) the Reform valorization of the rational, ethical, and universalistic aspects of Judaism.

In one sense, this second issue is really just the flip side of the first. However, as attitudes toward the value of ritual have changed, the Reform championing of the ethical has not ended.[6] Thus, these streams of thought have become more distinct.

Kashrut in the Early Years of Reform Judaism

Both anti-ritual sentiments and pro-ethical sentiments converged in the early years of Reform Judaism to produce in the 1885 PP a consensus against kashrut. Prior to this consensus, key Reformers had argued variously for the complete elimination of kashrut or various modifications of kashrut, with Geiger suggesting that an all-or-nothing approach should be taken.[7] Significantly, kashrut was viewed as overwhelmingly a ritual practice. Thus, the rejection of kashrut was largely a rejection of what the Reformers viewed as outdated rituals that impeded Jewish-gentile relations. Implicit in this rejection was the view that kashrut held no redeeming ethical value that might argue for some form of maintenance. Indeed, it was the *rejection* of the dietary laws that was viewed as ethical, for in eliminating Jewish-gentile boundaries, early Reformers saw themselves as participating in the dawn of the messianic era.[8]

We should note that the 1885 consensus on kashrut did not emerge without serious divisiveness. Remarkably little was written about kashrut by these early Reformers, so it is difficult to turn to texts to gain insight into this early period. However, we can better appreciate the early debate if we keep in mind that, on the issue of diet, what is *written* is surely much less important than what is *eaten*. Gunther Plaut, who is favorably cited by Knobel, suggests that the dearth of writings is likely due to the early Reform view that diet is a private matter, and simply because many Reformers had already abandoned the dietary laws.[9] We should add, however, that even if the early Reformers viewed eating as a private matter, it was and remains an unavoidably public act. Pointing to the great significance attached to diet, the vocal German Reformer Max Freudenthal (1868–1937) observed:

> The laws of Kashrut are generally considered by Jews themselves to be the watershed between Orthodoxy and Liberalism. He who keeps the dietary laws appears to the Liberal as an Orthodox Jew, and those who disregard them are, in return, decried by the Orthodox not only as Liberals but even as godless and un-Jewish.[10]

Thus, the paucity of public writings stands alongside the powerful non-verbal statement made as Reform rabbis and synagogues made their attitude toward the dietary laws abundantly apparent by the foods they ate or served in public.

Keeping this in mind, the Reform stance on the dietary laws may be one of the most communicated positions of early Reform. At an early rabbinical conference in Frankfort the reform of the dietary laws was among the issues about which the Jews of Breslau urged discussion, citing the need to reconcile actual practice with the law.[11] Though the conference failed to take up this request specifically, this is evidence of high self-consciousness around diet. Many Reform rabbis today can recall their own internal debate about the level of kashrut they would keep when dining with more traditional colleagues; not infrequently, especially in past years, this debate asked whether one ought to violate kashrut in front of traditional colleagues *on principle*.[12] It is hard to imagine this is only a contemporary phenomenon.

There is perhaps no better symbol of this largely unrecorded part of the early debate on kashrut than the *"t'reifah* banquet." This banquet, served to the first class of graduating rabbinic students at the newly formed Hebrew Union College and reported in the Jewish media, was supposed to be kosher, but ended up violating every law of kashrut except the prohibition on pork.[13] Whether the serving of nonkosher foods was deliberate or a catering error is not known with absolute certainty, but the event ultimately became a focus of much controversy and contributed to the formation of Conservative Judaism.[14]

Even if the incident was an error, as Isaac Mayer Wise maintained, the friction over kashrut, and the larger issues for which it was the chosen symbol, was hardly imagined. Thus, the early consensus against kashrut expressed in the 1885 PP was in part possible because events like the 1883 banquet had alienated at least some individuals who would have argued for a softer position. A crucial factor that allowed the rejection of kashrut in the 1885 PP was a willingness to alienate some traditional-leaning liberal Jews, and, in some cases, even a desire to alienate them.

Contemporary Reform Judaism and Kashrut

Overview

As in the early years of Reform Judaism, the twin issues of the status of ritual and of ethics bear on the contemporary Reform reception of kashrut. This time, however, the impact is more favorable to observing kashrut. Both the CCAR's 1979 responsum "Kashrut in Reform Judaism" and Peter Knobel's 1990 essay "Reform Judaism and Kashrut" (citations in endnote 1) document the contemporary trend toward renewed interest in ritual, generally, and kashrut, specifically. This paper will focus on updating their work and looking more closely at the way in which emphasizing the ethical possibilities of kashrut has been a central part of renewed interest in the dietary laws.

The Return to Ritual: Changing Attitudes or a Changed Situation?

Knobel is undoubtedly correct to argue that "the history of Reform Judaism's attitude toward kashrut should be viewed within the context of its attitude toward Jewish religious practice in general."[15]

Knobel, drawing on Michael Meyer's book *Response to Modernity*,[16] argues persuasively that openness to kashrut begins to advance as Reform Judaism becomes open to traditional observance in general. This return to ritual does not get seriously under way until after World War II;[17] the story since then is one of increasing openness to ritual observance. The two most recent publications that Knobel discusses are the 1979 publication of the *Gates of Mitzvah*, a useful landmark in the return to ritual, and the 1988 publication of a statement by the joint UAHC [now URJ][18] / CCAR Task Force on Religious Commitment. Knobel's discussion of the *Gates of Mitzvah* highlights that in this document "kashrut is now conceived as offering the possibility of sanctification," and provides various options for practice.[19] More incisively, Knobel points out that *Gates of Mitzvah* is "an attempt to broaden the definition of kashrut to include all dietary disciplines undertaken for Jewish religious reason as part of kashrut."[20] Knobel finds the statement of the Task Force on Religious Commitment with its vision of kashrut "as a mitzvah that can deepen a Reform Jew's spiritual life" an even more remarkable reversal of Reform's early hostility to kashrut.[21] Knobel concludes that "there has been a revolution in the attitude of Reform Judaism toward religious observance, and the extreme emphasis on universalism has been balanced by a reassertion of particularism."[22]

I would suggest that Knobel overstates the issue when he calls the changes "a revolution in . . . attitude" (p. 492). The "revolution," if it exists at all, is not in basic Reform attitudes, which seem only slightly modified, but in the situation of Reform Jews. The 1885 PP attack on kashrut is crucially located in a climate in which Reform Jews are striving to integrate the Jewish community within modern civilization *and find that the Jew is often still alienated.* It is this particular situation in which kashrut is experienced as a barrier and the framers of the 1885 PP are, perhaps, aware of this when they qualify their rejection as based upon "our present mental and spiritual state." The framers of the 1885 PP further imply that the ceremonial laws are rejected not only because they do not make a positive contribution, but because they pose a danger and, indeed, are "apt rather to obstruct than to further modern spiritual elevation" (from the 1888 PP). Part of that danger is precisely the dictary law's potent ability to separate Jew from gentile.

Seen in this light, the Reform rejection of kashrut is only partially a rejection of kashrut itself; it is also an attempt by Jews to integrate into the larger culture without rejecting Judaism. To the extent that the Reform rejection of kashrut (and ritual generally) is indeed predicated upon achieving integration, it can hardly be accounted as a "revolution" when, now that Reform Jewry in America is so integrated it fears its own assimilation, taboos on kashrut observance are themselves abandoned. It is worth noting as well that Reform Judaism has remained cautious enough on endorsing kashrut that even nine years after Knobel characterized the move toward greater observance as a "revolution," the mere use of the word "kashrut" was removed from the fourth draft (out of six) of what became the 1999 PP, since it caused too much controversy.[23] The 1999 PP, issuing what amounts to the same qualification seen in 1885, asserts only that some of the mitzvot Jews ought to study and fulfill "if they address us as individuals and as a community" might include the nameless mitzvot that "demand renewed attention as the result of the unique context of our own times." One has to turn to the much less widely read CCAR commentary to know with any certainty that kashrut is one of the mitzvot some of the CCAR rabbis had in mind.

As Reform Judaism now consciously works to lend distinctiveness to Reform Jewish life, given the high level of integration and assimilation Reform Jews have achieved, the laws of kashrut no longer necessarily are seen as harmful. Indeed, the very effect of kashrut that was previously a difficulty—namely its power to separate Jew and gentile—is now viewed as beneficial.

Moreover, as gentile America increasingly asserts its commitment to a vision of pluralism that accommodates diverse eating habits, Jews have to give up less in the way of integration to maintain their distinctiveness. Former CCAR president Richard Levy was a driving force behind the "Ten Principles for Reform Judaism," the first draft of what ultimately became the 1999 PP; he laid particular importance on the practice of kashrut, which is evident in the early drafts. In the first three renditions of the "Ten Principles for Reform Judaism" kashrut was given a place of pride and its sanctifying and ethical potential was stressed. In a highly publicized interview with *Reform Judaism*, the Reform Movement's official periodical, Levy was called upon to defend the "Ten Principles." The interviewer asked Levy to respond to the fact that "kashrut was abandoned, at least in part, because it was seen as a barrier separating Jews from other people."[24] Tellingly, Levy responds not only by defending the positive value of separation for contemporary Jews, but by pointing out that ethnic distinctiveness itself is no longer a burden in America. Levy writes:

> In fact, in today's society, separation, or diversity, is becoming the norm, particularly in dietary preferences. These days the host will ask, "Are you a vegetarian? Is there anything you can't eat?" And, of course, you can dine out with friends and eat different foods.[25]

We can see intimated here the same situation that we saw in 1885, namely that the Reform willingness to consider kashrut is predicated upon its non-interference with the "proper level" of Jewish integration. It thus appears that the situation has changed more than Reform attitudes.

Similarly, whereas early Reform was willing to shake up traditionally minded Jews by abandoning the dietary laws (as declared in the 1885 PP and seen in the aftermath of the *t'reifah* banquet if not the banquet itself),[26] contemporary Reform has expressed greater interest in maintaining good relations with the larger Jewish community.

This concern is expressed in the 1999 PP call to "reach out to all Jews across ideological . . . boundaries" and its "embrace [of] religious and cultural pluralism as an expression of the vitality of Jewish communal life," and is featured prominently in the recorded discussions about its various drafts. Here again, the apparent changes in attitudes about kashrut appear to be better characterized as changes in social situation and related attitudes about intra-Jewish unity.

Kashrut and Ethics

Overview

Not only can we see multiple factors that explain the present interest in kashrut that are unrelated to a fundamental shift in attitude about kashrut itself, but it is also clear that much in the traditional Reform critique of ritual and kashrut remains intact. Most notably, virtually no serious challenge to autonomy is presented in the official Reform statements that call for a move toward once-neglected rituals (though the issue of autonomy is debated).[27] Furthermore, since the return of interest in kashrut has gone hand in hand with the valorization of the ethical content of kashrut, it is difficult to say to what extent Reform Jews have really embraced a new openness to kashrut as a "strictly ritual" observance and to what extent Reform Judaism has simply discovered and/or invented an ethical basis for kashrut while maintaining its suspicion of strictly ritual commandments. For example, Richard Levy observes in the already mentioned interview with *Reform Judaism* that "a kosher diet can not only fulfill the mitzvot of forsaking forbidden foods in the Torah, but can also respond to ethical injunctions."[28] Statements like these preserve a great deal of ambiguity about the status of observing kashrut on the basis of its being commanded, for they do not allow the fact that kashrut is commanded to stand alone. Indeed, it is quite difficult to find Reform endorsements of kashrut that are not in part dependent on kashrut's being viewed as an ethical practice in addition to whatever else it might be.

That said, we must note that some recent Reform writings on kashrut do suggest that it is valid to observe kashrut on "the authority of ancient biblical and Rabbinic injunctions," as, for example, is stated in the *Gates of Mitzvah*.[29] This is, indeed, as Knobel has noted, a "far cry"[30] from the 1885 PP. One of the most significant breaks with the past in the 1999 PP is precisely its call to study "the whole array of mitzvot," which clearly includes the "Mosaic and Rabbinical laws as regulate diet, priestly purity, and dress" rejected in 1885. However, one wonders if traditional grounds for kashrut are found acceptable only because Reform rabbis, unlike their colleagues in 1885, are now confident that kashrut has ethical meaning relevant to contemporary Judaism. The Reform "return" to ritual in the case of kashrut and perhaps elsewhere is, in fact, regulated and constrained by the Reform valorization of the ethical and rational. Kashrut may be legitimately practiced on the basis of "ancient biblical and rabbinic injunctions," but—and here is the rub for true traditionalists—only because there are good rational and Jewish ethical reasons to adopt kashrut.

As presently expressed, official Reform statements casting kashrut in a positive light do not lean heavily on the inherent value of traditional Jewish rituals and virtually always mention—if not stress—the ethical and/or utilitarian considerations. Kashrut is suggested for its ability to enhance Jewish distinctiveness by, for example, helping create a Jewish home or, alternatively, for its potential to help one stand in "identification and solidarity with the worldwide Jewish community."[31]

Distinguishing the Reform Approach

Similarly, ethical aspects of kashrut that were ignored or did not exist at the time of the 1885 PP receive significant attention and are used to distinguish the uniqueness of the emerging Reform understanding of kashrut. For example, Richard Levy expresses his hope that

> keeping kosher . . . not be restricted to the separating of milk and meat, refraining from biblical *t'reif*, and accepting only traditional methods of *sh'chitah* (slaughter). A Reform approach to kashrut

should also encourage concern for *tzar baalei chayim*, the pain of living creatures cruelly penned in and fattened. Similarly, a Reform embrace of kashrut might well ban veal as well as biblical *t'reif*, and might prohibit fruits and vegetables grown with pesticides or harvested under inhuman conditions.[32]

Levy's remarks above aim to highlight the distinctive ethical nature of a "Reform approach to kashrut" and, by so doing, are arguing in a classically Reform polemical mode against a traditionalist/Orthodox understanding of kashrut. This aspect of the Reform discussion of kashrut and ethics is prominent in an explicitly polemical piece published in *Reform Judaism* by Simeon Maslin, then president of the CCAR, which highlights the issue of kosher slaughter. Regarding kashrut, Maslin asserts:

> All Jews, kosher or not, should be concerned about taking life for food and the way animals are treated before slaughter. For some this might mean humane rather than kosher slaughter. Others might define kashrut as abstaining from mammal meat entirely. . . . Still others might choose pure vegetarianism. Indeed, a growing number of Reform Jews are opting to keep kosher, not because they are commanded, but as a constant reminder of God's bounty, to make it possible for all Jews to eat at their tables, or for a variety of other Jewish affirming reasons. . . . Are Jews who require a more painful method of slaughter because they adhere to the methods of antiquity more authentic than Jews who, having studied the tradition and infused its spirit, have opted for a culinary regimen more consonant with contemporary understandings of a humane diet?[33]

I have quoted Maslin at length here because his comments bring out an interesting tension in the Reform discourse: Maslin both champions a Reform practice of kashrut because it may "make it possible for all Jews to eat at their tables," at the same time he endeavors to distinguish the superior potential of a Reform approach to kashrut. Thus, whereas we noted before that the return to ritual in Reform Judaism is partially buoyed by a desire to "reach out to all Jews across ideological and geographical boundaries" (1999 PP), there are important constraints on how far this accommodationist attitude stretches.

Historical Roots of Ethical Kashrut among Reformers

Further continuity with early Reform is suggested by the great deal of history behind Reform's championing the ethical basis of kashrut.[34] Bernhard Felsenthal, described by Plaut as a classical Reformer in most respects who was conservative in regard to change of dietary laws,[35] argued for kashrut as an ethical practice simply by virtue of its being a dietary discipline. Felsenthal wrote that the dietary laws have "a deeper ethical significance. . . . They teach us the lovely virtue of self-discipline and thereby assist us to become a holy people."[36] Other early Reformers, like Max Freudenthal, argued that the dietary laws are concerned with humane slaughter and are an expression of the prohibition against causing *tzaar baalei chayim*—cruelty to animals.[37] Significantly, Freudenthal was writing to defend kosher slaughter (as a humane method of killing animals) from anti-Semitic attacks in the guise of animal welfare concerns.[38] Such veiled anti-Semitic attacks on *sh'chitah* were in fact widespread in Europe generally, but especially in the German-speaking world;[39] in responding to such attacks it is likely that the traditional association of *tzaar baalei chayim* with the laws of kashrut was reinforced.

Following this history, virtually every recent Reform discussion of kashrut in the last twenty years has cited *tzaar baalei chayim* as one of the ethical teachings embedded in the practice of kashrut, several adding that, therefore, vegetarianism may serve as a practice of kashrut.[40] These same sources have sometimes also followed those early Reformers who attributed a more generic ethical valence to the basic act of dietary discipline.

What is new, however, is the argument that traditional Jewish values can or ought to reshape kashrut so as to create a broad ethical basis for the dietary laws. Knobel rightly points this out when he comments that

Gates of Mitzvah is "an attempt to broaden the definition of kashrut to include all dietary disciplines undertaken for Jewish religious reasons as part of kashrut."[41] Jewish ethical values related to health and wellness, animal welfare, ecological sustainability, and the treatment of human labor are now cited by Reform sources as potentially informing a new understanding of kashrut—often called "eco-kashrut." Rabbi Barry Schwartz, who chairs the Subcommittee on Eco-Kashrut of the present CCAR Task Force on Kashrut suggests that eco-kashrut can be envisioned as a "four part test of *bal tashchit* (excessive waste and environmental impact), *tzaar baalei chayim* (cruelty to animals), *sh'mirat haguf* (health), and *oshek* (labor exploitation)."[42] Such contemporary arguments for revising kashrut to give it a strong ethical basis are indeed new, though perhaps not particularly revolutionary, given the Reform willingness to modify so much in Jewish tradition on ethical grounds.

The Vegetarian-Kashrut Option

Basic Background of Vegetarianism in a Jewish Context

We can gain a more nuanced understanding of the contemporary turn to kashrut by looking at some of the specific options for kashrut being advocated by Reform leaders. One such proposal is the aforementioned vegetarian-kashrut option. As we have seen, virtually all Reform rabbinical discussions of kashrut since 1979 have cited *tzaar baalei chayim* in connection with kashrut. Most of these discussions have also favorably mentioned the vegetarian-kashrut option, including the CCAR's 1979 responsa on kashrut, the extended discussion of kashrut in the CCAR's *Gates of Mitzvah*, and a pair of addresses by CCAR presidents (Levy 1998, Maslin 1996). Moreover, as this paper was completed, a resolution advocating vegetarianism was being considered by the CCAR's Task Force on Kashrut.[43]

In addition to the potential ethical valence of vegetarianism, that diet's potential to help observant Jews maintain some level of kashrut has helped create a basic openness to vegetarianism. Significantly, even for those with no particular bias toward vegetarianism, choosing vegetarian options when dining out or suggesting vegetarian dishes in invitations to pot-luck meals is a widely accepted way to keep a certain level of traditional kashrut in many American Jewish circles. Thus, the question of vegetarianism has a certain organic connection to kashrut for some Jews.

However, the mainline Rabbinic tradition has typically discouraged vegetarianism and even established a connection between eating meat and the observance of the Sabbath and other holy days.[44] This is true despite the fact that there are powerful streams of thought in Judaism that cast vegetarianism in a positive light. Perhaps most prominently, a long exegetical tradition rooted in Talmud and maintained by the authoritative medieval biblical exegetes (including Rashi) and continuing into modern times has held that vegetarianism was God's first dietary command in Eden (Gen. 1:29).[45] Citing this fact, often along with the famous vision of human-animal harmony in Isaiah 11, a number of modern and contemporary Jews (including Rav Kook, the first rabbi of pre-state Israel) have advocated vegetarianism in idiosyncratic ways.[46]

Vegetarianism as a Messianic Return to Eden

The contemporary Reform leaders advocating for the vegetarian-kashrut option follow this intellectual current as well as a broader history of Reform messianism when they invoke images of a return to Edenic vegetarianism. For example, the proposed CCAR resolution advocating vegetarianism observes that "according to Genesis (1:29), God's primary and ideal dietary command is vegetarian." Similarly in an essay entitled "What Value Does Kashrut Have for Reform Jews Today?" which is available on the URJ website as part of its adult education program, we read that "kashrut was established as a compromise with the ideal of vegetarianism. . . . Ideally, we would all be vegetarians, following the utopian Garden of Eden story in Genesis 1."[47] In an essay entitled "Ethical Vegetarianism: The Perspective of a Reform

Jew," published in the *CCAR Journal,* a Texas-based rabbi explains his own journey to a vegetarian-kashrut practice, noting in his argument that "it is quite clear that in the Edenic state, Adam and Eve did not consume the flesh of other animals."[48] A final example is found in a feature article that advocates vegetarianism published in the Summer 1995 issue of *Reform Judaism,* where we read that God's vegetarian command in Genesis 1:29 "set before us . . . the ideal of creation."[49] The essay goes on to explain that the vegetarian ideal "reappears in the vision of the Prophet Isaiah . . . 'The wolf shall dwell with the lamb. . . .' The optimal vision of Creation is thus embodied in a vegetarian diet."[50] Yet, none of these Reform sources rests its case wholly upon such arguments.[51]

Present Reform Vegetarian Advocacy

Current Reform advocacy of the vegetarian-kashrut option, taking its cue in part from the discussion of eco-kashrut, most prominently cites arguments based on Jewish values pertaining to health, ecology, and animal welfare in support of vegetarianism.[52]

The structuring and history of the Task Force on Kashrut, where a resolution advocating vegetarianism now sits, says a great deal about where the vegetarian-kashrut option is located in the larger discussion and so is worth detailing here.[53] The task force was formed under the CCAR presidency of Charles Kroloff (who is also among those supportive of the proposed CCAR resolution on vegetarianism) and was charged to (1) make recommendations for a kashrut policy for CCAR meetings, and (2) develop guidelines and approaches to kashrut for the movement as a whole. To achieve those ends, four subcommittees were set up in the following areas: (1) recommendations for within the CCAR, (2) recommendations for the Reform Movement generally, (3) "eco-kashrut," and (4) preparations for presentations at the UAHC Biennial. Interestingly, the Eco-Kashrut Subcommittee is the only one with an explicit and specific theological/ethical vision guiding it; the other three committees have more practical charges. As a matter of procedure, it is likely that the Eco-Kashrut Subcommittee will be asked to present its findings to the other subcommittees.

Under the rubric of eco-kashrut, this subcommittee will present guidelines for how broad Jewish ethical values might be tied to the Reform practice of kashrut. In doing so it is looking at previous CCAR resolutions calling for participation in the United Farm Workers grape boycott (see resolutions from 1985, 1989) and the CCAR's support of legislation opposed to dangerous pesticides (see resolutions from 1984, 1989, 1990) as precursors to eco-kashrut thinking in the Reform Movement. The idea of eco-kashrut and vegetarianism along with it thus has a voice in the current project to develop Reform guidelines for kashrut. How seriously this voice will ultimately be taken is yet to be seen.

Historical Trends Related to the Vegetarian-Kashrut Option

Kashrut as a Scientific System: Health and Hygiene

Taking a step back, we can discern three distinct trends that feed into the vegetarian-kashrut option and, by extension, the entire issue of kashrut. First and most obvious is the already discussed renewal of interest in ritual. Second is a long-standing[54] desire among many Jews to find a rational, scientific basis for kashrut as has been manifested in attempts to argue that traditional kashrut is empirically more healthful or more hygienic than other diets.[55] While these attempts have proved largely unpersuasive, their historical pervasiveness does suggest a strong desire to unite healthful eating (as medically defined) and the practice of kashrut. I think it is fair to say that attempts to argue that traditional kashrut is more healthful have lost prominence, but the impulse they represent is unlikely to have disappeared completely.

Given the considerable extent to which secular medical and nutrition authorities have argued for the superior healthfulness of vegetarian over non-vegetarian diets,[56] and given the now twenty-year-old official Reform suggestion that vegetarianism may be a valid form of kashrut, it is not surprising that Reform advocates of vegetarianism argue for that diet based on health concerns. Certainly, the authors of this resolution are aiming to draw in the health conscious and we need not point to historical precedents to explain why superior healthfulness might persuade some people to adopt just about any reasonable diet. What I wish to emphasize, however, is that those advocating the vegetarian-kashrut option on health grounds follow, consciously or not, within a specifically Jewish historical trend. What may distinguish the new advocacy, however, is that their arguments are made on a more solid scientific basis (see previous endnote).

It seems probable that the vegetarian-kashrut option is buoyed by this overlap with health considerations. Rabbi Barry Schwartz reports that among his colleagues who are persuaded that vegetarianism is better for you, this fact is likely to be viewed as an argument in favor of the vegetarian-kashrut option.[57] Health arguments have also been linked with the increasing interest members of the CCAR are showing in the idea of "rabbinic wellness." For example, former CCAR president Charles Kroloff has argued for the proposed CCAR resolution endorsing vegetarianism on these grounds.[58]

What seems to have happened with the "health argument" for kashrut is similar to what happened historically with the "ethics argument": first it was argued that kashrut had an ethical basis, but now we see arguments that Jews ought to create an ethical practice of kashrut based on Jewish values (e.g., eco-kashrut). Similarly, many Jews in the past have argued that kashrut *is* more healthful; now a vocal minority argues that kashrut (traditional or not) ought to be practiced in such a way that it is *made* more healthful through vegetarianism or other dietary restrictions.

Judaism and Ecology

A final trend that has helped make possible and shape the vegetarian-kashrut option is the explosion of Jewish interest in ecology and the desire to uplift Jewish practices and values that have a positive ecological valence. While a serious review of the emergence of Jewish ecology is beyond this paper, we can note here that contemporary

Jewish ecological writing began to appear prominently in 1970 and the discussion has grown since then with no sign of slowing. We can also note that this discourse began with a defensive posture—countering critiques that the Bible and Judeo-Christian values were contributing factors to today's ecological woes.[59] While much Jewish ecological writing today still is defensive, the discourse is now dominated by the task of affirming and articulating a positive understanding of Jewish approaches to the environment and environmental problems. At least a vocal minority of those seriously involved in the discussion of Judaism and ecology view plant-based diets favorably because they use fewer resources, require less land, and cause less pollution,[60] as well as theological reasons related to our view of non-human creation.[61]

As the Judaism and ecology discussion has matured and become a significant intellectual stream in Reform Judaism,[62] the pro-vegetarian voices have also gained a wider audience and commanded more attention. Significantly, the CCAR resolution endorsing vegetarianism originated in the Committee on the Environment, a relatively new creation itself. Rabbi Barry Schwartz reports that in addition to the general return to ritual, interest in the vegetarian-kashrut option owes its greatest debt to the surge of interest in Jewish ecology.[63]

Distinguishing the Vegetarian-Kashrut Option
from Gentile Vegetarianism

Despite the variety of historical trends within Judaism that have led a minority of Jews to advocate vegetarianism as a means of keeping kosher, this kashrut option may have the rather unusual effect of making a kosher diet indistinguishable from gentile vegetarian diets. Thus, the question has arisen for some whether there is a proper Jewish basis for the vegetarian-kashrut option. Of course, Jews routinely engage in unquestionably Jewish practices in which gentiles also engage (for example, reading the Bible), so there is no logical reason to exclude vegetarianism as a form of kashrut because it may be similar to gentile practices. However, since Jewish tradition (Reform and otherwise) has long located kashrut's significance in part in its ability to distinguish Jew from gentile, it may be of importance that a form of kashrut looks like gentile practices. Indeed, as we have seen, the early Reform rejection of kashrut is in part because of the priority the movement assigned to integration and, similarly, the return to kashrut is related to the prioritization of maintaining distinctiveness.

At root the question of whether any form of kashrut, vegetarian or otherwise, needs to be distinct in practice from gentile diets, is a normative question that cannot be answered in a descriptive essay such as this, but rather must be debated by Jews as religionists. However, we can clarify several issues here regarding the vegetarian-kashrut option. First, depending on the form of vegetarian-kashrut advocated, such a diet may be quite distinct from gentile forms of vegetarianism.[64] Second, when gentile and kosher vegetarianism are the same in practice, the question of whether this dietary practice is a form of kashrut and thus Jewish will hinge upon an evaluation of motivation. Clearly, the Jewish leaders that have advocated for the vegetarian-kashrut option are not suggesting that any person who is vegetarian is keeping kosher, yet, in typically Reform fashion, neither are they setting forth specific, authoritative criteria for what constitutes Jewish observance.

Conclusion

In addition to the vegetarian-kashrut option's obvious connection with the turn toward more ritual observance, present advocacy of it rests upon intellectual streams that have a substantial history in Reform Judaism: the valorization of Jewish ethics generally; the association of kashrut with *tzar baalei chayim*; a desire to reconcile kashrut with contemporary understandings of health and hygiene; and the growth of Jewish ecology. Arguments for the vegetarian-kashrut option contain much that is continuous with the early Reform rejection of kashrut in their valorization of ethics, upholding of autonomy, and in the conspicuous absence of a defense of strictly ritual aspects of Judaism.

The intellectual continuity seen in the case of the vegetarian-kashrut option holds true, a fortiori, in the turn toward kashrut generally. The Reform evaluation of Jewish ritual and valorization of ethics has continuously been of central importance; however, now its effects are partially reversed. Reform Judaism still views the dietary laws as increasing separation between Jew and gentile; however, now this has a positive valence. Reform Jews continue to be aware of the power of kashrut to internally unify Jewry, but now view this potential with increased favor. Reform Judaism has maintained its dominant concern with the ethical and rational, but now kashrut is viewed as fitting (or made to fit) into these categories.

As is always the case with intellectual history, one could also stress the intellectual discontinuity. The 1885 PP's assertion that the dietary laws "fail to impress the modern Jew with a spirit of priestly holiness" is contradicted implicitly, for example, when the *Gates of Mitzvah* invites Reform Jews to decide if kashrut "would add *k'dushah* to their homes and their lives."[65] Similarly, Reform calls to recast kashrut in light of broad Jewish values were entirely absent in 1885.

I have stressed continuity here mainly because that aspect has been so neglected in the contemporary discourse. However, attention to continuity is also crucial because it allows one to be aware of how Reform thought and theology are coming closer to traditional observances *without* revising basic Reform tenets. The contemporary Reform interest in ritual and kashrut is not simply a *t'shuvah*, nor a revolutionary break with Reform intellectual history. Rather, the present discourse on kashrut partakes of each of these processes, and attention to these complexities ought to assist Reform self-understanding as well as a broad historical understanding of these noteworthy changes.

NOTES

1. For example, such early Reformers as Wiener, Creiznach, Felsenthal, and Geiger held different views. For discussion, see the useful surveys of the few primary sources available on this issue in:
> (1) Peter S. Knobel, "Reform Judaism and Kashrut," *Judaism* 39, no. 4 (1990): 488–89 and
> (2) Central Conference of American Rabbis Responsum, "Kashrut in Reform Judaism," (1979) [viewed on www.ccarnet.org on June 17, 2003].

2. Knobel, "Reform Judaism and Kashrut," 489.

3. Although the statement of principles itself does not specifically mention kashrut, the CCAR's own commentary to the principles does.

4. I use this particular phrasing to encompass both those rabbis who propose vegetarianism as merely one valid option among others, and those who see a moral mandate to practice vegetarianism. While at certain points in this paper these two levels of interest in vegetarianism will be distinguished, they will generally be dealt with simultaneously.

5. Knobel, "Reform Judaism and Kashrut," 489.

6. Of course, this is not to say that some individuals or congregations do not consciously pull resources from "ethical" activities like social justice programs and put them toward "ritual"-oriented programming. There is in Reform life an ongoing tension between these two poles of religious practice. Nonetheless, looking broadly at the Reform Movement, the dramatic return to ritual has by no means been paralleled by similarly dramatic attacks upon Reform social activism and political engagement. As we shall see in the case of kashrut, the streams that champion ritual and the streams that champion ethics may run together.

7. Those arguing for complete abandonment of the dietary laws include Holdheim, Einhorn, Kohler, Chorin, and the Leipzig Synod. Those arguing for modification of the dietary laws include Wiener and Creiznach. For sources and discussion see citations given in footnote 1.

8. For further discussion, see: (1) Knobel, "Reform Judaism and Kashrut," 489 and (2) the more extensive discussion in Jacob B. Agnus, "The Reform Movement," in *Understanding American Judaism*, ed. Jacob Neusner (New York: Ktav, 1975), 12–19.

9. W. Gunther Plaut, *The Rise of Reform Judaism* (New York: World Union for Progressive Judaism, 1963), p. 212.

10. As cited in: W. Gunther Plaut, *The Growth of Reform Judaism* (New York: World Union for Progressive Judaism, 1965), 266.

11. David Philipson, *The Reform Movement in Judaism* (New York: Macmillan, 1931), 189.

12. What I report here is admittedly anecdotal, but I trust it is not controversial. One popular-press article reports, "Richard Levy [former CCAR president] remembers well a conversation he had with a fellow student in his first year of rabbinical school. . . . The two rabbis-to-be were discussing Jewish dietary restrictions, and felt that Reform Jews should eat pork on principle" (Alexandra Wall, "Reform Rabbis Debate Virtues of a Veggie Diet," *Jewish Bulletin News of Northern California*, July 20,

2001, viewed at www.jewishsf.com/bk010720/ fp6a.shtrnl on June 23, 2003). Such stories are commonplace.

13. As has been emphasized by the recent research of Rabbi Lance Sussman, the avoidance of pork was viewed differently from other rules of kashrut in early Reform, so it is perhaps no accident that pork was avoided while other laws were flaunted. Seafood in particular was seen as healthful and therefore viewed more positively. Sussman's research is not yet published, but some of his key points are discussed in Debra Nussbaum Cohen, "Taste-House of Worship: A Menu for Reform," *Wall Street Journal*, July 6, 2001, W11.

14. Ronald H. Isaacs and Kerry M. Olitzky, *Critical Documents of Jewish History: A Sourcebook* (Northvale, NJ: Jason Aronson, 1995), 60.

15. Knobel, "Reform Judaism and Kashrut," 488.

16. Michael A. Meyer, *Response to Modernity* (New York, Oxford: Oxford University Press, 1988).

17. Ibid., 325.

18. Union of American Hebrew Congregations (now Union of Reform Judaism).

19. Knobel, "Reform Judaism and Kashrut," 491.

20. Ibid.

21. Ibid., p. 492.

22. Ibid.

23. For discussion, see speech of Richard Levy, then president of the CCAR, "Remarks to the UAHC Board of Trustees in Memphis Regarding 'Ten Principles of Reform Judaism,'" given December 5, 1998.

24. Richard Levy, "Is It Time to Chart a New Course for Reform Judaism?" (interview), *Reform Judaism*, Winter 1998, 4 (pagination follows online version).

25. Ibid., p. 5 (pagination follows online version).

26. Even if the *t'reifah* banquet itself was a catering error, the disputes that followed it more than suggest a willingness on the part of Reformers to alienate traditionalists over this issue. For example, Wise was hardly sympathetic with the ire of traditionalists over the incident. Conservative rabbi and scholar Neil Gillman, in his history of the Conservative Movement, emphasizes that, while Wise himself may have intended that the event be kosher, he nonetheless "bitterly denounced the traditionalists for their concern over what he disparaged as kitchen Judaism. 'It is about time to stop that noise over the culinary department of Judaism. The American Hebrew's religion centers not in kitchen and stomach. . . . It has some more important matters to attend to'" (Neal Gillman [quotation is Wise], *Conservative Judaism: The New Century* [New York: Behrman House, 1996], 25–26).

27. There are some voices calling for a new approach to autonomy. See, e.g., the following critique of autonomy regarding kashrut from a liberal perspective: Alan Henkin, "Kashrut and Autonomy," p. xx. However, in the official Reform statements on kashrut, individual autonomy has remained entirely intact even if more emphasis has been laid on the individual considering the larger community in his or her decision-making process.

28. Levy, "Is It Time to Chart," 3 (pagination follows online version).

29. Simeon Maslin, ed., *Gates of Mitzvah* (New York: CCAR Press, 1979), 132.

30. Knobel, "Reform Judaism and Kashrut," 491.

31. Maslin, *Gates of Mitzvah*, 132. The use of kashrut to foster intra-Jewish solidarity is also cited in the Reform responsum "Kashrut in Reform Judaism" (see note 1); in the CCAR's Commentary to the 1999 PP under their comments to the text "As individuals and as a community" (see p. 9 [pagination follows online version]), http://ccarnet.org/Articles/index.cfm?id=45&pge_prg_id=4687&pge_id=1656; and in Simeon Maslin, "Who Are Authentic Jews?" *Reform Judaism*, Summer 1996, 2 (pagination follows online version).

32. Levy, "Is It Time to Chart," 3 (pagination follows online version).

33. Maslin, "Who Are Authentic Jews?" 2–3.

34. The association of kashrut with concern for animals predates the modern period and is already highly developed in Maimonides, who writes in his discussion of kashrut in *Guide of the Perplexed*, "Since the necessity to have good food requires that animals be killed, the aim was to kill them in the easiest manner, and it was forbidden to torment them through killing them in a reprehensible manner" (Moses Maimonides, *The Guide of the Perplexed*, trans. Shlomo Pines [Chicago: University of Chicago Press, 1963], 3:48, 112a, p. 599.

35. Plaut, *Growth of Reform Judaism*, 265.

36. Cited in ibid., 266.

37. Cited in ibid., 267.

38. Ibid., 266.

39. Michael Metcalf, "Regulating Slaughter: Animal Protection and Anti-Semitism in Scandinavia, 1880–1941," in *Judaism and Animal Rights: Classical and Contemporary Responses*, ed. Roberta Kalechofsky (Marblehead, MA: Micah, 1992), 114–26.

40. See, e.g., Maslin, *Gates of Mitzvah*, 132; the 1979 CCAR responsum, "Kashrut in Reform Judaism"; the CCAR's Commentary to the 1999 PP, 9 (pagination follows online version); Maslin, "Who Are Authentic Jews?" 2 (pagination follows online version); and Levy, "Is It Time to Chart," 3 (pagination follows online version).

41. Knobel, "Reform Judaism and Kashrut," 491.

42. Quote from personal correspondence with Barry Schwartz, May 2002. In accord with Schwartz's comments regarding labor, the CCAR's Commentary to the 1999 PP suggests that the "oppression of those who work the fields to harvest our foods" might inform a Reform practice of kashrut (p. 10 [pagination follows online version]).

43. This proposed resolution is presently entitled "Resolution on Judaism, the Environment and Dietary Health."

44. For a highly informed, though polemical, discussion of how traditional Jewish teachings discourage vegetarianism, see the anti-vegetarian piece by David Bleich, "Vegetarianism and Judaism," in *Judaism and Environmental Ethics*, ed. Martin D. Yaffe (Boulder, CO: Lanham Lexington Books, 2001).

45. For a discussion of textual sources, see the pro-vegetarian book by Richard H. Schwartz, *Judaism and Vegetarianism* (New York: Lantern Books, 2001), 1–2.

46. For examples, see the list of brief biographies compiled in ibid., 171–78.

47. Mimi Platt Zimmerman, "What Value Does Kashrut Have for Reform Jews Today?" (UAHC Department of Adult Jewish Growth, August 26, 2000), 1 (pagination follows online version; viewed on http://uahc.org/torah/issue/000819.shtml_on June 29, 2003).

48. Edward Rosenthal, "Ethical Vegetarianism: The Perspective of a Reform Jew," *CCAR Journal* (Spring 1992), 50.

49. Harold M. Schulweis, "Thou Shalt Eat Vegetables," *Reform Judaism*, Summer 1995, 24.

50. Ibid.

51. A possible historical background to this current advocacy is that a handful of German Jews in the early 1900s and again in the 1920s advocated vegetarianism and Zionism in a messianic framework (personal discussion with Asher Biemann, May 2002). See, e.g., Leopold Schwarz, "Neu-Essäertum und Zionismus," in *Die Stimme der Wahrheit: Jahrbuch für wissenschaftlichen Zionismus: Erster Jahrgang*, ed. Lazar Schön (Würzburg: N. Philippi, 1905), 234–59. If there is such a historical link, perhaps through the several famous Yiddish writers who were vegetarian advocates and/or Rav Kook, it is not one about which contemporary Reform advocates of "messianic vegetarianism" seem conscious.

52. Reform sources citing all three arguments include Rosenthal (see note 48), Schulweis (see note 49), the proposed CCAR resolution endorsing vegetarianism, and an unpublished essay by Richard Litvak, "A Contemporary Perspective of Reform Judaism on the Spiritual and Ethical Dimensions of Eating," which Barry Schwartz informs me has been circulating among CCAR rabbis interested in eco-kashrut.

53. This information about the formation and structure of the Task Force on Kashrut was provided to me by Barry Schwartz, who chairs the Subcommittee on Eco-Kashrut, from a CCAR internal memo dated June 20, 2001.

54. As with the association of animal welfare and kashrut (see note 34), the tendency to link kashrut with health goes back at least as far as Maimonides, who argued that the food excluded by kashrut is less hygienic and less healthful. See Maimonides, *The Guide of the Perplexed*, trans. Pines, 3:48, 112a, pp. 588–99.

55. I will not detail this phenomenon here, but refer the interested reader to Jenna Weissman Joselit, "Culture on a Plate: What Our Dietary Choices Tell Us about Ourselves," *Reform Judaism*, Winter 1998, p. 28.

56. In 1997, the American Dietetic Association summarized extant nutritional research pertaining to vegetarianism and concluded, "Scientific data suggest positive relationships between a vegetarian diet and reduced risk for several chronic degenerative diseases and conditions, including obesity, coronary artery disease, hypertension, diabetes mellitus, and some types of cancer" (American Dietetic Association, "Position of the American Dietetic Association," *Journal of the American Dietetic Association* 97 [November 1997]: 11). Although the healthfulness of vegetarian diets is now widely acknowledged, there are of course a variety of opinions among individual specialists on this issue.

57. Personal interview with Barry Schwartz, May 2002.

58. Ibid.

59. Lynn White's 1967 essay, "The Historical Roots of Our Ecologic Crisis" is the most cited critique.

60. One widely respected scientific discussion of these and other effects of dietary choices is A. B. Durning and H. B. Brough, *Taking Stock: Animal Farming and the Environment*, Worldwatch Paper 103 (Washington, DC: Worldwatch Institute, 1991).

61. Among those who have advanced theological arguments for practicing kashrut through vegetarianism, perhaps the most prominent is the former president of the

Reconstructionist Rabbinical College, Arthur Green. See Arthur Green, *Seek My Face, Speak My Name* (Northvale, NJ: London: Jason Aronson, 1994), 87–89.

62. The increasing prominence of ecological concerns is witnessed in a variety of areas including: (1) the prominent inclusion of environmental concerns in the legislative agenda of the Reform Movement's political action branch, the Religious Action Center (see relevant sections of www.rac.org); (2) the handful of CCAR resolutions and responsa on the environment since the late 1970s; (3) the inclusion of ecologically minded language in the 1999 PP, which calls upon Jews "to protect the earth's biodiversity and natural resources"; and (4) the fact that the *CCAR Journal* devoted the entirety of its Winter 2001 issue to a symposium on "Judaism and the Environment."

63. Personal interview with Barry Schwartz, May 2002.

64. A practice of vegetarian-kashrut, for example, may include abstention not only from meat, but from nonkosher vegetable oils and spices that are likely to be contaminated with *t'reif*; such a practice also may require, as no gentile vegetarian diet would, the observance of traditional Jewish law on the contamination of cookware.

65. Maslin, *Gates of Mitzvah*, 133.

22

MEAT MINIMALISM
Were We Meant to Be Ethical Omnivores?

Karen R. Perolman

In the ever-expanding lexicon of food-related vocabulary, "flexitarian" is among the newest ways to explain one's ethical and omnivorous diet. Flexitarian, like "meat minimalist" and "weekday vegetarian," is a useful term to describe a growing movement of omnivores who are interested in maintaining an ethical diet without becoming vegetarians or vegans. In the Jewish food movement, this subgroup is gaining attention and speed as Jews attempt to find a way to resolve the conflict between their cultural and culinary desire to consume the meat of animals and the realities of the modern factory-farmed animal industry.

In the last decade, vegetarianism and, to some extent, veganism have become the most popular way in which Jews demonstrate their desire to reconcile Jewish ethics with the reality of the inherently unethical kosher and nonkosher meat industries; sidestepping all things meat related allows these Jews to express their desire to eat according to the laws of kashrut without consuming the meat of animals. However, vegetarianism is not a new way to eat; in fact, it is commonly accepted that the first human beings ate an exclusively vegetarian diet according to God's command in the Garden of Eden: "Look, I have given you all the seed-bearing plants on the face of the earth, and every tree that has in it seed-bearing fruit—these are yours to eat" (Gen. 1:29). The Talmud and, later, the nineteenth-century Italian biblical commentator Umberto Cassuto drew from this verse that the "natural" human diet is one free of meat, and that the original human beings ate only vegetation.[1]

Despite the growing numbers of Jewish vegetarians, most Jews still desire and eat a diet that includes the meat of animals. Yet, a certain amount of cognitive dissonance occurs when one wants both to eat according to Jewish law and values *and* to eat meat. For many Jews, eating meat is not an irrelevant religious pastime; rather it is one of the ways history, ritual, time, and culture are expressed. Simply look at the menu for any Jewish holiday and you'll find meat as the main course: brisket on Rosh HaShanah, matzah ball soup on Passover, chopped liver and chicken on Shabbat, and corned beef on rye for no reason at all. It is undeniable that meat plays an important and established role in holiday celebration, perhaps because of the Talmudic dictum "When the Temple was in existence, there could be no joy without meat" (Babylonian Talmud, *P'sachim* 109a). Temple or not, Jews still concur that eating meat elevates celebrations. Consider, for example, the Ashkenazic z'mirot that wax poetic on the abundance of meat served on Shabbat,[2] and *Birkat HaMazon* (Blessing after Meals), which contains a reference to *mat'nat basar v'dam* (the gifts of flesh and blood).[3] Meat sanctifies time, it would seem, symbolizing the use of "our very best" to elevate the day. For some, it is a weekly reminder of abundance bestowed upon us by a generous and caring God.

Despite the cultural and religious pressure to consume meat, kosher meat, especially ethically raised and slaughtered varieties, is an expensive luxury that is often unattainable. This epicurean expense echoes the plight of the ancient Israelites, who were only permitted to eat the meat of animals if they could also afford to own livestock and suffer the economic loss of the animal.[4] Regardless of the expense to a family to serve chicken soup on Friday evenings, *cholent* (traditional meat stew) for Shabbat lunch, or meat entrees at a bar mitzvah party, the value of the celebration apparently outweighs any monetary concern.

The "valuing" of meat and subsequent association of meat with wealth began in seventeenth-century Eastern Europe, when impoverished Jews idealized meat as the ultimate Shabbat meal. Despite their meager means, meat was the ultimate expression of *oneg* (the joy of) Shabbat. Once in America, it would seem, the prophecy of Sholem Aleichem became a reality: "In America you could have chicken soup and challah in the middle of the week!"[5] With each successive generation of Jews in America, meat became more and more a staple of daily meals. While meat and potatoes became standard for the weekday meals of American Jews, the Shabbat standards, including meat dishes like pot roast and brisket, were clung to with tenacity, perhaps as reminders of the past. Even today contemporary North American Jews, for the most part, maintain their carnivorous customs. An outward sign of prosperity, "meat meals" continue to be glorified even as kosher meat becomes financially exorbitant, ethically problematic, and altogether unhealthy.

Given the opposing values of traditional cuisine and contemporary ethics, how should an ethically minded, rational Reform Jew make decisions about what meat to eat? Some solve this problem by limiting their meat consumption to kosher animals only raised in ways that meet certain standards, including grass-fed or grass-finished beef, cage-free eggs, and poultry raised without hormones or antibiotics. Others choose to eat nonkosher meat that also adheres to these standards although not *hekshered* (labeled as kosher by a recognized kashrut certification authority). For these Jews, eating ethically raised, nonkosher animals is as important and sacred a choice as it is for those who choose to eat kosher meat. Many would identify with the current and growing "green kosher" movement, made up of those who understand kashrut from a broad perspective that includes ethical as well as halachic elements.

Perhaps the newest incarnation of the ethical omnivore is the Jew willing to eat standard kosher meat, but with less frequency and thus in less quantity. Aaron Potek, a student at Pardes in Jerusalem, is the founder of MOOSHY (Meat only on Shabbat, Happy Occasions, and

Yom Tov), a philosophy of reduced, yet consecrated meat eating. As Potek explains, "The idea behind [MOOSHY] is simple: limit the amount of meat you eat and sanctify the meat you do eat."[6] Drawing on the Talmudic principle of *ein simchah elah basar* ("there is no joy without meat" [Babylonian Talmud, *P'sachim* 109a]), Potek follows a "meat-minimalist" diet, eating meat only on Shabbat, Jewish holidays, and *s'machot* such as weddings and *b'nei mitzvah*. Potek acknowledges that the MOOSHY movement is a small one that will not necessarily create systematic change in the larger Jewish community. Yet, attention to the frequency and type of meat eaten is the first step toward the larger promise of "improv[ing] our world and act[ing] in a way I believe God intended."[7]

Like Potek, many of MOOSHY's followers define themselves as Conservative and Orthodox Jews; however, the religious meat-minimalist perspective is pluralistic. In fact, a "meat-light" diet similar to MOOSHY was one of the centerpieces of Rabbi Eric Yoffie's 2009 Union for Reform Judaism Biennial Address. Standing before three thousand Reform Jewish lay and professional leaders, Yoffie, president of the URJ, made the bold statement, "Let's make a Jewish decision to reduce significantly the amount of red meat that we eat."[8] Yoffie went on to explain why reducing meat consumption is indeed a Jewish issue: while meat consumption has dramatically increased, the natural resources necessary for the production of meat are rapidly being depleted. At the same time, Yoffie raised the health axiom that a diet heavy in meat products is more likely to lead to health problems, such as heart disease and cancer. According to Yoffie, Jews consume too much meat on account of the assumption that the only way to honor Shabbat and holidays is through the eating of meat. He concluded, "For the first twenty-five hundred years of our three-thousand year history, Jews consumed meat sparingly, and we can surely do the same."[9]

Across the Jewish spectrum, whether one decreases meat intake because of religious, environmental, or health concerns, a commitment to consume less meat is emerging as another thoughtful and important way for Jewish omnivores to remain true to both religious and ethical imperatives. This phenomenon is also becoming popularized within the larger "green food" movement. In his newest food instruction manual *Food Rules*, Michael Pollan suggests that one should "treat meat as a flavoring or special occasion food." Pollan also presents the simple Chinese proverb "Eating what stands on one leg [mushrooms and plant foods] is better than eating what stands on two legs [fowl], which is better than what stands on four legs [cows, pigs and other mammals]."[10] Similarly, in his vegetarian manifesto *Eating Animals*, Jonathan Safran Foer implores readers to examine the type and frequency of the meat they eat and to evaluate if it, in fact, corresponds to their values, be they religious or ethical.[11]

Where do these arguments leave the ethically minded Reform Jew? The answer is not as simple as "eat meat" or "don't eat meat." The argument we must have is the way in which we eat meat. How much? How often? For what reasons? One way we might begin this conversation is to take a closer look at our shopping carts, refrigerators, and dinner tables. Once we take stock of our current meat-eating habits, then we should take the advice of MOOSHY and Rabbi Yoffie to reduce our meat consumption. In order to be aligned with our Jewish values, we should ensure that meat does not become another food consumed easily and without thought. Limiting meat to special occasions like Shabbat and choosing vegetarian options frequently does not lessen our connection to Judaism's most iconic food; if anything, this serves to sanctify and honor it.

NOTES

1. Babylonian Talmud, *Sanhedrin* 59a–b; Umberto Cassuto, *A Commentary on the Book of Genesis: Part One—From Adam to Noah* (Jerusalem: Hebrew University Press, 1944), 58.

2. Examples include, but are not limited to *Mah Y'didut*, *Yom Zeh M'chubad*, *Ki Eshm'rah Shabbat* (from *A Limmud Shabbat* [London: Lancaster House, 2006]).

3. *A Limmud Shabbat*, 11.

4. Rashi, on Babylonian Talmud, *Sanhedrin* 59a–b.

5. Hasia R. Diner, *Hungering for America Italian, Irish, and Jewish Foodways in the Age of Immigration* (Cambridge, MA: Harvard University Press, 2001), 177.

6. Aaron Potek, "Mooshy: Balancing Morals and Morsels," *Presentense*, Winter 2009, 20, http://issuu.com/presentense/docs/pt7/22?mode=a_p (accessed January 15, 2010).

7. Ibid.

8. Rabbi Eric Yoffie, "2009 Biennial Shabbat Sermon." http://blogs.rj.org/reform/2009/11/president-yoffies-shabbat-serm.html.

9. Ibid.

10. Michael Pollan, *Food Rules: An Eater's Manual* (New York: Penguin Books, 2009), 53–55.

11. Jonathan Safran Foer, *Eating Animals* (New York: Back Bay Books, 2010).

23

BLOOD, SWEAT, AND TEARS

The Making of a Reform *Shochet*

JOSH WHINSTON AND GERSH LAZAROW

How two rabbinic students arrived at the idea that we needed to slaughter animals ourselves is as important a part of our story as the slaughter itself. Thinking about food and the process of how it comes to the table has become a national obsession over the past decade; Jews, however, have been concerned with this for millennia. Even before we decided to embark on a lengthy study of the laws of *sh'chitah*, ritual slaughter, our own eating habits were evolving. One of us was a recent vegetarian who came to vegetarianism for kosher reasons; the other an omnivore who ate only kosher meat. We were both dissatisfied with the state of the kosher meat industry and its seemingly blinkered attitude toward animal welfare and sustainable farming. While many grocers across the country were offering consumers real choice at the checkout, kosher shoppers seemed to be limited to only two or three options with almost no reliable information about the conditions under which that meat had been brought to market.

Our dissatisfaction was made only more intense after the revelations related to the Agriprocessors fiasco in Postville, Iowa, were made public at the end of 2007. The inhumane treatment of both workers and animals disgusted us. Then and there, we committed to learning everything we could about *sh'chitah*. We began meeting weekly, translating and discussing Rambam's *Mishneh Torah, Hilchot Sh'chitah*. Like the text, our discussion focused on the intricacies of ritual slaughter—how to cut, with what to cut, where to cut. We purchased scientific diagrams and explored bovine and fowl anatomy in ways we had not done even in high school biology class. Our initial goal was clear: become experts on the relevant *sh'chitah* texts. Over a seven-month period, we studied with our teacher, Dr. Stephen Passamaneck, analyzing and interpreting the text.

Throughout the study project, we joked about putting what we had learned to use. Yet, it is unclear when the exact moment occurred that we began to take our knowledge and ourselves more seriously. Our first task was to find a *mumcheh*, an expert, as the halachah stipulates that a *shochet* must be trained by another expert *shochet*.[1] Having no desire to slaughter alone, and wanting our animals to be slaughtered with the highest standards, we began a search for a *shochet* who would train us to slaughter. We both agreed that we would travel anywhere in the country to train. Sadly, we were unable to find a willing *shochet*. All of the *shochtim* we contacted had no desire to train two Reform rabbinical students in the art of kosher slaughter. Some even laughed at the idea. The one Conservative rabbi who is slaughtering in this country felt he was too new and inexperienced to train others. Therefore, since no teacher existed for us, we decided to proceed with the only real support coming from the texts of our tradition. In making this decision, we took heart from the fact that the *Shulchan Aruch* allows for one to eat the slaughter of an unfamiliar *shochet* if, on inquiry, he is knowledgeable of the laws and procedures.[2]

The *sh'chitah* procedure itself consists of a rapid transverse incision with an instrument of surgical sharpness, called a *chalaf*, which severs the major structures and vessels at the neck (*simanim*). The *Shulchan Aruch* makes it clear that the *chalaf* must be perfectly smooth without the minutest notch or irregularity.[3] As it became increasingly obvious that we were going to have to lead ourselves though this process, we spent a great deal of time mastering the requirements of the *chalaf* before making our way down to the kitchen supply store Sur La Table to purchase what we felt was as perfect a blade as we could find. The shop assistant thought we were insane, but we felt confident that we were well on our way.

With knife in hand, we then turned our attention fully to the actual requirements of the slaughter. The *Shulchan Aruch* details five halachic prerequisites that the *shochet* must ensure in order to correctly perform *sh'chitah*. When we finished studying with Dr. Passamaneck, we produced the only known translation of the key chapters from the *Shulchan Aruch* that detail these requirements:[4]

1. *Sh'hiyah*: there should be no interruption of the incision.
2. *D'rasah*: there should be no pressing of the *chalaf* against the neck, excluding use of an axe, hatchet, or guillotine.
3. *Chaladah*: the *chalaf* should not be covered by the hide of cattle, wool of sheep, or feathers of birds, and therefore the *chalaf* has to be of adequate length.
4. *Hagramah*: the incision must be at the appropriate site to sever the major structures and vessels at the neck.
5. *Ikur*: there must be no tearing of the vessels before or during the *sh'chitah* process.

Finally, we needed an animal to slaughter. We were confident in our knowledge but were by no means ready to slaughter livestock. We thought poultry, with its small size and simple anatomy, would be a more than sufficient measure of our knowledge. The challenge then became, where do two rabbinical students find live chickens in the middle of Los Angeles? We scoured the Internet for suitable suppliers but could find nothing locally. Our search seemed futile; we worried that Los Angeles's urban sprawl had beaten us, when on a whim we decided to try Chinatown. As it happens, the Hebrew Union College Los Angeles campus is situated just a few miles from the Los Angeles Chinatown, and before we could talk each other out of it, we were in the car. Within minutes we where driving down North Broadway, and to our astonishment, we saw a giant wooden chicken perched on top of a building, with the words Superior Poultry sprawled across the front. We parked our car, got out, entered the store, and realized that our seven-month journey was now rushing to a fairly daunting conclusion.

With the last puzzle piece in place, the time had arrived for us to put our months of learning into practice. Not knowing exactly how long the process was going to take us, we decided to return the next morning. Like the shop assistant at Sur La Table, the staff at Superior Poultry seemed most bemused by our presence. Believing fundamentally that the way an animal dies is as important as the way it lived, our plan called for us to source birds that were raised to the highest ethical standards. Regrettably, when we explained this to the Superior Poultry staff, we where informed that our only choice was between brown or white, not cage-free or hormone-free chickens. We purchased six white birds and had them boxed for the hour-long drive to our slaughter location. We had chosen to use a local summer camp, as it offered both the privacy we desired and the industrial kitchen we thought we might require.

On arrival at the camp, we released the birds into a pen and began to work setting up the slaughter site. To our surprise the text actually provided very little insight with regard to this task, and we found ourselves leaning heavily on the lessons we learned from watching hours of footage on YouTube. We knew that the birds would be calmed if they could be held by their feet with their heads hanging toward the ground. We knew that both hands would be needed to perform the actual slaughter, so we erected a gallows of sorts that would allow us to place the bird's feet into a slipknot that would pull tight under the bird's weight. We set up a cleaning station, which included boiling water and an ice bath, and then we checked our knife for imperfections.

Wearing rain slickers and gloves, we prepared to get dirty. One by one, we brought the birds out and placed their feet in the slipknot, letting them hang upside down as they began to relax. Once all wing flapping had ceased, being careful to hide the knife from the bird's view, we came up alongside the bird and gently took hold of its body. Placing the bird between our arms and body at an angle toward the ground, we once again waited as the bird calmed down and acclimated to its new position. Using our free hand, as instructed by the text, it was necessary to remove some of the feathers on the neck to better reveal the *simanim*, the major structures and vessels at the neck. Once found, we said the appropriate blessings and cut.

There is no doubt, whether or not we happened to make a kosher cut, we were learning as we were cutting. How heavy a hand to use while cutting was key to making the cut kosher. We needed to cut the *simanim* and, at the same time, not cut too deep in order to avoid hitting bone and causing a nick in our knife or the *simanim* themselves. The technicalities of a kosher cut kept us focused; the details of cutting helped us remove ourselves from the reality of what we were doing— taking a life. What forced us quickly back into the moment was the feeling of life leaving the body we were holding in our hands. Once the cut was made and the blood began to spill onto the ground, the birds continued to breathe for a few moments. More than the sight of the blood flowing from the neck, we will never forget feeling the bird's breast cease expanding and contracting. Feeling life leave a body is shocking and unforgettable.

More than we could have ever have imagined, the text spoke to us in this life-ceasing moment. Out of respect for the slaughtered animal and its life, tradition dictates that the *shochet* is obligated to cover the blood with earth and recite a blessing acknowledging the life that was taken. Time and time again, whether the cut was kosher or not, we found ourselves kneeling in front of the slaughtered bird, painstakingly ensuring that every drop of blood was collected and covered. It is difficult to describe how humbling this experience was and how much it affirmed the belief that our kashrut is not something we should outsource to either multinational companies or religious organizations that don't share our sensibilities, ethics, or values.

In April 2009 we slaughtered six chickens; upon examination we agreed that four of them were kosher. In so doing we became *shochtim*, in all likelihood the first *shochtim* to ever identify as Reform Jews. It was an incredible journey that began in disgust and awe. Our goal had never been to make *sh'chitah* part of our regular ritual practice, but rather to reaffirm our belief that real and lasting choice can only be made through knowledge and experience. To this day, one of us remains a vegetarian, and the other an omnivore who eats only kosher meat.

NOTES

1. The *Shulchan Aruch, Yoreh Dei-ah*: "It is customary not to allow a person to slaughter unless he is an observant Jew [see 2:1–2ff.] and a qualified scholar has certified that he knows the relevant laws [see 18:17, 23:1, 25:1], and it is customary that women not be slaughterers [see 1:1–2]."

2. *Shulchan Aruch, Yoreh Dei-ah* 1:1 "When that person is not in front of us, then it is OK to eat from that which he has slaughtered and to rely on the halachic assumption; but if he is in front of us, we must check if, in fact, he is an expert and if he knows the laws of ritual slaughter."

3. *Shulchan Aruch, Yoreh Dei-ah* 6:1: "The instrument must be free of blemishes on or close to its cutting edges that can 'catch' even an object as thin as a hair [see 18:2, 18:4–6, 18:10]. It should be checked (by touch) for such blemishes both before and after slaughtering with it [18:3, 18:9, 18:11–12]; this checking must be done very carefully by a qualified expert [18:17]. If a blemish is found after slaughter, the slaughter is invalid even though no blemish was present before slaughter [18:1; see also 18:11, 18:13, 18:15–16]."

4. For more details, see *Shulchan Aruch, Yoreh Dei-ah*, chaps. 23 and 24, available online at http://en.wikisource.org/wiki/Shulchan_Aruch/Yoreh_Deah#Ritual_Slaughter.

24

REAL LIFE / REAL FOOD
A Letter to My Vegetarian Husband

ZOË KLEIN

To: My vegetarian husband
From: His guilt-ridden wife, who keeps falling off the vegetable cart

We are both rabbis. We've studied the same texts. We've turned
the same verses over and over, examining them like gems under
a magnifying glass, full of refractions of color and light. We both
understand that only after Noah's sacrificial offerings did God say,
"Any small animal that is alive shall be food for you, like green
grasses" (Gen. 9:3). The sanction to eat meat is given the moment
after God realizes "the human mind inclines to evil from youth
onward" (Gen. 8:21). Perhaps that was the violence God saw Noah's
generation commit. The carnivorous drive of both man and beast so
horrified heaven that the ducts of the deep were opened and the land
welled over with torrential tears.

We have both turned over the verse "You shall not boil a kid in its
mother's milk" (Exod. 23:19, 34:26; Deut. 14:21). In Exodus 23, this
verse follows verses on sacrifice, festal offerings, and choice first fruits.

Biblical scholars understand it to be referring to ancient Egyptian sacrifices, not necessarily how we prepare our food. But we've also drunk from the Talmud and been fed by the commentators, who understand it as a prohibition against cooking milk and meat together. We've encountered the fences built around that law.

You remember all the late nights when I was finishing my rabbinic thesis, "Animal Sacrifice and the Continual Offering in the Second Temple Period." In my studies, I learned that the deep-rooted instinct to sacrifice grew out of basic archaic taboos on eating flesh and the need to reconcile mortal frailties with the gods upon whom man believed his well-being depended. After the Flood, meat eating is God's concession to an imperfect mankind, and man, being acutely aware of his imperfection and ashamed before the Creator for his hunger for flesh, attempts to elevate the entire process, legitimizing it by turning the animal into an offering. God, apologetically, is invited to the table. I remember what Jacob Milgrom wrote in *Studies in Cultic Theology and Terminology*: "Man will have meat for his food and will kill to get it. The Bible has therefore worked out a system of restrictions whereby man may satiate his lust for animal flesh and yet not be dehumanized in the process."[1]

I remember when we were dating, I felt ashamed when I had a hot dog. I would have a stick of spearmint gum, like a smoker, before seeing you. When I was pregnant, I wanted my body to be like Eden for our child, where only the fruit of most trees and the green of the earth were food, where there was no killing—an idyllic serenity of species cohabiting. But my body craved more iron than spinach could provide.

I love that there are never bones in our kitchen. I love that when you take me to kosher vegetarian restaurants, I can close my eyes and point to anything on the menu and know it will be fresh, healthy, and good. Chicken-less nuggets are packed in our children's lunches.

I try, when confronted with a burger, to remember the starry eyes of the little cow in our daughter's book. I try to eat low on the food chain: fish before chicken before beef. And then Friday nights, the preschool presents trays of savory meat *cholent*.

Judaism recognizes our *yetzer hara* (evil inclination) and teaches us to harness it. It understands that we crave meat and, instead of saying do not eat it, commands us not to mix death with life, to separate out the blood, which is its life force, and to not mix it with milk, which represents birth and life. To mix them is to accept the world as it is—fragmented, haphazard, where people die suddenly or too slowly, too young, death and life at random. Rather, we separate them, indicating that everything should happen in its proper time. To everything there is a season. And someday, God willing, there will be that final season, when every day is Shabbat, when we reenter Eden.

Until that day, I repent, and attempt, and repent, and attempt again to join you in expressing adoration for the wild, bristling, and breathing world through the choices I make. Until that day, when the lioness with the heart of a lamb will lay down peacefully with her lamb, who has the giant heart of a lion.

NOTE

1. Jacob Milgrom, *Studies in Cultic Theology and Terminology* (Leiden, The Netherlands: E.J. Brill, 1983), p. 104.

Part Five

Concern for Oppressed Food Workers: *Oshek*

In his reprinted article, "*Oshek*: The Meeting Point of Ritual Piety and Moral Purity in a Contemporary Reform Kashrut" (originally published in the *CCAR Journal*, Winter 2004), Richard Litvak defines *oshek*, the oppression of a laborer, and applies this value to Reform dietary practice. In doing so, Litvak reminds us of Reform Judaism's proud history of supporting the United Farm Workers. Recalling this important period in our past, Peter E. Kasdan ("A Look Back at the Reform Movement's Response to the United Farm Workers Grape Boycott") shares a unique, personal view of this social action uprising, which involved so many in the Reform Movement. In "Our Dark Addictions: Chocolate, Coffee, and Tea," Deborah Prinz widens our discussion of workers' rights by delving into the abuses of workers in the chocolate industry and by educating us about fair trade solutions. While Joseph Aaron Skoot's "Let Your Table Be to You a Temple" is found in part 3, on *bal tashchit*, his essay also offers insight into the plight of modern farmers and speaks to the theme of this section as well. In the "Real Life / Real Food" chapter, Robert J. Marx ("Post-Postville and Onward") shares his point of view on the aftermath of the closing of this kosher slaughterhouse in Iowa, exploring its impact on the immigrant workers.

I had the honor to invite these writers to contribute to this section. We are blessed to have them shed light on *oshek* issues, but these authors have too few peers. While there are certainly many passionate Reform Jewish leaders involved in social justice causes, the number of Jews actively fighting for agricultural workers' rights no longer matches our involvement in the 1970s. I hope these articles will inspire our generation of Reform Jews to hear the prophetic call for justice and to work toward that goal.

25

OSHEK

The Meeting Point of Ritual Piety and Moral Purity in a
Contemporary Reform Kashrut

RICHARD LITVAK

The study of *oshek* gives the contemporary Reform Jew a way of looking at the nexus of ritual practice and social justice in sanctification of our daily meals. *Oshek*, the oppression of a laborer, is forbidden by the Torah (Lev. 19:13–14). It is a transgression against God as well as against the exploited worker (Lev. 19:11–13). *Oshek* is first prohibited in the "Holiness Code" in Leviticus 19:13: *Lo taashok et rei-acha*, "Do not oppress your neighbor. Do not withhold that which is due your neighbor and do not rob him. The wages earned by a day laborer shall not remain overnight with you until the morning." It occurs again in Deuteronomy 24:14–15: *Lu taashok sachir oni v'evyon mei-achecha o m'geir'cha asher b'artz'cha bisharecha*, "You shall not abuse a needy and destitute laborer, whether a fellow countryman or a stranger in one of the communities of your land. You must pay him his wages on the same day, before the sun sets, for he is needy and he sets his heart on it; else he will cry to the Lord against you and you will incur

Adapted with permission from Richard Litvak, "*Osheq*: The Meeting Point of Ritual Piety and Moral Purity in a Contemporary Reform Kashrut," *CCAR Journal*, Winter 2004, 38–44.

guilt." Writing in eleventh-century France, Rashi interpreted this text prohibiting *oshek* to apply particularly to the farm worker. *V'eilav hu noseh et nafsho,* "It is the farm worker who risks his *nefesh,* his life, climbing up a ladder or hanging from a tree to do his work."[1] The classic sacred sources of Judaism call on us to actively oppose the oppression or exploitation of the farm worker who frequently toils under dangerous conditions.[2]

What then is the relationship between Jewish dietary ritual and the prohibition of *oshek*? The prophet Isaiah preached that exploitation of the laborer actually nullifies the value of a dietary ritual observance (Isa. 57:14–58:14). In these passages, Isaiah proclaimed that God is unresponsive to the ritual piety of fasting while the laborer is oppressed. Instead, God desires a fast comprised of breaking every yoke, sharing one's bread with the hungry, housing the homeless, and clothing the naked. This view became so essential to Judaism that Isaiah's words became the haftarah portion for the Day of Atonement. It provides the linkage every Yom Kippur between fulfilling the dietary ritual of fasting and the ethical responsibilities of social justice. Isaiah's ancient words described the social justice goals we help fulfill when we become part of the contemporary farm workers' movement.[3]

In biblical times, one of the essential ritual food offerings a worshiper would bring to the Temple was the *olah,* the whole burnt offering (Lev. 1:3–17). Isaiah preached specifically that God hates the *olah* that comes from robbery—*ki ani Adonai oheiv mishpat sonei gazeil b'olah* (Isa. 61:8). The Mishnah takes up the theme of the invalidation of a ritual object that has been acquired through stealing. It states that a stolen palm branch is invalid for use in the obligatory ritual waving of the *lulav* (*Sukkot* 29b). In the Gemara, Rabbi Yochanan, in the name of Rabbi Shimon ben Yochai, explains that using a stolen *lulav* would be invalid because it would be trying to fulfill a ritual precept through a moral transgression (*Sukkot* 29b–30a). In *Midrash Rabbah,* Rabbi Tanchum b. Chanilai links stealing with the invalidation of a bird offering (*Vayikra Rabbah* 3). Because the bird flies around stealing its food from here and there, it is not fit for an offering. Rashi adds in his commentary at the beginning of Leviticus—*lo hikriv mi gazal*—ritual food offerings cannot be consecrated from that which has been stolen.[4] The new JPS translation of Isaiah's words on this subject speaks to the application of these texts to the subject of *oshek*. It notes that the robbery that invalidates the ritual food offering of the *olah* is the "robbing of wages" (of the agricultural laborer) (Isa. 61:8). Our food is not fit for ritual sanctification until we have tried to separate it from the stolen wages of an exploited farm worker.

How does this connect to dietary food rituals that are still practiced today? From Rabbinic times to our own times the recitation of the *Motzi* is a central ritual by which we consecrate our food to God.

In a discussion of the warrant for the recitation of the *Motzi* and other food *b'rachot*, Rabbi Chanina bar Pappa says, "Whoever has enjoyment from this world without (saying) a blessing, it is as if he has robbed the Holy One and the community of Israel" (Babylonian Talmud, *B'rachot* 35a–b). Not recognizing God as the source of creation before partaking of the food is a form of spiritual robbery that desecrates its holiness. But there is also a moral dimension in Rabbinic literature to the recitation of a *Motzi*. It is forbidden to make a *b'rachah* over food that is stolen from another human being.[5] Our *Motzi* must be preceded by moral action.

The Central Conference of American Rabbis made the social activism connection between *oshek* and sanctified eating when it passed a resolution in 1976 supporting the rights of farm workers to organize and bargain collectively. In support of the United Farm Workers, it called upon

> all persons of good will to seek out and purchase UFW Black Eagle label grapes and iceberg lettuce to affirm those growers who have bargained in good faith and as an incentive to growers who are procrastinating in negotiations. . . . Be it further resolved that the CCAR call on its constituents to support California type collective bargaining legislation for farm workers in Florida and in other states where the United Farm Workers have begun an organizing drive, and are seeking support for such labor legislation.[6]

Today, the plight of the farm worker in America continues to cry out to us. The average farm worker earns only eight thousand dollars a year[7]—way below the federal poverty level. A U.S. Department of Labor study in 1992 determined that the majority of migrants and former migrant farm workers live in poverty.[8] The Wagner Act provided extensive federal labor rights for many workers; however, it does not cover agricultural laborers. Only a few states have extended these rights to farm workers. One-third of all farm workers say that they have had children working with them in the fields.[9] The General Accounting Office concluded that farm workers "are not adequately protected by regulations and programs; their health and well-being are at risk."[10] Due to stoop labor, pesticide dangers, and transportation and farm equipment injuries, among other hazards, farm work is considered to be one of the five most dangerous occupations in the nation.[11] The Environmental Protection Agency estimates that as many as three hundred thousand agricultural workers are poisoned each year by pesticides.[12] The words of Deuteronomy reverberate today: the farm worker still risks his *nefesh*, his life, in the fields. Reminiscent of Rashi's description of the dangers of farm labor, today's fruit pickers often climb high ladders while carrying bags weighing up to ninety-five pounds.[13] These patterns of *oshek* are found all across America. They exist among the berry pickers in California, the mushroom workers in Florida, the pickle cucumber farm workers in South Carolina, and the apple harvesters in Washington and New York State.[14] In addition, farm workers are particularly easily exploited because many of them are undocumented workers.[15] Deuteronomy instructs us not to abuse a documented worker but also not to abuse the undocumented worker. Our conference has also called on us to struggle against this form of oppression of farm workers.[16]

The Central Conference of American Rabbis has not only supported the rights of farm workers in the days of Cesar Chavez; today the CCAR is a member of the National Farm Workers Ministry (www. nfwm.org), an interfaith organization that works to end the exploitation of America's farm workers. Through it, rabbis and laypeople, individuals and synagogue social action committees can easily obtain current information about products that are the subject of boycotts because of their company's practice of *oshek*. Information is available as well about food products of companies that have provided safe working conditions and recognized the rights of farm laborers to organize and collective bargain. Wallet-sized guides are even available to take to the grocery store. Just as one would read labels for that which is ritually kosher or *t'reif*, we can read labels and purchase those that are ethically kosher, or not purchase those that are ethically *t'reif*, in regard to *oshek*. Our food purchases can sanctify our meals.

What else can we do? It is estimated by the United Farm Workers that raising the cost of a basket of berries by five cents would raise most berry pickers above the poverty level.[17] Before reciting the *Motzi*, acknowledging our ritual gratitude to God, we can regularly place a few coins in the *tzedakah* box, acknowledging our moral responsibility to God and the fellow human beings who are partners with God in providing us our daily food. Simlilarly we can place special *tzedakah* boxes for this purpose in the kitchens of our synagogues. We can periodically send that *tzedakah* on to Farm Workers Organizations whose names and addresses are listed on the National Farm Worker Ministry website.

The redress of *oshek* often requires political action as well. The National Farm Worker's Ministry provides information about letter-writing campaigns to companies whose products result from the exploitation of farm workers. We can contact food store managers and ask them to stop carrying these food products and to start carrying those that deal justly in these matters. Similar information is available regarding restaurants. Refraining from eating at a popular pizza chain that purchases the majority of mushrooms harvested by exploited labor, and letting its managers know, is another way of practicing this dimension of the sanctification of food. Pausing before the recitation of the *Motzi* to write and address a letter on this subject to a national food purveyor, a local restaurant manager, or a national restaurant chain can also sanctify the food we then consume.

Our sacred sources teach us to pause before we eat for the ritual recitation of a *b'rachah*. In expressing our gratitude to God, we transform what otherwise would be stealing into a sanctified gift from the Divine. To ensure the validity of our blessing, these sources also urge us to work so that the food on our table is not desecrated by the exploitation of the farm laborer. This nexus of ritual piety and moral purity provides one important element in the practice of a contemporary Reform kashrut.

NOTES

1. *Pentateuch with Rashi Commentary*, ed. M. Rosenbaum and A. M. Silbermann (New York: Hebrew Publishing Company, 1970), 119.

2. Ibid.

3. National Farm Workers Ministry website: www.nfwm.org. St. Louis, MO, 2003.

4. *Pentateuch with Rashi Commentary*, ed. M. Rosenbaum and A. M. Silbermann (New York: Hebrew Publishing Company, 1970), 2b.

5. Israel Meir HaKohen, *Sefer Mishnah B'rurah* 696:31, vol. 6 (New York: M.M.Y. Zaks, 1946), 326.

6. Resolution on Farm Workers, adopted by the CCAR at its Eighty-Seventh Annual Convention in San Francisco, 1976. Another resolution of support for farm laborers was passed in March 1979 at the annual convention in Phoenix, Arizona, condemning the use of easily exploited foreign laborers to frustrate collective bargaining by the farm workers. (See also CCAR Responsa 7561.4—CCAR Responsa Committee review of the Jewish sources supporting the rights of the laborer, including the right to union organizing and collective bargaining. The responsa affirms the Responsa Committee's support for these rights for laborers today.) The CCAR also passed resolutions on behalf of farm workers in 1973, 1979, 1980, 1986, and 1989.

7. National Farm Workers Ministry website, www.nfwm.org.

8. Ibid.

9. Ibid.

10. Ibid.

11. Ibid.

12. Ibid.

13. Ibid.

14. Ibid.

15. Ibid.

16. See note 6 above.

17. *Five Cents for Fairness: The Case for Change in the Strawberry Fields*, a project of the Strawberry Workers Campaign, November 1996—a project of the AFL-CIO and the United Farm Workers, p. 3.

26

OUR DARK ADDICTIONS
Chocolate, Coffee, and Tea

Deborah Prinz

It hurt my heart deeply to think about it. . . . They enjoy something I suffered to make. I worked hard for them but saw no benefit. They are eating my flesh.[1]

These words of a young man rescued from slavery on an Ivory Coast cocoa plantation reveal the sinister side of chocolate. Chocolate, as well as coffee and tea, the popular beverages that first saturated Europe in the seventeenth century,[2] stir up very basic Jewish ethical issues. Beyond a sometimes gluttonous overconsumption of chocolate calories or over-caffeinating from tea and coffee, we may, knowingly or not, also imbibe sin, as in the High Holy Day liturgy's *al cheit shechatanu l'fanecha b'maachal uv'mishteh* (for the sin we have committed before you through food and drink). These transgressions result in bitter lives for individual laborers and local populations, and threaten the sustainability of the earth.

The tasty temptations of chocolate do not always mix well with Judaism's concern about the ethics of *oshek*, which literally means "withholding wages" or "monetary oppression," but generally refers to honest and fair labor practices. Demand for chocolate, coffee, and tea creates a great disconnect between the standard of living of most growers of cocoa beans (cacao), coffee, and tea on the one hand and that of the producers and consumers of these luxury products on the other.[3] Today's chocolate industry often obscures the tragic psychological and physical torture endured by children to obtain the cocoa beans needed to satiate the developed world's chocolate addictions. The complexities of chocolate ethics both reflect and surpass the challenges of tea and coffee. Many subsistence cocoa bean growers have no knowledge of that final treat of chocolate, while generally coffee and tea farmers do experience some form of those beverages in their own cultures. Also, chocolate requires much more processing.

The wrongs perpetrated to produce chocolate started with its very discovery and use by Europeans. Cocoa beans were colonial extract products appropriated by Europe through the conquests of Columbus and Cortes. Timothy Walker, writing about slave labor and chocolate in Portuguese-dominated Brazil, notes that

> prior to the 1880's . . . at every stage of Brazilian cacao production, coerced human labor played a role in the gathering and process-ing of this valuable commodity . . . [which] included indigenous peoples, coerced work of free blacks, mixed race laborers and Eu-ropean convicts forced to emigrate to Brazil.[4]

Ironically, at about the same time that Cadbury,[5] one of several Quaker-founded and owned chocolate companies in Britain of the eighteenth century, sought to create a utopian community for its workers in Bournville, it was embroiled in a controversy about pur-chasing cocoa beans from slave labor plantations in São Tomé and Pr'ncipe.[6] Novelist Jorge Amado captures the shame of the Brazilian cacao business:

> For cacao was money, cacao was power, cacao was the whole of life; it was not merely something planted in the black and sap-giving earth: it was inside themselves. Growing within them, it cast over every heart a malignant shade, slaying all good impulses.[7]

Today, money and profit still sadly tempt farmers and producers into the child labor and child slavery market. Growers in places such as Ivory Coast and Ghana claim that the low prices of cacao require labor of their own or enslaved children. Unfortunately, the Ivory Coast law that workers must be at least eighteen is rarely enforced. Currently, some twelve thousand children, often kidnapped from their families or sometimes sold by a family member in Mali, work in the Ivory Coast or Ghana. They are not paid for dangerous work with machetes, are not allowed any personal possessions, are imprisoned at night, are denied schooling, are forced to work long hours, and are left with untreated wounds after beatings. Leaders of a Mali human rights association estimate that child slaves are found on at least 90 percent of the Ivory Coast cocoa plantations. Over half of the world's chocolate may be defiled by the cruel treatment of children.[8] This *shanda* should melt away.

The 2005 Harkin-Engel Protocol, also known as the Cocoa Protocol, written by Senator Tom Harkin (D-IA) and Representative Eliot Engel (D-NY), sought to provide certification to eliminate the worst forms of child labor. Eight multinationals have signed onto the Protocol including Guittard, Nestlé, Hershey, M&M/Mars, and Callebaut. Unfortunately, however, it has not been fully implemented, and the initial deadline for its complete implementation has passed.[9]

Some multinationals have attempted to ameliorate the harsh realities of child slave labor by other means. Cadbury, for instance, offers its line of organic and fair trade Green and Black's along with other well-meaning initiatives. Through gestures such as its "Cocoa Partnership," Cadbury donated five thousand bicycles and over two and a half tons of books to the people of Ghana. These gestures, along with its single line of fair trade Dairy Milk bars, seem only symbolic,[10] obfuscating darker chocolate ethics.

In order to provide fair compensation to coffee, tea, and cocoa farmers, several fair trade certification systems seek to establish a minimum price above market value. Chocolate producers such as Theo,[11] Shaman,[12] Divine,[13] Zotter,[14] Equal Exchange,[15] and Dagoba[16] claim fair trade certification. These fair trade agreements establish criteria and standards for payment with the aim of providing increased income to farmers.[17] However, some analysts, as well as chocolatiers, question the success of these fair trade options, in part since fair trade chocolate makes up only about 1 percent of the global supply. Only one of these companies, Divine, is farmer owned. Several chocolate makers prefer to sidestep the fair trade certification costs, claiming that their farmers benefit more from their direct contact and superior financial arrangements. Sean Askinosie[18] gives back 10 percent of the profits from his company to his farmers in Mexico and Ecuador to enable them to participate in his business philosophy "a stake in the outcome." In doing so, he seeks to increase the quality of the cocoa bean and also improve the lives of the farmers. Another company, Taza, which labels itself "ethically traded," incentivizes quality, visiting farmers at least once a year to inspect workplace standards and conducting its finances with each farmer transparently and publicly. This company hopes soon to acquire third-party certification.[19] Kallari takes another approach. Its cooperative of some 850 farmers in Ecuador reaps 100 percent profit of the growing and processing of chocolate there. This business plan, based on local and organic production, yields four times the profit for the farmers, six times as much as if they sold to local traders or brokers.[20] The Bolivian company El Ciebo[21] profits the growers 100 percent as well. Yet a different formula, Terra Nostra's Equitable Trade certification, claims to go beyond fair trade by running a cooperative that collects and invests member fees in site-specific development projects that "enhance and nurture vibrant, healthy communities and the ecosystems from which these traded materials are derived."[22] A Massachusetts worker-owned co-op, Equal Exchange,[23] sells fair trade and organic coffee, tea, and chocolate, trading directly with democratically organized small-farmer cooperatives, paying a guaranteed minimum price, and supporting sustainable farming practices.

While such fair trade and other arrangements may benefit the farmers of coffee, cocoa, and tea, they cannot fully guarantee that these products are free of child labor or slave labor of children, as documented in recent reports.[24] To shun eating chocolate spoiled by *oshek*, a discerning Jewish chocolate lover might prefer to purchase bars of single-origin beans to avoid corrupt, bulked beans from West Africa. However, sometimes even those single-origin products may include beans sourced from Africa, since the European Union requires that only 10 percent of the bar must be from the country stated as the origin, and the United States currently has no controls in this area at all.[25] Lobbying for the full implementation of the standards sought by Harkin-Engel would help eliminate the crime of child slavery, as would protests directed at the relevant purveyors.

While *oshek*-suffused chocolate may be of the greatest concern, other Jewish values may inform our chocolate diet as well. Conglomerates such as Hershey and Godiva boast kashrut certifications[26] to adhere to Jewish dietary laws. These are not ethical standards, nor are they intended to be. Smaller, artisanal chocolate purveyors cannot always afford a *hechsher*. Some chocolate companies generously demonstrate their dedication to social service by folding their earnings into good works to assist farmer communities. One company supports rescue dogs by selling kosher-for-Passover chocolate in the shape of matzah called "Don't Passover Me Bark."[27]

The certified organic, fair trade Santa Cruz–based company Shaman claims that its chocolate profits support the Huichol Indians of the Sierra Madre mountains of Mexico. This enables the Huichol to keep their traditions alive, including their "healing and transformational shamanism."[28] These and other admirable projects may delight our sweet tooth while alleviating our guilt about the great income gap between chocolate grower and consumer. However, supporting shamanism raises questions about *chukat hagoyim*[29] (following the ways of gentiles) and *avodah zarah*[30] (idolatry). This particular endeavor may not be appropriate for Jews.

Jewish ideas about not wasting that which has potential for future use, known as *bal tashchit*, resonate when considering recycling and sustainability in connection with chocolate. For example, Original Beans commits to "restoring our planet's most valuable forests" with conservation training programs and buffer zones protecting old-growth rain forests. The use of fossil fuels in production is offset through monitored reforestation programs.[31] Hershey's subsidiary Dagoba markets its chocolate as "good for people and for the planet" with its commitment to "Full Circle Sustainability," which seeks a positive change in "ecology, equity, community and quality." Its projects include reforesting Costa Rica's Upala Cacao Cooperative with forty-five thousand seedlings and underwriting green space in several cities.[32]

Certainly using recycled paper and low-impact inks in packaging, developing green factories, and implementing low-energy practices such as those claimed by some chocolatiers would be valuable.[33] Some companies also recycle unused cocoa shells into mulch.[34] While organic, sustainable chocolate is not always packaged in recycled wrappers, the two do go together for Endangered Species Chocolate—fair trade, organic, *hechshered*, and LEED[35] certified—which donates 10 percent of its net profit to protect endangered animals, habitats, and people.[36] Organic certification supports the resources of the rain forest, as does rain forest certification.[37]

Cocoa companies boast rain forest certification such as that provided by Rainforest Alliance, which seeks to conserve the forest canopy in growing cacao, protects wildlife, and works toward sustainability. Plantations Arriba Chocolate[38] first carried the seal, joined by Newman's Own[39] and others. Mars[40] and Kraft[41] have partnered with the Rainforest Alliance to train farmers in the Ivory Coast and Ghana about the standards. Blommers,[42] Mars, and Kraft have developed rain forest benchmarks for some of their chocolate lines.[43]

While such initiatives as organic farming, recycled packaging, planting forests, rain forest accreditation, and fair trade certifications apply to tea and coffee as well, additional sustainability issues foam up around chocolate. Coffee, tea, and chocolate challenge the popular admonition to eat unprocessed, local, fresh foods from the perimeters of the grocery store. Further, while coffee and tea require some minor modification of the plant product through roasting of the natural coffee bean or drying of the tea leaf, solid chocolate as we know it, love it, and devour it today requires intense processing. Chocolate customers living in the cooler, wealthier Northern Hemisphere import cocoa beans out of their equatorial habitat and transport them long distances. The end product requires multiple energy-sapping steps, including fermenting, drying, roasting, winnowing, grinding, conching, and tempering. Only then is chocolate shipped to the retailer.

Given these intense outputs of energy in most chocolate preparation, Taza's minimal stone grinding based on techniques from Mexico may make sense.[44] Sourcing beans from Central or South America or Hawaii and processing them in the United States may diminish chocolate's carbon footprint, rather than importing chocolate from Belgium, France, Switzerland, or other distant countries.[45]

Raw chocolate skips several production steps and may be an alternative as well. Makers of raw chocolate claim that after fermenting the beans, when temperature control is difficult, further preparation of the chocolate stays under 118 degrees. Vanessa of Gnosis Chocolate[46] imports pastes of stone-ground cacao from Ecuador, Peru, and Bali to fashion her raw, organic, and hand-prepared chocolate. Nutritionist and author David Wolfe counts raw cacao as one of the world's superfoods: "The cacao bean has always been and will always be Nature's number one weight loss and high energy food."[47] He argues it would be more nutritional to eat chocolate in its rawer state, either the cocoa bean, the cocoa nibs (without the shell), or other minimally processed forms. Unfortunately, suppliers of raw cocoa beans sometimes use natural gas in the drying process, which may mean that ostensibly raw chocolate may be full of poly-aromatic hydrocarbons.[48]

Unless consumers really pay close attention, they may unintentionally purchase chocolate, coffee, and tea that harm the environment, local populations, laborers, and themselves. Faced with a mélange of options when selecting chocolate, a liberal Jew might be informed by Jewish principles and also take a very nuanced approach to certifications, service projects, ingredients listings, type of processing, and country of origin. The earliest chocolate lovers, the Mayans and Aztecs, thought chocolate had divine grace. We, too, could savor our chocolate with a sense of the spiritual. Ultimately, we might approach our chocolate, coffee, and tea intake with the wisdom of Rabbenu Bachya ben Asher: "See how one's eating is considered a perfect act of worship like one of the forms of the divine sacrifices."[49]

NOTES

1. Brian Woods and Kate Blewett, *Slavery: A Global Investigation* (London: True Vision, BBC, 2001); view at http://freedocumentaries.org/film.php?id=192.

2. Ross W. Jamieson, "The Essence of Commodification: Caffeine Dependencies in the Early Modern World," *Journal of Social History* 35, no. 2 (Winter 2001): 269–94.

3. Chocolate, tea, and coffee were the first European drinks concocted with boiled water. Long before that, each began as part of an indigenous culture. Tea was drunk in China, coffee in Ethiopia and Yemen, chocolate in Central America. Early coffee's consumption occurred in religious settings in Yemen. Myths related to the origins of tea connect it with royalty. Mayans and Aztecs drank cold chocolate with exotic spices in cultic ceremonies; chocolate came to be known as a sacred food, food of the gods, *theobroma*. Coffee and tea traveled to Europe through tourist culture. As the markets for these consumables expanded, plantings were transported elsewhere—coffee to South America, tea to India, and cocoa to Africa. See http://en.wikipedia.org/wiki/Tea; http://en.wikipedia.org/wiki/Coffee; http://en.wikipedia.org/wiki/Chocolate.

4. Timothy Walker, "Slave Labor and Chocolate in Brazil: The Culture of Cacao Plantations in Amazonia and Bahia (17th–19th Centuries)," *Food and Foodways* 15 (January 2007): 79.

5. http://www.cadbury.co.uk/home/Pages/home.aspx (accessed April, 2009).

6. Lowell J. Satre, *Chocolate on Trial: Slavery, Politics and the Ethics of Business* (Athens: Ohio State University Press, 2005); Carol Off, *Bitter Chocolate: Investigating the Dark Side of the World's Most Seductive Sweet* (New York: Random House, 2006), 96; Sudarsan Raghavan, "Two Boys Tell of Descent into Slavery," *JSOnline Milwaukee Journal Sentinel*, June 25, 2001, jsonline.com; Christian Parenti, "Chocolate's Bittersweet Economy," money.CNN.com, February 15, 2008.

7. Jorge Amado, *The Violent Land*, trans. Samuel Putnam (New York: Alfred Knopf, 1965), 273.

8. Lowell J. Satre, *Chocolate on Trial: Slavery, Politics and the Ethics of Business*; Carol Off, *Bitter Chocolate: Investigating the Dark Side of the World's Most Seductive Sweet*; Brian Woods and Kate Blewett, *Slavery*; http://en.wikipedia.org/wiki/Children_in_cocoa_production. Put the issue of the abuses and scandals of child slave trafficking right into the Passover seder using a text found at http://www.globalexchange.org/campaigns/fairtrade/cocoa/Passover.

9. http://en.wikipedia.org/wiki/Cocoa_Protocol. In lieu of proper legal enforcement, avoiding these abuse-tainted chocolates is not easy. Companies such

as Cadbury, Hershey, and Godiva "bulk" their beans. They buy from middlemen and cannot accurately identify how much, if any, originates in Ghana or the Ivory Coast, where child slave labor is most prevalent. As one Godiva representative suggested in an e-mail (April 2010), since 80 percent of all cocoa comes from West Africa, it is likely that the bulked cocoa Godiva uses contains some tainted cocoa.

10. http://www.cadbury.com/ourresponsibilities/cadburycocoapartnership/Pages/cadburycocoapartnership.aspx; Cadbury's Green and Black's Maya Gold was the first product to go fair trade in the United Kingdom, in 1994.

11. http://www.theochocolate.com, located in Seattle.

12. http://www.shamanchocolates.com, located in Santa Cruz.

13. http://www.divinechocolate.com, located in England.

14. http://www.zotterchocolate.co.uk, made in Austria.

15. http://www.equalexchange.coop; American Jewish World Services and Equal Exchange have partnered to promote and sell fair trade, kosher chocolate and coffee. See http://jcarrot.org/introducing-better-beans-fair-trade-kosher-coffee-and-chocolate.

16. http://www.dagobachocolate.com, located in Oregon.

17. http://en.wikipedia.org/wiki/Fair_trade; http://www.transfairusa.org/; http://www.wfto.com.

18. http://www.askinosie.com, located in Missouri.

19. http://www.tazachocolate.com, located in Massachusetts; see more about third-party certification through ICS, Quality Assurance International, at http://en.wikipedia.org/wiki/Quality_Assurance_International.

20. http://www.kallari.com; Judy Logback, lecture, April 8, 2010, at Food Emporium Chocolate Room, New York; Jill Santopietro, "When Chocolate Is a Way of Life," *New York Times*, November 5, 2008.

21. www.elceibo.org, located in Bolivia.

22. http://www.terranostrachocolate.com, located in Vancouver; http://www.terranostrachocolate.com/equitradeback.php.

23. http://www.equalexchange.coop/our-co-op.

24. See note 6.

25. Judy Logback, e-mail message to author, May 22, 2010.

26. Valhrona, Elite, Hershey, Valhrona, Divine, and others. See http://www.kantrowitz.com/chocolate/ for a list of kosher chocolate and candy makers.

27. http://rescucchocolate.com, located in Brooklyn.

28. http://www.shamanchocolates.com, located in Santa Cruz.

29. http://www.myjewishlearning.com/beliefs/Issues/Jews_and_Non-Jews/Legal_Issues/Non-Jew_in_Jewish_Law.shtml.

30. http://en.wikipedia.org/wiki/Avodah Zarah.

31. http://www.originalbeans.com cleverly allows you to enter the lot number of your chocolate bar in order to see the trees planted in response to a particular batch of chocolate.

32. http://www.dagobachocolate.com/circle.asp.

33. Companies such as Taza, Original Beans, Askinosie, Dagoba, and Malie Kai package with recycled materials.

34. Taza and Askinosie.

35. http://en.wikipedia.org/wiki/Leadership_in_Energy_and_Environmental_Design.

36. http://www.chocolatebar.com, located in Indianapolis.

37. http://www.rainforest-alliance.org/marketplace.cfm?id=main.

38. http://www.vintageplantations.com, located in New York.

39. http://www.newmansownorganics.com/food_chocolate.html.

40. http://www.mars.com/global/index.aspx.

41. http://www.kraftfoods.co.uk/kraft/page?siteid=kraft-prd&locale=uken1&PagecRef=483&Mid=483.

42. http://www.blommer.com/default.htm.

43. www.rainforest-alliance.org.

44. The cocoa beans intended for beverage use undergo simpler processing on a stone metate or through an electric stone grinder, as in Guatemala and Mexico. To see this: http://www.jews-onthechocolatetrail.org/2009/01/chocolate-in-mexico/. The result is very different from the packaged, highly processed cocoa known elsewhere.

45. In Hawaii, Jim Walsh developed a plantation of criollo cacao beans in 1986 called Hawaiian Vintage chocolate; http://www.hawaiianchocolate.com. Also, in Hawaii, Malei Kai grows on the north shore of Oahu Island; http://www.maliekai.com/.

46. http://www.gnosischocolate.com.

47. David Wolfe, *Superfoods: The Food and Medicine of the Future* (Berkeley, CA: North Atlantic Books, 2009), 36.

48. Judy Logback, e-mail message to author, May 22, 2010.

49. Bachya ben Asher ben Hlava, *Shulchan Shel Arba*, 497, cited in Jonathan Brumberg-Kraus, "'Torah on the Table': A Sensual Morality," in *Food and Morality: Proceedings of the Oxford Symposium on Food and Cookery 2007*, ed. Susan R. Friedland (Great Britain: Prospect Books, 2007), 47.

27

A LOOK BACK AT THE REFORM MOVEMENT'S RESPONSE TO THE UNITED FARM WORKERS GRAPE BOYCOTT

PETER E. KASDAN

> You shall not abuse a needy and destitute laborer, whether a fellow Israelite or a stranger in one of the communities of your land.
>
> *(Deut. 24:14)*

> Each time a man or woman stands up for justice, the heavens sing and the world rejoices. Each time a man or woman stands up for justice and is struck down, the heavens weep and the world mourns. Farm workers everywhere are angry and worried, but we are not going to fall into the trap that our oppressors have fallen into. We do not need to destroy to win. We are a movement that builds and does not destroy.
>
> *(Cesar Chavez, April 1975)*

George Santayana, in his *The Life of Reason*, wrote, "Those who cannot remember the past are condemned to relive it."[1] This, then, is an attempt to remember some personal history that bound this writer to historic events in which the religious values of our Reform Jewish Movement became intertwined with the destinies of America's migrant worker population. It began in November 1961 with these words of conscience:

UAHC RESOLUTION ON MIGRANT FARMERS

In recent years the American conscience has been aroused by the many privations and discriminations visited upon America's migratory farm workers. These men and women, who perform such useful and necessary work for all of us, experience distress and disadvantage which make them the "excluded" or "forgotten" Americans.

Because of our commitment to human dignity and social justice, the Union of American Hebrew Congregations at this 46th Biennial Assembly, calls upon the federal government and all state governments and interstate agencies to take vigorous action to seek a humane solution for this important social problem.

We urge our national Commission on Social Action, and all congregations, to conduct educational programs to make our membership aware of and sensitive to the unjust abuses experienced by these workers and the human suffering involved in this social issue. We call upon the Commission on Social Action to join with like-minded groups of all faiths to ameliorate this problem of social distress and to seek through legislation and education to raise the status of these farm workers from the present level of degradation to a position of dignity and equality in accordance with our religious and democratic traditions.

I began my studies at HUC-JIR, Cincinnati, in September 1961. I knew something about the UAHC but had no idea, at all, what took place at its conventions, nor how such events would affect me as a Jew. That naivete remained with me during those five years of study. Fast-forward to June 1966. My twenty-six classmates and I were ordained at the Plum Street Temple; we looked forward to our first congregational jobs. Coincidently, during that very same summer, the United Farm Workers (UFW) Union was being formed in a merger of Cesar Chavez's National Farm Workers of America (NFWA) and the Filipino American AWOC (Agricultural Workers Organizing Committee). The NFWA was attempting to organize the workers at the DiGiorgio Fruit Corporation (the fictional Gregorio Fruit Corporation in John Steinbeck's *The Grapes of Wrath*) and had staged a successful strike and boycott of DiGiorgio's produce. The grower was forced to agree to an election among its workers but brought in the Teamsters Union to oppose Chavez's NFWA. To counter that move, the AWOC merged with the NFWA to form the United Farm Workers and quickly affiliated with the AFL-CIO, the national labor federation. The DiGiorgio workers voted for the UFW.

In October 1969 the UAHC's General Assembly, meeting in Miami, Florida, passed a resolution on "Farm Workers and the Grape Strike." In the early years of my rabbinic career, I had just begun my tenure at Temple Shaari Emeth, Englishtown, New Jersey. HUC-JIR had prepared me to "teach and preach." What did I know of boycotts and farm workers? Of pesticides and labor unions? The Union's resolution on "Farm Workers and the Grape Strike" would serve as a turning point in my career, indeed in my Jewish life, as I took the words of the resolution to heart.

UAHC RESOLUTION ON FARM WORKERS
AND GRAPE STRIKE

WHEREAS, like other farm workers, the grape pickers of California and Arizona do not enjoy the benefits of the National Labor Relations Act or other federal legislation mandating a collective bargaining process. These grape pickers, among the poorest working people in our land of plenty, have appealed to the conscience of the country to support them in their desperate struggle to secure a collective bargaining agreement with the growers of table grapes. We cannot stay indifferent to their appeal, nor to the right of other farm workers to a fair share of the fruit of their labors.

THEREFORE, THE 50TH GENERAL ASSEMBLY OF THE UAHC RESOLVES:

1. to urge the Congress of the United States to extend collective bargaining rights to farm workers by an appropriate amendment to the National Labor Relations Act:

2. to affirm its support for the grape pickers of California and Arizona by urging all its members and affiliates to join in the

boycott of table grapes from those states until a collective bargaining agreement has been reached;

3. to call on the Commission on Social Action to help all UAHC congregations and affiliates in the implementation of the boycott until such action is taken by the Congress of the United States.

It was the second resolution that got me going; I began to research the farm workers movement. I discovered that there was a National Farm Worker Ministry and that there were, among the dozens of priests and ministers already involved in the Farm Worker Ministry, a few rabbis serving as well. Among them was Rabbi Joseph Glaser, then the UAHC's regional director in San Francisco, California. In 1966, Cesar Chavez had turned to him to mediate the UFW's dispute with the wine-grape growers who supplied the Manischewitz Company with grapes for their kosher wine. Joe, almost single-handedly, was able to persuade the executives at Manischewitz to support the workers; they, in turn, used their influence with the growers, and the UFW began gaining new contracts for its workers. I wrote to Rabbi Glaser, asking for his advice as to how I might also become involved in the Farm Worker Ministry. His phone call followed just a week later, and he became my mentor in matters of social justice.

In the summer of 1970, attempting to keep the UFW out of California's lettuce and vegetable fields, most Salinas Valley growers signed "sweetheart" contracts with the Teamsters Union. Some ten thousand Central Coast farm workers responded by walking out on strike. The UFW used the boycott to convince some large vegetable companies to abandon their Teamster agreements and to sign UFW contracts. Chavez called for a nationwide boycott of non-union lettuce. I began boycotting non-UFW head lettuce and urging my congregants and friends to join our family in supporting both the local and the national migrant worker community.

In the spring of 1971, when I was asked to become the rabbi at Temple Emanu-El, in Livingston, New Jersey, I was already heavily involved in the farm workers movement. I did not know that one day I would welcome Cesar Chavez to our temple's sanctuary, nor could I have known then that Cesar and his family would be "live-in" guests in our home, sitting at our table, even participating in our seder. For the next fifteen years, my congregation and I pursued social justice for the farm workers. We took the lead in the head lettuce boycott that marked the decade of the 1970s. On May 14, 1973, Temple Emanu-El's board of trustees passed a resolution calling head lettuce *t'reifah*—not fit for human consumption.

TEMPLE EMANU-EL RESOLUTION ON HEAD LETTUCE

Whereas, throughout our history, our judges and sages declared that food produced through the exploitation of people is not *kasher*—not fit for consumption by Jews and

Whereas, the Migrant Lettuce Workers are waging a lettuce boycott and strike to receive basic decent conditions, facilities and wages and an end to racism on their jobs, the use of child labor and harmful pesticides, Temple Emanu-El supports the actions of the United Farm Workers Union.

Further, in an effort to combine moral encouragement with positive action, Temple Emanu-El will not serve head lettuce unless harvested under the UFWU contract, at any function sponsored by the Temple or any of the Temple's organizations. The Temple further commits itself to urge our members and all who use the Temple's facilities to follow the practice of the Temple.

In 1982 Republican George Deukmejian was elected governor of California. It wasn't long before his political appointees shut down enforcement of the state's Farm Labor Law, which his predecessor, Governor Jerry Brown, had secured for the farm workers. It was seen as a betrayal of the trust of the state's weakest citizens, a return to the "business as usual" days of the 1960s and 1970s. In 1984 Cesar Chavez announced yet another grape boycott, and just two years later, he began the "Wrath of Grapes" Campaign, hoping to draw public attention to the pesticide poisoning of grape workers and their children. In response to the "Wrath of Grapes" Campaign, at its August 11, 1986 meeting, Temple Emanu-El's board of trustees passed the following resolution in support of this new grape boycott:

TEMPLE EMANU-EL'S RESOLUTION
ON TABLE GRAPE BOYCOTT

Whereas, the Migrant Farm Workers are waging a boycott against table grapes grown with the use of pesticides harmful to farm workers and the consumer; Temple Emanu-El supports the actions of the United Farm Worker Union (as does the UAHC, the CCAR and the Joint Commission on Social Action of Reform Judaism). In an effort to combine moral encouragement with positive action, Temple Emanu-El will not serve table grapes, unless they are harvested under UFWU contract, at any function sponsored by the Temple or any of the Temple's organizations. The Temple further commits itself to inform its membership of this policy and requires all who use the Temple's facilities to follow the practice of the Temple as regards the use of table grapes.

In June 1989, at its 100th Annual Convention, the CCAR again reaffirmed its commitment to the grape boycott, calling on "its members, their congregations, and organizations to support the Grape Boycott until the aforementioned problems [i.e., the use of life-threatening pesticides and the right of farm workers to be protected from abuse] have been rectified."

Most people have no idea at all just how important the Jewish community and the Jewish value system were to Cesar Chavez, nor of his love for the people and the State of Israel. Cesar visited Israel; he left there "in love" with the *kibbutz* system. He brought back not just Israeli agricultural techniques, but also the belief that creating a *kibbutz* at La Paz would allow all who lived there—the workers and the president of the UFW and their families—to sit together in the dining room and to share their meals together, each of them having contributed an equal portion of their salaries to the food collective.

Cesar Chavez was a powerful human being and, yet, a very simple man. He was not a great orator, yet he could motivate hundreds of thousands of American citizens, of all ages, to go into their local supermarket and demand that the store honor the boycott. He could also embrace you, as if you were the only person in the room, though the room was overflowing, and make you feel that you were his brother or sister. He was a tireless worker on behalf of other human beings and as president of an AFL-CIO affiliated union, he took the same weekly wage as the lowliest of his workers.

Cesar died on April 23, 1993, in Arizona, where he had gone to defend the UFW against a multimillion dollar lawsuit brought against the union by the large vegetable grower Bruce Church, Inc. We are constantly in need of modern heroes—people to guide us and to goad us, to light a fire within us that will force us to fulfill our Jewish values. Cesar was such a hero to those of us who knew and worked side by side with him. We include him, along with the generations of our families, in our recitation of *Kaddish* on his *yahrzeit*. He was, and remains, one of the *lamed-vav tzaddikim*, one of the righteous of our generation.

NOTE

1. George Santayana, *The Life of Reason, or the Phases of Human Progress* (New York: Scribner's, 1917), 284.

28

REAL LIFE / REAL FOOD
Post-Postville and Onward

Robert J. Marx

On May 12, 2008, agents representing the U.S. Government Immigration and Custom Enforcement (ICE) swooped into Postville, a small town in the northeastern corner of Iowa, and arrested 390 workers employed by the country's largest kosher meat packing plant. Postville had already earned more notoriety than it might have desired. Its kosher meat packing plant had been cited on numerous occasions for health and safety problems; its workers were largely immigrants from Guatemala and Mexico who spoke little English; and the plant's Chasidic managers, with their long beards and black hats, seemed every bit as foreign. At the time of the ICE raid, Agriprocessors, owned by the Brooklyn-based Rubashkin family, was the largest slaughterer of kosher meat in the country. It produced over 60 percent of the kosher beef and 40 percent of the kosher chickens sold in the United States. But the treatment of its workers was anything but morally kosher.

A month after the ICE raid, over fifteen hundred of us, Jews drawn from cities all over the Midwest joined by members of other religious communities, traveled to Postville. We came to protest what we regarded as a dual injustice: the exploitation of the workers by Agriprocessors and the raid by our government's immigration service. We wanted not only to protest, but also to listen, to learn, and to see what we could do to help. The prophet Jeremiah once complained that too often we listen without hearing. That humid Sunday in Iowa there was plenty of listening—and even more sadness.

We needed no translator to understand the stories. The conditions at the plant were horrific—"medieval" was what one government official called them. Young children were illegally employed; rudimentary sanitary rules were ignored; workers were induced to buy stolen social security numbers so that they could remain in the country. If there was a ray of sun, it was that, for a time, these desperate immigrants were able to earn a precarious living, at least enough to keep their families together. And then came "the raid"—the raid that shattered everything: fathers deported or in jail; mothers forced to wear ankle (GPS) bracelets; children too terrified even to cry. Most of the residents of Postville wanted Agriprocessors to succeed despite the immigrant workers and "strange" managers, for the plant brought a promise of prosperity to Postville. Now that hope would have to wait for another day.

There is a postscript to the Postville story. The ICE raid hardly marked the end of Shalom Rubashkin's problems. As the manager of Agriprocessors, he faced accusations regarding both the treatment of his workers and his financial dealings. Paradoxically, he was found innocent of any crime involving the exploitation of workers but was convicted of bank fraud and was sentenced to a twenty-seven-year prison term. As of this writing, that sentence is being appealed. That corporate financial crime can be punished so severely, while the exploitation of workers can find such easy vindication, is another of the dilemmas our commerce-friendly society has yet to confront. Regardless of what the outcome of the appeal process will be, these verdicts raise important additional questions about what the word "kosher" really means.

· Part Six ·

Hechsher: Who Decides
What Is Kosher?

Hechsher, "certification," has been an influential part of modern kashrut since 1923, when the first *hechsher* was granted by the Orthodox Union. In my article "Considering *Hechsher*," I evaluate the place of certifications in Reform dietary practice, pointing out their strengths and weaknesses. Ariana Silverman ("We Answer to an Even Higher Authority") documents the new types of certification that strive to assure that ritual kashrut also upholds ethical values. In "But Is the *Mashgichah* Kosher?" I share my experiences as a *mashgichah*, overseeing a kosher bakery (I am no longer serving the bakery discussed in my article). As I recall in this article, reprinted from the *CCAR Journal* (Spring 2001), the question quickly transformed from whether the bread was kosher to whether I, a Reform woman rabbi, was kosher. This intrinsic question—who, not what, is kosher—unfortunately, seems to become a primary emphasis in the kosher world today. In seeking to promote kashrut to the Reform world, I hope to refocus the discussion on the food and the values it reflects.

In "Wine: Our Symbol of Joy," Terje Z. Lande and Oren Postrel educate us about kosher wine, giving Reform Jews the tools with which to make educated choices. In the "Real Life / Real Food" chapter,

Deborah Bodin Cohen ("*Kiddush* and Mad Dog 20-20—A Kosher Combination?") reveals the darker issues embedded in the production of some kosher wines. Both articles prove that appearance does not reveal the whole story and that assumptions about what is truly kosher can easily be dissolved.

29

CONSIDERING *HECHSHER*

Mary L. Zamore

Hechsher, or kosher certification, has become commonplace on food labels, as those little symbols permeate the marketplace more and more each year. In fact, Integrated Marketing Communications, a firm that tracks trends in the kosher industry, estimates that in 2003 there were more than eighty thousand certified kosher products in the United States.[1] Therefore, most North American customers are used to seeing the host of letters, symbols, and Hebrew words that certify that the food product was overseen by a *mashgiach* (inspector), usually a rabbi, guaranteeing that the product is fully kosher. For the kosher-keeping consumer, these symbols make grocery shopping easier. One simply searches for the product with the *hechsher*, knowing that it is kosher.

As Reform Jews, we need to decide whether or not we want to take advantage of this convenient approach to kashrut. Of course, this depends in part on the level of kashrut the individual Reform Jew is keeping. These kosher certifications facilitate a stringently kosher life-style by ensuring that marked products are fully kosher at every minute detail of production. While kosher-keeping Reform Jews will seek out such products, generally Reform Jews are not concerned with such a deeply detailed approach to kashrut. Yet, since *hechsher* holds such a prominent place in the American marketplace and since Jews interested in ritual kashrut will regularly encounter choices concerning *hechsher*, it is important to explore the world of *hechsher* through Reform eyes.

When incorporating ritual kashrut into one's dietary practice, the first question is, to what extent is one concerned about the kashrut of a particular food product? Some Reform Jews take a visual approach to their food: "It looks kosher, therefore it is kosher to me." Many liberal Jews who keep ritually kosher read labels, using that criterion to decide whether a particular item is sufficiently kosher. On the other hand, there are many ingredients that are unfamiliar, and navigating through multisyllabic chemical names can be tricky and frustrating. In addition, the Food and Drug Administration (FDA) does not require full disclosure of the origins of ingredients like "natural flavors," which may be from plant or animal sources.[2] Therefore, depending on kosher certification either all the time or for specific foods can be helpful. In chapter 30, Ariana Silverman explores the development of kosher certifications and its connection to the lengthening of our food chain.

This Item Is Sponsored by the Letter "K"

Federal trademark law mandates that a letter of the alphabet cannot be a registered trademark. Therefore, when one sees a plain "K," this does not indicate that the product has been certified by an independent, outside third party. Rather, use of the plain "K" indicates that the food manufacturer has deemed its product to be kosher.[3] In this way, the manufacturer does not need to pay anyone to certify that the standard of kashrut is being upheld. One might say that they are not answerable to anyone but the consumer. The exception to the "K" rule is when the manufacturer actually does pay for supervision but does not advertise it on the label. In these limited cases, the *mashgiach* is usually listed on the company's website. For most liberal Jews the manufacturer's use of "K" can be helpful when trying to select a product quickly.

The "K," however, does not usually reflect the highest standards of kashrut. The product may be made on shared equipment or stored in a vat that was manufactured using *t'reif.* There is no way to tell, although, as legal liability becomes more of an issue to manufacturers, ingredient labeling is becoming more transparent. A label may announce that the product was produced on shared machinery or contains milk derivatives, for example. While the primary concern is disclosing potential food allergens, the informative labeling benefits those who keep kosher.

Hechsher and Supporting an Entire Industry

When one decides to purchase foods exclusively bearing a *hechsher*, the consumer is indirectly supporting these certifying agencies. However, it should be noted that certain *hechshers* are so pervasive in the marketplace that almost all consumers, wittingly or unwittingly, are indirectly supporting the main agencies. As in any mix of power and religion, the consumer is supporting, albeit indirectly, a religious organization that may or may not share the same worldview on kashrut, Israel, religious pluralism, or on any number of other issues. Only a careful examination of each individual agency and its leading rabbis would help you decide what to support. Again, this is as cumbersome, or perhaps more so, than personally analyzing multisyllabic ingredients and trying to discern their kashrut. Sometimes products are certified by individual rabbis, and it may be easier to evaluate one's comfort level with the product and rabbi.

Just like the Jewish community itself, there is a range of stringency for *hechshers.* These concerns reflect supervision at different levels, starting with the standard definition of kashrut ranging to very involved, detailed anxieties about every level of production. Presently, in the mainstream to ultra-Orthodox communities, there is an ever narrowing of the definition of what is kosher. For example, many rabbis have instructed their communities to stop eating certain produce (naturally kosher), because of an obsessive concern with bugs (not kosher) hiding within the fruit and vegetables. For example, strawberries, raspberries, broccoli, and brussels sprouts have been almost entirely removed entirely from some Jews' diets. Clearly, this is not the spirit with which Reform Jews approach kashrut, and there is no need to support or mimic this wing of the kosher-oriented community.

The Role of Secular Certifications

Sometimes Jews who keep kosher rely on secular certifications and labels to guide their ritual kashrut. For example, many families who eat *kitniyot* on Passover will depend on gluten-free labels to guide their holiday purchases, avoiding foods with the five grains (wheat, rye, oats, barley, and spelt) that need special treatment during Pesach. Consumers seeking pareve foods may depend on vegan labels. Again, these labels are not intended for aiding kashrut and, therefore, are not usually concerned with issues of shared equipment, auxiliary ingredients (like the oil or lard that may grease the machinery), or chemicals that are derivatives of *t'reif*. Ultimately, the concern for most liberal Jews is just the listed ingredients.

Beyond Kosher

Kosher certification is solely concerned with ritual matters. This, of course, has been a great criticism of the Orthodox Union, the certifying agent for the notorious Rubashkin slaughterhouse in Postville, Iowa. As Ariana Silverman discusses in chapter 30, there is a new crop of Jewish labels that seek to certify the ethics of food production in both factories and restaurants. All these new certifications are given to products or eating establishments that are already certified kosher. This means that the owner must pay two different independent parties to attest to whatever is being certified. Even a financially robust business may find this to be a budgetary burden. As Terje Z. Lande and

Oren Postrel point out concerning wine, and Deborah Prinz explores concerning chocolate, certification (kosher or ethical) is expensive and often out of reach for new or small producers. For these struggling companies, profits are often elusive or slim, and paying for one, or even two, certification agencies and implementing their recommendations would be impossible. For, example, I was recently asked to oversee an ice-cream parlor. The deal breaker concerning becoming fully kosher was the gummy bears. The franchise owner felt he could not afford the switch to gummy bears produced with kosher gelatin rather than the more typical version made from a protein derived from the collagen inside animal skin and bones.[4]

The slow or local eating movement fosters having a personal relationship with the producers of one's food. Buying food from a CSA or farmers' market or eating at a restaurant dedicated to slow food allows one to ask questions, exploring the production of your food. Rather than depending on a third party to investigate and evaluate, the consumer can have a personal dialogue with the food supplier and, in turn, can shape the food chain by letting her opinions be known.

When eating in a restaurant, it may be sufficient to ask what broth is used in the soup. However, there is a certain comfort and ease (as described by Zoë Klein in chapter 24) in being able to order anything off the menu in a kosher or strictly vegetarian or vegan restaurant.

Last Thoughts

Ultimately, one must match the level of kashrut observance to his adherence to *hechsher*. While there is a level of convenience in utilizing the guidance of these certifications, there is also a narrowing of the culinary experience and interactions. Also, when considering *hechsher*, one must decide whether to support, albeit indirectly, the political goals of the agencies that provide the oversight. As secondary certification of ethical values takes hold in the Jewish community, Reform Jews will have the opportunity to evaluate their worth as well.

NOTES

1. Lisë Stern, *How to Keep Kosher* (New York: William Morrow, 2004), 40.

2. Ibid., 41.

3. Shimon Apisdorf, *Kosher for the Clueless But Curious* (Baltimore: Leviathan Press, 2005), 41.

4. Most liberal kosher-keeping Jews feel comfortable eating conventional gelatin, as the protein is so far removed from its original source. This is according to the liberal application of the halachic principle *davar chadash* (new thing), meaning that the substance is so altered in the production that it bears little resemblance to the original. Strict vegetarians avoid conventional gelatin and kosher gelatin if it is produced from fish bones. Many kosher gelatins are made from seaweed.

30

WE ANSWER TO AN EVEN HIGHER AUTHORITY

ARIANA SILVERMAN

Food choices are not arbitrary. Rather, food choices are expressions of our priorities. Whether consciously or not, people make food choices based on the questions they ask, how they answer those questions, and how they prioritize the answers. Since the formulation of biblical law, Jews have asked whether ingredients fit within the parameters of what is acceptable to eat. The biblical Hebrew root *k-sh-r* eventually came to mean "to be right, pleasing, fit; to be pronounced fit; to be ritually permitted."[1] As the laws of kashrut evolved, Jews grew particularly sensitive to two basic questions: "Where did it come from?" and "Is it 'fit' to eat?" These questions, in essence, are about food chains and gatekeepers.

The Lengthening of the Food Chain and the Role of Kosher Certification as Gatekeeper

One of the greatest changes in kosher eating is the breakdown of Jews' ability to know the path of their food and, therefore, to make individual or communal decisions about whether it is "fit" to eat. For most of

Jewish history, upholding the laws of kashrut was facilitated by the capacity to keep a close eye on food production. Until the early part of the twentieth century, the food chain for all consumers was very short. In the Jewish American immigrant community, Jewish consumers could buy food exclusively from their Jewish neighbors who were butchers, bakers, peddlers, or small shop owners.

The "gatekeepers" of the dining table were Jewish women.[2] They were the ones who purchased and prepared the food, and therefore, they were the ones responsible for ensuring that the food served on the table aligned with their values. A Jewish woman could usually tell you exactly how the food was made, where she purchased the ingredients, and in most cases, the name of the seller. These interpersonal relationships meant that she could decide, perhaps in consultation with religious authorities or other members of the community, whether a particular food vendor could be trusted. She also often had a direct relationship with the raw ingredients themselves. If she wanted a chicken for dinner, she went to the butcher and saw the live chicken before it was slaughtered.

These women's lives, however, were about to be transformed. As Joan Nathan explains in "A Social History of Jewish Food in America," "In 1925, the average American housewife made all her food at home. By 1965, 75–90% of the food she prepared had undergone some sort of factory processing."[3] This liberated women from the kitchen, allowing them to spend less time and energy preparing food. However, it also decreased their role as gatekeepers in the food chain. The bags, bottles, and boxes that replaced open bins often concealed the product itself. They also concealed where it came from.

When Jews could no longer trace their food back to its sources, they become more dependent on certifiers to ensure that the food they were eating was in consonance with Jewish law. In 1923, the Orthodox Union (OU) began its "official kashrut supervision and certification program."[4] This allowed Jews who kept kosher to have a sense that someone was serving as a gatekeeper, and a *hechsher* indicated that a food product was "fit" to eat.

A radical departure from the local Jewish butchers and bakers of past generations, the twenty-first-century marketplace promotes thousands of products that bear a kosher *hechsher*, with approximately five thousand new kosher products hitting the shelves in 2009.[5] They collectively contain ingredients from all over the world. China is among the largest producers of kosher ingredients, with over two thousand companies that produce kosher items.[6] This is no longer a food chain in which buyer and seller know one another, whether Jew or non-Jew. Workers in China are producing ingredients that are bought by anonymous executives at multinational corporations to be mixed together in laboratories by anonymous chemists and then packaged in factories by anonymous line workers to be shipped to the anonymous managers of supermarket chains, where they are stocked by anonymous employees and then scanned at the checkout by the one person you may actually meet—that is, if you do not use the self-checkout. In other words, as Samantha Shapiro reported in the *New York Times*, "Jews no longer know that their meat is kosher because they know the person who killed it but because of the symbol that appears on the shrink-wrap at the grocery store."[7]

While the length of the food chain has led to cheaper prices, it has also produced opacity and anonymity, meaning that we now know very little about how our food is made. There are dozens of kosher certifying agencies[8] whose *hechsherim* indicate whether a product was made with kosher ingredients and in kosher processing facilities, but not how the environment, animals, or workers were affected along the food chain. Somewhere along the way, it is quite possible that the values that matter to us as Jews, beyond halachic compliance, are not being upheld. Unfortunately, when part of the kosher food chain was revealed in 2004, this proved to be the case.

The Unseen Costs of the Kosher Food Chain: Agriprocessors

Aaron Rubashkin, a member of a Lubavitch Chasidic family, came to the United States from Europe in 1952[9] and started a Brooklyn butcher shop.[10] In 1987, he bought a defunct meat factory in Postville, Iowa.[11] He, and later, his son, Sholom Rubashkin, turned it into the largest kosher meatpacking plant in the country—Agriprocessors. By 2004, Agriprocessors was supplying about 60 percent of the nation's kosher meat and 40 percent of the nation's kosher poultry.[12]

On November 30, 2004, the People for the Ethical Treatment of Animals (PETA) released a videotape of the slaughtering practices at Agriprocessors.[13] Steers' throats were slit according to kosher law; however, the animals were not experiencing a quick, painless death. Rather, as reported in the *New York Times*, the video documented that after their throats were slit, "animals with dangling windpipes stand up or try to; in one case, death takes three minutes."[14]

In response to a request from the Orthodox Union,[15] Agriprocessors agreed to changes that included giving *shochtim* a stun gun, which could knock steers unconscious if they thrash about after their throats have been slit.[16] Unfortunately, Agriprocessor's treatment of animals was not the only problem.

In May 2006, Nathaniel Popper of the *Forward* broke a story that highlighted the abuses of the workers at Agriprocessors. Although Agriprocessors was one of hundreds of slaughterhouses in which illegal immigrants were working for low wages and no benefits, Popper reported that "even in the unhappy world of meatpacking, people with comparative knowledge of AgriProcessors [*sic*] and other plants . . . say that AgriProcessors stands out for its poor treatment of workers."[17]

In May 2008, Popper's discoveries became national news when a raid on the Agriprocessors plant led to the detainment of 389 illegal immigrants.[18] Following the raids, workers reported a range of atrocities that spanned the spectrum of worker abuse. They reported child labor, lack of safety training, extremely long work shifts, forced overtime without overtime pay, and verbal, sexual, and physical abuse.[19] Workers also reported that the managers threatened to report their illegal status if they complained. Iowa labor authorities documented dozens of cases of underage workers and issued citations for safety violations but failed to obtain a conviction on criminal child-labor charges. Federal prosecutors also filed charges against Agriprocessors and Sholom Rubashkin for money laundering,[20] labor law violations, bank fraud, mail and wire fraud, and nonpayment for livestock.[21] As of June 2010, Rubashkin had been convicted in federal court of 86 fraud charges.[22]

Shortening the Food Chain and Emerging Gatekeepers

Traditional kosher certifiers still fill the vital role of monitoring halachic compliance. However, the Agriprocessors scandal, coupled with the burgeoning secular food movement, motivated the re-creation of shorter Jewish food chains and gatekeepers who monitor issues other than traditional halachah.[23] Some Jews have started independent kosher meat businesses. Kosher Conscience, a poultry- and meat-buying cooperative in New York, was conceived by Simon Feil in 2006. Feil, who had attended Orthodox day school and a yeshivah in Israel, was shocked after seeing the PETA videos. Feil explained, "When I realized that kosher didn't also mean humane, I had two choices: to become a vegetarian or create kosher meat that also adhered to Jewish values across the spectrum."[24] In November 2007, Kosher Conscience sold its first organic, free-range kosher turkeys for Thanksgiving.

Mitzvah Meat, which also sells kosher, ethically raised and slaughtered, grass-fed meat from local New York State farms, had its first sales in August 2008 and is now slightly larger than Kosher Conscience. Dr. Maya Shetreat-Klein started Mitzvah Meat because she believes in the health benefits of naturally raised meat. However, she also appreciates the environmental, animal welfare, and "spiritual" benefits of being more connected with the "animal and the person raising it."[25] In July 2007, Devorah Kimelman-Block of Silver Spring, Maryland, started KOL (Kosher, Organic, Local) Foods, which is currently the largest distributor of ethical kosher meat, shipping online orders to forty eight states. Kimelman-Block declared, "My Bubbie ate kosher grass-fed beef before there was such a thing as industrially produced meat and I wanted to be able to do the same."[26] The number of independent, ethical kosher meat businesses is continuing to grow, as more and more like-minded Jews seek to provide ethical kosher meat, both locally and regionally.

The Conservative Movement and Magen Tzedek

In response to the article published in the *Forward* in May 2006, the Conservative Movement felt it needed to take action. The movement's Rabbinical Assembly (RA) and the United Synagogue of Conservative Judaism (USCJ) formed a commission to go to Postville and see the plant for themselves. They made several visits in August and September of 2006. Among the commission's members was Rabbi Morris Allen of Mendota Heights, Minnesota. Rabbi Allen cites this trip, along with a desire to promote kosher practice in his synagogue, as among the reasons he spearheaded the Hekhsher Tzedek campaign.[27]

In December 2006, under Rabbi Allen's leadership, the RA and USCJ began a joint project to create a *"hekhsher tzedek"* (justice seal) that would indicate to consumers that certain kosher products met the ethical standards outlined by the organization's Hekhsher Tzedek Commission. In 2008 the CCAR passed a resolution in support of Hekhsher Tzedek, promising to work with it in cooperation and encouraging Reform Jews to consider the guidelines established by the commission. In 2009 at the Union for Reform Judaism's 70th General Assembly, a resolution was passed which addressed many food values, including praising "the Conservative Movement for creating a new system of kosher certification that takes into account ethical factors."[28] The use of the word *hekhsher* upset many in the Orthodox community who feared that a *"hekhsher tzedek"* would be viewed as a competing kosher certification. So in December 2008, the Hekhsher Tzedek Commission changed the name of the seal from "Hekhsher Tzedek"[29] to "Magen Tzedek."[30]

The mission of the Hekhsher Tzedek Commission is to

> bring the Jewish commitment to ethics and social justice directly into the marketplace . . . and the home. The Commission's seal of approval, the Magen Tzedek, will help assure consumers that

kosher food products were produced in keeping with the highest possible Jewish ethical values and ideals for social justice in the area of labor concerns, animal welfare, environmental impact, consumer issues and corporate integrity.

The Magen Tzedek, the world's first Jewish ethical certification seal, synthesizes the aspirations of a burgeoning international movement for sustainable, responsible consumption and promotes increased sensitivity to the vast and complex web of global relationships that bring food to our tables.[31]

Magen Tzedek is meant to essentially function as a gatekeeper. While not a kosher certification, the Magen Tzedek seal will give consumers some information about the food chain of a kosher product. Consumers will know that its production met certain criteria regarding labor concerns, animal welfare, environmental impact, consumer trust, and corporate integrity. In May 2010, Rabbi Allen predicted that "over the course of the next year we will be in the marketplace."[32]

Uri L'Tzedek, Peulat Shachir, and Bema'aglei Tzedek

Some in the Orthodox Movement have taken up the cause of rewarding ethical kosher businesses with their own seal of approval. Uri L'Tzedek, which means "rise up to justice," was founded by Shmuly Yanklowitz and Ari Hart while they were rabbinical students at Yeshivat Chovevei Torah in New York. Uri L'Tzedek is

an Orthodox social justice organization guided by Torah values and dedicated to combating suffering and oppression. Through community based education, leadership development and action, Uri L'Tzedek creates discourse, inspires leaders, and empowers the Jewish community towards creating a more just world.[33]

In December 2008, they announced their intention to award a seal of ethical business practices, called Tav HaYosher (ethical seal), to kosher restaurants that meet three elements in their treatment of workers. They include "the right to fair pay, the right to fair time, and the right to a safe work environment."[34] In meeting these standards, "all criteria are derived strictly from US, State, and local law."[35] For example, the "right to fair pay" means that all workers must be paid at least the minimum wage appropriate for their job, and this applies to both documented and undocumented workers. "Fair time" includes overtime pay, one day off per week, and appropriate breaks for hours worked. "A safe work environment" includes an anti-discrimination clause, Occupational Safety and Health Administration (OSHA) regulations governing restaurant safety, and the right to unionize.

Uri L'Tzedek announced the first seven recipients on May 12, 2009, the one-year anniversary of the infamous raid on Agriprocessors.[36] As of June 2010, the seal had been awarded to almost forty businesses in New York, New Jersey, Maryland, Illinois, and Pennsylvania.[37]

In Los Angeles, an organization called Peulat Sachir[38]: Ethical Labor Initiative embarked on a similar mission. It was started by Rabbi Daniel Korobkin, spiritual leader of Kehillat Yavneh in LA's Hancock Park neighborhood, Rabbi Elazar Muskin of Young Israel of Century City, and Rabbi Yosef Kanefsky of B'nai David-Judea Congregation.[39] They offer "a covenant agreement to any business owner who complies with the six basic areas of labor law as required by the state of California," deferring, like Uri L'Tzedek, to American law. The basic areas include: (1) minimum wage, (2) payment of overtime wages, (3) provision of meal and rest breaks, (4) leave policy, (5) workers' compensation insurance, and (6) discrimination/harassment policies.[40] The business owner would sign a covenant, pledging to treat his or her workers fairly, with the expectation that the businesses would be self-policing. Unlike the Tav HaYosher, the certification could be granted to businesses outside the food industry—any local business that serves Jews, including synagogues, bookstores, and attorneys' and physicians' offices.[41] They awarded their first compliance certificates to two restaurants and two synagogues just before Passover 2009.[42]

Both organizations are based in part on the work of an Israeli organization, Bema'aglei Tzedek (circles of justice), which awards its Tav Chevrati (social seal) certification to Israeli businesses that "respect the legally-mandated rights of their employees and are accessible to people with disabilities."[43] The tagline of the Tav Chevrati initiative is "Cuisine with a Conscience."[44] Founded in 2004, Bema'aglei Tzedek is a social change organization dedicated to addressing many of Israel's societal ills, but as one of its supporters noted in *Sh'ma* magazine, it is "probably best known for being a pioneer in the field of ethical kashrut."[45] The certification has been awarded to approximately 350 establishments throughout Israel.

The Reform Movement

While the majority of Reform Jews do not look for a kosher *hechsher* on their food, it is nonetheless incumbent upon us to demand and support a higher standard of ethical behavior from the Jewish food industry. In addition to praising the work of the Hekhsher Tzedek Commission,[46] the Reform Movement has launched the "Green Table, Just Table" Initiative[47] to encourage Reform Jews to adopt ethical eating guidelines for themselves and for their synagogue communities. Synagogue guidelines enable synagogues to act as gatekeepers, giving sanction to foods that meet certain requirements. Additionally, Reform Jews can shorten the food chain by participating in a Community Supported Agriculture (CSA) program, including the Jewish CSAs spearheaded by Hazon.[48]

We now live in a world in which many food chains have become environmentally disastrous and inhumane. When faced with the complexities of modern life, Reform Jews have sought the prophetic voice and looked to our tradition for wisdom and insight. We must do so again now. The question facing Reform Jews is not confined to our beliefs about kashrut and custom. The question facing Reform Jews is whether the ethical mandate we seek as Jews applies to the very sources of our sustenance. In the beginning, Jews knew the Source of their food. It is time to look back to the sources.

NOTES

1. Marcus Jastrow, *Dictionary of the Talmud* (1903), 677–78.

2. For more on this idea, and how it can be seen in Europe, see Ruth Ann Abusch-Magder, "Kashrut: The Possibility and Limits of Women's Domestic Power," in *Food and Judaism* (Omaha, NE: Creighton University Press, distributed by the University of Nebraska Press, 2005), 169–92.

3. Joan Nathan, "A Social History of Jewish Food in America," in *Food and Judaism* (Omaha, NE: Creighton University Press, distributed by the University of Nebraska Press, 2005), 7.

4. Ibid., 8.

5. Julie Wiener, "Inside the Business of Kosher," *Jewish Week* (New York), October 27, 2009.

6. Ibid.

7. Samantha Shapiro, "The Kosher Wars," *New York Times*, October 12, 2008.

8. See, e.g., http://www.kashrut.com/agencies/.

9. Nathaniel Popper, "In Iowa Meat Plant, Kosher 'Jungle' Breeds Fear, Injury, Short Pay," *Forward*, May 26, 2006.

10. Julia Preston, "Rabbis Debate Kosher Ethics at Meat Plant," *New York Times*, August 22, 2008.

11. Susan Saulny, "Hundreds Are Arrested in U.S. Sweep of Meat Plant," *New York Times*, May 13, 2008.

12. Shapiro, "Kosher Wars."

13. Preston, "Rabbis Debate Kosher Ethics at Meat Plant."

14. Donald G. McNeil Jr., "Videos Cited in Calling Kosher Slaughterhouse Inhumane," *New York Times*, December 1, 2004; see also Aaron Gross, "When Kosher Isn't Kosher," *Tikkun*, March/April 2005.

15. Donald G. McNeil, Jr., "Kosher Authority Seeks Change in Steer Killings," *New York Times*, December 3, 2004.

16. "Slaughterhouse to Change Its Process," *New York Times*, December 9, 2004.

17. Popper, "In Iowa Meat Plant."

18. Preston, "Rabbis Debate Kosher Ethics at Meat Plant."

19. Julia Preston, "After Iowa Raid, Immigrants Fuel Labor Inquiries," *New York Times*, July 27, 2008.

20. Ben Harris, "More Charges against Rubashkin," *JTA*, January 19, 2009.

21. Rebecca Dube, "New Owner of Agriprocessors Faces Old Questions about Its Plans for Company," *Forward*, July 31, 2009.

22. "Rubashkin Convicted on 86 Charges," *JTA*, November 12, 2009.

23. Sue Fishkoff, "The Greening of Kashrut," *Hadassah Magazine*, February 2009, 30–31.

24. Julie Wiener, "Beefing Up Eco-Kosher," *Jewish Week* (New York), September 30, 2009.

25. Ibid.

26. Cheryl Kolin, "The Latest in Brisket: Grass-Fed Kosher Beef," *Jewish Advocate*, September 11, 2009.

27. Preston, "Rabbis Debate Kosher Ethics at Meat Plant."

28. See the CCAR Resolution "Kashrut and Hekhsher Tzedek" (http://data.ccarnet.org/cgi-bin/resodisp.pl?file=kashrut&year=2008A) and the URJ Resolution "Worker Rights, Ethical Consumerism and the Kosher Food Industry" (http://urj.org/about/union/governance/reso/?syspage=article&item_id=1909). See also the URJ Resolution "Eating Jewishly" (http://urj.org/about/union/governance/reso/?syspage=article&item_id=27522).

29. Ben Harris, "With New Name, Ethical Kashrut Seal Can Appear alongside the O.U.," *JTA*, December 26, 2008.

30. *Magen* can mean both "star" and "shield."

31. "Mission Statement," Magen Tzedek, http://magentzedek.org/?page_id=17 (accessed June 18, 2010).

32. Amy Klein, "Conservatives' Ethical Seal Nearing Kosher Marketplace," *JTA*, May 25, 2010.

33. "Mission & 3 Pillars," Uri L Tzedek, http://www.utzedek.org/whoweare/mission-a-3-pillars.html (accessed June 18, 2010).

34. "Standards," Uri L Tzedek, http://www.utzedek.org/tavhayosher/standards.html (accessed June 18, 2010).

35. Ibid.

36. Sue Fishkoff, "N.Y. Food Establishments Earn New Ethics Seal," *JTA*, May 12, 2009.

37. "Restaurant List/Map," Uri L Tzedek, http://www.utzedek.org/tavhayosher/restaurant-listmap.html (accessed June 18, 2010).

38. *Peulat sachir* means "the wages of a laborer." Peulat Sachir derives its name from the injunction in Leviticus 19:13 that prohibits holding a worker's wages until the morning. It does not appear that they are currently active.

39. Sue Fishkoff, "Orthodox Groups to Offer Ethical Seals for Businesses," *JTA*, December 15, 2008.

40. Rabbi N. Daniel Korobin, "Ethics Plan Would Raise Sanctity of Business," *Jewish Journal*, March 18, 2009.

41. Fishkoff, "Orthodox Groups to Offer Ethical Seals for Businesses."

42. Fishkoff, "N.Y. Food Establishments Earn New Ethics Seal."

43. "Tav Chevrati," http://www.mtzedek.org.il/english/TavChevrati.asp (accessed June 16, 2010).

44. Ibid.

45. Dyonna Ginsburg, "A Journey into the Ethics of Kashrut," *Sh'ma* (November 2009): 20.

46. See note 28 above.

47. See http://urj.org/life/food/.

48. For more information on starting a CSA, see http://urj.org/life/food/?syspage=document&item_id=27140. For information on Hazon's CSA Program, see http://www.hazon.org/go.php?q=/food/CSA/aboutHazonCSA.html.

31

BUT IS THE *MASHGICHAH* KOSHER?

Mary L. Zamore

Admittedly, I have taken for granted all the letters typed on official synagogue letterhead that are crookedly taped to bakery and restaurant windows, and I have given no thought to the wide variety of symbols that blend into the labels of the many groceries I buy contentedly. However, the lessons of the last two years have brought these symbols and letters into a new light for me. As I carefully scrutinize the kashrut certificates in delis, I catch myself wondering about the rabbi behind the *hashgachah* and whether people object to his position.

In addition to my responsibilities as a congregational rabbi, I am a Reform *mashgichah*, overseeing a neighborhood bakery. Several weeks after I was ordained, I fell into this job by accident, or perhaps, I should say that the job fell into me by accident. Working too late on a Friday afternoon, I received a stranger into my study who was looking for a rabbi, any rabbi. The stranger turned out to be the owner of a local bakery that needed a new *mashgiach*. Filled with enthusiasm, but lacking

Adapted with permission from Mary L. Zamore, "But Is the *Mashgichah* Kosher?" *CCAR Journal*, Spring 2001, 77–80.

experience, I accepted this responsibility without fully understanding the implications of my actions. Like most functions in the practical rabbinate, I envisioned using my HUC-JIR training as a foundation on which I could build through study and the support of my colleagues. However, over the last two years, I have been confronted with many challenges, the intensity of which I would have never predicted.

When I was asked to oversee the bakery, I explained to the non-Jewish owners that a Reform woman rabbi may not be their best choice. I warned them that the bulk of their customers who are from the greater Jewish community might not be pleased. They insisted that they wanted me. At first, I mused that the bakery's owners thought I would be a pushover—a Reform, woman rabbi with no standards. So, I did everything in my power to impress upon them the seriousness with which I was assuming my responsibilities. They did not mind. Even when local rabbis threatened to denounce the bakery's kashrut, and even when one synagogue withdrew all their *oneg* and party business, they still insisted on retaining me. Truly, I do not know why the owners decided to take this stand jeopardizing their business of twelve years. I was embarrassed that my Jewish community presented itself in such a bad light to the greater community and I was impressed at the dedication of the bakery owners. Their commitment to the Jewish community, albeit profitable, is commendable.

I have always struggled with the meaning of kashrut. While I find that the connections to God, my tradition, and my community that kashrut creates are spiritually fulfilling, I feel uncomfortable with the logistical burdens it can produce. Keeping kosher takes time and effort. In addition, I am conscious of the barriers to the nonkosher community that kashrut can erect. Eating together builds connections; a restricted diet can encumber dining with others. While in college, my search led me to the decision to keep kosher in a way that balances the benefits with my concerns. Today, my home is kosher with two sets of dishes, although I do not require *hechsher* on all the food products I bring into my house. I eat vegetarian or fish out. I thought overseeing the bakery would force me to confront kashrut in the most direct way and, perhaps, help me to resolve my questions. I believed overseeing the bakery would be a service to the greater Jewish community, giving me a connection to many Jews beyond my own congregants.

The majority of the bakery's business comes from the Reform and Conservative congregations in the area; there are other local bakeries that serve the Orthodox community. I knew that for the bakery I would need to require a higher standard of kashrut than that which I keep at home or that which my synagogue keeps. Continuing the initial *hashgachah* work of a Conservative colleague, I just had to oversee and maintain the kashrut there. In other words, it was supposed to be relatively easy work. After all, an established kosher bakery with few new recipes creates not the same amount of worry as a restaurant, for example.

Initially, things went smoothly. I read. I studied. I spoke to Conservative and Orthodox rabbis who oversee bakeries and restaurants. These colleagues readily answered my questions and shared their experiences with me, addressing me warmly, as colleagues should. In addition, the bakery's former *mashgiach* reassured me that I could do the job properly. And so I did. Then the phone calls started. Strangely enough, three local Conservative rabbis called within the same week, announcing their intention to withdraw their synagogues' *oneg* and challah contracts. Threatening to renounce the bakery to the community, the first complainer told me I could not be trusted to oversee the bakery. I am a member of the CCAR, which has renounced halachah, he explained. Over a series of heated phone calls I asked him to consider sitting down with me and hearing for himself what I actually do at the bakery. I asked him to judge my actions rather than to make assumptions. I later found out that none of these rabbis believed that I personally observed kashrut. He finally agreed. Our discussion was difficult and challenging, but in the end, he accepted my *hechsher* and even gave me a friendly welcome to the community. He has since defended me to his colleagues and community. In fact, the second rabbi accepted my *hechsher* because of the recommendations of the first.

The third was the greatest disappointment. He simply called and said he was renouncing my *hechsher* to his community. Again, I asked him to sit and talk with me. He refused. I asked him to just think about it. He refused. His reasons: first, I am a Reform rabbi and he would never, ever trust a Reform or Conservative *hechsher*. Period. His other reason—I have not studied those sections of the *Shulchan Aruch* that address kashrut. While I was disgusted by the rude manner in which he treated me, I accepted his advice and added the pertinent sections from the *Shulchan Aruch* to my studies.

I did not expect to go unnoticed as a Reform, woman *mashgichah*. After all, my feminine name jumps off the kashrut certificate hanging in the bakery, alerting consumers that a liberal rabbi is overseeing the bakery. I expected questions about my standards. I have clearly informed my colleagues that I am willing to answer any questions and am willing to accept that my standards or interpretations of laws may not match those of a specific colleague. But I am not willing to accept stereotypes and prejudice. Just because I am a Reform rabbi does not mean that I am incapable of overseeing a kosher bakery. I know my predecessor was not subjected to any questions about his own kashrut or his work at the bakery.

I recently sat down to defend my *hechsher* with a Conservative rabbi who had just moved into our community. I called him to introduce myself and to explain that I oversee the bakery from which his new synagogue purchases cookies and challah. I invited him to express any concerns; he asked for a complete tour of the bakery. After the one-and-a-half-hour tour and intense grilling, he approved the bakery for dairy, but not for pareve use. While there were many moments during our meeting when I regretted making the initial phone call, I respected this rabbi's questions, as he is a trained *mashgiach* and he has overseen bakeries and restaurants in the past. Some of the other rabbis asked questions that revealed little knowledge of cooking, save the kashrut of a bakery. Although I appreciated his knowledgeable approach, I doubt if he regularly insists on overseeing the entire inspection of other bakeries. At one point, this rabbi turned to me and asked point blank, "Why would you want to oversee a bakery?" I tried to describe my feelings about Judaism, God, *K'lal Yisrael*, and kashrut. However, I could not help wondering to myself, what rabbi asks a colleague why one would want to officiate at a wedding or visit the sick.

I believe that ultimately my patience will pay off. I feel that, by demonstrating to my colleagues and to their congregants, I can be a qualified, capable *mashgichah*. Eventually I will break their stereotypes and, perhaps, build some connections within the Jewish community. Yet, I am disappointed that my colleagues have not treated me as an equal; that they have been more concerned with declaring me *t'reif* than worrying about the kashrut at the bakery. All I have asked is that they merely spend the time to find out what I actually do, rather than making assumptions about Reform rabbis. I ask to be judged by what I do, not by who I am.

I am certainly not the only Reform rabbi functioning as a *mashgiach*. There are Reform rabbis who oversee the kashrut of nursing homes, schools, and other institutions. Without a doubt, every congregational rabbi helps set policy concerning synagogue kitchens. With the vote of confidence kashrut has gained through the *Statement of Principles*, perhaps the Reform Movement will someday have a certification program for *mashgichim/mashgichot*, as we now successfully offer for *mohalim/mohalot*. As I do my work at the bakery, I feel the weight of public scrutiny. I know that if I make a mistake, not only am I judged; so, too, is the entire Reform rabbinate. It would be comforting to have more direct support through training by my own movement.

When I see my congregation's nursery school children carrying home their challot on Friday afternoon, I know that I am doing work of which I can be proud. I am doing work for my Reform community and, more so, for my greater Jewish community. And, by means of this sacred task, I strengthen my bond to God through food. In turn, may God strengthen me to do my work with dignity.

And may the *milchigs* and pareves stay separate. Amen.

32

WINE

Our Symbol of Joy

TERJE Z. LANDE AND OREN POSTREL

For most Reform Jews, the expression "kosher wine" conjures the image of sitting around the Passover table forcing down a sickly sweet liquid that burns the throat. In fact, ironically, for some it is not a Jewish holiday without that taste. However, there is much more to the Jewish relationship with wine. In order to make informed decisions about the role of wine in one's personal kashrut, it helps to appreciate its function in Jewish ritual and to become educated about the current state of kosher and nonkosher wine making.

Historical and Ritual Context

In much of the Jewish ritual tradition, the consumption of wine is a central ingredient. Wine is considered a primary symbol of joy in Judaism. Wine is thought to enhance personal and communal happiness and denotes comfort and sustenance.

Jewish text provides rich imagery connected with wine. In the Bible, wine is associated with the profound nature of human experience, such as in the sensual and loving relationship in Song of Songs 1:2, "Let him kiss me with the kisses of his mouth, for his love is better than wine." Wine is also used to describe the complacency and threat of Israel's greatest enemies by the prophet Jeremiah, who spoke: "Moab has been at ease from his youth, and he has settled on his lees and has not been emptied from vessel to vessel" (Jer. 48:11). Unlike in the Christian tradition, in which wine is transfigured into Jesus, in Judaism wine is only wine. Wine is never intended to imply anything more than the joyous pleasure it imparts and our ability to experience *hidur mitzvah* (beautification of a ritual). According to the Psalmist, "Wine gladdens the heart of man" (Ps. 104:15). As our symbol of joy and celebration, wine, like bread, claims a sufficiently high status to have its own specially formulated blessing created by the Rabbis of the Talmud: *borei p'ri hagafen* (Creator of the fruit of the vine). From the Talmud (*M'gilah* 16b), we have the salutation before drinking wine: *l'chayim* (to life). With few but notable exceptions, wine is included in every ritual moment in the life of a Jew. The Rabbis of the Talmud instituted that on every Shabbat eve and every Shabbat day wine is used while invoking the name of God in order to sanctify this period of rest. Wine is used at rituals that mark change of personal status, such as entering into the covenant of Judaism and becoming a married person.

The exceptions for consumption of wine include public days of mourning, such as the nine days leading up to Tishah B'Av,[1] when it is customary to abstain from wine to accentuate the spirit of loss and mourning, marking the destruction of both Temples. Nor is wine consumed as part of Jewish mourning customs or at the signing of a divorce decree, the *get*. Since wine is so closely connected to moments of joy, it makes sense that it would not be used in these situations.

In the Hebrew Bible, we are introduced to the fermented juice of the vinifera grape[2] after Noah's traumatic witnessing of God's global flood intended to rid the world of corruption. As Noah emerges from the ark, he plants a vineyard and soon after becomes intoxicated from the wine. In that compromised state, he is drawn into corrupt behavior with his own sons. Noah's imbibing and its consequences lead to future

Jewish attitudes toward alcohol consumption. The overconsumption of wine is frequently blamed by the Jewish textual tradition for unleashing deleterious behavior with punishable consequences. For example, a blessing spoken while intoxicated, the Talmud teaches, is thought to be a *to-eivah*, an abomination. While wine drinking is permitted and even encouraged, drinking to excess is not. The exception to this general approach is Purim, when, according to the Gemara (*M'gilah* 7b), Jews are commanded to drink until one can no longer distinguish between "cursed is Haman" and "blessed is Mordecai." On the other hand, wine is described in the Talmud as inducing a liberating effect on consciousness. Rav Huna, a great wine collector and appreciator, describes wine in Tractate *Bava Batra* (12b) as a way to open the heart to reason.

In our modern context, however, it is important to be sensitive to those who struggle with alcoholism (see CCAR Responsa 5755.16 for further discussion) and, in addition, not to press alcohol on children. Some rabbis ask the congregants to raise their cup of "grape product" rather than "wine" in thanksgiving when it is time for *Kiddush*.

What Makes Wine Kosher and Why Does It Matter?

As Reform Jews embrace ritual kashrut, it is important to be educated about the choices concerning wine. First, this chapter will explore the differences between wines that are certified kosher and those that have no *hechsher*.

While many Jews are surprised to learn that there is more to kosher wine than the Manischewitz Concord Grape variety, high-quality kosher wines are now produced in all major wine-making countries, including France, Italy, Austria, Hungary, Spain, Portugal, Argentina, Chile, United States, Australia, New Zealand, South Africa, Cyprus, and of course, Israel. What, then, makes a wine kosher?

Outside of the Land of Israel,[3] there are two main factors that determine whether or not a wine qualifies for an Orthodox *hechsher*:

1. Any person involved in handling the wine from the time the grapes are crushed to the time of bottling must be an "observant Jew," meaning one who observes an Orthodox-defined Shabbat.
2. All ingredients, tools, and utensils used in the entire wine-making process must be certified kosher.

The first of these requirements specifically concerns the issue of *yayin nesech* (libation wine), ensuring that the wine was not made or used for pagan sacrificial purposes. This was a huge concern for the Talmudic Rabbis and even today seems to be of continuing concern within the Orthodox community.[4] While these concerns were valid in ancient times, from a progressive, Reform Jewish perspective, they should have no validity today with regard to commercially produced wines. This suspicion of gentiles (or even nonobservant Jews) also led to the category of *mevushal* wines, the process of heating wine to the point where according to halachah the liquid is no longer considered a libation wine. While this legal loophole is difficult for liberal Jews to comprehend, a kosher wine that has gone through this process can never lose its kosher status, regardless of who subsequently touches it.

An additional reason for these arcane laws was to dissuade social contact with non-Jews, as it was believed that drinking wine together would lead to intermarriage. Strangely enough, the laws of kashrut do not prohibit Jews from sharing their kosher wine with non-Jews, nor do the laws apply to liquor or other fermented drinks. Although it has been proved beyond a doubt that it is possible to make excellent wines that are *mevushal*,[5] Rachel S. Mikva (chapter 4) is correct in pointing out that this approach is an offensive concept that Reform Jews should reject.

From a Reform Jewish standpoint, especially as it concerns having an educated, informed relationship to the food and drink we consume, the second set of kosher requirements should be the focus of our attention. Whereas most consumers would consider a bottle of wine to consist of 100 percent grapes from an ingredient perspective, the wine-making process may in fact include a number of other ingredients or agents. It is important to note that, in most cases, the wineries are under no legal obligation to inform the consumer about these additives on their labels.

The primary purpose of these added ingredients is to "fine," or to clarify and filter, the wine. In order to remove particles and grape parts or even to alter or modify the taste of the wine, vintners may utilize both organic and nonorganic components such as egg whites, fish bladders, milk protein, or bentonite.[6] Historically, some countries also used ox blood for this purpose, a practice that was prohibited by the European Union only as recently as 1999.[7] While fining practices may vary from place to place, the end consumer may be oblivious, as the label requirements in most countries do not compel producers to declare these ingredients. The notable exception is Australia, which has required full disclosure since 1994.

From a kashrut perspective, undisclosed ingredients are a significant problem. As these ingredients are intentionally introduced, they are not nullified by the one-sixtieth rule.[8] This Talmudic principle allows for accidental contamination up to one-sixtieth of a cooked or manufactured food if the contamination does not affect the taste of the item. In the case of the fining of wine, the ingredients are intentionally added and may alter the taste of the wine. Hence, one may unwittingly end up with a bottle of wine that is "dairy" or, worse, blatantly *t'reif* unless one knows the practices of a particular winery. The irony is that, with the exception of Australia (and certified vegan wines), a *hechsher* on the bottle is the only consumer protection that will guarantee that a bottle of wine is pareve (wines certified as vegetarian may have been fined using dairy products). This practice is clearly a concern also for those with severe food allergies.

Similarly, for those who observe Passover, the question becomes one of *chameitz*: has the yeast used in fermenting the wine ever been in contact with one of the prohibited grains? As Alroy (1990) points out, this could happen if the vat was cleaned with a grain-based agent such as vodka.[9] Another point of concern would be if winemakers add other types of yeast to speed up the fermentation process.[10] Again, only a *hechsher* can guarantee that the bottle on your seder table is *chameitz* free.

Israel and Wine: Historical, Spiritual, and Economic Connections

Grapes and the production of wine have been inextricably linked to Israel since biblical times. In fact, clusters of grapes were one of only three objects that the twelve spies brought back from the Promised Land to the Israelites waiting in the wilderness to exemplify the bounty of the Land (Num. 13:23–26). The importance of wine for both Temple and general personal use is attested to by the more than three thousand references to wine in the Talmud[11] and by the fact that wine was produced in ancient Israel until the Moslem conquest.

Wine making was reintroduced in the second half of the nineteenth century, with the aim of providing an economic foundation for the early Zionist immigrants. However, Israeli wines of high quality were not produced until the last twenty to twenty-five years. The introduction of modern techniques allowed wine makers to realize the full potential of Israel's varied soils and climates. Today, there are more than 140 wineries in Israel, producing more than thirty-six million bottles per year.[12] While most of these wines are made under rabbinic supervision, many of the smaller wineries cannot afford to incur the cost of certification, and a small number deliberately choose not to be certified for ideological reasons. Some of the leading Israeli wineries (both *hechshered* and non-*hechshered*) now produce wines that are sought after by wine lovers around the world.

There are few experiences that allow a more direct and spiritual connection to a place (some may call it *terroir*) than the enjoyment of a wine made from grapes grown in a single vineyard. With consistently high-quality wines from Israel now being available throughout North

America, there is no reason why Reform Jews should not be encouraged to choose Israeli wines, even outside of the usual Passover buying season. Not only is this one way of supporting Israel economically, but it also strengthens our spiritual bonds to the Land itself. As Israeli winemaker Shuki Yashuv told the *Washington Post*, wine making should be seen as an expression of Zionism: "Wine is a deep connection to my origin and gives me a very primitive sense of belonging to this place. Wine is an expression of normalcy, which is not so self-evident for Jews."[13]

A Role for Kosher Wine in Reform Kashrut?

In the classic *t'shuvah* (responsa) on whether or not all wines are kosher in the eyes of the Conservative Movement, Rabbi Israel Silverman (1977) held that all wines produced in modern factories should be allowed, as "no human being touches it." Even so, he still recommended that when fulfilling a ritual obligation, *hechshered* wines should be used, especially those produced in Israel. However, knowledge of the wine-making process reveals that many wines cannot be defined as "untouched," but rather actively treated during the production process; it is difficult to apply the same generalization today.

From a Reform Jewish perspective, it is up to the individual to make educated choices. If one wants to follow a stricter level of kashrut, it may make sense to use wines that are either *hechshered* or certified vegan both for regular drinking with meals and for ritual purposes. For those who want to be more lenient, it may be meaningful to separate the two purposes and use only *hechshered* or certified vegan wines for *Kiddush*, while enjoying other wines for regular consumption.

Congregations need to create and maintain a comfortable, noncoercive atmosphere concerning wine in communal settings, especially on Purim. Grape juice should always be available and clearly marked. It is incumbent on both clergy and lay leadership to model the responsible drinking that Jewish tradition calls for. An integral part of this is to ensure the inclusion of alcohol education in our religious schools.

As consumers, it is important to push for clear labeling practices for the sake of both religious and health purposes. Regardless of what level of observance you are comfortable with, it is, for all the reasons mentioned above, worth seeking out some wines from Israel. Next time you are visiting your local wine store, inquire about Israeli wines; next time the congregation travels to Israel, make sure to visit a winery.

Wine remains one of the primary symbols of joy within Judaism. May we continue to enjoy responsibly the pleasure it imparts and, through it, to experience *hidur mitzvah*—the beautification of sacred rituals. *L'chayim*!

NOTES

1. Except for Shabbat *Kiddush*.

2. The type of grape from which modern wines are produced.

3. In Israel, agricultural requirements such as *sh'mitah* (leaving the land fallow every seventh year) and *orlah* (not harvesting new plantings until they are four years old), as well as a symbolic tribute to the Temple, also apply.

4. Avrohom Juravel and Zev Baruch, "Uncorking the Secrets of Kosher Wine," *Jewish Action*, Spring 2007.

5. See, e.g., Daniel Rogov's descriptions of U.S.-made *mevushal* wines in *Rogov's Guide to Kosher Wines*. (Jerusalem: The Toby Press, 2010).

6. A derivative of clay. For a full discussion of fining agents, see Caroline Pyevich, "Why Is Wine So Fined?" *Vegetarian Journal* 16, no. 1 (January/February 1997).

7. Council Regulation (EC) No. 1493/1999.

8. Odelia Alroy argues in the article "Kosher Wine" in *Judaism* 39 (1990): 452–60 that as long as the intention is to remove these agents, then the one-sixtieth rule will apply. However, according to Klein, anything that was added with intent cannot subsequently be annulled through this mechanism (Isaac Klein, *A Guide to Jewish Religious Practice* [New York: Jewish Theological Seminary, 1979]).

9. Alroy, "Kosher Wine."

10. See Sergio Esposito, *Passion on the Vine* (New York: Broadway Books, 2008), 149, for discussion on Italian practices.

11. A search on the word "wine" in *Judaica Classics: Talmud*.

12. Daniel Rogov, *Rogov's Guide to Israeli Wines* (Jerusalem: The Toby Press, 2010).

13. Linda Gradstein, "Israel's Wines: A Culture Uncorked," *Washington Post*, June 7, 2009.

33

REAL LIFE / REAL FOOD
Kiddush and Mad Dog 20-20—A Kosher Combination?

DEBORAH BODIN COHEN

In 1990, I graduated from University of Michigan and, like so many other recent graduates, moved to Washington, D.C., to work in the world of politics and public policy. I joined the staff of the Advocacy Institute, as a monitor of the alcoholic beverage industry and its marketing. My first assignment: tracking Cisco, a new low-end, fortified wine.

Bottled to look like a wine cooler and full of sugar to taste like one, Cisco contains four to five times more alcohol. By drinking just one bottle, an average-sized person would be legally drunk. Cheap and easy on the palate of novice drinkers, Cisco quickly became popular among teenagers and college students, who dubbed it "liquid crack." In emergency rooms across the country, doctors treated for alcohol poisoning young people who drank Cisco. Eventually, the Federal Trade Commission stepped in and forced changes in Cisco's appearance and marketing.[1]

One day my boss passed by my desk and asked, "You know that Manischewitz Concord Grape that your grandmother serves on Passover? The same company that makes your grandmother's Manishewitz also produces and markets Cisco." The maker of Manischewitz,

Centerra Wine Company (named Canandaigua Wine Company until 2006), in addition to kosher wines, produces two of the most popular fortified wines, Cisco and Richards Wild Irish Rose. Cisco and Richards Wild Irish Rose are not kosher and have a higher alcohol content and lower price tag than Manischewitz. Richards Wild Irish Rose, with 30 million bottles in sales annually,[2] has been a flagship product of the company since 1954. Centerra Wine Company shares the $125 million fortified wine market with two other wineries: Mogen David and E. & J. Gallo.[3] In comparison, the kosher wine market is about one-fifth the size of the fortified wine market. Kosher wines have about $27 million in yearly sales in the United States; Manischewitz and Mogen David make up 88 percent of these sales.[4]

Fortified wines, also called "bum wine" and "hooch," are available almost exclusively in poor urban areas and college campuses and are shunned by most liquor stores in middle class and affluent areas.[5] A 375-milliliter pocket flask of fortified wine sells for under three dollars and contains the equivalent of four to five shots of vodka; its high sugar content placates hunger, an important consideration when choosing between a meal and drink. The word "wino" came into use during the Depression to describe those unfortunate souls who turned to fortified wine to forget their troubles.

As Reform Jews, we search for holiness through working for social justice. Fortified wines' purpose is enabling street alcoholics and young people to get drunk—hardly a holy or just mission. Yet, wine is one of the only kosher products that Reform Jews universally purchase. As Jews, we use kosher wine to sanctify our most sacred events—marriage, *b'rit milah*, Passover, Shabbat. The root of *Kiddush*, the blessing over wine, means "holiness."

Mogen David Winery's fortified wine, named MD 20-20, is an especially disturbing example of the problem with these wines. On the street, MD 20-20 is called "Mad Dog 20-20." Rappers sing about Mad Dog 20-20's potency. On college campuses, fraternity members "Mad Dog" prospective recruits—knocking at their doors at daybreak and forcing them to drink a bottle quickly. *Magen David* means "Star of David." It is the holy symbol of our people. Can the profaning of such a holy symbol truly be considered kosher?

NOTES

1. "Canandaigua Wine Co. Agrees to Advertising, Packaging Changes for Cisco Fortified Wine to Settle FTC Charges," Federal Trade Commission Press Release, March 12, 1991.

2. Stephane Fitch, "Up from the Gutter," *Forbes*, March 20, 2000.

3. David Dietz, "The Bottom of the Barrel," *San Francisco Chronicle*, July 7, 1996.

4. W. Blake Gray, "Kosher Keepers: Many of the Wines Enjoyed by Passover Observers Are Splendid Enough for Everyone, Year-Round," *SFGate*, April 14, 2005.

5. Michael Wilson, "For $2, a Wine for Those Who Can't Be Bothered with a Cork," *New York Times*, February 4, 2010.

Part Seven

———

Guarding Our Health:
Sh'mirat HaGuf

As our generation engages in a discussion of where we have gone wrong concerning our health, we often find ourselves mindlessly munching on cookies at the *Oneg Shabbat* and serving pizza and soda at youth group functions. Ignoring the call for a new approach to eating, the majority of our Jewish institutions are still functioning in a vacuum where healthy food is concerned. This chapter provides the foundation for a broad discussion on the issues surrounding our health. In this way, Reform Jews can combine their interest in contemporary health issues with the inspiration of our ancient Jewish texts. William Cutter ("Palates, Pilates, Politics: A Prophetic Vision for Eating") shares his personal journey to health, while showing us how the Jewish tradition can and cannot guide our food choices. Cutter also challenges us to look beyond our own health to include concern for the food insecure. In part 8, Neal Gold's "Let All Who Are Hungry Come and Eat: Food Ethics, *Tzedakah*, and How We Celebrate" creates an interesting dialogue with Cutter's questions concerning the role of food at our life-cycle events. Also found in part 8, Michael Namath and Rachel Cohen's "Raising Our Voices for Food Justice" demonstrates how the American Farm Bill has shaped the American diet and has affected our health.

Applying the model of the Pharisaic fellowship tables, Doug Sagal ("Of Pharisees and Allergies: *Shulchan Shalom*") broadens our conversation by teaching us how to be inclusive of those with food allergies and sensitivities. Sagal's exploration of the Pharisaic fellowship tables complements Ellen Lippmann and Trisha Arlin's "We Eat First: A Congregational Snapshot," found in part 9. Sagal explores the obligation a community has to accommodate those with special eating needs. This is becoming a more urgent question as our institutions struggle to welcome children with deadly allergies. Although this article reflects a specific health context, we can extend the questions raised by Sagal to challenge us to think about how to accommodate those with other needs (like vegetarians or Jews who keep strictly kosher). This gives our communities much to think about.

Any discussion of Reform dietary practice must recognize the struggle of some members of our community to have a healthy relationship with food. Therefore, Ruth A. Zlotnick ("Returning Food to Its Rightful Place: Eating Disorders in the Jewish Community") sensitizes us to the challenges of eating disorders and reminds us to educate our communities about these illnesses. In the Real Life / Real Food section, Julie Pelc Adler ("Redefining Healthy Eating, For Life") urges us to draw lessons from Shabbat in order to enjoy our food at every meal.

Part 7 dares us to create healthier options for our communities—to rid our synagogues of endless candy for children and sugary drinks for all. As William Cutter points out, our Jewish institutions spend little time on teaching or modeling healthy eating; we rarely incorporate such values into our life-cycle events. The challenge is to create welcoming tables that also nurture our individual health. As the Jewish community tackles this directive, I urge our community to share our successes. Hopefully the changes that support healthy living will also sustain the environment.

34

PALATES, PILATES, POLITICS

A Prophetic Vision for Eating

WILLIAM CUTTER

The Contrary Logic of How We Eat

Our colleague, liturgist Dahlia Marx, opens her book *When I Sleep and When I Awaken*, "If you want to know the heart of the Jew, listen to how we pray."[1] I begin this chapter with a slight reversal of that affirmation: if you want to know what makes the Jewish heart beat faster, watch how we eat. We may accompany our eating with rituals of prayer and blessing, but the fact is we eat more than we pray. The passion for eating has come at a cost that cannot easily be alleviated amid the crosscurrents of advice about what is ethical, what is healthy, and what is sustainable; but now is a good time to do some serious thinking about our complex affair with food.

We find ourselves in an era in which we are obsessed with health, yet neglectful, and at the same time we have been unable, in spite of notable efforts, to attend to the demon hunger in the world. While we are certainly more attentive to aspects of nutrition, we, the well-off, fill our restaurants—emporiums of pleasure but not of nutrition—almost every night, while the poor can barely afford food at all. There is more food writing, more television entertainment about food, and more food talk than ever to fill our leisure hours. My task in this chapter is to make a case, in Reform Jewish terms, for healthy eating in the midst of these crosscurrents and amid a passionate interest in what we put in our mouths. As long as we honor the palates of people (their likes and dislikes and the limits on Nazirite aspirations), we can also attend to the pilates (the physical health of people) and the politics (communal care for all).

We Begin in Text but Conclude in Reality, Logic, and Program

I bring to this chapter my own skepticism about Jewish texts as norm setting, combined with my love for studying those texts, an apparent contradiction that I hope to reconcile here. I bring to the table over thirty years of careful consideration of what to eat, preceded by an equal number of years of abuse through dining on fatted calves and fowl and relaxing under the smoke of unfiltered cigarettes. I was the product of an immigrant culture that celebrated because our family could afford to eat large quantities of animal meat. My aesthetic was quantity. Only years later, under the stress of personal illness, did I begin to understand that I really could do something about eating for health that didn't compromise my aesthetic sensibility. I think I was fairly typical. Now that there is a new spirit in the land and a fresh consciousness about nutrition, it is also true that we progressive Jews are driven less by the compulsions of our immigrant status or a need to demonstrate our "arrival" into American culture. Perhaps in such a climate, young men will enter their forties with less fat on their bellies and less nicotine in their lungs than I did.

This hard-won awareness of eating for health has not come from the ancient texts of Jewish life but from living. But if we will ask whether there is some Jewish literature that can get us started in our quest for health, or if healthful eating can be a valid way to enter our rich textual heritage, or if thinking about culinary responsibility is a way to probe the history of effective Jewish social justice, then we have a valid exercise on which to embark. It is surely easier to draw on Jewish texts to justify feeding the poor than to argue for eating broccoli (although there are plenty of classic texts that argue for eating vegetables). Let me state here the values upon which I will build my case for the mitzvah of bio-nutrition and gustatory moderation. The case relies on a simple principle in Judaism, to do what is "straight and good" (Prov. 2:20), what is, in other words, self-evident,[2] and associated with a variety of subordinate themes that will support that wisdom. Rabbinic respect for the body can serve only as the most general inspiration and cannot guide us toward specific behaviors. Overriding principles serve as better starting points in the discussion than as conclusions about normative behavior.

So what are some of those overriding principles beyond "the good" urged by Proverbs? What are the principles that begin our discussion, the ideas that we can reframe into starting points for our consideration of nutrition? "Improvement of the world" (*tikkun olam*), viewing God as good and as enabling good (*hatov v'hameitiv*), defining the importance of land in terms of its healthy yield (*haaretz hatovah asher natan lach*), preserving nature's resources (*bal tashchit*), living in the image of God (*b'tzelem Elohim*), caring for our bodies (*sh'mirat haguf*), acting with intentionality (*kavanah*), understanding boundaries (*hasagat g'vul*), and finally, celebrating once in awhile at both fixed seasons and spontaneous occasions (*v'samachta b'chagecha*)—all of these texts can reflect on the place of food in our lives, and encourage moderation and wisdom in eating, but none of them navigate toward one or another specific practice in our time. The specifics will work only if informed by scientific information and rational discourse. Surrounding all of these values of normative restraint must be the respect for the passions and fancies that food prompts in our contemporary communities of plenty, and the respect for eating as a reflection of our more or less licit but boundless passion for what tastes good.

Each of these overarching principles is an opportunity for extensive discourse. Along with these principles, the texts contain fascinating stories about rabbis at meals, about communities that have tried to create healthy environments, and about the effectiveness of certain foods for achieving effective bodily function. Post-Talmudic literature even demonstrates an acceptance of changes wrought by scientific discovery that support the general principles. The lore about the beauty of Rabbi Yochanan and Resh Lakish (Babylonian Talmud, *B'rachot* 5b) or about performing a mitzvah by visiting the bathhouse (*Vayikra Rabbah* 34:3) is enough to argue that tradition permits us to take our bodies seriously. The *Yotzer* morning prayer about the orifices of our bodies certainly is the warrant, liturgically speaking, for persistent and daily consciousness about physical limits and attention to the tangible flesh. What it really suggests is that we start the day by stimulating that consciousness. So we begin from there but are left with individual decisions about individual ethical and nutritional choices in individual circumstances: Is organic food healthier? Which foods really help us maintain our health? Is there any way to know the bona fides of nutrition advisors? And how might we influence our congregations and especially our children toward sensible nutrition? If nutrition and attention to food are part of *tikkun olam*, then perhaps Rabbi Yoffie hit the bull's-eye during his 2009 Biennial address, even though the subject of food seemed lightweight compared to the more global geopolitical or loftier metaphysical questions he might have chosen to discuss.

Nutrition Leadership in an Age of Abundance

At a wedding I recently attended (and actually helped pay for) the quantity of hors d'oeuvres was a sight to behold—a point of immense pride, the residue of which is a warm memory and happily diminished pocketbook. It was an aesthetic affirmation of the union of a wonderful young couple, and a signifier of beauty and pleasure.

Mary Douglas was certainly right when she noted that the food we eat reflects our values, and insofar as she was right, I might blush to think what values accompanied our families' big fat weddings.[3] For that short amount of time, all the parents involved in this wedding were eager to demonstrate love for their kids and wanted to be gracious hosts. You could decipher our meal, but I cannot affirm whether the code had to do with a modern kashrut, a sense of aesthetic style, a concern for social justice (because we donated a percentage of the cost to hunger programs), or health. But I think health probably figured least in our calculus. And of this I am certain: while the abundance of that meal bespoke a gracious impulse, it also has something to do with why America can't seem to eat more healthfully than it does.

Cultures continue to reflect their values through food, and therefore generosity and abundance continue to characterize weddings. It would seem dour to concentrate too much on health at a wedding. Yet more substantive aspects of nutrition and particular components of our lives that are involved with food have certainly moved front and center of the contemporary Jewish agenda. We hear of change abroad in the world, of new projects and a new literature (of which the current book is an example), and we might imagine a time when the balance between health and abundance will readjust.[4]

Yet in none of these cases has the change toward more self-conscious healthful eating emanated from the Jewish tradition—at least not in practice. As is so often the case, we Jews are in a kind of rear guard of larger cultural trends, and they are trends that are largely influenced by economic necessity, awareness of suffering in the world, and young people seeking a way to define the world in their terms. Indeed, viewed through a Freudian prism, one might say that we in the older generation have graciously left room for the younger generation to surpass us in just this area. Food, in many ways, was the one untended area that needed to be attended. Trimming the fat has become a way of "being thinner than our parents."

Even if we are more the product of our times than followers of Jewish tradition, and even if many of the old norms have dissipated, and even if our entire formerly immigrant culture may now feel guilt about eating too much of our grandmother's chicken, this essay is meant to challenge us to navigate within that turbulent current of new norms and new values in order to chart a healthier twenty-first century. Culinary restraint, moderation, mindfulness about what we eat, and concern with how others eat and provide our food can become Jewish values, if we choose to make them so. The texts can invite us to deliberate but so far, it seems, have directed us only so far.[5]

My Story: How I Came to Care

I began my own journey toward healthier eating in the midst of a period of a gargantuan appetite, my passion for hard work, the pressures of a successful career, and a love of whatever it is in cigarettes that provided so many illusions. I was forty years old and was satisfied every year when the chest x-ray revealed no shadows. What I did not understand, and what my Judaism had not helped me understand, is that most of disease and almost all of health is a slowly accumulating business. Health is much closer to Maimonides's notions of an ever-evolving striving for perfection than it is to a solution to specific problems; it is much closer to a broad calculus of common sense than to quick solutions in which a particular menu, designer exercise, and meditation program can secure long life. We are trained, in our culture, to seek remedies to specific illnesses and otherwise assume we are healthy. This "near truth" gets in the way of gradualism—the true lesson of Jewish salvation, which few textbooks, seminaries, or pulpits actually teach.

The specifics have always been baffling. While recovering in the cardiac intensive care unit of our local hospital with a clear case of myocardial infarction, some diet and nutrition issues were raised immediately, though in a haphazard fashion: some nurses whispered into my ear what not to eat if I ever got well; hospital dieticians laid out protocols for healthy diet; a Cleveland Clinic doctor asserted that all chocolate was poison; and an anxious wife and mother were zealous to protect me from poison, but they disagreed about what the poison was. There was a ton of reading matter about lipids, cholesterol, adrenalin formation, bowels, and more, and the age of Pritikin, Ornish, and Zen cuisine had arrived. A terrible time to have a heart attack! I was bombarded with notions about healthy eating and, need I note, a nauseating litany of confirmations of my "type A" behavior. So while being bombarded, advised, and cajoled, I slowly carved out my own sense of nutrition. And, should any reader doubt the efficacy of saving one life: a young cardiologist "took me under his wing" and helped debunk the quick-solution promoters by cautioning me that my bypass surgery was only an apparent quick fix. Since that time I have attended workshops, paid expensive consultation fees, bought a ton of vitamins I have not taken faithfully, and flirted with every promising piece of research about how to eat. I remain, at seventy-three years old, overwhelmed by choices and the evidence. Today I am still eating, still mildly overweight, and finally pretty healthy.

Think of the factors that drive us to eat what we eat: sustainable farming competes with the march of global capitalism; the intimacy of farming one's own fruit and vegetables competes with an overbearing professional schedule (gardening between meetings is not quite sustainable); and the values of spartan life compete against the ever-growing impulses to eat more elaborate and nuanced cuisine, fostering surely the greatest restaurant culture ever known to humankind. Sometimes the battering of food information can be humorous—by the food consciousness movements and by the assertions of ethical, cultural, religious, or health superiority. In an ancient world, notes Israeli scholar Ruhama Weiss, the Rabbinic meal was a site for contention, competition, and self-elevation, over which blessings and religious procedures held precedence. We have replaced this description of the ancients with a refashioned contention and self-elevation about what passes for acceptable nutritional habits.[6] The new hierarchy has less to do with blessings than with the health of our community. It is a good change, although no less combative or quirky.

Jews appreciate good food and lots of it. But the Rabbinic attention to health has been less critical and is certainly less known, and very rarely does one hear Jews formally talking about good health habits when it comes to food. Can the Jewish tradition, which sometimes seems to have fostered diabetes, really foster healthy eating? Can a thriving bourgeoisie that lives better than any middle class in the history of the world really affirm its commitment to feed the poor? We shall see. And which part of all of this can be driven by the occasional glimpse into what our Jewish tradition offers by way of guidance? Is the Jewish tradition capable of including my love of good food with my desire to eat healthfully? Will the Talmud help me be conscious of the hungry people lying in doorways just around the corner from my home? And can the prophets, who *did* make me conscious of those poor people, ever guide me toward particular solutions? And where—even in Maimonides—will I find the inspiration to take care of my body any more convincingly than from the admonitions of a good-looking personal trainer named Rick or Stacy?

So let's revisit the potential for change in the midst of the realities of palate, to see how Jewish tradition might provide us with hooks for thinking about healthy eating. In the way in which Reform Judaism has really been able to re-form classic texts, I have already cited many opportunities for reflecting on better eating. None is more suitable, I think, than the notion in *Sanhedrin* 37a that "if you save a life, you save the entire world." And this epigram would imply that we must be careful to eat those things that at least won't jeopardize a life. It would also mean that people in certain professional positions have the opportunity to save many worlds, and many times over at that. It is a rhetorical nicety that I believe has inspired people who do good works in our Western world. But what if we were to say—without the purely rhetorical "authority" sought in that phrase—that one who tries to save the world has the real opportunity to save (at least) one life? Ah, there would be the urge to look at social policy in a new way, and the opportunity for our people to really do something both culinary and moral for the benefit of the world. It is what my young doctor did for me those many years ago. In fact, we have to turn many of our epigrams on their heads in order to gain a new perspective on the meaning of old texts: "Where are you going?" said the young student to his (modern liberal) rabbi as they both entered the restaurant. "I am on my way to perform a mitzvah!" I will turn all of my eating into a mitzvah, and only when I succeed will I bless with a clean conscience.

But by going back to old texts, we challenge ourselves to examine what used to be versus what is today. The legendary Hebrew philologist Jacob Preuss left us many chapters on food in his compendium on biblical and Talmudic medicine. Preuss's work has been translated by the great contemporary scholar-physician Fred Rosner, who acknowledges that the Jewish tradition has bequeathed much more folklore than science about health. But what seems like folklore today was once medical practice, and what seems like medical practice today may someday seem like folklore. The field is open for contemporary progressive Jews to search for sensible ways to actualize the general principles of Jewish traditional literature, based on the best science we can muster. Jewish tradition offers a comfortable beginning to a very serious conversation, and the prophets offer an inspiration for attention to things that escape our consideration because of the very pressures and social realities that overshadow our attention to the real needs of our culture. The Talmud urges the Rabbis not to institute decrees that people cannot tolerate, and the prophets suggest that there a very few moral values that we cannot tolerate—that are beyond our grasp. That is the tension of our modern lives, is it not? We should live in the image of God; we should provide food for the hungry; we should address ourselves to whatever behaviors contribute to *tikkun olam*; we should embrace *tikkun olam* as part of care of our bodies. What we need is an acknowledgment of the proper role of Jewish authority in our lives in general and of the use of the literary tradition to occupy us on our journey to eat as well as we can, as carefully as we can, and to try to provide that privilege to others.

Perhaps we should return to the notion of the meal as a test of hierarchy (see note 4), but in this instance a hierarchy not about the proper blessings that usher in our eating, but about the kind of eating that ushers in blessing.

NOTES

1. Dahlia Marx, *When I Sleep and When I Awaken* [in Hebrew—on the prayers between day and night] (Tel Aviv: Yedioth Aharonot Press, 2010). And when new blessings for food and eating will be developed, Dahlia Marx will be among those leading the design.

2. See the writings of Aryeh Cohen on this topic.

3. Mary Douglas, "Deciphering a Meal," in Carole Counihan and Penny Van Esterik (eds.), *Food and Culture: A Reader* (New York: Routledge, 1997), 36.

4. At the URJ Biennial Convention of 2009, Rabbi Eric Yoffie, http://urj.org/about/union/leadership/yoffie/?syspage=article&item_id=27481.

5. For an example of intellectual interest in this area, see Jonathan Safran Foer, *Eating Animals* (New York, Back Bay Books, 2010).

6. Ruhama Weiss, *Ochlim L'daat (Meal Tests): The Meal in the World of the Sages* (Israel: Hakibbutz Hameuchad, 2010). See also, David C. Kraemer, *Jewish Eating and Identity through the Ages* (New York: Routledge Advances in Sociology, 2007).

The author thanks his students Bradley Jay Cohen and Jessica Yve Gross for enlightenment on this subject and for inspriation.

35

OF PHARISEES AND ALLERGIES

Shulchan Shalom

DOUG SAGAL

Some scholars hold that early Rabbinic Judaism, the Judaism that molded the religion we practice today, began as table fellowships. The Torah demands that a certain portion of foods produced be designated as Temple offerings, in part for consumption by priests (Lev. 2:8–10). Once designated, these are forever forbidden for consumption by non-priests or for non-Temple purposes. Only food that was "tithed," that is, a portion of which was dutifully set aside for the Temple, was permissible for non-priests to consume. Eating improperly tithed food was considered a sin. Scholars and others who scrupulously maintained these commandments of tithing, as well as the laws of ritual purity, would gather for meals together, confident that the food they consumed had been ritually processed according to the Torah and was, therefore, permissible to eat. The early Pharisees (proto-rabbis of the first and second century C.E.) made a careful distinction between those who were faithful in consuming only properly tithed foods eaten in a state of ritual purity (such persons were known by the name *chaver*) and those who did not eat properly tithed food and were not careful in matters of purity (designated *am haaretz*). One who merely ate properly tithed foods but was not strict in matters of ritual purity was considered "in between" the *chaver* and the *am haaretz* and was deemed "trustworthy" (*ne-eman*).

Mishnah D'mai 2:2–3 states in part:

> He that undertakes to be trustworthy must give (the proper) tithe from what he eats and from what he sells and from what he buys. And he may not be a guest of an *am haaretz*. Rabbi Y'hudah, however, states that he that is the guest of an *am haaretz* may still be considered trustworthy. . . . He that wishes to become a *chaver* may *not* sell to an *am haaretz* food that is wet or dry, and may *not* be a (table) guest of an *am haaretz* [emphasis mine].

Professor Jonathan Brumberg-Krauss of Wheaton College argues that the purpose of these "eating clubs" or table fellowships was actually to be *inclusive*, to encourage those who were not part of the Pharisaic community to join. The goal was to increase participation in the type of Judaism that was evolving in the Second Temple era, particularly in the face of competing sects, such as nascent Christianity.

As Dr. Brumberg-Krauss writes:

> Table fellowship was the principle practice used by the Pharisees to win adherents to their religious movement in the first century C.E. The Pharisees' gathering together to eat properly tithed food in a state of ritual purity, and the procedures for acquiring food and maintaining households or other spaces fit for such gatherings, were strategies to influence non-Pharisees to conform to a Pharisaic way of life.[1]

Further, during the course of these early Pharisaic meals, the principles and ideas of Judaism would be recalled, discussed, expanded upon, and disseminated. According to this "table fellowship theory," it was at these meals, in the company of others and surrounded by food, that the roots of modern Judaism were planted, and members of the Jewish community who were not part of the group were encouraged to join.

In addition, the early Sages valued the dining table as a place of potential holiness. They taught that if persons sit at the table and speak words of Torah, God's presence dwells among them (*Pirkei Avot* 3:3). They called the dining table a *mikdash m'at*, a "miniature altar," that could achieve the sanctity of the ancient altar in Jerusalem if the practices of Judaism were incorporated into the act of eating. Once the Temple was destroyed, the dining table became a potential point of contact between humanity and God.[2]

In sum, Judaism has long valued food as a compelling magnet for gathering and the building of community. In the modern synagogue, one of the ways that this ancient tradition is preserved is the widespread custom of refreshments after Shabbat worship, variously called *Oneg Shabbat* or *Kiddush*. The *Oneg Shabbat* provides a place for the community to join together for refreshment, both of body and soul. These informal gatherings after worship provide an opportunity for congregation members to connect with one another, for new or potential members to be greeted and welcomed, for clergy to interact with worshipers, and for congregants to catch up with each other. The weekly ritual of post-worship gathering "at the *Oneg*" performs a function almost as important as the service itself.

But what if some are excluded from that table, through no fault of their own?

Modern medicine can increasingly identify those who are susceptible to allergies from certain foods, such as gluten or peanuts. Those suffering from these food allergies can experience symptoms ranging from discomfort and hives to even anaphylactic shock and cardiac arrhythmia. Eating certain foods, sitting at a table that contains those food products, or even eating foods that were placed in proximity to those products can bring on symptoms, and even death.

Like many good ideas, the notion that a Shabbat *Oneg* should be open to those with food allergies and other food intolerances (such as celiac disease) came from a congregant at Temple Emanu-El, Westfield, New Jersey. One mother noticed her son gazing longingly at the treats assembled on the tables during the *Oneg Shabbat* following worship, unable to eat them because of his severe food allergies. She approached me and asked if it would be possible to provide a separate table of treats, gluten and nut free, for those unable to partake of the "regular" *Oneg*. We assembled a small group of families interested in the idea, and they volunteered to both provide the appropriate foods and stand behind the table during the *Oneg* to welcome those with food allergies and to politely ask those without to enjoy treats from the "regular" *Oneg*. Food was placed on the table with its containers so that ingredients could be read. To the evening announcements, we added a line "welcoming those with food allergies to our table to enjoy the gluten- and nut-free snacks." It was decided that the special foods would be provided once a month, at our *Hallellu* musical service, which draws large numbers of worshipers of all ages.

The members of the small committee and I chose the name *Shulchan Shalom* to designate this special table. *Shulchan* means table, and *shalom* in its most literal sense means "whole." We wanted our worshipers to feel that they were part of the community, not only when worshiping, but also when enjoying the festive *Oneg* that followed. The message we tried to send is that we as a community are not truly "whole" until everyone can be a full participant.

In the first year, those who enjoyed the special foods bore the costs of the food to be purchased. In the second year, the committee asked that the congregation assume the expenses, given that many worshipers, including those coming from outside the community, were now enjoying the opportunity to participate fully in the *Oneg*. We debated our responsibility to bear the cost of this monthly expense. We asked, what is the obligation of the community to provide special foods for what, in the end, remained a small percentage of worshipers? We reminded ourselves that food is an integral part of the Jewish experience and that our tradition teaches us to elevate the act of eating into a holy deed. We recalled the ancient tradition of table fellowships and the role that they played in the development of Judaism. In the end, we decided that welcoming as many worshipers as possible to our "table" was part and parcel of our congregational vision to open doorways into Jewish life. Therefore, beginning in the second year, the board of trustees, recognizing the importance of the *Shulchan Shalom* to our vision, began budgeting for the necessary expenses, and they continue to do so to this day. Even in our current economy, no one has ever proposed eliminating this expenditure.

The Pharisees of old were meticulous about the duty to tithe properly and to eat foods in the proper state of ritual purity. As evidenced by the material in the Mishnah, they debated who could be welcomed to the table and who must be excluded from participation. They tried to encourage the observance of the laws of tithing and purity, in order to enable as many as possible to partake of both food and fellowship. Since the destruction of the Temple and the cessation of many of the laws regarding tithing and ritual purity, such issues are less vital to modern progressive Jews. However, the issues remain poignantly the same. When we make decisions regarding food, who is included, and who excluded? Are those with food allergies and intolerances welcomed at the table, or must they forgo sharing in the common meal? To what extent does a particular Jewish community change its practices to accommodate as many as possible?

It has been nearly eight years since we began our *Shulchan Shalom*, and I consider it a triumph that a new generation of young people cannot remember a time when there were no treats for them at the *Oneg*.

NOTES

1. Jonathan Brumberg-Strauss, "Were the Pharisees a Conversionist Sect? Table Fellowship as a Strategy of Conversion," in *Jewish Missionary Activity in the Hellenistic and Roman Worlds*, ed. A.-J. Levine and R. Pervo (Scholars Press, forthcoming), 161–92. See also Jacob Neusner, *From Politics to Piety: The Emergence of Pharisaic Judaism*, 2nd ed. (New York: Ktav, 1979), 80.

2. Ezekiel 11:16; Babylonian Talmud, *M'gilah* 29a; and many sources. See also Simeon J. Maslin, ed., *Gates of Mitzvah: A Guide to the Jewish Life Cycle* (New York: CCAR Press, 1979), 37.

36

RETURNING FOOD TO ITS RIGHTFUL PLACE

Eating Disorders in the Jewish Community

RUTH A. ZLOTNICK

Food and Judaism are inextricably linked to one another. We are heirs to a profound and engaging tradition, one that encourages us—through action, study, and prayer—to affirm life and enrich our daily relationships. Food can symbolize the Jewish tradition and the culture that has emerged from it. Ask any adult to reminisce about childhood experiences during Jewish holidays, and the response often involves food. Challah, hamantaschen, matzah ball soup—our memories are imbued with the scents and tastes of the foods we ate as children. One of the reasons for this may be that cultural values and beliefs are passed along to families and the community during food preparation or at mealtime. Thus, even Jews who live in families that have more than one cultural heritage or Jews who are only nominally attached to the religion of Judaism might identify with certain foods as symbols of Jewish culture.

Moreover, many of us were raised with the philosophy that it is always better to have too much rather than too little food at a special event. Holiday tables are laden with dish upon dish placed before the family, while relatives urge one another to "Eat, eat!" Some people speculate that this phenomenon may be attributed to our history, during much of which we experienced periods of dire deprivation and starvation. As a result, for example, during the Yom Kippur War of 1973, some Holocaust survivors in Israel amassed food in far greater quantities than did their neighbors. Perhaps the power of Jewish history subconsciously plays itself out every time we gather with food as our centerpiece.

This sets the scene for eating disorders (anorexia, bulimia, and binge eating / compulsive overeating) to become silent yet destructive forces in our families and our community. Anorexia is characterized by significant weight loss, often as a result of self-imposed starvation. People with anorexia cannot maintain their body at the minimum ideal weight for their age and height. They are profoundly fearful of gaining weight, perceive themselves as fat, and deny the seriousness of their weight loss. Their intense fear of gaining weight often becomes a preoccupation with food, calories, and exercising. More people die from anorexia than from any other psychiatric disorder.

Bulimia is marked by a cycle of binge eating—consuming a large amount of food in short time periods with an accompanying sense of being out of control—followed by some form of purging—behaviors that compensate for the experience of binge eating. Purging behaviors run the gamut from vomiting to excessive use of laxatives or diuretics to obsessive exercising. Bulimia can result in a variety of medical problems, from dental and esophageal disorders to kidney and gastrointestinal damage. In some cases, bulimia nervosa leads to death.

Like bulimia, binge eating / compulsive overeating entails consuming a large amount of food in short time periods with an accompanying sense of being out of control. However, in this case, the food binge *is not* followed by a purging episode. Often people with this disorder eat very quickly or until they are uncomfortably full, after which they feel intense shame. Binge eaters / compulsive overeaters often exhibit such classic symptoms of depression as lethargy, isolation, and mood swings.

A recent adage contends that eating disorders are the Jewish addiction of choice. This adage is inexact on two fronts. First, it implies that

Jews are not vulnerable to other sorts of addictions, like alcoholism and drug abuse. They are. Second, it implies that Jews are diagnosed with eating disorders more than other groups. They are not. However, eating disorders do manifest themselves in a unique way within the Jewish community. Jews, especially but not exclusively Jewish women, are particularly vulnerable to eating disorders. People who are high achieving, well educated, and middle class are more susceptible to eating disorders than other people are. And this is often an accurate description of many of our families in Reform congregations.

Those who work in the field of eating disorders insist that the following underlying truth cannot be reiterated enough: Eating disorders are not about food. They are about emotions and psychological well-being. Thus food becomes a metaphor for larger emotional needs. Hunger and nourishment are no longer connected to the nutritional value of the food on the plate but to meeting emotional needs that are not satisfied in other ways. For many anorexics, self-starvation is a way to deny their emotional needs and to attempt to exert their power by controlling what they consume. The sensation of food in the stomach, of feeling "full," fills the anorexic with fear or disgust. Binge eaters claim that food helps them to fill an inner emptiness, stuffing down anger or filling up on love. For those who purge, vomiting is often regarded as punishment for having "consumed too much," but it does not quell the need for love or to voice anger.

Because food in the Jewish community is often viewed as a symbol of our culture, it is an easy object to abuse in the quest for emotional satiation. As one woman in recovery from anorexia has said, "In Jewish culture, food represents love. By not eating her food, I was rejecting my mother's love. It was my way of separating from her." A middle-aged man currently battling compulsive eating disorder concurs: "Many Jewish people tend to stuff themselves with food to block out emotions. My family never talked about their true feelings. Instead, everybody overate and complained about being full." These same dynamics propel the cycle of bingeing and purging: "I started in high school. My mother and grandmother were beautiful women, and I knew I could never live up to their expectations for me to be like them. I would try and fail, try and fail. This was mirrored in my bulimia."

Occasions on which families gather for the Jewish holidays can be particularly nerve-racking for people with eating disorders. With every course, family members make comments and suggestions: "Try the kugel"; "Oh, take another piece. You can afford it"; "Sweetie, you've had enough dessert." Every holiday presents its own challenges. Anorexics often regard Yom Kippur as a day of licit fasting, a day in which everyone else experiences the "high" of self-starvation. For binge eaters, the overabundance of sweets at an *Oneg Shabbat* can be both tempting and painful. Passover seders, Yom Kippur break-fasts, and Chanukah latke-eating parties can all be extremely anxiety-provoking for those with eating disorders. Yet family members at these events often do not even realize that their loved one is counting calories, pushing food around on the plate, running to the bathroom to vomit, or inspecting each bite that everyone else is taking. All this reveals another truth about eating disorders: Jewish families have a difficult time accepting that a loved one is self-destructive.

Like other forms of self-injurious behaviors, eating disorders affect every member of the family, undermining, in the words of one parent, "the myth of the perfect Jewish family." As one mother put it, "I think Jewish parents overidentify with their children. We didn't want to accept my daughter's anorexia. We were stonewalled by denial. Her anorexia was an acknowledgment that there were problems in the entire family system." Siblings, too, learn a great deal by the way in which a family accepts or denies a loved one's eating disorder.

As a community, we have begun to chip away at the denial that compels us to say "not my loved one" or "not in my synagogue" when we see someone engaged in self-destructive behaviors. In the last decade, there has been a wealth of resources that have emerged to assist Jewish families that are impacted by eating disorders. If you fear that a loved one may be suffering from an eating disorder, there are certain signs to look for. For example, there may be cause for concern if your loved one has gained or lost an excessive amount of weight during a short period of time. Perhaps they have exhibited significant changes in their eating behavior, such as excessive dieting, eating alone behind closed doors, refusing to eat certain foods, or hurrying to the bathroom after meals. Or they may seem preoccupied with food, weight, or counting calories. People with eating disorders may weigh themselves more than once a day, cook for others without eating themselves, or wear baggy clothes in order to hide their body. They might also display signs of depression, such as irritability or mood swings, or give the impression that they are withdrawing from relationships.

Eating disorders may be a contemporary phenomenon impacting Jewish families, yet we are fortunate to receive an ancient tradition that can aid in one's recovery. Jewish values can pave the way to a healthy relationship to food and nourishment. Our Sages teach that in each generation since the destruction of the Temple, every table in every Jewish home has become an altar—that is, a center for the sacred in our lives. Judaism emphasizes that food should be enjoyed as one of the gifts of Creation, but it should be enjoyed in moderation. People are encouraged to eat enough to maintain the health of their body—not too much and not too little. According to tradition, every meal begins and ends with a *b'rachah*, a blessing, of gratitude for the food we are about to eat, which enables us to live, to work, and to love. Kashrut can also be a means to attaining a deeper reverence for the way in which we nourish ourselves, leading to an experience of wholeness in the world.

Eating disorders are unlike any other addiction because our survival depends upon our food intake, and therefore the individual who suffers from eating disorders can never be far from the object of their self-destruction. The key to a wholesome relationship with food is a wholesome relationship with the self. In Judaism, we believe that all human beings are created *b'tzelem Elohim*—in God's image. For people with eating disorders, this belief has been submerged. As a community, we can help return a sense of their own sacredness to people with eating disorders by being sensitive to their needs at family and temple events, by focusing on who people are rather than how they look, and by reaching out to the entire family, not just the individual with the eating disorder. Together we can return food to its rightful place: not as a weapon that our loved ones use to destroy themselves but as a pleasurable part of our Jewish experiences and memories and as a means to nourish the best in ourselves. As Rabbi Akiva taught in *Pirkei Avot* 3:14, "Human beings are loved because they are made in God's image." We can help people with eating disorders discover that they, too, are loved and that they, too, have within themselves a spark of the Divine.

37

REAL LIFE / REAL FOOD
Redefining Healthy Eating, For Life

JULIE PELC ADLER

I'm sitting at my regular table at my favorite local diner eating a grilled blueberry muffin. Rachel is the waitress. She's here every weekday morning, serving up scrambled organic eggs, fair trade coffee, and a welcome midwestern attitude entrenched in Santa Monica, California. My vegetarian soy-bacon is fried crisp, just as I like it. As I eat, I'm fiddling with my smartphone, checking Facebook statuses, peeking at my work e-mail, and exchanging text messages with a colleague about a meeting later today.

I am here, but I am not present. I barely taste the muffin with its buttery goodness. I'm not aware of the presence of my fellow diners. Rachel has refilled my coffee, but absorbed in my phone, I fail to acknowledge the kindness.

Jewish tradition commands us to guard our bodies and keep them healthy, as we were created in the image of God. For most of us, the term "healthy eating" conjures thoughts of restrictive diets, carefully measured fat and calorie intakes, and rigorous measurements of various body parts. However, "health" is much more holistic.

There is a profound tradition deeply ingrained in Jewish life of *oneg* (enjoyment) and of *Shabbat* (resting in the present). Shabbat creeps onto our calendars every week with the command to *shamor* (guard) and to *zachor* (remember). We rest from the frantic and frenetic creation of the everyday; we sink into *oneg*, embracing the here-and-now. We delight in slow, relaxed meals with friends and family; we sing; we bless; we offer gratitude. We sanctify time together with those we love.

Honoring this Shabbat spirit of *oneg* is what it means to "choose life" (Deut. 30:19). When we monitor our eating to support health, we must remember to measure the health of our mind-sets, not just our waistlines. Created in God's image, we are taught that it is our duty to care for ourselves—our whole selves. As Maimonides wrote, "We must strive to maintain a healthy body so that we can serve God."[1] Crash dieting and extreme restriction do not support health any more than gorging ourselves on junk food and neglecting to exercise. Yet, healthy eating is more than making the right food choices. We are responsible for our mental health, as well as our physical health.

Keeping our Shabbat attitude in mind, we must remember that we *eat to live*; our choices must support and encourage *life*. Choosing life includes making choices to support holistic health: healthy minds, healthy communities, healthy spirits, and healthy bodies. Sometimes, "healthy eating" can include a blueberry muffin prepared on a buttered skillet, an extra cup of warm coffee delivered with a smile, and a table free from distractions and work.

It is time we reclaim the full meaning of "healthy" eating. Then we can conscientiously make choices for which we can raise our coffee cups and exclaim with full joy and gratitude, "*L'chayim!*"

NOTE

1. *Mishneh Torah, Hilchot Dei-ot* 3:5.

Part Eight

Justice: *Tzedek*

A s each of us creates a personal dietary practice and shapes our communal kashrut, *tzedek* (justice) and *tzedakah* (charity) must be integrated into our food ideologies. The Reform Movement has its roots deeply planted in social justice activism. Therefore, the impulse for social justice must join with our passion for kashrut. In "Let All Who Are Hungry Come and Eat: Food Ethics, *Tzedakah*, and How We Celebrate" Neal Gold offers an important criticism of the abundant food at our life-cycle events. He suggests a better approach that would certainly serve to distribute food resources more fairly by discouraging food waste. Gold's model also has the potential to be gentler to our waistlines and to the environment. Irwin Zeplowitz ("Pricing Our-selves Out of the Market: Is Eating Kosher [Ritually and Ethically] a Privilege of the Rich?") warns us against creating an elitist food prac-tice that is accessible only to the wealthy or hyper-motivated. Speaking in terms of justice and the reality of consumerism, Zeplowitz infuses our discussion with a dose of needed realism.

Michael Namath and Rachel Cohen ("Raising Our Voices for Food Justice") broaden our vision of food justice to help us understand the current state of the American food policy. Educating us about the history of the American Farm Bill, Namath and Cohen weigh its strengths and weakness. They suggest a new model that could bring healthier food choices to the food insecure. This discussion of American economic policy also opens our eyes to a source of the American health crisis.

In the Real Life / Real Food section, Linda Motzkin and Jonathan Rubenstein ("Bread, Torah, and *Tikkun*") share with us the story of Slice of Heaven Breads, the bakery project housed in their synagogue. This social justice project inspires us by demonstrating what one community can achieve through food.

38

LET ALL WHO ARE HUNGRY COME AND EAT
Food Ethics, *Tzedakah*, and How We Celebrate

Neal Gold

In Mordecai Spector's (1858–1925) classic Yiddish story "A Meal for the Poor,"[1] a wealthy Jewish citizen named Reb Yitzchok Berkover is preparing for the wedding of his youngest daughter. Reflecting the ethos of the shtetl, all the poorest members of the community, including those who beg for *tzedakah* in the marketplace, are to be honored guests at the celebration.

However, Reb Yitzchok's daughter's wedding will not be like all the other *s'machot* of the town, because this time the poor are tired of being taken for granted. This group of schnorrers will not be paid off by one hot meal and lip service about how beloved they are. These men and women take a stand—by going on strike.

On strike! They will boycott Reb Yitzchok's wedding unless their demands are heard. And if the reader says, "Who cares? They should be happy for what they can get," it goes to show how far removed we are from the values of the Old World. Reb Yitzchok is mortified, because if the poor are not part of his child's wedding feast, then his reputation as a man of generosity will be destroyed. He is, as they say, over a barrel.

Reb Yitzchok's conundrum illustrates our spiritual situation. Few of us live in communities where we are expected to host poor and hungry people as part of our celebrations. But there is a provocative connection between the story and us: namely, food ethics are often located at the crossroads of religious practice and our most deeply held values.

In his tour-de-force commentary on the Book of Leviticus, Dr. Jacob Milgrom spells this out. Leviticus, with all its arcana of sacrifices and offerings, is also the earliest place where Jewish food laws are detailed. This is Milgrom's thesis about Leviticus:

> Values are what Leviticus is all about. They pervade every chapter and almost every verse. Many may be surprised to read this, since the dominant view of Leviticus is that it consists only of rituals, such as sacrifices and impurities. This, too, is true: Leviticus *does* discuss rituals. However, underlying the rituals, the careful reader will find an intricate web of values that purports to model how we should relate to God and to one another.[2]

What applies for all of Leviticus applies for its sections, too, including chapter 12, where we find the Torah's primary exposition of the laws of kashrut. Suddenly, the food laws of Leviticus become startlingly relevant: food becomes the realm for a meditation on life and death, of our values and convictions.

We note here that the rabbinical laws of *tzedakah* evolved directly from the Torah's food laws. In ancient Israel, the safety nets that were established for the most desperate members of society inevitably focused on the agriculture:

> When you reap the harvest of your land, you shall not reap all the way to the edges of your field, or gather the gleanings of your harvest. You shall not pick your vineyard bare, or gather the fallen fruit of your vineyard; you shall leave them for the poor and the stranger: I the Eternal am your God.
>
> (Lev. 19:9–10)

Thus, biblical society developed a system around the cultivation of food wherein certain parts of the field *did not in fact belong to the landowner, but became the property of the hungry and homeless members of society, who were entitled to come and take what rightfully belonged to them.*[3] Aspects of this system included the following:

- *Pei-ah*: The edges of the field, which were not to be harvested but left for poor people.
- *Leket*: The gleanings that fell from the hands of those who gathered the harvest. The gleaners could not make a "second pass" to collect what they dropped; these now belonged to the hungry gatherers.
- *Shich'chah*: The forgotten sheaves that had been overlooked by the reapers would also become the property of the poor and hungry people.
- *Peret* and *Oleilot*: Special categories that applied similarly to the grape harvest, namely those clusters that were underdeveloped or fell to the ground before or during the harvest.

As Jewish society evolved, moving beyond an agricultural base and even beyond the Land of Israel, other institutions came into place to provide a safety net for the most desperate and hurting members of the community. The essence of this safety net, however, is found in the Torah's ethic around the cultivation of food.

Throughout Jewish history, the interconnection of food ethics and other values of justice, generosity, and basic decency played itself out in interesting and occasionally startling ways. The sixteenth-century code of Jewish law the *Shulchan Aruch* records a remarkable law:

> A person should immediately offer to the waiter anything that is being served that has an [enticing] aroma, as well as anything else that anyone would have a strong appetite for. It is a particularly fine practice to give the waiter something immediately from each kind of food.[4]

Our generosity should extend not only to people who are most obviously hurting and needy. In this rather extreme example, the Rabbis tell us that the person serving the food might be tantalized by delicious food that he is not permitted to taste. It is an act of decency and sensitivity to share a taste with him! Perhaps this represents the Rabbis in one of their most idealistic moments. Nonetheless, in the radical nature of this ideal, we can be inspired to allow mealtime to make us more generous and more humane.

Characteristic of Jewish life is the *s'udat mitzvah*, or "mitzvah meal." Jewish communities have celebrated holidays, life-cycle milestones, and sacred moments (including the conclusion of studying a tractate of Talmud) with food and drink since our earliest days. In the Torah, Abraham marks Isaac's development with just such a celebration: "The child grew up and was weaned, and on Isaac's weaning day, Abraham held a great feast" (Gen. 21:8). Subsequently, the Talmud and codes of Jewish law describe that mealtime celebrations are essential—and even required—aspects of commemorating these moments.[5] One hallmark of the *s'udat mitzvah* is that there is no differentiation between the "religious part" and the "party part" of a Jewish celebration. At a *b'rit milah*, a bar/bat mitzvah celebration, a wedding, and so on, the ritual events and celebratory events are, religiously speaking, all of a piece. Considering the contemporary American Jewish celebration, I would go one step further than that: *how* we celebrate says much more about our religious and moral values than even the ritual itself!

What values does the typical American *simchah* convey? Are our milestones celebrations of gratitude to God and opportunities for others to share that gratitude? Or are they demonstrations of crass consumption, waste, and disregard for the great need that lies just beyond the periphery of the party? Furthermore, we should consider that life-cycle celebrations are often the main locus where non-Jews witness Jewish practice in action. Every celebrant should ask, what statements about our communal or family values are on display to our neighbors at our celebration?

How easy (and worthwhile) it is to decry the spiritual carnage of the Jewish American bar mitzvah or wedding scene by describing how coarse and excessive some of our *s'machot* have become. Indeed, countless rabbis have done so over the years. Our task here is to offer some alternatives, to integrate the principles of tzedakah and *chesed* into our celebrations.

Food of course plays a central role in our parties; therefore, food can become the focal point for celebrating with dignity and a sense of justice. Many communities celebrate with the assistance of food rescue programs.[6] These are organizations that collect perfectly edible food from hotels, reception halls, restaurants, caterers, schools, synagogues, and so on, and redistribute the food to people in need. In New York City, for instance, the vans of City Harvest are ubiquitous as they collect leftover food to deliver to food pantries, soup kitchens, and other places where food is distributed to hungry people.

At our congregation, Temple Shir Tikva in Wayland, Massachusetts, we encourage families who are celebrating *s'machot* always to ask the caterer, "Do you donate leftover food?" After enough Jews bombard their caterers with this question, the caterers will understand that it is unacceptable to throw away perfectly good food when people in America are going hungry. If the caterer answers yes and explains how, then this part of the mitzvah has been fulfilled.[7] If the caterer does not donate as a rule, our families are encouraged to contact our local food rescue program[8] in order to get the leftovers to a local shelter, food pantry, or soup kitchen. They are likewise encouraged to give leftover flower arrangements and centerpieces to patients or residents, to nurses stations, and to waiting rooms of local hospitals or nursing homes.

Several years ago, I regularly visited the Ramaz School, an Orthodox Jewish day school in New York. At lunchtime, I observed a remarkable ritual of the students and faculty. Of course, after the meal they would all recite *Birkat HaMazon*. Then—just as ritually, just as religiously—they would place all the edible, leftover food on a long table covered with aluminum foil. Each student had a role in the assembly line, as the food was methodically wrapped and prepared for City Harvest to come and collect it. Just as *Birkat HaMazon* was a religious duty for this community, so, too, was *bal tashchit*—ensuring that food that would be valuable to somebody else would not be needlessly destroyed.

Our communities should strive for nothing less. It would be a worthy endeavor for synagogues, camps, and NFTY to create an infrastructure of food harvesting anywhere in our community where it does not yet exist.

Similarly, the phenomenon of MAZON—A Jewish Response to Hunger[9] has been a primary conduit for Jewish communities to incorporate the mitzvah of *tzedakah* into their celebrations. Founded in 1985, MAZON was organized in the spirit of the ethos that is reflected in "A Meal for the Poor," as a bridge between the abundance of resources in the American Jewish community and the desperate need felt by the millions of hungry people in the world. Noting that "historically, rabbis did not allow celebrations to begin until the community's poor and hungry people were seated and fed," MAZON created an infrastructure for Jewish communities to do so symbolically by donating 3 percent of the cost of a *simchah* to its anti-hunger programs. To give to MAZON, or similar *tz'dakot*, a proportion of the food costs of a celebration is an echo of inviting needy people to share in the event itself.

In the climax of "A Meal for the Poor," Reb Yitzchok finally realizes that he owes the poor members of the town more than they owe him. He gives in to their demands, giving them a rare moment of power and self-respect. And so, they finally agree to attend his daughter's wedding. The feast can go on in an appropriately *menschlich* manner:

> After the meal the musicians began to play again, and the poor danced around in a great ring, holding Reb Yitzchok by the hands. Reb Yitzchok danced out into the very center of the ring made by the poor. His satin coat tails flew like the wings of an eagle. His eyes, from which tears of joy were freely running, seemed to be staring straight upward, while his thoughts soared higher than the Seventh Heaven. He laughed and he cried at the same time, like a child. And all the while, he kept embracing the poor, each in turn. He hugged them affectionately and kissed their cheeks.

"Brothers!" he cried out to them, dancing. "We must be merry! Let us be merry as only Jews know how to be merry! Fiddlers! Play something a little faster, louder, livelier, stronger!"

That is how a Jew is happy.

That is how a real Jewish wedding ought to be.

The poor, as well as the rest of the wedding guests, clapped their hands in time to the music.

In short, as I have told you, [dear reader,] I've been to a Jewish wedding.[10]

Certainly, "A Meal for the Poor" is a satire. But the community being satirized has pathologies remarkably similar to our own. The chasm between rich and poor is decried in Spector's shtetl; in America that chasm is wider than it has ever been. People who are poor and hungry in our communities have even less power than those in the story "A Meal for the Poor." After all, how can someone who is invisible possibly go "on strike"?

Beneath the surface of Jewish food laws is a meta-ethic of Jewish life that maintains that all people are interconnected and responsible for one another. Make no mistake, Jews are certainly entitled to a *s'udat mitzvah* at joyous milestones in their lives. But tradition calls upon us to make those moments of celebration times in which the character of the entire community is elevated, when the highest values of our tradition are revealed. They are opportunities for *tzedakah* and for *bal tashchit*. All too often, they are displays of precisely the opposite: conspicuous waste and grotesque overconsumption.

Integrating the values of tzedakah, *bal tashchit*, and Jewish food ethics into our celebrations, as well as our day-to-day living, is more than simply the right thing to do. It will also amplify these moments by deepening our sense of gratitude, awe, and interconnectedness that lies at the root of spiritual living. It is our goal—indeed, our mandate—to make each wedding, bris, bat/bar mitzvah, and every other *simchah* an opportunity for our community and our guests to echo Spector's narrator by saying, "I've been to a Jewish celebration."

NOTES

1. Mordecai Spector, "A Meal for the Poor," trans. Milton Hindus, in *A Treasury of Yiddish Stories*, ed. Irving Howe and Eliezer Greenberg (New York: Penguin Books, 1989), 250–55.

2. Jacob Milgrom, *Leviticus: A Continental Commentary* (Minneapolis: Fortress Press, 2004), 1.

3. For further discussion of this ancient system, see Frank M. Loewenberg, *From Charity to Social Justice: The Emergence of Communal Institutions for the Support of the Poor in Ancient Judaism* (New Brunswick, NJ: Transaction Publishers, 2001), 92–96.

4. *Shulchan Aruch, Orach Chayim* 169:1.

5. See, for instance, Babylonian Talmud, *P'sachim* 113b and commentaries, which holds that one who does not attend a *s'udat mitzvah* at a *b'rit milah* is "barred from heaven." This is the source of the tradition that one does not issue formal invitations to a *b'rit milah*, but rather simply announces the time and place of the *s'udah*. Similar sources are found for celebrations around a wedding, bar mitzvah, *pidyon haben*, and the first meal upon returning from a funeral.

6. No one who donates food in good faith can be held liable, civilly or criminally, for someone who gets sick from the donated food. It is a federal law: The Bill Emerson Good Samaritan Food Donation Act of 1996. See www.usda.gov/news/pubs/gleaning/appc.htm. It is important to know this, as "liability" is often an excuse that is used when food gets dumped.

7. It is important to note that some hotels give leftover food to their staff and employees. From our perspective, this is perfectly acceptable; our job here is to ensure that good food is not being dumped.

8. MetroWest Food Harvest, Framingham, MA, a service of South Middlesex Opportunity Council, http://www.smoc.org/index.asp?pgid=82.

9. www.mazon.org.

10. Spector, "A Meal for the Poor," 254–55.

39

PRICING OURSELVES OUT OF THE MARKET

Is Eating Kosher (Ritually and Ethically) a Privilege of the Rich?

IRWIN ZEPLOWITZ

As we seek to define a Reform approach to food, we should be asking: Can we *afford* to eat the way we *want* to eat? Or, more properly, will our kashrut, however defined, be "affordable"? For if we want to be practical and not just idealistic about kashrut, we would be foolish to ignore the cost involved. While it is impossible to define what "affordable" means objectively, anyone who has lived paycheck to paycheck knows what it is not. While affordability is a more essential issue for the poor, it is also a concern for those who are financially secure. I am faced, as are all consumers, with a very real decision every time I go shopping: am I willing to pay more for something because I think it is the "right" kind of food to buy, or will I opt for what is cheaper (if not cheapest)? More critically for those who argue for particular standards of behavior for us as Jews: will our moral or Jewish values of what is *kasher* ("fit" or "proper" for us) make our dietary desideratum just a privilege for those with enough discretionary income, commitment to Jewish tradition, or moral fervor to ignore the cost?

Many who keep kosher because God commands it find kashrut a financial burden.[1] Weighing the compelling desire to serve God against the cost, one may choose to give up other things in order to eat in the way one believes is divinely ordained. In a liberal Jewish context, where keeping kosher may not be based solely (if at all) on divine demand, the added expense of keeping kosher can become a challenge to the very premise.

Contemporary liberal Jewish conversations about food are often framed in an ethical context. For example, what is most compassionate or "best" for the animals we eat (how they are raised or slaughtered)? Is it "right" to eat meat or to consume it in such large quantity? If workers are "unjustly" treated, can we lay claim to the food really being *kasher*? Are farmers "fairly" compensated? These are worthy questions. Yet, they are not the only ones we ought to be asking. In making a moral claim on behalf of the agricultural laborers and factory workers who produce our food, should we not also seek what is in the best financial interest of consumers? If people cannot afford the food we *want* them to eat, we must either find ways to produce food more reasonably or develop arguments with sufficient suasion to convince people that they should pay more for food deemed kosher (whether ritual or ethical). If not, we may well have to be less lofty in our expectations.

Kashrut is a communal definition of what is proper food. We should be wary, then, of standards to which our community will not adhere, regardless of their possible lofty aims. As the Talmud teaches, "One should not impose a restriction on the community unless the majority will follow it" (Babylonian Talmud, *Bava Batra* 60b; *Bava Kama* 79b). Thus, my assertion that what is ethically "best" or most "proper" for us as Jews (using health, the environment, sustainability, a sense of *K'lal Yisrael* or anything else as criteria) will not be enough unless the food we produce is competitively priced. Simply put, too high a standard may establish an ideal that most people are simply unwilling to pay to attain. Thus, in defining the criteria for a Reform kashrut, we should also be asking, "Can we afford it?" For if not, we will, in essence, price ourselves out of the market, ideologically and practically.

This is not an argument against making the attempt. On the contrary, it is laudable to think more deeply about our food. If we seek a life of holiness, surely it should involve so elemental and instinctual a desire as eating. How, though, can we maximize the moral intent in kashrut? Should we establish an ideal few will attain—much less seek—or accept compromises that balance affordability with ethical desirability?

The value of affordability is deeply linked to a sense of social justice. What I am arguing for, therefore, is that as we define what is kosher for us as Reform Jews, we do so with the goal of making proper food available for the most number of people, not just those rich enough to afford it or pious enough to be willing to give up other things to do so.

It can be argued that the virtue of raising animals in a more "moral" or compassionate manner is worth the extra cost. If it is healthier to eat food with fewer hormones and chemical additives and without having to be shipped long distances, there may be a long-term financial savings not only for individuals, but also communally. These and other arguments for more sustainable farming, with high ethical standards for the treatment of animals and those who work with them, are intellectually sound, but they will not move most people unless and until the food produced is reasonably priced.

The issue of affordability has a foundation in Reform Judaism's long-time emphasis on social justice, but it is also in keeping with a Judaism that has long emphasized food in a context of equitable distribution of resources. The biblical definition of animals we can and cannot eat was *not* the sole concern of the Torah about what we eat. Food was to be shared with those in need through *pei-ah*, leaving a section of a field unharvested (Lev. 19:9, 23:22); *maaseir oni*, setting aside one-tenth of produce (Deut. 14:28); and *leket*, leaving fallen produce on the ground during harvest (Lev. 19:9, 23:22). In another biblical example, it is possible to conclude that the food given to *kohanim* was an unfair demand of an elite class of individuals, but it can also be seen as an attempt to redistribute resources to those who did not have the land—and thereby the means—to raise their own food. The blessing that comes with eating (Deut. 8:10) is not for sustenance alone, but sees *v'savata*, "satisfaction," as a prerequisite. It is not enough, therefore, to provide nourishing food. The Torah presupposes that we must enjoy it—a challenging task, indeed, for one who is too poor to provide adequate nourishment.

The idea of being "satisfied" with our food challenges those whose sole criterion in making purchases is the actual price one pays. Inexpensive food often comes with ancillary costs—to the preservation of our environment, the proper treatment of workers, the well-being of the animals raised, or our health. Can I truly be "satisfied" knowing the chicken I am eating was slaughtered in a kosher way but lived its life in a cage cooped up with little room to move, loaded up with hormones that may affect my long-term health, and slaughtered by someone without adequate health-care benefits? I can ignore all this, but a consciousness of *v'savata* pushes me to consider that the ultimate cost may, indeed, not be worth the cheaper price I pay at the market. In defining kashrut for ourselves, we need, therefore, to ask additional questions: How do we establish paying the real value of raising food in as sustainable and healthy a way as possible, yet not making it too expensive for most people? What can we do to educate people about the true "value" involved with paying somewhat more for our food? Is cheaper food truly worth the price?

Rabbinic Judaism established, through legend and law, wide-ranging means to provide food for all. The Talmudic Sages allowed great latitude for the fixing of prices in the market but placed greater limits on goods that were considered *chayei nefesh* (things on which life depends).[2] In that era, communal charities were established to distribute food to visitors in the community as well as those who were impoverished. The Sages of the Talmud did not speak about "animal rights," but they believed that we have a moral responsibility to care for other species. That being said, Rabbinic Judaism places sustenance of human life above that of animals.[3] Furthermore, it was considered praiseworthy to support those who did not have sufficient resources to eat. One story tells how Rabbi Akiva's daughter averted a death fated for her by giving a poor person food at her wedding. This, Akiva claimed, was a source for "*tzedakah* saves from death." In providing righteously for others, it is not only those in need who are saved, but ourselves (Babylonian Talmud, *Shabbat* 156b).

Among the most radical attempts to keep prices reasonable occurred in seventeenth-century Moravia. At that time the Shabbat meal of choice was fish. Fish merchants, aware of this, established a cartel, and in a classic tale of supply and demand, the price of fish skyrocketed, so much so that the poorer Jews in the community were hard pressed to afford what was considered de rigueur for their Erev Shabbat meal. In a bold attempt to undercut the exorbitant prices being charged, the Jewish residents organized a boycott of fish, and the leading authority of the time supported them, arguing that the fish was *t'reifah* (unfit to eat).[4] This conscious reversal of the Torah's dictates and thousands of years of Rabbinic law was clearly related to a meta-halachic understanding that those of every socioeconomic status—not only the well-to-do—should have access to affordable food for it to be considered kosher.

As we consider what is kosher to eat, I would like us to also consider that sustainable farming and eating ought to have the greatest *social* benefit—that is, feeding the most people for the most minimal "cost" (financial cost, in both the short and the long term, including also long-term health and environmental costs). In the headlong rush to support locally grown, organic, mostly vegetarian food, let us not forget the need for affordability as a key element of social justice.

Some practical suggestions:

- First, we should do some realistic soul searching (*cheshbon hanefesh*) about what we claim we want and what we are willing to pay for as consumers. If affordability always trumps my religious and moral concerns, then I need to ask myself, "How committed am I really to a Reform kashrut?" We cannot push our community so much that they ignore the claims we make for a contemporary kashrut, but we can and should educate people to ask themselves whether the inexpensive food they have come to expect is truly "worth" the cost in other ways. There is a spiritual benefit/gain that comes from eating in a Jewish way.

- Second, let us advocate in the Jewish (and larger) world a theology of limits. Eating less in general and less meat in particular really is a way to better mesh the supply with the demand. Judaism advocates the many advantages that come with the control of our appetites.

- Third, we should find ways to encourage businesses (local farmers, but also larger supermarket chains) to bring the kind of food we define as ethically "proper" to market, since the economy of scale will bring down prices across the board. What we buy as consumers will determine what the producers will sell. Our institutions should make considered, conscious choices for buying food we deem kosher, setting a model for individual behavior.

- Fourth, we ought to provide specific, attainable means for communities, families, and individuals to find ways to buy the food they ideally would like to, in ways they can afford. This may mean establishing CSAs (Community Supported Agriculture), providing web-based resources for people to find kosher meat that is "free range," or educating people how to more easily plant organic gardens at home, at their synagogue, or in their community.

- Fifth, let us continue to reach out to Conservative rabbis who are working on the Magen Tzedek certification to create a greater voice in the Jewish world about what *kasher* ("proper" and ethical eating) means in our time.[5]

- Sixth, growing out of the Jewish understanding of *tzedek* (equity and fairness), we must advocate that the food we seek for ourselves be available to all, particularly since access to healthy, affordable food is extremely limited in poorer communities and to those of more modest means. One method (among others) would be to encourage local governments to give incentives (e.g., tax breaks or establishing tax-free zones) for community markets, to entice growers to set up farmers' markets in more than well-to-do neighborhoods and communities. We must seek ways to enable people to use food stamps at these markets. We can also engage in community organizing to buy, or get donated, land for local community gardens.

• Finally, we need to find the communal "stomach" for engaging in political action, to—among other things—seek ways to lessen (if not halt) governmental subsidies for particular food industries, to advocate for reasonable standards for schools to use in providing food for students, and to create incentives for people to grow some of their own food. Food pantries are important, but we must keep in mind the dictum that the highest level of righteousness (*tzedakah*) is giving people the means to support themselves.

Food is a gift from God, and we have been given enough to sustain and satisfy ourselves. Only when all can sit at the table and eat in such a manner can we justifiably say a complete blessing. We can afford to eat better. Let us just be sure that in seeking what is kosher we do not price ourselves out of the market.

NOTES

1. Rachel Kahn-Troster, "Kashrut: Reining in Expenses," *Sh'ma* 40, no. 669 (April 2010), www.shma.com/2010/04/kashrut-reining-in-expenses; Shmuley Boteach, "Too Expensive and Lonely to Be Jewish," http://www.huffingtonpost.com/rabbi-shmuley-boteach/too-expensive-and-lonely_b_173065.html.

2. For a full discussion on this, see Meir Tamari, "Trading in Basic Commodities," in *With All Your Possessions: Jewish Ethics and Economic Life* (New York: Free Press, 1987), 88–89.

3. As, for example, in the ruling that we feed animals before ourselves but give water to ourselves before our animals (because the latter is related to the maintenance of life, not just fulfilling one's appetite).

4. *T'shuvot HaTzemach Tzedek*, sec. 28.

5. See http://magentzedek.org.

40

RAISING OUR VOICES FOR FOOD JUSTICE

MICHAEL NAMATH AND RACHEL COHEN

One Friday night after Shabbat services, a poor man with a shaggy beard and ragged clothes followed a group of people to the home of one of the wealthiest families in town. As he walked toward the house, he could smell the delicious food that had been prepared. When he reached the door, the host stopped him before he could enter the house, explaining that they simply did not have enough room at the table.

The next week the same poor man was able to borrow elegant clothes and again followed the group of people to the wealthy home. This time the host welcomed him inside. When the food was placed on the table, the poor man began to stuff his pockets with the food.

Everyone at the table was horrified by the sight of this man putting food into his pockets. Finally, the host asked the man what he was doing. The man answered, "When I came to your home in torn clothes, you turned me away. When I came back dressed in fine clothing, you welcomed me as a guest. My clothes made all the difference. Since they were invited in, I'm feeding my dinner to my hungry clothes."

(Based on a folktale found in Dov Noy's A Tale for Each Month*)*

Too often we fail to look at the people who are affected by our economic policies. Instead, we see numbers on a page and make decisions based on what is practical, forgetting that those numbers represent people. Our tradition holds deep lessons about our food system and the policies that shape it—about everything from how we grow our food to how we treat farm workers to what we do with leftovers. When we look at the food system, with its effects on the environment, the economy, and our health, through the lens of these Jewish values, the costs and benefits of various food policies become clearer and a vision of a more just food system emerges. With a major "food fight" under way at the political level, with competing policies that stand for very different ideals for the future of our food system, putting these values into practice are more important than ever before.

The evolution of the American food system in the twentieth century has been dominated by one overarching policy: the Farm Bill. The first Farm Bills were agriculture subsidies that emerged during the Great Depression, a time when small family farmers desperately needed government money to stay afloat. Through a complex series of farm subsidies and a wide variety of farm and nutrition programs, the Farm Bill has shaped a system of industrial agriculture that focuses on one overarching goal: the production of a tremendous quantity of cheap food. The Farm Bill is reauthorized every five years and now dictates the distribution of hundreds of millions of dollars to the American agricultural industry.

Our modern industrial food system, centered around policies like the Farm Bill, succeeds tremendously at producing corn and soy, the basic sources of much of our caloric intake, cheaply and efficiently. The evolution of the Farm Bill to its modern incarnation as an omnibus policy propping up cheap food makes sense in light of its origins—a time when supporting small farmers and growing the food supply were of vital national importance.

Today our nation produces mass quantities of food—enough to feed everyone in the United States with plenty to spare—on limited land. U.S. farmers produced 334 million metric tons of corn in 2009, a 180 percent increase over 1960s' production levels, using only 34 percent more land. We produce 40 percent of the world's corn and soy supplies, exporting a tremendous amount to developing countries.[1] Agribusiness giants like Archer Daniels Midland and Monsanto consistently rank in the Fortune 500 and reap billions of profits each year.

The importance of a stable and abundant food supply should not be overlooked or understated. After all, ensuring that everyone has enough food to eat is a Jewish value exhorted in the Torah and supported in the midrash: "When you are asked in the world-to-come, 'What was your work?' and you answer, 'I fed the hungry,' you will be told, 'This is the gate of the Lord, enter into it, you who have fed the hungry'" (*Midrash T'hillim* 118:17).

With government support for efficient production of cheap food, we can feed people not only in our country, but also around the world. This policy speaks clearly to our Jewish values around hunger and health: all people deserve access to food as a basic human right, no person should go hungry, and when there are people in need, we are obligated to help. In Deuteronomy 15:7–11 we are clearly commanded that when there is a poor person among us, we must not turn away, but rather we must provide as much help as is needed:

> If, however, there is a needy person among you, one of your kin in any of your settlements in the land that the Eternal your God is giving you, do not harden your heart and shut your hand against your needy kin. Rather, you must open your hand and lend whatever is sufficient to meet the need.
>
> Deuteronomy 15:7–8

If the goal is to provide affordable and abundant sustenance efficiently, then the Farm Bill is a case study in successful public policy. Although food insecurity remains a challenge due to inequitable distribution, the simple reality is that, as a nation, we produce more food than ever before, and the Farm Bill is part of the reason. The cupboards of millions of Americans, as well as agribusiness giants, are full.

However, our food system and the policies that shape it have come under an enormous amount of criticism in recent years from the environmental, economic justice, and international development communities. Under Farm Bill policies, our nation's agricultural system produces more food (mostly corn) than ever before, but it is becoming increasingly clear that this system has a wide variety of adverse and unintended consequences. The challenge of our modern food system is maintaining this unprecedented level of productivity without destroying our environment and causing a vast array of other unintended consequences for global health and hunger.

As Michael Pollan explains in reference to our current federal food policy, "This focus on quantity may have made sense in a time of food scarcity, but today it gives us a school-lunch program that feeds chicken nuggets and Tater Tots to overweight and diabetic children."[2] The negative impact on health goes hand in hand with the unprecedented energy consumption associated with global food distribution, the greenhouse gases spewing from factory farms, and the negative impacts on farmers in the developing world.

Having enough food for all—and ensuring that those most in need have access to the most essential resource for survival—is an important, and deeply Jewish, goal. However, we also value environmental stewardship and sustainability and can see that, among other negative effects, our industrial agricultural system despoils our environment and degrades our land so that future food growth may be inhibited. The earliest verses of Genesis include the clear exhortation "to work [the earth] and to keep it" (Gen. 2:15), not just to use our resources to bring forth what we need—namely, food—but to be thoughtful guardians of our planet for current and future generations.

So, how do we reconcile or balance these values and goals: the need to have enough food for all, and the need to ensure the long-term sustainability of our food system and encourage the production and access to good, healthy food for all? If it is a question of quality versus quantity, and the Farm Bill represents quantity, then what is the alternative? One emerging idea, based on a successful model in place in Pennsylvania, is the Fresh Food Financing Initiative, created in 2004.

The Pennsylvania initiative responds to the reality that the Farm Bill produces massive amounts of food, but this food is largely unhealthy, and healthy alternatives are often inaccessible. People in rural communities lack access to local food sources, a fierce irony in a once agrarian society that is now served by highly centralized agriculture.

Many in urban communities, particularly low-income communities, have few places to purchase healthy food; grocery stores do not exist in those communities, and instead neighborhood residents shop at gas stations, convenience stores, and fast-food restaurants. The Fresh Food Financing Initiative in Pennsylvania has led to the creation or improvement of nearly seventy grocery stores in traditionally underserved areas, increasing access to healthy food and creating millions in private investment in a healthier food system. Advocates hope that replicating the Pennsylvania example on a national level would improve nutrition and increase access to healthy food while growing local economies. In short, it would combat the negative unintended consequences of policies like the Farm Bill.

The push for local, organic, and other alternatives to industrial agriculture is grounded in the need for healthy food and environmental stewardship, goals that reflect Jewish values as important as the impulse to feed everyone for as little cost as possible. From Leviticus to Maimonides, we are commanded to keep our bodies healthy, so that we might better serve God (or pursue *tikkun olam*). The commandment *bal tashchit*, which enjoins, "Do not destroy things from which humanity may benefit," reminds us to be good caretakers of our limited natural resources (Deut. 20:19–20). The environmental and health effects of industrial agriculture—the contaminating sewage pools common at Concentrated Animal Feeding Operations (CAFOs, or factory farms), the air pollution and energy consumption that results from moving the average food item fifteen hundred miles from farm to fork, and the exploding levels of childhood obesity—make it increasingly clear that our Jewish tradition demands a change.

The philosophy behind the Fresh Food Financing Initiative argues for a different set of food justice values than our traditional food policy: it's not just the quantity of food that matters, but quality, location, impact, and access. This vision of food justice means that all people should be able to obtain healthy food in their communities, not just buy massive quantities of cheap corn-based processed food products. It requires a turn away from subsidized corn and soy to a focus on producing fresh fruit and vegetables and consuming food grown within a few dozen miles of our homes instead of thousands of miles away. After all, the Talmud teaches that "it is forbidden to live in a city that does not have a green garden" (*Kiddushin* 4:12).

Approaches like the Fresh Food Financing Initiative do not disregard or oppose the goal of supplying abundant and affordable food, but rather add to traditional views of effective food policy. These approaches argue that the quality and accessibility of food we produce matters, not just the quantity.

What is wrong with this alternative model, one that emphasizes quality and honors our obligations to protect our individual health and our environment? The most trenchant critique of the sustainable agricultural movement is that it simply cannot produce affordable food for all. Our society is built on cheap food, and many people struggle even when prices of common commodities are low. So, while shopping at Whole Foods and farmers' markets might be a nice way to make the wealthy feel better about their carbon footprint, these solutions will never be practical for all Americans.

Yet, our current food policy is already failing to provide food for all. The Farm Bill and the industrial food system it supports have led to tremendous centralization of the food supply, leaving tremendous gaps in the food system. Some communities—not just around the world but here in the United States—lack access to fresh and healthy food, and these "food deserts," as they have come to be called, grow as the food system becomes more and more centralized.

Again, policies like Fresh Food Finance respond; in addition to promoting quality over quantity of food, Fresh Food Finance is largely about democratizing the food system. This means focusing on growing and eating local food, getting to know your farmers, and reengaging children with their food. But how do we build public policy, on a federal level, that encourages such intensely local activity? The major challenge for policies like Fresh Food Finance is that they are based on the specific needs of local communities and are not easy to "scale up" to the national level.

"Think globally, act (or farm) locally" can be read as the motto for the new food movement happening throughout North America and other parts of the world. This phenomenon is impacting on the Jewish world as well, as Jews connect food concerns to our Jewish values. Jewish farmers are gathering at Kayam Farm outside Baltimore, and activists are coming together for the annual, ever-growing Hazon food conference. But we know that while reconnecting with our own food and land is a laudable and Jewish goal, it alone is not enough. If our true goal is food justice, we cannot limit our actions to our own selves, our families, and our Jewish community. Rather, moving from a vision to a reality of food justice for all people requires raising our voices in support of policies that will create the just food future we envision.

We cannot meaningfully reform our food system without going beyond local action, as important as these personal and communal food changes may be. We need to advocate for policies that allow alternative food systems to "scale up" and compete. While new approaches like Fresh Food Financing Initiative are unlikely to replace the Farm Bill any time soon (and we likely wouldn't want them to), there is clearly value added by examining new approaches to food production and distribution that tackle some of these challenges of scale and affordability. We need to examine the options to see what can work at the national level to ensure that we have enough food for all, but also that it is good and healthy food.

The problems of our industrial food system are not new. As Secretary Tom Vilsack of the Department of Agriculture, explains, "It's not just that what we've been doing the last few years to support farmers and rural communities hasn't been working. It's that what we've been doing for the last few *decades* hasn't been working."[3] We have the resources to implement our Jewish values of food security, personal health, and environmental sustainability, but we need to think creatively about shaping policies that honor them, drawing from the success of our Farm Bill past while moving toward a new food future. Jewish values that consider health, economic justice, and environmental sustainability support a food system that not only provides enough for all, but also ensures that all people have access to good food. There must be a balance between Farm Bill–style subsidies that do ensure affordable, yet poor-quality food for all and an exclusive push for organic produce and localized food production through policies like Fresh Food Financing Initiative. Our Jewish values demand that we raise our voices for food policy reform and that we demand nothing less than a truly just food system.

NOTES

1. Wolfram Schlenker and Michael J. Roberts. "Nonlinear Temperature Effects Indicate Severe Damages to U.S. Crop Yields under Climate Change," *U.S. National Library of Medicine*, August 28, 2009, http://www.ncbi.nlm.nih.gov/pubmed/19717432.

2. Michael Pollan, "Farmer in Chief," *New York Times Magazine*, October 9, 2008.

3. Eric Hoffner, "Meet a Young Farmer Leading a Greenhorn 'Guerrilla' Movement," *Grist Magazine*, March 23, 2010, http://www.grist.org/article/greenhorn-guerilla/.

41

REAL LIFE / REAL FOOD
Bread, Torah, and *Tikkun*

LINDA MOTZKIN AND JONATHAN RUBENSTEIN

It's Friday morning in Temple Sinai's kitchen—also known as Slice of Heaven Breads, a nonprofit, all-volunteer bakery. The kitchen, renovated as a commercial bakery with a grant from a local philanthropy, is humming with activity. The dough for about eighty challahs— including white, whole-wheat, vegan, raisin, and seeded varieties—is rising.

The regular volunteers have arrived: a radical Catholic with Quaker leanings, a congregant in protracted recovery from a traumatic brain injury, a young Jew laid off from a financial services job, a man with Down syndrome, and a staffed group of adults from a local agency for people with developmental disabilities. On any given day there will also be toddlers with a parent or grandparent, *b'nei mitzvah* students, and youths doing community service.

When the first dough has risen, we stand in a circle around the beautiful wooden baking counter. We separate a small piece from the dough and visualize the ingredients it contains (all organic and/or locally produced), where they come from, who labors to provide them, and what we are doing with them: making bread and providing sustenance for the Shabbat tables of Jewish members of the community and for customers of all persuasions; donating the proceeds of our sales to food programs and other causes; providing loaves to Jewish and non-Jewish residents of local facilities for the aged; and donating bread and other baked goods for fundraising activities of local nonprofit organizations. We sound a chime, join hands, and stand together in silence to consider our blessings, and then we say the blessing over the mitzvah of separating the challah.

This interlude is brief, because we have work to do. Everyone sets to a task: cutting and weighing out the dough, dividing each weighed piece into smaller pieces for braiding. Then we make four-, five-, or six-braid loaves or more complex ones for special occasions such as weddings or *b'nei mitzvah*.

The work proceeds rhythmically, steadily, joyfully. The loaves are braided, covered, left to rise, glazed, baked, removed from the oven, set on cooling racks; later they are bagged, labeled, and sorted. Some of the regulars take their time helping differently abled braiders complete their loaves; others make sure the production continues expeditiously. Finally, more volunteers arrive—often *b'nei mitzvah* students fulfilling their mitzvah service—to deliver the loaves designated for the elderly and infirm recipients.

One synagogue, one community, in its small way is seeking to bring about *tikkun* by linking community building, direct service, ethical eating, and healing of the earth. We do this through our commitment to use locally produced and organic ingredients in our products; by teaching and modeling sustainability, just production, and ethical consumption; by supporting organizations dedicated to hunger, poverty, and disaster relief; by welcoming into our community people of differing abilities and needs; by giving the first fruits of our baking—loaves made by many hands and many spirits—to people for whom the bread and the delivery visit are a blessing; and by teaching the empowering, elemental craft of bread making.

Part Nine

Spirituality

While some Jews quip that all Jewish holidays boil down to "They tried to kill us. We survived. Let's eat," the Jewish relationship with food has a much deeper spirituality. In "Food Preparation as a Holy Act: *Hafrashat Challah*," Ruth Abusch-Magder immerses us in the ritual of taking challah to demonstrate the Jewish approach to food preparation. Through this finite ritual, she teaches us much about rituals at the ancient Temple, theology, and liturgical blessings. Building on this last theme, Bennett F. Miller ("The Joy and Privilege of Blessings Before and After a Meal") makes the old new again by refocusing our attention on the variety of food blessings and *Birkat HaMazon*, the Blessing after Meals. He helps us consider their place in Reform dietary practice; he shines new meaning onto their ancient words.

Ellen Lippmann and Trisha Arlin's "We Eat First: A Congregational Snapshot" builds beautifully on the model of the Pharisaic fellowship tables, as taught by Doug Sagal ("Of Pharisees and Allergies: *Shulchan Shalom*") in part 7. While most us of know that food is important to our creating community, Lippmann and Arlin infuse a new passion into that goal. In "What I Eat Is Who I Am: Kashrut and Identity," Peter Knobel explores the role of food in the crucible of identity formation. In doing so, he recalls how the earlier generations of Reform Jews approached food and identity and offers a model for today. Knobel reflects on the Reform relationship to other Jews, as well as to the greater world.

While it may seem counterintuitive, it is vital to include fasting in any discussion of kashrut. Our dietary practice is equally defined by what we do eat and by when we do not eat. In "*Tzom*: Fasting as a Religious/Spiritual Practice," Sue Levi Elwell provides a comprehensive survey of the use of fasting in Judaism, including both ritual and social justice fasts. Elwell provides innovative, original blessings to use before, during, and after fasting. She also addresses what to do if one cannot fast. Sharing a story about Yom Kippur fasting, Donald A. Weber ("An Introduction to Hunger") recalls an interactive sermon he gave one year in order to teach his congregation empathy for the food insecure. Just reading his article will impress an important lesson on us all.

42

FOOD PREPARATION AS A HOLY ACT

Hafrashat Challah

RUTH ABUSCH-MAGDER

Once, I sat with a rabbinic colleague who asked me of my spiritual practice. I told him about my weekly bread baking, an admission that left him entirely unsure how to respond.

My Shabbat preparation begins each week when I take the flour out of the cupboard, mix it with salt, water, yeast, eggs, and oil and let it rise. The process of kneading, of pushing and pulling the dough, is thoroughly satisfying. I say blessings, follow ancient rules, add my own meditation. It is a deeply spiritual act.

When thinking of the spiritual elements of food in traditional Judaism, our attention is often diverted by questions of kashrut or by the blessings that bracket our culinary consumption. Yet, baking bread is among the most ancient of Jewish spiritual endeavors. The Rabbinic rituals that are embedded in the process of making bread recall directly the rites of the ancient Temple in Jerusalem. This process is known as *hafrashat challah*, the separating of *challah*. Done in the quiet of the kitchen long before the full potential of the dough has been realized as bread, this small ritual speaks to a broader vision of partnership in which people, together with God, work toward bringing redemption to the world—a vision in which bread stands for all forms of sustenance and the potential of the world-to-come.

In contemporary Jewish life, the term *challah* is often synonymous with the eggy braided loaves consumed in honor of Shabbat.[1] While challah bread has the potential to feed the body, the ritual of *hafrashat challah* has the potential to feed our souls. *Hafrashat challah* offers a spiritual challenge to the convenience of breakfast bars and drive-through restaurants. It demands that we consider what we put in our mouths and the process by which we prepare food.

Hafrashat challah refers to the ritual of removing a piece of the un-baked dough, blessing it,[2] and setting it aside. The portion of *challah* is then disposed of either by burning or throwing it away. Whatever its fate, this dough may not be consumed. In the halachic literature, there is some disagreement about the amounts of flour that must be used before the obligation to separate *challah* kicks in. There is also discussion about the amount that must be removed. In addition, there are different expectations for those who bake at home as opposed to those who rely on the sale of bread for income. Although as liberal Jews we may be less concerned with the details of this particular obligation, the ritual, its history, and its meaning open up critical conversations and opportunities for spiritual expression.

Our modern conversation about separating *challah* must begin with its biblical roots. In Numbers 15:17–21, the people of Israel, upon entering the Land, are commanded:

> The Eternal One spoke to Moses, saying: Speak to the Israelite people and say to them: When you enter the land to which I am taking you and you eat of the bread of the land, you shall set some aside as a gift to the Eternal: as the first yield of your baking, you shall set aside a loaf as a gift; you shall set it aside as a gift like the gift from the threshing floor. You shall make a gift to the Eternal from the first yield of your baking, throughout the ages.

In the time that the Holy Temple stood in Jerusalem, these verses were understood to be the backbone of the system of tithing of bread, the setting aside of loaves for the *kohanim*, who did not own land, work the land, harvest their own wheat, or bake their own bread. The destruction of the Temple meant the cessation or transmutation of the general systems of sacrifice and tithing. By comparison, the practice of taking *challah* remained surprisingly close to its ancient roots. Already in the Mishnaic period, those involved with baking were obligated to say a *b'rachah* (blessing) for the commandment of *hafrashat challah* as they set aside a portion of the dough to be burned—like the sacrifices of old.

Though it was not inevitable that taking *challah* endured after the destruction of the Temple in Jerusalem, it is not really surprising. Having lost the altars and places of gathering, the people were not entirely without some form of physical and spiritual sustenance. Even the poorest of the poor had bread, and that bread connected them to the past, as it also held out hope for a future redemption. The endurance of taking *challah* beyond not only the Temple, but also the Land of Israel, reinforces the exalted position of bread in Judaism.

Even in biblical times, the word *lechem*, "bread," had multiple meanings. In addition to referring specifically to baked loaves, the word was used interchangeably to refer to a complete meal or even food in general. In addition, the word "bread" was sometimes associated with toil.[3] The biblical equation of bread with all forms of comestible sustenance is reinforced by the later development of pronouncing blessings over food. Rabbinic tradition holds that blessings must be said before consuming any food. While there are blessings for every category of food, once the blessing over bread, the *Motzi*, is said at the start of a meal, no other subsequent blessings are necessary. Bread is the paradigmatic food, and its blessing preempts all others.

Yet, the Rabbinic blessing over bread suggests so much more than an appreciation of caloric sustenance. The *Motzi* celebrates God as "the One who brings forth bread from the earth." While this is a beautiful vision, it is an abstraction of the natural state; bread does not grow from the ground. In this way, it differs from the concrete nature of the general food blessings, which, with the exception of the *Kiddush* over wine, reflects the basic means by which a food comes to be; apples and

oranges, for example, are eaten after acknowledging God as "the Creator of the fruits of trees." Moreover, the *Motzi* should be read together
with *Birkat HaMazon*, "the Blessing after Meals." Not only does the
eating of bread trigger the obligation to recite the full grace, but also,
as Rabbi Lawrence Hoffman points out, both blessings share a vision
of a messianic time when we return to the ease and abundance of Eden,
when food will simply come forth from the earth and there will be no
hunger.[4] In other words, we will have reached the messianic era when
bread comes forth from the earth with such ease that all have bread in
the fullest meaning of the word.

This messianic vision of God pulling forth bread from the earth
puts an important frame on the commandment to take *challah*. Until
redemption is achieved, it is the baker who must partner with God to
bring forth bread from the earth and feed the hungry. Therefore, the
making of bread is no ordinary act; it is one of covenant, a sacred connection between the Divine, who created grain, and the people who
transform that grain into the essence of sustenance. In our modern
era, we in the Western, developed world are increasingly disconnected
from the process by which food is made; it is easy to lose sight of the
miracle that is food. The blessings before eating can be critical in helping us restore a connection to God as a provider of food.

Rabbi Mordechai Yosef Leiner of Isbitza, the Mei HaShiloach,
wrote in his commentary on *Parashat T'rumah* that we come to understand the role of God in being *motzi lechem min haaretz* (the One who
brings forth bread from the earth) when we put bread into the oven and
cannot control which portion of the dough bakes first. But those who
take *challah* encounter God's role in bringing forth our sustenance long
before the dough begins to bake. They come to experience bread—and
by extension all food—as part of a dependence on God. When I first
began to make challah, I focused on finding the right recipe, getting the
yeast to rise properly. If only I practiced enough, had the right recipe,
the right flour, the right location in my oven, I would be in control
of the results. I have with time become quite a proficient baker; I am
able to produce excellent *challot* with great predictability. Yet, the act

of taking *challah* serves as a reminder, that despite my skill and no matter the pride I take in my final loaves, I am not fully in control. In this process, as in all my areas of endeavor, I am in partnership with God.

I am not the first bread baker, regardless of gender, to connect with God during the process of making bread. Historically, the work of making bread fell primarily to women. As early as the Mishnaic period, taking *challah* was designated as one of three commandments specifically connected with women.[5] Whether trying to make the most of the limited opportunities for spiritual expression, responding to a broader understanding of bread as a sacred food, or both, women developed many rituals and customs that spoke to the holiness of the act of *hafrashat challah*. Some women would recite psalms as they worked. Others saw the preparation of dough as a time to offer special prayers, words of praise and petition.[6] These customs and the associated liturgy model female spirituality, sacred creativity, personal agency, and direct divine connection.

Today most Jews, like most citizens of the industrialized world, do not make their own bread. Indeed, much of the bread we consume comes from factories where, if the bread is kosher, *challah* has been taken in a perfunctory way. The spiritual element, like much of the bread we consume, has been sealed off from nature by plastic. The loss of this seemingly minor ritual moment is greater than the convenience gained.

We should consider reintroducing the taking of *challah* in contemporary Reform communities. Kitchens in synagogues might be open during Hebrew school so that parents could perform the ritual together. The kitchens of JCCs might be open in conjunction with adult programming so that seniors could gather to take *challah*. Dough might be made available, with educational materials, so that individuals or families might experience taking *challah*. Given the rhythms of contemporary Western life, it is however, unrealistic to imagine most individuals making a shift to baking bread in such a way that the taking of *challah* is likely to become routine. Ironically, it is this very modern reality, in which we are generally disconnected from food preparation, that makes the spiritual lessons gained from this ritual all the more pressing. For those who do not bake bread ever or infrequently, we can incorporate the teachings of *hafrashat challah* into lessons about food production, *tzedakah*, and spirituality.

Taking *challah* is a humbling experience that reminds us that we are not fully in control of our own experience. It also connects us to the ancient roots of Judaism, which intertwined agriculture and religion, tying together the most fundamental elements of life with a vision of divinity. It is a ritual that not only helps us establish a positive relationship with the rituals of the Temple, but also allows us to connect with the rich female legacy that celebrates what has historically been women's work and brings to the surface the inheritance left to *all* Jews by generations of Jewish women. Taking *challah* serves as a reminder to us that we are God's partners in bringing about redemption. Additionally, in a broader culture that values personal spiritual expression, taking *challah* brings us an opportunity to enter into personal contemplation with the framework of established ritual. The symbolic significance of bread, as emblematic of all food and of sustenance more generally, imbues the many meanings of this ritual with import for every element of life.

When God exiled Adam and Eve from Eden, they were told that they would have to toil for their sustenance. Today, as in no other time in history, many possess the power not to engage in the work of food preparation. Yet, as our discussion of *hafrashat challah* suggests, there is more to preparing food than the physical effort exerted. Taking *challah* provides us with a chance to see our relationship with food within the context of a covenantal relationship with God—to view it not only as a relationship of gratitude, but also as a reminder of our own obligation to work to redeem the world.

NOTES

1. Though originally an Eastern European culinary tradition, the naming of these Shabbat loaves draws on biblical verses that according to lexicographers and scholars equates the Hebrew term *challah* with "loaves" (Francis Brown, S. Driver, and

C. Briggs, *Brown-Driver-Briggs Hebrew and English Lexicon* [Peabody, MA: Hendrickson Publishers, 1996], 319).

2. There are two versions of the blessing for taking *challah*. They vary only slightly in the conclusion of the blessing. The Ashkenazic version is as follows: *Baruch atah, Adonai Eloheinu, Melech haolam, asher kid'shanu b'mitzvotav, v'tzvivanu l'hafrish challah* (some add: *min ha-isah*). The Sephardic version is as follows: *Baruch atah, Adonai Eloheinu, Melech haolam, asher kid'shanu b'mitzvotav, v'tzvivanu l'hafrish challah t'rumah*. "Blessed are You, *Adonai* our God, Sovereign of the universe, who hallows us with mitzvot, commanding us to separate *challah*" (some add: "from the dough"; Sephardic version adds: *t'rumah* [offering]).

3. The first mention comes in Gen. 3:19, where Adam and Eve's need to sweat for their bread is symbolic of all toil. By contrast to the work that Adam and Eve would have to do, in Exodus 16, where the word *lechem* is used for the manna, we come to understand that "bread" can be a holy gift. A third meaning of *lechem* emerges from the many verses where the word is understood to be synonymous with a meal or with all forms of eating. In Gen. 37:25, for example, Joseph's brothers sit down to eat *lechem*, which is best understood as a meal. Though there is variation as to how different versions translate the term *lechem*, in this and other instances, the *JPS Tanakh* understands *lechem* as a meal, and the *Brown-Driver-Briggs* explains that the word *lechem* can be understood as "*bread*, the ordinary food of early Hebrews" (p. 536). In Exod. 34:28, Moses abstains from eating *lechem* or drinking water in preparation for ascending to Mount Sinai to receive the Torah. It is absurd to imagine our great leader abstaining from bread and water while indulging in cake and wine; we are clearly not meant to be so literal in our understanding. Just as water is meant to stand in for all liquid refreshment, bread symbolizes all food.

4. Lawrence Hoffman, *The Way into Jewish Prayer* (Woodstock, VT: Jewish Lights Publishing, 2000), 140.

5. The other two women's obligations are *nidah* and *nerot*, the obligations of menstrual purity and the lighting of candles on Shabbat and holy days.

6. Many examples of prayers said by women during the taking of *challah* have come down to us through the generations: Aliza Lavie, ed., *A Jewish Woman's Prayer Book* (New York: Spiegel and Grau, 2008), 184–93; Tracy Guren Klirs, ed., *Merit of Our Mothers: A Bilingual Anthology of Jewish Women's Prayers* (Cincinnati: Hebrew Union College Press, 1992), 12; Dinah Berland, ed., *Hours of Devotion: Fanny Neuda's Book of Prayers for Jewish Women* (New York: Schocken Books, 2007), 39.

THE JOY AND PRIVILEGE OF BLESSINGS
BEFORE AND AFTER A MEAL

Bennett F. Miller

Michael Pollan, author of *Omnivore's Dilemma*, writes that eating "is an ecological act, and a political act, too."[1] For Jews, eating is also a religious and spiritual act. Our tradition informs us that food is not simply the result of nature or agriculture; what we eat and consume represent the gifts given to us by the Divine. The Psalmist declares, "The earth is the Eternal's and the fullness thereof" (Psalm 24:1).

As Jews entered the world of modernity, much of our tradition was set aside. Fully engaged members of contemporary society, America's Jews were doing all that they could to assimilate into the general culture; in doing so, it often meant setting aside rituals and practices that were perceived as belonging to a distant past or as being part of a particularism that no longer held meaning for Jews.

In 1999, when the Central Conference of American Rabbis produced "A Statement of Principles for Reform Judaism," it did so with a clear historical understanding that Reform Judaism was unique in its approach to our tradition's past and its future. The preamble states the following:

> The great contribution of Reform Judaism is that it has enabled
> the Jewish people to introduce innovation while preserving tradi-
> tion, to embrace diversity while asserting commonality, to affirm

beliefs without rejecting those who doubt, and to bring faith to sacred texts without sacrificing critical scholarship.[2]

At the same time that Reform Judaism is integrating an awareness of preserving tradition with a drive to introduce innovation, twenty-first century America is also experiencing a newfound understanding and appreciation for food and our relationship to it. Ecological and political issues regarding food and its development, production, effect on diet, and relationship to a democratic society are represented in the daily discourse of ideas through the media and the publication of literature and film. As diet has become big business, eating and consumption have become central themes in our culture's daily discourse.

As a result, Reform Jews once again are looking to our tradition to develop sacred meaning to our relationship with food and diet. What better place than the world of blessings! After all, blessings (*b'rachot*) represent the language of gratitude, praise, and petition. This essay, then, is divided into two sections: first, about food blessings for before one eats; the second, food blessings for after one eats.

Blessings Surrounding Food: Before Eating

The recitation of a blessing (*b'rachah*) before doing something demonstrates that the action we are about to perform will be transformed from an instinctual exercise to a sacred event. This is especially true in regard to food consumption.

An example of this is found in the Talmud:

> Our Rabbis have taught: it is forbidden to a man to enjoy anything of this world without a blessing, and if anyone enjoys anything of this world without a blessing, he commits sacrilege. What is his remedy? He should consult a wise man. But what will the wise man do for him? He has already committed the offence! Raba said: What this means is that he should consult a wise man beforehand, so that he would teach him blessings, so that he should not commit sacrilege.
> (Babylonian Talmud, *B'rachot* 35a)

Certainly, Reform Jews do not consider overlooking the recitation of blessings to be sacrilege. However, we can find meaning in this text, which emphasizes the importance of blessings. "Consulting a wise man" may very well mean looking to the wisdom of the sages of our tradition. The language of blessing is the opportunity to celebrate and appreciate the good fortune that has befallen us, the opportunities for meaningful living that are given to us, and the gifts of our lives. What the Rabbis have given to us in the language of blessing represents a vocabulary of sacred words, designed for every experience in life that we encounter.

The opening formula for nearly every blessing sets the meaning and purpose of its recitation. When one recites בָּרוּךְ אַתָּה יְיָ אֱלֹהֵינוּ מֶלֶךְ הָעוֹלָם both the words and the action are placed into a context. We recognize that our action connects us to the Divine, that there is a sacredness to the meaning of our action, and that what we are about to do is not to be considered ordinary or mundane. We are praising God for being *Melech haolam*, "Sovereign of the universe." Such a statement indicates our awareness that there is a direct connection between this world and the world of the Divine. Therefore, each step in the process of the action we are about to perform or the thanksgiving we are expressing has relevance and importance to us.

The *Motzi*[3] may be the most commonly used blessing of this genre. Familiar to the overwhelming majority of Jews, *Motzi* is often associated with eating a challah on Shabbat or at a festive meal, bar or bat mitzvah, wedding, or bris. In its specificity, *Motzi* is a blessing to be recited before one eats bread. After all, the blessing is a statement of thanks to God "who brings forth bread from the earth."

בָּרוּךְ אַתָּה יְיָ אֱלֹהֵינוּ מֶלֶךְ הָעוֹלָם הַמּוֹצִיא לֶחֶם מִן הָאָרֶץ.

Motzi serves as a direct reminder that bread (and all food) is a gift; without the Divine, no such gift exists. Yet, the recitation of *Motzi* also reminds us of our connection to the earth itself; it reminds us to care for the earth and to be cognizant of the importance of the world in which we live and its impact on our daily lives. By extension, such recitation should remind us of the role played by those who till the earth, bring forth its produce, and are involved in the production of the food we are about to eat. After all, the blessing refers to bringing forth bread, not grain, from the earth. Thus, reciting *Motzi* is an important theological and sociological (and even political) statement. Involved in its expression are ecological values, concerns for the rights of workers, and hope for a world that reflects the divine purpose. It is fair to say that, taken seriously, *Motzi* is a powerful statement recited to remind us of the complexity and sacredness of our world and the privilege we have to live in it.

For many Reform Jews, the *Motzi* has become a generic blessing recited before eating anything.[4] As our sensitivity regarding food consumption becomes heightened, we should understand that many food specific blessings exist. Why would our tradition provide us with more than generic food blessings? Perhaps to aid us in our understanding of the biodiversity of the world in which we live. Moderns understand that every species provides meaning and purpose to the order of our universe. Fruit and vegetables are not the same. They each have a role to play in the human diet. As their respective blessings teach us, bread and cake do not grow, are not taken from the ground; much more is required in their production. Grains such as wheat, oats, and barley (to name just a few) are plants that require refinement in order for them to become the staples that sustain humans. Thus, expanding our communal knowledge to include the full variety of food blessings may be more appropriate than using *Motzi* as a generic food blessing. Our tradition provides the following blessings to be recited before eating:[5]

Over (non-bread) foods made from wheat, oats, rye, barley, and spelt:

בָּרוּךְ אַתָּה יְיָ אֱלֹהֵינוּ מֶלֶךְ הָעוֹלָם בּוֹרֵא מִינֵי מְזוֹנוֹת.

Blessed are You, Adonai our God, Sovereign of the universe,
Creator of many kinds of food.

Over wine:

בָּרוּךְ אַתָּה יְיָ אֱלֹהֵינוּ מֶלֶךְ הָעוֹלָם בּוֹרֵא פְּרִי הַגָּפֶן.

Blessed are You, Adonai our God, Sovereign of the universe,
Creator of the fruit of the vine.

Over tree fruit:

בָּרוּךְ אַתָּה יְיָ אֱלֹהֵינוּ מֶלֶךְ הָעוֹלָם בּוֹרֵא פְּרִי הָעֵץ.

Blessed are You, Adonai our God, Sovereign of the universe,
Creator of the fruit of the tree.

Over fruit from the earth:

בָּרוּךְ אַתָּה יְיָ אֱלֹהֵינוּ מֶלֶךְ הָעוֹלָם בּוֹרֵא פְּרִי הָאֲדָמָה.

Blessed are You, Adonai our God, Sovereign of the universe,
Creator of the fruit of the earth.

Over meat, fish, milk, eggs, and cheese, as well as beverages (other than wine):

בָּרוּךְ אַתָּה יְיָ אֱלֹהֵינוּ מֶלֶךְ הָעוֹלָם שֶׁהַכֹּל נִהְיֶה בִּדְבָרוֹ.

Blessed are You, Adonai our God, Sovereign of the universe,
by whose word all things come into being.[6]

Our tradition recognizes that with blessing, an act such as eating becomes transformed into the realm of the sacred. One of the hallmarks of Reform Judaism is that our actions should be based on meaning, not on mere recitation. In the case of food blessings, their recitation should serve to heighten our sense of meaning, our awareness of the role that food plays in our lives. Saying *Motzi* or one of the other blessings before eating should heighten our sense of social justice regarding our responsibility for the care of the earth and the workers who have labored to take the raw products from the earth to the table. Such blessings should also serve as reminders to us of our own freedom and our need to be aware of the poor and impoverished in our communities. It is all too easy to simply think of food as something to be consumed. Our actions should not reflect our animal instincts; rather, they should reveal the "divine image" in each of us. Reciting blessings before we eat should not be understood as formula or ritual but as heightening our sense of wonder, our connection to the Divine, our connection to Judaism, and a reflection of our own meaning and purpose in life.

Blessings Surrounding Food: After Eating

Reform Jews should be grateful to the North American Federation of Temple Youth (NFTY). Over the course of the last fifty years, NFTY has provided the Reform Movement with creativity in the area of social action, liturgy, music, and programs. It has also restored and revitalized much of our tradition in many areas, including the world of blessings. The Blessing after Meals (*Birkat HaMazon*) is included among the transformative innovations that NFTY has initiated. At NFTY events and URJ summer camps, *Birkat HaMazon* has been revitalized. Several generations of youths have shared in the joy of reciting *Birkat HaMazon* after meals. They have returned to their homes and to their synagogues knowing this blessing. Today, the *Birkat* has become a staple of Reform practice.[7]

While it is true that most Reform Jews do not recite blessings after they eat everyday meals,[8] there is a growing awareness in Reform circles that its recitation serves as an authentic form of Jewish expression of gratitude. We find in the Torah the following words: "When you have eaten your fill, give thanks to the Eternal your God for the good land given to you" (Deut. 8:10). This passage serves as the proof text for *Birkat HaMazon*, the first of all blessings regarding eating and food. It reflects the historical relationship between God and the Jews. When we complete our meal, we are to remind ourselves that the food we have eaten is a gift to us from God, just as the manna in the desert was a gift to us from God that sustained us during our wandering years.[9]

The recitation of the *Birkat* serves as a form of thanksgiving. If one reads the preceding verses in the same chapter of Deuteronomy, it becomes clear that reciting *Birkat* is a form of thanksgiving for the fulfillment of the covenant between God and our ancestors; the covenant through which God gave us the Land of Israel, manna to sustain us in the desert, food from the land, provided us with all of our needs, and more. In reciting the *Birkat*, our words serve as a form of fulfillment of our part of the charge outlined in Deuteronomy, "to faithfully observe all the Instruction" (Deut. 8:1) that God has enjoined upon us.

There is another important reason for reciting the *Birkat*. The Mishnah informs us that "three who have eaten are to recite the *Birkat HaMazon*" (*Mishnah B'rachot* 7:1). Why should this be so important to the Rabbis? The eating of food is a reflection of our own human character. When we eat alone, we eat for survival. The only thing that matters is satisfying our individual need. Yet, eating in community transforms the physical act into a social, spiritual, and/or religious expression. For the Rabbis, eating in community served as an act of humility. When we eat together, we take care of one another and we nurture each other. For example, over a meal, we often ask about each other's welfare. Eating in community should be seen not as a "right" or entitlement of being human, but rather as a privilege and honor, for doing so means sharing "in community" with our fellow beings and with the Divine.

So often in America today, people eat alone, in cars, or in fast-food restaurants. Americans are deeply influenced by the consumerism of our times, and our eating habits have become a reflection of our isolation from one another and of our connection to things. Our tradition stands in contrast to such behavior, and *Birkat HaMazon* recognizes that eating together is important, because gathering over food represents living in community all the time. Recently, Rabbi Eric Yoffie, president of the Union for Reform Judaism, called on our communities to devote more attention to eating together on Shabbat, to revitalizing our sense of communal meals.[10] There is a growing awareness that eating in community serves many important functions. Similarly, we have witnessed the growth of the "family meal movement." There is a growing understanding that families who eat together are healthier, have lives that are more organized, and have a deeper sense of shared values.

Birkat HaMazon raises eating to an even higher level. Reminding us of God's gifts, this extended set of blessings recognizes that through Divine providence the individual receives nourishment to be sustained physically, Torah to carry out the covenant, and Jerusalem and Zion to be sustained spiritually. *Birkat HaMazon* serves to remind the individual and the Jewish community that what sustains us is not only the physical, but the theological and the covenantal nature of life as well.

While most Reform Jews recite an abbreviated version of the traditional *Birkat HaMazon*, the following normative selections are worth examining:[11]

1. The preamble: When one recites the *Birkat*, one should invite others (more than three) to participate as well. (*Mishnah B'rachot* 7:1 infers that one "summons" the other.) So, *Birkat* begins with a Jew over bar mitzvah age extending the invitation: "Let us praise God!" And the others who have eaten respond, "Praised be the name of God, now and forever!" Of course, if one is not in the company of others, *Birkat* can still be recited, and certainly should be.

חֲבֵרִים וַחֲבֵרוֹת, נְבָרֵךְ! יְהִי שֵׁם יְיָ מְבֹרָךְ מֵעַתָּה וְעַד עוֹלָם!

Let us praise God! Praised be the name of God,
now and forever!

2. The blessing of thanks for nourishment: This is the central theme of *Birkat*. Through God's grace and mercy, nourishment is provided to all who live. In reciting this blessing, we are keenly aware that food is a precious gift from the Divine.

בָּרוּךְ אַתָּה יְיָ, אֱלֹהֵינוּ מֶלֶךְ הָעוֹלָם, הַזָּן אֶת הָעוֹלָם כֻּלּוֹ בְּטוּבוֹ בְּחֵן בְּחֶסֶד וּבְרַחֲמִים. הוּא נוֹתֵן לֶחֶם לְכָל בָּשָׂר כִּי לְעוֹלָם חַסְדּוֹ. וּבְטוּבוֹ הַגָּדוֹל תָּמִיד לֹא חָסַר לָנוּ, וְאַל יֶחְסַר לָנוּ מָזוֹן לְעוֹלָם וָעֶד. בַּעֲבוּר שְׁמוֹ הַגָּדוֹל, כִּי הוּא אֵל זָן וּמְפַרְנֵס לַכֹּל וּמֵטִיב לַכֹּל, וּמֵכִין מָזוֹן לְכָל בְּרִיּוֹתָיו אֲשֶׁר בָּרָא. בָּרוּךְ אַתָּה יְיָ, הַזָּן אֶת הַכֹּל.

Sovereign God of the universe, we praise You: Your goodness
sustains the world.
You are the God of grace, love, and compassion, the Source of
bread for all who live;
for Your love is everlasting. In Your great goodness we need never
lack for food;
You provide food enough for all. We praise You, O God, Source of
food for all who live.

3. Thanksgiving for our heritage: This is the second blessing of
Birkat. It expresses gratitude for the heritage that our people
were given when Joshua entered the Land of Israel. In doing so,
we are reminded of our connection to our ancestors going back
in time to Abraham and Sarah.[12]

כַּכָּתוּב: וְאָכַלְתָּ וְשָׂבָעְתָּ, וּבֵרַכְתָּ אֶת יְיָ אֱלֹהֶיךָ עַל הָאָרֶץ הַטּוֹבָה אֲשֶׁר נָתַן לָךְ.
בָּרוּךְ אַתָּה יְיָ, עַל הָאָרֶץ וְעַל הַמָּזוֹן.

As it is written: When you have eaten and are satisfied,
give praise to your God who has given you this good earth.
We praise You, O God, for the earth and for its sustenance.

4. It is also within this second blessing that we find *Birkat*'s foundational text. *Birkat* includes the very text of Torah (Deut. 8:10)
upon which the entire blessing is based.

וְאָכַלְתָּ וְשָׂבָעְתָּ, וּבֵרַכְתָּ אֶת יְיָ אֱלֹהֶיךָ עַל הָאָרֶץ הַטּוֹבָה אֲשֶׁר נָתַן לָךְ.

When you have eaten and are satisfied, give praise to your God who
has given you this good earth.

5. The blessing for Jerusalem: Jerusalem in our tradition is the holy abode of the Eternal. Together with the Land of Israel, Jerusalem serves as the spiritual possession of the Jewish people. Including this blessing in *Birkat* helps us to recognize that our relationship with the Eternal is not simply about nourishment and survival; it also reflects our connection to our physical and spiritual past, both considered essential for the contemporary Jew.

וּבְנֵה יְרוּשָׁלַיִם עִיר הַקֹּדֶשׁ בִּמְהֵרָה בְיָמֵינוּ. בָּרוּךְ אַתָּה יְיָ, בּוֹנֵה בְּרַחֲמָיו יְרוּשָׁלָיִם. אָמֵן.

Let Jerusalem, the holy city, be renewed in our time.
We praise You, Adonai, in compassion You rebuild Jerusalem.
  Amen.

6. God's mercy: Included in *Birkat* are a number of entreaties to *HaRachaman* (the All Merciful). They serve as requests to God, petitions for our loved ones, for a time of goodness and for kindness to our hosts. There are also other specific insertions. They serve as reminders of the cycle of the year and the importance of the Festivals. In the twenty-first century Jews should have a greater awareness of the rotation of the year and its impact on a person's life and the way Jewish identity is shaped. Perhaps that is why in our tradition the Festivals are about receiving the Law at Sinai, celebrating our freedom from slavery, and expressing gratitude for the miracle of the bounty that is produced from the earth.

הָרַחֲמָן, הוּא יְבָרֵךְ אוֹתָנוּ וְאֶת כָּל אֲשֶׁר לָנוּ, כְּמוֹ שֶׁנִּתְבָּרְכוּ אֲבוֹתֵינוּ, אַבְרָהָם, יִצְחָק וְיַעֲקֹב, וְאִמּוֹתֵינוּ שָׂרָה, רִבְקָה, רָחֵל וְלֵאָה, בַּכֹּל, מִכֹּל, כֹּל, כֵּן יְבָרֵךְ אוֹתָנוּ כֻּלָּנוּ יַחַד בִּבְרָכָה שְׁלֵמָה, וְנֹאמַר: אָמֵן.

Merciful One, bless us and all our dear ones; as You blessed our
  ancestors Abraham, Isaac, and Jacob, Sarah, Rebekah, Rachel,
  and Leah, so bless us, one and all; and let us say: Amen.

(On Shabbat) הָרַחֲמָן, הוּא יַנְחִילֵנוּ יוֹם שֶׁכֻּלּוֹ שַׁבָּת וּמְנוּחָה לְחַיֵּי הָעוֹלָמִים.

Merciful One, help us to see the coming of a time when all is
 Shabbat.

(On *Yom Tov*) הָרַחֲמָן, הוּא יַנְחִילֵנוּ יוֹם שֶׁכֻּלּוֹ טוֹב.

Merciful One, help us to see the coming of a time when all is good.

(Rosh HaShanah) הָרַחֲמָן, הוּא יְחַדֵּשׁ עָלֵינוּ אֶת הַשָּׁנָה הַזֹּאת לְטוֹבָה וְלִבְרָכָה.

Merciful One, bring us a year of renewed good and blessing.

7. Peace for all: *Birkat* concludes with a blessing for peace. After
 all, what good is food and nourishment if there is no peace? This
 is the existential request of all human beings. In this blessing,
 included is the hope for peace for all humanity and specifically
 in the Land of Israel as well.

עֹשֶׂה שָׁלוֹם בִּמְרוֹמָיו, הוּא יַעֲשֶׂה שָׁלוֹם עָלֵינוּ וְעַל כָּל יִשְׂרָאֵל, וְעַל כָּל יוֹשְׁבֵי
תֵבֵל, וְאִמְרוּ אָמֵן.
יְיָ עֹז לְעַמּוֹ יִתֵּן. יְיָ יְבָרֵךְ אֶת עַמּוֹ בַשָּׁלוֹם.

May the Source of peace grant peace
 to us, to all Israel, and to all the world.
May Adonai grant strength to our people.
 May Adonai bless our people with peace.

8. On Shabbat: More than any other, the Shabbat table is the
 transformative ritual in Jewish life. Everything about the Shabbat meal serves to heighten the level of one's spiritual connection to life. Therefore, added to *Birkat HaMazon* is the
 recitation of Psalm 126. It reflects an optimistic spirit of re-
 unification between God and the People of Israel in the Land
 of Israel. In effect, these words from the *Tanach* bring together
 everything to be included in the *Birkat HaMazon* that will be
 recited.

שִׁיר הַמַּעֲלוֹת, בְּשׁוּב יְיָ אֶת שִׁיבַת צִיּוֹן, הָיִינוּ כְּחֹלְמִים. אָז יִמָּלֵא שְׂחוֹק פִּינוּ
וּלְשׁוֹנֵנוּ רִנָּה. אָז יֹאמְרוּ בַגּוֹיִם, הִגְדִּיל יְיָ לַעֲשׂוֹת עִם אֵלֶּה. הִגְדִּיל יְיָ לַעֲשׂוֹת
עִמָּנוּ, הָיִינוּ שְׂמֵחִים. שׁוּבָה יְיָ אֶת שְׁבִיתֵנוּ, כַּאֲפִיקִים בַּנֶּגֶב. הַזֹּרְעִים בְּדִמְעָה,
בְּרִנָּה יִקְצֹרוּ. הָלוֹךְ יֵלֵךְ וּבָכֹה נֹשֵׂא מֶשֶׁךְ הַזָּרַע, בֹּא יָבֹא בְרִנָּה נֹשֵׂא אֲלֻמֹּתָיו.

A song of ascents. When Adonai restores the fortunes of Zion, we
see it as in a dream, our mouths shall be filled with laughter, our
tongues, with songs of joy. Then shall they say among the nations,
"Adonai has done great things for them!" Adonai will do great
things for us and we shall rejoice. Restore our fortunes, Adonai, like
watercourses in the Negev. They who sow in tears shall reap with
songs of joy. Those who go forth weeping, carrying the seed-bag,
shall come back with songs of joy, carrying their sheaves.

I remember a moment many years ago regarding *Birkat* that was
incredibly instructional. We were at camp and we started to recite
Birkat HaMazon. As is often the case, the campers began to add cute
one-liners and bang on the tables. One of the rabbis stood up and asked
us to stop singing the blessing. I recall him saying, "If you understood
the words of what you are singing, you would never behave as you are
doing now!"[13] All of us stopped singing, and we used the next hour as
a time to study the words of *Birkat HaMazon*. It became a powerful
personal growth moment, and the recitation of *Birkat* has never been
the same for me.

Birkat HaMazon is not only a song of blessing; it is also a text from
which we should learn. As outlined above, *Birkat* invites us to reflect
on the meaning of covenant, on our relationship to God, to Torah, and
to Israel, and on the notion that there is a direct connection between
eating and bringing about peace.

It should be noted that in the traditional *Birkat HaMazon*, there is
a passage from Psalms just before the concluding verse of the text. It
reads, "I have been young and now I am old; yet I have not seen the
righteous forsaken, nor his seed begging for bread" (Ps. 37:25). It is not
found in most Reform versions of *Birkat*. Could it be that too many of

us have seen righteous people "begging for bread" and therefore we find the text unacceptable? Or perhaps it is a source of embarrassment to know that such people in our time exist, or that as witnesses to the Holocaust we are all too well aware of how the righteous have been forsaken. However, for me, this text serves as an important statement, as a reminder of what it means to live in a world that is godless, but also what it means to live in a world where God's sovereignty is carried out. Maybe that is why these words precede the Psalmist's vision, "May Adonai grant strength to our people. May Adonai bless our people with peace" (Ps. 29:11).

We moderns live in a fast-food world in which we focus on the economy of production and consumption of food. More and more we are coming to understand that such an approach to nourishment and sustenance cheapens the meaning of our own lives and reduces our eating activities to nothing more than acts of survival. Our tradition compels us to understand that our approach to food and eating must be more than satisfying our basic needs; what we eat and how we eat should be understood as both privilege and gift. To our ancestors, food was a reflection of God's goodness and mercy; it also connected us to our covenant.

I believe that rabbis and educators, parents and grandparents, too, should use *Birkat HaMazon* as an important instructional tool for what it means to be a Jew in the twenty-first century. In the same way that *Birkat HaMazon* has become a staple in Reform Jewish youth circles, so too, it should become a staple in the education of our people and in our daily, Shabbat, and Festival practice.[14] As a way of increasing the use of *Birkat HaMazon* in our communities and in our homes, we should devote time to study its text, providing learning opportunities for adults and children alike to reflect on the meaning of the words, to discuss commentaries to the text, and then to learn its melody and make it part of our daily personal and communal practice. In doing so, *Birkat HaMazon* just might serve as a powerful transformative text for the next generation of Reform Jews seeking meaning and purpose in life.

NOTES

1. Michael Pollan, *Omnivore's Dilemma* (New York: Penguin Books 2007), 11.

2. Preamble to "A Statement of Principles of Reform Judaism," Central Conference of American Rabbis, 1999. http://ccarnet.org/documentsandpositions/platforms/.

3. Sometimes this blessing is erroneously referred to as "the *HaMotzi*," although the article "the" is already embedded in the Hebrew word. *Motzi* is not a formal title; neither is *HaMotzi*. It is simply the first distinguishing word in the blessing, a common practice for determining the name of a prayer or recitation.

4. This misuse has a basis in Jewish law, as once *Motzi* is recited no other specific food blessings are required during a meal. The ancient world viewed bread as defining a meal.

5. There are also blessings for various kinds of prepared foods and even for smelling the fragrance of plants, fruits, or spices. For a fuller list of such blessings, see Joseph Hertz, *The Authorized Daily Prayer Book*, rev. ed. (New York: Bloch Publishing, 1987), 984–92.

6. *Food for Thought: Hazon's Sourcebook on Jews, Food & Contemporary Life*, 14.

7. Just as with *Motzi*, *Birkat HaMazon* is often referred to simply as *Birkat*.

8. See "Is Dietary Practice Now in the Reform Mainstream?" by Richard N. Levy and Marc Gertz, chapter 8 in this volume.

9. See *The Pentateuch*, translation and commentary by Samson Raphael Hirsch (New York: Feldheim Publishers, 2007), *B'midbar*, 294.

10. See "Presidential Address," Union for Reform Judaism Biennial Convention, Toronto, November 2009. http://urj.org/about/union/leadership/yoffie/?syspage=article&item_id=27481.

11. Hebrew text of *Birkat HaMazon* is from *On the Doorposts of Your House*, revised edition edited by Chaim Stern (New York: Central Conference of American Rabbis, 2010), 23–40. It should be noted that there is not any one official Reform version of *Birkat HaMazon*. This speaks to the creativity and vitality of Reform Judaism. A very popular *Birkat HaMazon* may be found in the NFTY *Birkon Mikdash M'at* (New York: URJ Press, 2005). In fact, there are two versions included in this booklet: a short version (used at most NFTY and URJ events) and a longer version. Educators might want to compare and contrast the traditional *Birkat HaMazon* with these two other versions to teach about differences in ideology and theology between Reform Judaism and traditional Judaism.

12. Elie Munk, *The World of Prayer*, trans. Henry Biberfeld (Jerusalem: Feldheim Publishers, 1961), 213.

13. Rabbi Sheldon Gordon z″l, at Olin Sang Ruby Union Institute, summer 1968.

14. As we teach *Birkat HaMazon*, we can offer alternatives to the normative Reform form. Some people use בָּרוּךְ אַתָּה יְיָ, הַזָּן אֶת הַכֹּל. as the shortest form of *Birkat*. It is useful as an introduction to the ritual practice or for rushed settings. Also, Rabbi Shefa Gold has popularized a shorter alternative version of *Birkat* using "an interpretive blessing" based on the Babylonian Talmud, *B'rachot* 40b. It can be found at www.ritualwell.org.

44

WE EAT FIRST

A Congregational Snapshot

ELLEN LIPPMANN AND TRISHA ARLIN

Kolot Chayeinu, a seventeen-year-old independent progressive congregation, was founded on an understanding of the role food can play in establishing community, based on ancient Jewish table fellowships and modern Jewish cafeterias. At Kolot Chayeinu we eat together at every opportunity, tapping into the deep roots of Jewish connection and identity. Food is memory, ritual, and welcoming, an invitation to and a binder of community, and it has been so since our congregation's inception.

B'reishit: The Beginning

Rabbi Ellen Lippmann arrived in New York City in 1979, returning to the place of her parents' birth, in awe of the panoply of Jewish possibilities. Soon after, she had a lunch at the Garden Cafeteria, one of the last Lower East Side Jewish cafeterias, with its bland, overcooked vegetables, brown bread, and the liveliest conversation among and between tables that she'd ever experienced. We would never put up with that food any more, but she was drawn to the passionate need for talk. The Garden Cafeteria became the shul-café of her dreams. Rabbi Lippmann started Kolot Chayeinu with that dream in mind, cognizant of what happens in shuls, where even the dullest davening turns into a buzz of enthusiasm with the beginning of the *Oneg Shabbat* or the *Kiddush*. "Why not flip the order?" she asked. "Why not eat first, and bring that buzz into the prayer or study?" And so we do.

Shacharit: Breakfast

The food arrives first. Bags, backpacks, shopping carts come through the door, filled with bagels or matzah, cream cheese, tofu, hummus, and anything else this week's breakfast bringer craves: donuts, gluten-free rice crackers, yogurt, fruit, kugel, juice, and always, coffee. It looks delicious as it is arranged on the kitchen table in baskets and on plates. Each person arriving stops to "oooh" and "aaahh" as we gather in a circle, hold hands, and sing the ancient blessing: . . . *hamotzi lechem min haaretz*. The words seem to bring others, and soon the room is filled with faces and voices and smiles and laughter and sometimes, even tears. Shabbat has begun at Kolot Chayeinu. Kolot is a Shabbat morning community at heart, and breakfast is the entry point, the way in, the transition from home and street to prayer and community.

When we eat a Kolot breakfast before prayer, when we share our food and our morning selves with each other, we remember who this community is and why we are there, that we are linked to the people in the room as *chaverim*, friends, fellow travelers, and that we can connect to God more easily with them than without them.

It is a kind of kashrut, this way of eating. Not rule-bound, exactly, but we have our set rituals and new ones; it is all a way to connect to the holy through food. *Kasher*, in addition to being related to the restrictions about eating, also means "right, proper, well-joined."[1] We are well-joined, indeed, when blessing and food and people and place all come together.

The congregation hears the same introduction to the *Motzi* before every meal. We join together, everyone touching someone who is eventually touching the bagel or the challah. The rabbi evokes the power of eating together to bridge separations between people and speaks of the chain of creation that led to this moment, from God to the seed to the earth to the farmer, from harvest to milling to baking to distribution to retail to the Kolot volunteer who purchased the challah and brought it to shul so we could stand there to thank God for this bread of the earth. Every time the rabbi does this, the regulars laugh. They know the lines of the story so well that sometimes they say it with her, almost word for word. Some occasionally chafe at the sameness but recognize it as a genuine ritual, as much a part of who we are as the traditional blessing for food. We are linked by touch and blessing, intertwined like that challah as we give thanks to God. This food and the rabbi's words introduce and normalize God's presence in our community as much and maybe more than any prayer.

The food, the gathering, the honest talk fill a deep need, offering relaxation, nurturing, pleasure, and contentment to those who arrive in time to partake. It is the Pesach seder, the rebbe's *tisch*, the family table, and *Mah Tovu* rolled into one. *Mah tovu ohalecha, Yaakov*: How good is this tent of meeting. Is this what our ancestors meant when they called God *HaMakom*—a place where everything comes together?[2]

A few months ago, a congregant, speaking with Modern Orthodox friends, mentioned that Kolot Chayeinu eats before services but not always afterwards. They laughed and all but patted her on the head, as if to say, what a cute and wacky shul. She later reported that she wanted to tell them, yes, well, maybe we're a little wacky, but that's not how it feels. It feels like a great big hug, the kind you get when a family has invited you into their home. Come on in, you look hungry, eat, then we'll talk, we'll pray, we'll find fellowship.

Every *b'rachah* is a moment of stopped time, a mini-Shabbat when we separate the holy from the mundane. A meal is like that as well. We stop, we sit, we connect. The rituals of eating and praying together are parallel, with a beginning, middle, and end, repetition, group participation, private moments, high points, calm conclusions, and formal closings.

Once that food-fueled connection is made and true conversation begun, real prayer can follow. *Modeh ani l'fanecha*: How grateful we are for this day, for this gathering, for the gift of awakening to the day. Every time we say *Baruch atah . . .* and give thanks for food or drink, we leave our narrow selves and become part of an expansive community. We are reminding ourselves to pay attention to the world with its small and large moments for which we can be grateful. We are saying, "We are in this together." We are leaning back into God[3] as we rest from the hard day or week, the pain we suffer, the yearnings we hold deep. We encourage humility and open-heartedness. These blessings we say or sing before or after eating hold centuries of wisdom and experience, eons of struggle and triumph, years of simple joys.

Minchah: Lunch

After services we make *Kiddush* together at Kolot Chayeinu and often have lunch as well. Here too the talk flows—reflection on the service, the *d'rash*, the Torah reading, the news of the day or of someone's illness or joy. Again, the ritual, the drink, the food in hand offers transition, connection, contentment: *V'shamru v'nei Yisrael et haShabbat.*[4] How did God mean us to celebrate Shabbat if not with rest and joy and gratitude and food—bread or cake or hummus and pita on a table, a glass of wine or juice in the hand? How else would we Jews celebrate? How can a Jewish community teach that kind of gratitude without living it?

Once a month or so we have a Shabbat Café: lunch and learning, the place where food and "Torah"—authors, community concerns, national issues, prayer—come together. We are reminded of the midrash in which Shimon bar Yochai teaches his students that Torah is something to be consumed, not only read with eyes and mind, but also taken in as nurture and, we would add, nutrient.[5]

Maariv: Dinner

Surprisingly, Kolot Chayeinu rarely has Shabbat dinner together. Years ago, though, there was a monthly vegetarian potluck followed by a short *Kabbalat Shabbat* service. We were much smaller in number, and it was still possible for us all to sit down together to share a full Shabbat dinner. We often had first-time visitors, people who were either dipping their secular toes into Judaism for the first time or who had fled from the sexist and unimaginative temples of their youth and were now looking for a way back in that fit with who they had become. At dinner they'd find themselves munching on pasta salad and lentils, and somehow the eating let them see the rabbi as an actual human being who laughed and asked questions while passing the seltzer. For many, it was the "mundane" act of eating together that actually moved them from cynical distance to deep engagement in the Jewish community and practice.

HaAtid Lavo: What's Next?

Kolot Chayeinu began as a kind of *chavurah*, albeit with a rabbi. We have grown from eight founders to more than 315 adult members and 200 kids. Questions of community have arisen at every stage of growth: How can people still get to know each other when there are more members and more natural groupings by affinity? How do we cross those boundaries? We meet in rented space and have no office, so food and the Internet are our places of connection. We thought that we would have a café, a place for nonformal learning, art, guided and spontaneous conversation, and more. We are not there, yet we maintain that dream and eat together at every opportunity. Parents provide food for children's classes, based on nutrition guidelines from teachers. Committees and task forces meet in homes, always with at least a little nosh. The annual congregational meeting starts with supper. Staff meets around food, and so does the board, finding the in-person connection of sharing a meal a needed alternative to e-mail and phone conversation.

Recently, new issues have arisen. The gluten-free have begun to rebel against the steady diet of bagels at breakfast. A resident food expert has taken over Shabbat lunch, insisting on a wide variety of vegetarian foods from all the cuisines of Brooklyn. He is also suggesting that we resist soft drinks in favor of good New York City tap water, conceding that if we yearn for carbonation, we should invest in our own seltzer machine. And plans are afoot for a food page on our new website. Perhaps it will include shared recipes, discussions between the vegans and meat eaters, thoughts about the eco-kosher movement, Uri L'Tzedek or Tav Chavrati.

Some members insist on chicken for a communal Shabbat dinner, saying, "It isn't Shabbat without chicken!" Others are vegan, urging us all to give up meat, eggs, and even dairy. Others want us to avoid processed food. Some keep eco-kosher, insisting that if there is chicken, it should be kosher, but it should also be free-range and organic. Each person is passionate and adamant about his or her opinion, sure that if the rest would only see the light, the right decision would be made. And so, we balance: our occasional communal Shabbat dinners have both a kosher (and if we can, free-range and organic) chicken buffet table and a vegetarian table, and preregistrations indicate a nearly even split between them.

After one recent Kabbalat Shabbat service, a series of meetings about an important (though possibly not so interesting) congregational topic were announced. Afterwards there was a thoughtful, less than enthusiastic pause. Then the announcer said, "Oh, and there will be food." We all smiled and laughed, and then and there, many of us decided to go to the meeting. Why not? At Kolot Chayeinu we eat first. And it works.

NOTES

1. Marcus Jastrow, *Dictionary of the Talmud* (Jerusalem: Harov Publishing, n.d.), 677.

2. We love this phrasing by Rabbi Nancy Fuchs-Kreimer.

3. Thanks to Linda Thal for giving us this language as she received it from Rabbi Jonathan Omer-Man.

4. From the Sabbath liturgy. Literally, "The Children of Israel shall guard the Sabbath" (Exod. 31:16).

5. From the *M'chilta* of Rabbi Shimon bar Yochai to Exodus 13:17.

45

WHAT I EAT IS WHO I AM
Kashrut and Identity

PETER KNOBEL

Eating is a visceral experience. It not only sustains our bodies, but also leaves an imprint on our psyches. Eating is obviously a basic necessity to sustain life, yet eating is also deeply connected to identity. What we eat and what we refrain from eating says a great deal about who we are and how we understand ourselves in relationship to other Jews and other human beings.

In Torah we have clear regulations about which animals and fish may be consumed and which are prohibited (Leviticus 11, Deuteronomy 14). Historically the dietary laws (kashrut) have been a way of encouraging Jewish social intercourse and limiting interaction with non-Jews. Dietary rules create boundaries. This is well illustrated when Joseph eats with his brothers before he reveals his true identity to them. The text says, "They served him [Joseph] separately and them separately and the Egyptians who usually ate with him separately, for the Egyptians could not eat food with the Hebrews, since it was an abomination to the Egyptians" (Gen. 43:32).

Kashrut has played a significant role in connecting Jews to one another and achieving a sense of common identity. However, disputes about kashrut have created divisions within the Jewish community regarding the creation of boundary lines distinguishing one stream from another or one school of interpretation from the other. Decisions about dietary restrictions are often grounded in the philosophy of a particular stream.

The best and clearest example comes from classical Reform Judaism and its 1885 Pittsburgh Platform with its thoroughgoing universalism and its rejection of bodily mitzvot. In rejecting peoplehood, the rejection of kashrut makes complete sense. Classical Reformers understood how important the dietary laws had been to the past formulations of Judaism and that the new Judaism they were creating required a radical change to symbolize the new philosophy:

> We hold that all such Mosaic and Rabbinical laws as regulate diet, priestly purity, and dress originated in ages and under the influence of ideas entirely foreign to our present mental and spiritual state. They fail to impress the modern Jew with a spirit of priestly holiness; their observance in our days is apt rather to obstruct than to further modern spiritual elevation.[1]

If the goal was integration into society, kashrut was a barrier. Meals played an important role in nineteenth-century social and business relationships, as they do today. If the essence of religion is ethical behavior, then what goes into the mouth is not as important as what comes out of the mouth. This Enlightenment-inspired Reform community wanted to assimilate into educated society and to emphasize ethical behavior. That legacy shaped Reform Judaism. Personally, I remember participating in youth group events where the food was deliberately not *kasher* as a way of emphasizing the ethical dimension of Judaism.

Biblical law identifies the purpose of kashrut with *k'dushah* (holiness). As we find at the end of the list of animals that are permitted and prohibited, "You shall sanctify yourselves and be holy" (Lev. 11:44). These eating practices identified those who observed them as belonging to the covenant community that had set itself apart from other communities to serve God. Kashrut's goal, *k'dushah* (holiness), is to connect the Jew to God, to primary values, and to the Jewish people, but it is also to make the Jew distinct from his/her neighbors. While this is still the standard rationale for observing kashrut, it was not always a sufficient reason for all thinkers. For example, Maimonides, in *Guide of the Perplexed* (3:48), suggests that the main reason for kashrut is healthy eating. Modern Jews are still trying to shake the misconception that abstaining from pork is solely to avoid trichinosis.

The concept of *k'dushah* as separation is most clear with respect to Rabbinic kashrut, with its elaborate regulations such as separate meat and dairy dishes and utensils, requiring the foods be certified as *kasher* by competent authorities, and even requiring the inspection of lettuce to ensure that they are no insects that might be consumed. However, the simple decision of keeping biblically kosher—that is, refraining from pork and/or shellfish, and/or not mixing meat and dairy—makes those who observe biblical kashrut constantly aware of their identity as Jews and allows those with whom they dine to identify them as Jews. Many liberal Jews find this a satisfying approach to kashrut.

Today, an ever-expanding range of culinary identities are being mixed with Jewish ritual law. For example, kashrut may be blended with a vegetarian or vegan diet. This hybrid diet is often observed for reasons of health, as well as Jewish ethics. These practices require greater explanation both for the one who observes and for the outside world. Yet, they are, in fact, fertile soil for creative interpretation of traditional texts and values. As discussed in depth in other chapters in this book, if one wants to emphasize the essential harmony of nature, as exemplified in the story of Creation, vegetarian and vegan diets can be powerful examples of Jewish dietary discipline. In addition, the argument can be made that the vegetable protein that is needed to produce animal protein could best be used to feed more of the world's hungry people. This motivation for vegetarian/vegan kashrut deepens one's identity with social justice issues. Interestingly enough, it is easier for the vegetarian and vegan to make their homes open to more halachically observant Jews. In some ways, the broader food identity can create a greater connection to traditional Jews. The kosher vegetarian or vegan is one of many blended food identities in the Jewish world.

Informed by secular dietary and Jewish ethical concerns, as well as by Jewish tradition, many Jews combine kashrut with other values such as concern for the environment, workers' rights, animal rights, or health. While these, too, require some conscious explanation, these approaches have the potential for combining both the Jewish universalistic value of concern for all creation with the particularistic value of the special role of the Jewish people being a "light unto the nations."

Other dietary disciplines can also help reinforce Jewish identity. The eating of certain foods as part of the observation of Jewish Holy Days and Festivals helps to establish identity and connections with *K'lal Yis-rael.* The eating of matzah and refraining from leaven bind Jews in the celebration of the liberation from Egyptian bondage. The folk foods, like latkes (potato pancakes) and *sufganiyot* (jelly donuts) on Chanukah, become a measure of identity. Childhood family holiday meals later in adult life create broader associations with Jewish identity. An outgrowth of these folk foods, kosher-style eating has created what is often disparagingly been called gastronomic Judaism. However, sensual memory, especially smells and tastes, are powerful instruments for creating the feeling of belonging to a group even if the connection seems tangential to the outside observer. Retaining a stronger connection to standard kashrut, some Jews wish to make a distinction between home as a sacred Jewish space and the rest of their secular lives. These Jews observe kashrut only in their homes and have no dietary restrictions when they are outside their homes. While this phenomenon of "keeping kosher in" is sometimes labeled hypocritical in the Jewish world, Reform Judaism considers this a valid expression of Jewish identity.

Central to the ability of any particular form of kashrut to serve as part of Jewish identity formation is that it must on a conscious or unconscious level connect one to other Jews. About thirty years ago, I was engaged with some congregants in an informal study session on Yom Kippur afternoon. Someone asked me about my own level of kashrut. Having grown up in a classical Reform environment, I did not keep any form of kashrut at that time. Then, one woman, a Holocaust survivor, said to me. "You eat the flesh of the swine?" The answer was, of course,

"Yes." That was a revelatory moment. I realized that I needed a dietary practice that reminded me every time I sat down to eat that I was Jewish. As a result, I gave up all pork products, not because I did not like them. In fact, a serious foodie, I miss eating them to this very day, but refraining from eating pork immediately identified me with the Jewish people. It reminded me that in times of persecution, anti-Semites often tried to humiliate Jews by making them eat forbidden foods, especially pork. Yet, even in times of extremis (e.g., the Shoah), some Jews, even when starving, refused to eat forbidden foods as a sign of loyalty to the covenant and resistance to persecution. Refraining from pork has had a powerful affect on my identity as a Jew.

It is essential for Jews who have adopted alternative Jewish dietary practices to identify their particular dietary restrictions and eating habits with the term "kashrut." Some in the Reform Movement want to avoid the term "kashrut," because it is too connected to Orthodoxy or because they believe only one kind of dietary discipline can legitimately be called kashrut. Yet, the use of traditional terminology is essential to identification with *K'lal Yisrael*. Reform Jews need to accept traditional categories if they are to understand themselves as part of *K'lal Yisrael*. Recovering traditional language and categories will also force others to see Reform Jews as part of *K'lal Yisrael*. This does not mean that those Jews who believe kashrut is defined only by the halachah (Jewish law) will accept Reform interpretations of kashrut. However, in arguing that Reform practice is not kashrut, they, by implication, include Reform Judaism within the observant community. While this might seem an outrageous claim at first, the need on the part of halachic Jews to address Reform practice makes those practices part of the greater Jewish community and its identity formation.

Classical Reform Judaism was an important stage in the development of Judaism as it emerged from the ghettoized world of pre-Emancipation Europe and took root in the uniquely fertile soil of the United States. Today our needs and concerns are different. Now that we are fully integrated into Western society, we need concrete ways to strengthen our identity. Great ideas are reinforced by powerful ritual observances that move us spiritually and intellectually. Reform Judaism's pluralism means that no single standard of kashrut is possible. Returning to a Jewish practice that makes the most basic life-sustaining action—namely, eating—into a means of serving God and identifying with the Jewish people has transformative possibilities. Abraham Joshua Heschel said about his marching with Dr. Martin Luther King Jr. that his feet were praying. Kashrut, however defined but taken seriously, means that our stomachs will be praying, and we will feel our Jewish identity in our *kishkes*.

NOTE

1. "The Pittsburgh Platform," 1885, www.ccarnet.org.

46

TZOM

Fasting as a Religious/Spiritual Practice

SUE LEVI ELWELL

Intentional approaches to both eating and food offer opportunities for transforming the ordinary into the sacred. For Jews, any reconsideration of our relationship with eating includes a consideration of fasting. We celebrate our choices of not only what and how and with whom we eat, but also when we eat. We intentionally create, not disrupt, the very rhythm of life by eating and abstaining from food.

We are heirs of a rich legacy of intentional abstinence from food and drink. Fasting provides a singular opportunity to interrupt our lives and to focus not on gathering, preparing, and ingesting and digesting food, but on a cessation of all those activities for a discrete period of time. By intentionally choosing to fast, we are turning our attention away from feeding ourselves and those for whom we are responsible. The opening that we create by this turning is significant.

In his widely used *Guide to Jewish Religious Practice*, Isaac Klein delineates three types of historical fasts: statutory public fasts, public fasts decreed on special occasions, and private fasts. The most prominent and widely observed fast is the twenty-four-hour fast of Yom Kippur, the only fast "explicitly commanded in the Torah."[1] Five other "statutory public fasts" are mentioned in the *Tanach*: the Fast of Esther (13

Adar); the fasts on the ninth of Av, on the seventeenth of Tammuz, and on the tenth of Tevet; and the Fast of Gedaliah (3 Tishrei). However, it should be noted that few Reform Jews observe these fasts. Except for the Fast of Esther, these fasts are connected to the destruction of Jerusalem and the Temple and the loss of Jewish sovereignty. In *Mishneh Torah, Hilchot Taaniyot*, Maimonides writes about public fasts that were decreed by religious authorities in response to a range of threats to the well-being of the Jewish community.[2] Private or individual fasts include fasting on the day of one's wedding, fasting on a parent's *yahrzeit*, fasting by members of *chevrei kadisha* (as well visiting the cemetery) in preparation for their annual dinner,[3] and the fast of the firstborn on the eve of Passover.[4]

Twenty-first-century Jews are the heirs of this rich tradition of fasting. And we are heirs, too, to a tradition that mandates responsibility to and engagement in communal life, even as we live in a culture of individualism and self-absorption. We will consider first the challenges and possibilities of communal fasts, then examine individual fasts, and finally address those who choose not to or cannot fast. This essay concludes with suggested *kavanot* for entering into, supporting, or concluding a fast, as well as stating one's intention to abstain from fasting.

Communal Fasts

Yom Kippur is the preeminent Jewish fast, and the only one indicated in the Torah. Leviticus 16:29 states, "In the seventh month, on the tenth day of the month, you shall practice self-denial."[5] Throughout the ages, scholars, interpreters, and the Jewish people have considered "self-denial" to mean abstaining from food and water, in part because of its use with the more widely used root *tzadi-vav-mem* in Psalm 35:13 and Isaiah 58:3–5. Both terms, which appear throughout the *Tanach*, refer to both communal and individual expressions of petition and penance.

A communal fast has great power to both create and sustain community. Just as sharing food is an essential tool for bringing people together, a sense of shared intention in eschewing food can forge connections between people. Eating together brings individuals to a shared table, and once together, not only food, but also ideas are shared. This dynamic is enhanced and extended in a communal fast. When individuals commit themselves to a shared fast, there are three clear opportunities for connection: gathering for a shared meal to prepare for the fast, gathering for mutual support and perhaps commiseration during the course of the fast, and coming together once again to conclude or break the fast. Yom Kippur offers an excellent and the most familiar example of communal fasting. Most who fast gather with others for a meal that precedes the *Kol Nidrei* prayers, and many who fast find community in synagogue, where the fast is mentioned in the liturgy and is often referenced in non-liturgical comments, messages, *d'rashot*, or sermons. Yom Kippur also affords a unique opportunity for worshipers to stay for extended hours in synagogue and to distance themselves from socializing and from food. Finally, the break fast is an essential aspect of any fast, whether communal or individual. The fact that many synagogues hold communal break fasts, offering either small or substantial meals, or arrange for congregants to gather in one another's homes reflects the importance of ritualizing not only the beginning but also the conclusion of this major fast in the Jewish year.

The Yom Kippur fast has been the most consistently observed throughout Jewish history by observant and nonobservant Jews alike, in part because it provides an opportunity for individuals to claim a connection with tradition and community by engaging in a powerful yet time-bound spiritual act. Additionally, the Yom Kippur fast is unique among the fasts in the *Tanach* because it is not connected with either historical or mythopoetic Jewish events; fasting on Yom Kippur enables one who fasts to connect with the Jewish people without confronting the complex and, for some moderns, troubling issues connected with Jerusalem, Zion, and the loss of Jewish sovereignty. For those who attend synagogue services, the reading of Isaiah 58 underscores the imperative of complementing one's abstinence from food with just acts:

> Is this the fast I look for? A day of self-affliction? Is not rather this the fast I look for: to unlock the shackles of injustice, to undo the fetters of bondage, to let the oppressed go free, and to break every cruel chain? Is it not to share your bread with the hungry, and to bring the homeless poor into your house? When you see the naked, to clothe them, and never to hide yourself from your own kin?
>
> (Isaiah 58:5–7)

Even as the prophet's words challenge each listener, they may also serve as a source of pride of the richness of a tradition that asks not for simple "self-affliction," but demands that we who enjoy plenty are responsible for acknowledging and working toward redressing the imbalance in the distribution of the earth's bounty.

This explicit liturgical link between social justice work and communal fasting is reflected in a number of fasts undertaken by contemporary activist groups. Since 1950, small groups of Jews in various parts of the world have called for and observed communal fasts. In the 1980s, fasts and hunger strikes were organized across the United States and Canada to support Soviet Jews who had launched hunger strikes to protest their unwarranted and unlawful incarceration and their inability to emigrate from the Soviet Union. Two recent fasts underscore the range of religious and political expressions in the twenty-first-century Jewish world. On June 18, 2009, eighty rabbis fasted with Rabbi David Saperstein, director of the Religious Action Center of Reform Judaism, as a protest and as "an emblem of solidarity with the people of Darfur." Saperstein began a three-day, water-only fast on the evening of Monday, June 15, and invited rabbis of all four major streams of American Judaism (Reform, Reconstructionist, Conservative, and Orthodox) to join him for the final stretch of his fast.[6] In July 2009, in response to the Israeli blockade in Gaza, American Reconstructionist rabbis Brian Walt and Brent Rosen initiated Ta'anit Tzedek: Jewish Fast for Gaza, a water-only fast to be observed on the third Thursday of every month from sunrise to sunset. Their invitation reminded participants that "a communal fast is held in times of crisis both as an expression of mourning and a call to repentance."[7]

Individual Fasts

The most significant individual fast in the Torah is Moses's abstinence from food and drink for forty days and nights on Mount Sinai. Exodus 34:28 states, "And he was there with the Eternal forty days and forty nights; he ate no bread and drank no water; and he wrote down on the tablets the terms of the covenant, the Ten Commandments." When Moses retells the story in Deuteronomy 9, he reports a second forty-day period of fasting. The midrash teaches that this supernatural abstinence raised him to the status of celestial, non-corporeal beings and prepared him to meet with the Holy One. Embodied readers know that a fast of several hours produces a somewhat altered state of consciousness; how much more so a fast of days and weeks! "As Moses came down from the mountain bearing the two tablets of the Pact, Moses was not aware that the skin of his face was radiant, since he had spoken with God" (Exod. 34:29). Both his body and his spirit were transformed by his fast and his encounter.

While Jewish tradition focuses on communal, rather than individual fasts, a full or partial fast to mark singular personal events, particularly one's wedding and the observance of a parent's *yahrzeit*, offers a unique opportunity to focus on and be attentive to one's relationship with oneself, one's beloveds, and with the Source of all love.[8] In addition to the fast of the firstborn that is observed primarily by traditional Jews on Erev Pesach, some may choose to refrain from eating or drinking to prepare themselves for communal service, such serving as *sh'lichei tzibur*. And some contemporary Jews may fast as a way to atone for or distance themselves from negative behaviors or actions.

It is not uncommon today to fast in preparation for medical tests or procedures. We may consider these periods of intentional abstinence as an opportunity for reflection or spiritual growth. At times of intense engagement or at times of stress, we may find ourselves forgetting or unable to eat. Recognizing the spiritual energy of such times may help us to be more intentional about naming and claiming this abstinence as intentional rather than accidental.

Prayers for Initiating a Fast: Liturgical Innovations

There is no fixed tradition of prayers for beginning a fast. However, following the final meal that is eaten before beginning a fast, individuals or family members might choose to follow tradition and cover the dining table with a clean cloth. Instead of setting the table for a meal, the table is set for study and laden with books that will provide nourishment throughout the fasting period. The following prayers could be recited:

בָּרוּךְ אַתָּה יְיָ, אֱלֹהֵינוּ מֶלֶךְ הָעוֹלָם שֶׁהַכֹּל נִהְיֶה בִּדְבָרוֹ.

or

ברוכה אַתָּ יה, אֱלֹהֵינוּ רוֹחַ הָעוֹלָם
שֶׁהַכֹּל נִהְיֶה בִּדְבָרה.

Blessed are You, our God, Sovereign/Soul of the world,
who creates all things by Your word.

This short prayer is usually used for foods and drink that do not grow from or on the earth. Considering God's word as the source of fasting transforms the prayer as sanctifying the initiation of a fast.

Another alternative, which is offered here for the first time, might be the following:

בָּרוּךְ אַתָּה מַעְיָן חַיֵּינוּ הַפּוֹתֵחַ אֶת לִבֵּנוּ וְגוֹמְלֵנוּ שֹׂבַע. הֱיֵה עִמָּנוּ
בְּשָׁעָה זוּ שֶׁל כַּוָּנָה לָצוּם.

or

בְּרוּכָה אַתְּ מַעְיַן חַיֵּינוּ הַפּוֹתַחַת אֶת לִבֵּנוּ וְגוֹמְלֵנוּ שֹבַע. הֱיִי עִמָּנוּ
בְּשָׁעָה זוֹ שֶׁל כַּוָּנָה לָצוּם.

Blessed is the Source of All who opens us to Your nourishment.
Be with us during this time of intentional fasting.

One might conclude with the traditional appreciation for reaching
this time:

בָּרוּךְ אַתָּה יְיָ אֱלֹהֵינוּ מֶלֶךְ הָעוֹלָם, שֶׁהֶחֱיָנוּ וְקִיְּמָנוּ וְהִגִּיעָנוּ לַזְּמַן הַזֶּה.

or

בְּרוּכָה אַתְּ יָהּ אֱלֹהֵינוּ רוּחַ הָעוֹלָם, שֶׁהֶחֱיַתְנוּ וְקִיְּמַתְנוּ וְהִגִּיעַתְנוּ לַזְּמַן הַזֶּה.

Blessed are You, our God, Sovereign/Soul of the world, who keeps
us in life, sustains us, and enables us to reach this season.

Prayers during a Fast

In addition to liturgical and textual sources of support that are offered
during communal prayers, one who fasts might recite the following,
traditionally recited after a light meal:

בָּרוּךְ אַתָּה יְיָ אֱלֹהֵינוּ מֶלֶךְ הָעוֹלָם, בּוֹרֵא נְפָשׁוֹת רַבּוֹת וְחֶסְרוֹנָן, עַל כָּל מַה
שֶׁבָּרָא לְהַחֲיוֹת בָּהֶם נֶפֶשׁ כָּל חָי. בָּרוּךְ חֵי הָעוֹלָמִים.

or

בְּרוּכָה אַתְּ יָהּ, אֱלֹהֵינוּ רוּחַ הָעוֹלָם, בּוֹרֵאת נְפָשׁוֹת רַבּוֹת וְחֶסְרוֹנָן,
עַל כָּל מַה שֶׁבָּרָאת לְהַחֲיוֹת בָּהֶם נֶפֶשׁ כָּל חָי. בְּרוּכָה חֵי הָעוֹלָמִים

Blessed are You, our God, Sovereign/Soul of the universe,
who creates many creatures and their needs.
For all that You have created to sustain the life of all living beings,
praised are You, Life of the universe.

Rabbi Jonathan Slater points out that "this blessing . . . states outright that God has created us as beings with needs. Lack is a fundamental, existential fact, built into the nature of Creation. When we recite this blessing we are invited to confess the truth of our existence: we need support."[9] These words may help us as we make our way through a period of intentional abstinence from food and drink.

Prayers for Concluding a Fast

The wide range of traditional prayers upon eating different foods serves as the conclusion of most fasts. However, some might wish to add this new prayer:

בָּרוּךְ הַמּוֹלִיכֵנִי יְשִׁירוֹת בְּעֵת תְּפִלָּה וּתְשׁוּבָה. תֵּן לִי תְּבוּנָה
וְכַוָּנָה עִם חֲזָרָתִי לַאֲכִילַת מָזוֹן. מִי יִתֵּן וְהָאֵרוֹת לָהֶן זָכִיתִי בִּזְמַן
הַצּוֹם תַּמְשֵׁכְנָה לְהָאִיר אֶת דַּרְכִּי. בָּרוּךְ אַתָּה, מְקוֹר הַכֹּל.

or

בְּרוּכָה הַמּוֹלִיכַתְנִי יְשִׁירוֹת בְּעֵת תְּפִלָּה וּתְשׁוּבָה. תְּנִי לִי תְּבוּנָה
וְכַוָּנָה עִם חֲזָרָתִי לַאֲכִילַת מָזוֹן. מִי יִתֵּן וְהָאֵרוֹת לָהֶן זָכִיתִי בִּזְמַן
הַצּוֹם תַּמְשֵׁכְנָה לְהָאִיר אֶת דַּרְכִּי. בְּרוּכָה אַתְּ, מְקוֹר הַכֹּל.

Blessed is the One who has guided me through this time
of reflection and turning. As I return to the practice of physical
sustenance, may I be mindful and intentional. May my insights
gleaned from this period of abstinence sustain me as I go forth.
Blessed are You, Source of all.

When We Can and Cannot Participate in Communal Fasts

Our desire and ability to abstain from eating varies throughout our lives. For many, reaching the age of bar or bat mitzvah brings with it permission and opportunity to practice fasting for the first time. Many who are exploring or who choose Judaism look forward to fasting with the Jewish community. However, not everyone can or should fast. For those struggling with eating disorders, any fast may provide negative reinforcement to self-destructive behavior patterns.

For some women, observing Yom Kippur during pregnancy or lactation may be the first time they have intentionally refrained from fasting. Similarly, health-care professionals may discourage individuals undergoing certain treatments, those with particular nutritional needs, or those over a certain age from engaging in a full fast.

Individuals who wish to fast and are discouraged from doing so may struggle with this prohibition. They may consider (in consultation with their health care professional) a partial fast that enables them to take in sufficient nourishment, but nevertheless reminds them, each time they do eat, that they are differentiating this as a time of intentional fasting.

Prayers for Those Who Cannot Fast

Traditionally, there is a special addition to *Birkat HaMazon* for those who are unable to fast on communal fast days. However, after working with those who cannot fast, Rabbi Simkha Y. Weintraub of the National Center for Jewish Healing composed a powerful contemporary innovation to this practice. Here is a short excerpt from his "Meditation before Yom Kippur for One Who Cannot Fast":

> You know, dear God, that it is not my intent
> To be apart from our people and our tradition.
> My current state of health makes it unsuitable for me to fast

> So, dear God, I turn to You now in serenity and openness:
> Help me in the coming year to do my best in guarding my health.

Help us, Your children, learn how to protect our bodies from
harm.
Help us to support others in caring for their *tzelem Elokim*,
their Image of God.
Teach us to help one another grow and thrive in Body, Mind,
and Spirit. . . .[10]

An alternative prayer offering:

מַעְיָן חַיֵּנוּ, חוֹקֵר כְּלָיוֹת וָלֵב: לַמְרוֹת שֶׁאֵינִי צָם(ָה)/ה הַיּוֹם הֲרֵי אֲנִי
מִצְטָרֵף/פֶת לַנִּמְנָעִים מֵאוֹכֶל וּשְׁתִיָּה לְהִתְרַכֵּז פְּנִימָה. וְשָׁעוֹת
אֵלּוּ שֶׁל הִרְהוּר הַנֶּפֶשׁ יַעֲשִׂירוּ אֶת נִשְׁמָתִי וְיַאַפְשְׁרוּ לִי
לְהַמְשִׁיךְ לְשָׁרֶתְךָ בְּלֵב שָׂמֵחַ.

Source of all, you know my heart. Although I do not fast today,
I join those who abstain from food and drink to focus within.
May these hours of prayer and contemplation nourish my spirit,
and may I continue to serve you with a joyful heart.

Conclusion

For most Reform Jews, fasting is associated primarily with Yom Kippur. However, our tradition is rich with the use of fasting both as an experience shared with a community in times of fear, repentance, or grief
and as an individual expression of remorse, redirection, or cleansing.
As we discover new ways to eat, both in community and as individual
Jews, may we continue to explore a range of spiritual experiences when
we intentionally abstain from food and drink. New worlds await us
when we intentionally connect our minds and spirits with our bodies,
through eating and not eating, drinking and not drinking, stretching
our capacities in ways that open us to surprise, delight, and discovery.
May each of us be nourished by both fasting and eating as we deepen
our connection to our people and to the Holy One, the Source of all
sustenance.

NOTES

1. Isaac Klein, *Guide to Jewish Religious Practice* (New York: Jewish Theological Seminary of America, 1979), 242.

2. Ibid., 243.

3. Ibid., 252–53.

4. Some communities have observed a fast after a Torah has been dropped. See Mark S. Glickman, "Synagogue: After the Fall," *Reform Judaism*, Spring 2008 (http://reformjudaismmag.org/Articles/index.cfm?id=1333).

5. In *The Five Books of Moses: A Translation with Commentary* (New York: Norton, 2004), Robert Alter translates *t'anu et nafshoteichem* as "you shall afflict yourselves."

6. http://fastdarfur.org/.

7. http://fastforgaza.net.

8. It is difficult to gauge how many individuals observe the custom of fasting on one's wedding day. Some of the most popular Jewish wedding guides include a reference to and description of such a fast, e.g., Anita Diamant, *The New Jewish Wedding Book* (New York: Fireside Books, 2001), 159; Gabrielle Kaplan-Mayer, *The Creative Jewish Wedding Book: A Hands-On Guide to New & Old Traditions* (Woodstock, VT: Jewish Lights, 2009), 121. In his *Jewish Views of the Afterlife* (Lanham, MD: Rowman & Littlefield, 2009), Simcha Paull Raphael notes that fasting on the occasion of a parent's *yahrzeit* is "not a widely followed custom" (p. 443).

9. Jonathan Slater, *Mindful Jewish Living: Compassionate Practice* (New York: Aviv Press, 2004), 307.

10. http://urj.org/kd/_temp/C5A38805-A509-BEF1-33606C3CC686540F/Yom%20Kippur%20Meditation%20for%20No%20Fasting.pdf.

With deep thanks to Rabbis Simkha Y. Weintraub, Oren Hayon, and Linda Motzkin.

47

REAL LIFE / REAL FOOD
An Introduction to Hunger

Donald A. Weber

When the Rabbis wrote, "If there is no bread, there is no Torah" (*Pirkei Avot* 3:21), they were not speaking metaphorically. A person who is hungry—or whose children are hungry—will not take time to study, or teach, or relax, or help others; he or she will focus on nothing other than food.

How, I wondered, could I get my congregation of well-off, well-fed Jews to understand what hunger really feels like? Many of them have said, "I'm starving," but to them "starving" means they are an hour late for dinner. In order to feel the urgency of hunger, they would need to feel . . . *hungry*.

When are Jews most hungry? On Yom Kippur, of course. But are they hungry enough, even after fasting, to be willing "to tear up your loaves for the hungry" (Isaiah 58:7), as our Yom Kippur haftarah reading commands? We needed more, and on Yom Kippur Day 1988, I tried to give—and ask for—more.

When it came time for the sermon, I asked people to raise their hands if they were *really, really hungry*. As I expected, about a third of the congregation responded. So I said, "Maybe this will help."

With great ceremony, I brought out a brown paper shopping bag. With the assistance of the cantor, I removed its contents: a loaf of rye bread, a package of deli-cut corned beef, a large container of cole slaw and another of potato salad, and a half-dozen sour pickles. I heard several people muttering, "Very funny," but the muttering stopped when we opened the packages and . . . began making sandwiches. On the bimah. On Yom Kippur.

We didn't just *make* the sandwiches; we *created* them. Russian dressing on the bread; beautiful slices of meat laid in perfect order, stacked high, the way New Yorkers make sandwiches; ladles full of cole slaw, big enough to be seen in the back row of the sanctuary; and sour pickles, laid out and cut lengthwise to release their fragrance.

I could tell how far back the smells had traveled by the groans coming from the congregation.

When we finished our nearly ten-minute "torture by deli," I said, "*Now* how many of you are *really, really hungry?*"

Everyone's hands went up.

"Do you know that it is still *seven hours* until you can have anything to eat?"

More groans. Deeper groans.

"Do you know there are people who are *hungrier than you*, who have no idea when they will have anything to eat?"

The room was silent.

They listened. They really listened.

More than twenty years later, people still talk about that sermon. Even people who were not present when I gave it somehow "remember" it. Most importantly, more than twenty years later, Temple Rodeph Torah still defines itself as a congregation that puts feeding the hungry above almost everything else we do.

Im ein kemach, ein Torah. If there is no food, there is no Torah.

Part Ten

Making Your Choices: *Shalom*

The buffet has been laid out and there are many choices from which to select your dietary practice. Of course, no one eats alone all the time. Therefore, there are different levels to creating Reform kashrut. In "Your Personal Kashrut: *Sh'leimut* and *Sh'lom Bayit*," I suggest a process for individuals and households to select their Reform dietary practice. Exploring the challenges to finding a personal and household kashrut, I draw on the Jewish values of *sh'leimut* (feeling whole or balanced) and *sh'lom bayit* (having peace in one's home) to help guide the process. In "Creating a Reform Communal Dietary Policy," Jeffrey Brown expands the table to the institutional level. Brown provides an educational approach to creating a communal food policy. Here he gives an overview of his process; at www.ccarebook.org you can find the unabridged version of his resources.

Finally, in "Kosher Christmas Dinner," I highlight the challenges of keeping kosher in an interfaith family. In the liberal Jewish world, the overwhelming majority of us have non-Jewish family members in either our nuclear or extended families. Certainly, we all have non-Jewish friends. I hope the reflections I share resonate for many and help us to sit around the same table in peace.

48

YOUR PERSONAL KASHRUT:
SH'LEIMUT AND *SH'LOM BAYIT*

MARY L. ZAMORE

Please note that the following guide is designed to help the individual navigate through the choices this book has set before our community, or this section can be used as a teaching model.

After spending time reading about food choices, it would not be surprising to be confused about what to eat. Given the breadth and depth of questions raised and choices offered, it may be easier if manna fell from the sky at mealtimes. However, the purpose of this volume is not to overwhelm you, but rather to provoke thought, discussion, and ultimately, action.

The choice of a dietary practice is deeply personal, yet ultimately communal. We relate around food, through food, and over food. In chapter 49, "Creating a Reform Communal Dietary Policy," Jeffrey Brown addresses the creation of institutional food guidelines. However, before we consider organized groups with formal food policies, let us turn to our individual choices and the noninstitutional settings in which we eat.

As already stated, eating is a social activity. Our food choices are influenced by those with whom we share meals and create homes. Therefore, the articulation of a personal dietary practice has an effect on and is shaped by those with whom we break bread. We will discuss individual food choices and then return to the complexities of sharing meals and kitchens. It is important to clarify one's own dietary needs and goals before trying to navigate social interactions.

Where to Start

Many facets of kashrut have been presented in this volume. The buffet of sacred choices has been put before you, and now you may be interested in reforming your diet. Some choices may have an immediate appeal; others less so. If you are feeling overwhelmed by the choices on the metaphoric buffet, here is an exercise to clarify your thoughts:

1. You may want to start by making a list of your present dietary practices, include those choices of which you feel proud and those with which you struggle.
2. Then, make a list of past dietary practices (if they differ from your present diet), including those choices of which you feel proud and those with which you struggle.
3. Compare the past list with the present list. Highlight the practices to which you hope to return, if there are any. If you have abandoned any food practices to which you hope to return, take a minute to reflect on why these practices have slipped out of your daily life.
4. Now, reflecting on the choices presented in this volume, as well as your past habits, make a list of those practices you would like to incorporate into your personal kashrut in the near future.

This exercise is meant to help you focus on a handful of changes at a time. Very few of us are capable of or comfortable with making huge paradigm shifts in our diets. For the minority who function well quitting food habits "cold turkey" and starting new ones rapidly, enjoy implementing your new personal kashrut. However, know that it is likely that you will still need to allow time for your family and friends to adjust to your new dietary expectations. There is no reason to delay the changes that only have an impact on you as an individual, but those changes that affect others as well will need sensitive communication. We will return to this communal issue later.

Most people need a gradual approach in changing their eating habits. By comparing your past, present, and future dietary practices, you will see what really counts to you and what challenges you. You will see the gap between your ideal kashrut and reality. Start by prioritizing the top food values you want to integrate into your life. These can be big, meta-values, like eating with less of an impact on the environment, or smaller, more finite goals, like not mixing meat and milk. Figure out what challenges stand between you and your ideal practice. For example, we are often stymied by careless preparation, lack of time in general, tight finances, or awkward social interactions. Each of these types of challenges can undermine good intentions, but honest self-reflection and preparation usually take care of most difficulties. It helps to reflect on which challenges have an impact on your food choices, as this self-awareness can help you find solutions.

One approach calls for starting with the goals about which you feel the most passionate. This assumes that your passion will carry you through any challenges that may arise. It is important that your fervor not cause you to overlook the needs and feelings of those with whom you share a home or other food settings. The opposite approach focuses on the changes that are the easiest to incorporate into your life. If you are on a limited food budget, pick the changes that are most affordable; if you are tight on food preparation time, pick the changes that are most accessible.

With either approach, set yourself up for success. Do not overwhelm yourself with unobtainable goals. It is better to start slowly. As you integrate the changes into your dietary practice, you can add more changes when you feel ready.[1] You also need to plan in advance when (or if) you are willing to make exceptions, what you are going to do when confronted with challenges, and what you are going to do if mistakes (on your part or by others) are made. If you are not willing to make exceptions, then you will have to make plans to accommodate your needs. Planning for these bumps will help you stay committed to your desired kashrut.

The guiding Jewish value throughout this process of shaping your personal kashrut is *sh'leimut*, "wholeness." Sharing the same root as *shalom*, "peace," *sh'leimut* guides us toward food decisions that feel right and fit our personalities and lives. Creating a personal kashrut should not be painful, guilt-ridden, or forced. That is not to say that it should be effortless either. The effort is part of the point. As Peter Knobel explores in chapter 45, "What I Eat Is Who I Am: Kashrut and Identity," Jewish identity is expressed and strengthened through our food choices. Feeling the difference between eating with abandon and with restraint is appropriate. Personally, one of the things I appreciate about keeping kosher is that my Judaism is with me at every meal. In my own home, I only feel that a little bit. However, out in the greater world, my food choices accentuate my Jewish identity, perhaps to others, but more importantly to myself. The further I am from home, the more I appreciate this. While traveling, I may be sitting in a restaurant in a town with apparently no Jews. However, I will be scanning the menu, searching for the foods that support my kashrut. Pausing to think before I eat is part of the exercise of keeping kosher. This comfort with my Jewish identity is also a form of *sh'leimut*.

An Example to Illustrate This Approach

Robert Reform Jew has decided to embrace several practices discussed in this book. He has decided to give up all pork products, eat less meat in general, and buy fair trade and/or organic products when available. Robert lives alone, so he is in charge of his own kitchen. He has a stockpile of bacon and of pure beef hamburgers, which were on sale recently. Next month he is visiting his adult son and his family, staying at their home for two weeks. His daughter-in-law always makes her delicious ham as a welcoming dinner. In light of his tight budget, Robert is concerned about the price of organic vegetables and fair trade coffee, tea, and chocolate. Perhaps, in the future he will give up crustaceans, but he is not completely sure about that right now. He believes these are the right food choices, but he is also worried about the higher prices associated with these dietary practices.

Robert decides to do this: He donates his bacon to the local soup kitchen and decides to eat his way slowly through the frozen hamburgers, using them at a much slower rate than in the past. He will enjoy red meat once a week from now on, maybe more if there is a special occasion. Rather than making a big deal of not eating pork, Robert decides to enjoy his daughter-in-law's dinner but not to consume any other pork products from that day forward. If not eating pork is still Jewishly fulfilling after a few months of trying out this new practice, Robert plans to share the news of his new kashrut with his family and ask his daughter-in-law what he can do to make mealtime easier for her, since she is the family cook. Finally, Robert decides to switch over to buying fair trade coffee, but not chocolate, since this single change fits his budget for now. This will apply to his home only, unless he can convince his boss to change the coffee purchases (and budget) at work. In addition, Robert will buy organic produce when it is affordable enough; otherwise he will supplement with conventional produce. Next spring he will look into joining an organic CSA in order to save money and support a good cause. Hopefully, he will also save money by eating less meat and therefore have the funds to support his other food choices.

The next week Robert is invited to a neighbor's barbecue and is offered a hot dog. Robert has already had red meat this week, but he enjoys the treat. However, later that evening he realizes that there may have been pork in the frankfurter. Next time, he will have to ask about the brand or stick with other choices. He should probably buy a few kosher franks to keep in the freezer just in case. Our fictitious Robert Reform Jew has learned the joys and challenges of defining a new personal food ethic. In time, other challenges will arise, but he's off to a fine start.

Interaction with Family and Friends

Let us return to the issue of communal eating. Many of us share our homes with others and, therefore, our kitchens, mealtimes, and wallets on a daily basis. Just like our fictitious Robert Reform Jew, single people, of course, also deal with these issues, perhaps at a different frequency. Needless to say, if you are thinking of making significant changes in your eating habits, it is vital to let your spouse or partner know about your thoughts. At its best, this is a wonderful opportunity to share from the heart the values about which you care. Such a discussion should give each partner time to listen carefully, talk openly, and respond with thoughtful questions. It is important to anticipate the impact your proposed changes will make on food preparation, socializing, nuclear and extended family interactions, family finances, and your shared vision of child rearing. Food affects everything.

The guiding Jewish principle must be *sh'lom bayit*, literally "peace at home." This value guides us toward a domestic harmony in which both partners' opinions and feelings matter. As I write in chapter 50:

> Compromise means bending without harboring resentment and certainly not relinquishing one's ideals completely. Compromise means that you are willing to sacrifice at the same time that you recognize what another has sacrificed for your sake. While there are certainly bumps along the way, ultimately *sh'lom bayit* prevails through elevating the values of love and respect over ego and orthopraxy.

If partners have disparate visions of the household's food values, then it may take more than one conversation to come to agreement. These issues become more complex when there are already tensions concerning communication, family relations, or child rearing. If implementing a family food ethic becomes heated, it may help to step back and consider the true sources of friction—food or other issues.

Children and Kashrut

As you, or you and your partner, come to a decision on your household's kashrut, it is important to keep in mind that there must be special sensitivity in introducing children to new eating habits. This, of course, depends on the age of the child involved. Young children can easily transition through most food changes. While sudden changes can be problematic for children this age, who love predictability, a gradual approach works well. Grade school children can be positively engaged to learn about the food values you want to uphold. Many age-appropriate resources are available, depending on the values you are introducing. If you expect your child to adhere to certain dietary practices all the time, it is important to help your child navigate social situations outside of the home, like school, camp, play dates, and visits to extended family. Preparation and communication are key. It is important to clarify your child's needs to supervising adults and to help provide nutritious and enticing alternatives for your child. A child who feels deprived and socially awkward will not accept new food practices. Sometimes it helps to provide yummy goodies for all the children involved in your child's social circle. This way your child can feel proud of your family's new food choices.

Post–bar/bat mitzvah teens need a different approach. It may be helpful to have an open family discussion about the changes you want to make and about the expectations you have for your teen, while respecting your teen's feelings. Again, *sh'lom bayit* should be the guiding principle. It may be helpful to know some common methods that (ritual) kosher-keeping Reform families use for teenagers. Some report that after bar/bat mitzvah they leave the choice of keeping kosher up to their children. In their homes, everything is kosher and no *t'reif* may be brought into the house, but outside of the home, teens are actively encouraged to make their own choices, even at family meals at restaurants. Other parents ask that their children respect their family rules even outside the home when they are together as a family. Otherwise, when teens are eating without family, they are welcome to make their own food choices. Still other parents believe that thirteen is too young to be encouraged to make these choices independently. They wait until teens express a desire to differentiate from their parents' kashrut. Then, the parents deal with the "in or out of family settings" issue. All of these approaches can be used for teens when introducing new food values.

Extended Family and Friends

In this age, it seems that every person at a social gathering has a special dietary need. In fact, it is becoming standard hosting protocol to ask guests if they have such a need, and when setting menus, hosts usually take into account different food needs, announced or unannounced. Therefore, adding your own needs to the mix should not be shocking. That said, you should make it as easy as possible for your family and friends to eat with you by announcing your needs in advance and offering to help prepare something or pick the restaurant.

Enjoy the Adventure

Finally, as you create your personal and household food ethic, know that what works today may not work for tomorrow. In Reform Judaism, we are encouraged to try on new rituals and ideologies. Therefore, your personal kashrut will certainly evolve over time. Lapses provide an opportunity to reevaluate. You can reuse the exercise at the beginning of this chapter to reflect on your future vision. It is OK to try out new food choices, only to discard them later. You will surely want to add other choices to your personal kashrut over time. Finding a rabbi or other mentor, as well as a community with which to discuss the complexities of food issues and challenges, will help you to grow in your knowledge and passion. Enjoy the adventure!

NOTE

1. An extended discussion of progressively incorporating ritual kashrut into one's life is offered by Shimon Apisdorf, *Kosher for the Clueless But Curious* (Baltimore: Leviathan Press, 2005). While this reflects a strictly Orthodox approach to ritual kashrut, the gradual process described is helpful to liberal Jews, as well.

49

CREATING A REFORM COMMUNAL DIETARY POLICY

Jeffrey Brown

This book introduces the reader to the marvelous buffet of food choices that are available to today's liberal Jews. As we have seen, the traditional Jewish categories of kosher and *t'reif* no longer suffice to adequately differentiate the kinds of food choices that committed Jews might make in their everyday lives. Today, Reform Jews do not just wrestle with whether or not to eat a cheeseburger; they also consider the way that the cow was raised and whether the cow's "handlers" were fairly compensated.

The question now is, *how* do we go about making choices from the metaphorical buffet? More specifically, how do we make those choices in Reform communal settings[1]—in our synagogues, our camps, and at our regional and national gatherings?

Let me begin with a disclaimer: the agenda that I bring to this conversation is not what I hope Reform communities will decide to eat or not eat. Whether communities elect to go vegetarian or to mix meat and dairy—in this context, I do not particularly care. What I do passionately care about is the *process* by which our Reform communities go about making these all-important decisions.

There are any number of Jewish communal decision-making processes that exist in American Jewish life today. For example, in Orthodox circles (and in some Conservative communities as well), the rabbi
wields a near-autocratic sense of power and influence, particularly in
the realm of ritual affairs (a category that includes dietary policy in
traditional settings). In this sense, the rabbi is known as the *mara d'atra*
(the legal decisor of the local community in which that rabbi serves).
*In these traditional settings, it is the rabbi alone who decides what the com-
munity eats in the communal space.* The primary challenge of employing
this model of Jewish communal decision making is that it devalues the
opinions and concerns of the laity.

One of the great innovations that Reform Judaism brought to Jewish life in the nineteenth century was a shift in the balance of power
in communal life. With the arrival of the Enlightenment, individuals
became empowered to make choices for themselves about how to live
the ritual aspects of their Jewish lives; as a result, the opinions of their
rabbis mattered less.[2]

The evolution of the power of the laity, in terms of Jewish communal decision-making today, can be illustrated by the use of community
organizing in Reform settings.[3] This approach endorses the laity's central role in Jewish communal decision making. Their feedback (often
given in the facilitated setting of a focus group) goes on to determine
the course of Jewish life in this particular model of the contemporary
Jewish community. The approach of community organizing is, on a
certain level, the polar opposite of the *mara d'atra* model. The former
is almost exclusively concerned with the needs and desires of the laity,
running the risk of not taking into account the wisdom that a trained,
professional Jewish leader (like a rabbi) can provide.

The process that I suggest for a community that wants to write or
revise its institutional dietary policy stakes out a middle ground between the *mara d'atra* and community organizing models. Ideally, the
policy statements that our communities craft will reflect a *consensus*
that is achieved between the unique vision of its professional leader(s)
and the laity.[4]

What follows is a summary of a five-session curriculum on communal decision making. The full guide can be found at www .ccarebook.org.

The First Meeting

With the support of lay leadership, a committee facilitator (ideally the congregation's rabbi) will bring together a representative cross-section of the congregation. The first meeting sets the tone of this communal process.

The meeting might take place outside of the synagogue—perhaps at a supermarket, farmers' market, or even a farm[5]—any place that might invite participants to reflect on their relationship to food.

1. Open the meeting with a mixer, simultaneously giving group members the chance to introduce themselves and to share a little about their own connections to food.
2. Guide the group in an exercise that will define traditional kashrut.[6] This exercise is found in the online version of this guide.
3. Conclude with a discussion that challenges participants to reflect on the essential values of their institution.[7] Those values will be revisited in our final session, when the group makes its decisions about what will be permitted and prohibited in its policy.

The Second Meeting

This meeting and the next one should be devoted, in part, to an in-depth study of the "basics" of traditional kashrut. While Reform communities may ultimately decide not to include traditional Jewish dietary parameters in their communal food policies, any informed decision making on the subject requires knowledge, so that communities know why they are choosing not to observe certain rituals.

In the second meeting, the focus is on permitted and prohibited species. Interestingly, the traditional prohibition of certain species (like pork and shellfish) has been the most widely observed aspect of traditional kashrut in Reform communal settings.[8] (Incidentally, abstention from pork may also be one of the most widely observed of *all* daily ritual commandments by *individual* Reform Jews.)[9] Given the widespread resonance that species abstention has within our movement, it seems that this is the logical starting place for any discussion that seeks to reevaluate a community's dietary policy.

1. Lead an exercise to introduce the group to the taxonomy of kashrut. A basic understanding of these categories is a necessary first step in teaching participants about traditional kashrut.
2. Guide the group through an in-depth study of Torah texts concerning species prohibitions. This highlights how traditional Jewish law established its taxonomy—not just of the dietary laws in general, but of the different species of animals in particular.
3. Conclude with a fun review exercise. Using actual menu items from the noted New York City restaurant Jean Georges, participants are quizzed on which species of animals are permitted and which are prohibited, according to the Torah.[10]

The Third Meeting

The choices we make within the realm of Jewish eating are not just legal ones (choices that are, or are not, in keeping with the traditional laws of kashrut). They are also cultural ones. For many of us (and our communities) our cultural sense of *Jewishness*—our Jewish identities—is tied to the kinds of foods that we eat (regardless of whether or not they are technically kosher).[11]

1. Use a brief film clip from the Woody Allen movie *Hannah and Her Sisters* to provide participants with the chance to begin

considering how our food choices are related to the cultural side of our Jewish identities The conversation is an important one, because it will also lay the groundwork for the fourth meeting's discussion about more contemporary values that impact our food decision making.

2. Conclude with an in-depth text study on materials relating to two other important aspects of traditional Jewish eating: (1) the separation of meat and dairy; and (2) special dietary rules in effect only during Passover.

   a. Before we can do that text study, participants need to spend a few minutes being introduced to some basic Jewish legal texts and to the historical chronology associated with them. The historical development of halachah figures prominently in any discussion of kashrut. The traditional norms of Jewish eating were not established at Sinai. They were not even concretized with the final redaction of the Babylonian Talmud around 500 C.E. What we call kashrut today was still in formation as Maimonides was writing his law code the *Mishneh Torah* in the twelfth century, and even as fellow codifier Joseph Caro was writing the *Shulchan Aruch* in the sixteenth century!

   b. What are we Reform Jews to make of the fact that parts of kashrut were established so late in Jewish history? How (if at all) should these realizations affect the way we think about our sense of obligation to Jewish law? Are we more apt to be swayed by the call of an ancient practice or a modern one?[12]

The Fourth Meeting

In this final meeting before the committee gathers to draft its dietary policy, the group must directly confront the question of what Reform Judaism has historically thought about Jewish eating.

The meeting should begin with a head-on confrontation of the still pervasive stereotype that "Reform Jews are allowed to eat anything."

1. Begin by studying the *t'reifah* banquet and the Pittsburgh Platform of 1885, which may (or may not) reflect the ethos behind the banquet.[13] Look at relevant excerpts from the later platforms of the Reform Movement. This text study exercise will reveal the Reform Movement's ongoing "return to tradition"—a pendulum shift that arguably began not too long after 1885.

    This survey of the platforms is not meant to influence committees one way or the other. The intended purpose is to remind groups that the Reform Judaism of today can authentically accommodate a wide range of choices when it comes to traditional kashrut. We do not see kashrut as an all-or-nothing enterprise.

2. Lead a discussion on ethical kashrut. Since the 1970s, the liberal Jewish food lexicon has expanded to include "ethical kashrut."[14] Any Reform community that is seeking to write a new dietary policy must consider ethical kashrut as well. To what extent will issues like the following[15] influence the creation of new communal dietary standards? The fourth meeting will conclude with a discussion of these values, providing the basis for informed decision making in the final meeting.

    a. Respect for animals (*tzaar baalei chayim*): Perhaps this means going fully vegetarian, flexitarian (mostly vegetarian),[16] or abstaining from the meat of animals raised in "factory farm" conditions.

    b. Protecting the earth (*shomeir adamah*): Perhaps this could include a greater level of respect for the natural cycle of food production. One could avoid fruits and vegetables sprayed with pesticides or foods that have been genetically manipulated.

    c. Protecting one's own body (*sh'mirat haguf*): This might take the form of abstaining from foods with carcinogens, antibiotics, or hormones. *Sh'mirat haguf* also raises awareness of eating disorders in which food becomes a weapon against ourselves.

    d. Sharing food with the poor (*tzedakah*): Communities that decide to make this a core value of their dietary policies might go out of their way to ensure that for any communal or festive meal, a portion of its cost be donated to a hunger organization.

  e. Pursue peace and justice (*rodeif shalom* and *rodeif tzedek*): Avoid food produced by companies or countries that violate basic ethics.

  f. Holiness (*k'dushah*): Being spiritually mindful is an essential component of Jewish eating. When we eat, we should consider calling to mind where our food comes from, as we bless it / give thanks for it.[17]

The Fifth Meeting

The final meeting of the committee will be devoted to the actual decision-making process, as well as some discussion about the best way to frame, publicize, and implement the decision.

In theory, the decision making itself should be relatively straightforward at this point (though coming to a consensus within the group will be a challenge for some communities).

In the four previous sessions, participants were given opportunities to

- Reflect on the values that make their own institutions unique.
- Study about some of the traditional aspects of kashrut.
- Consider Reform Judaism's evolving perspective on the dietary laws.
- Think about contemporary issues relating to "ethical kashrut."

Steps to Decision-Making

1. Encourage participants to use the provided questionnaire, online at www.ccarebook.org, to organize their decision making.
2. Once the decision making has been completed, the curriculum provides resources for the committee to consider how best to

frame the new policy (e.g., as a stand-alone document, as part of the catering policy, etc.) and how best to communicate the new dietary policy to the rest of the community. To do this, committees are encouraged to study three actual dietary policies from Reform congregations.

Once the committee finalizes its plan on how to frame and publicize the policy, then it has completed its initial work. There will always be opportunities in the future to evaluate how the new policy is working.

In the meantime, communities might celebrate their new policies with a sacred and celebratory meal, featuring foods approved by the new policy. *B'tei-avon!*

NOTES

1. I mean to establish a contrast, here, between the unique factors taken into account in an individual's decision-making process (and perhaps also a family's) and the unique factors taken into account in a communal setting.

2. Michael A. Meyer, *Response to Modernity: A History of the Reform Movement of Judaism* (Detroit: Wayne State University Press, 1995), 100ff. The emphasis on the Reform rabbi of mid-nineteenth-century Germany was for him to be a "model for the modern Jew," not a legal decisor.

3. Union for Reform Judaism, "Just Congregations," Union for Reform Judaism, http://urj.org/socialaction/training/justcongregations/. The URJ's well-publicized "Just Congregations" initiative roots itself within the realm of social activism. Note, however, how this methodology is already evolving into a new and much broader approach to Jewish communal decision making: Sue Fishkoff, "New Jew Cool," *Reform Judaism*, Fall 2004; Jeremy S. Morrison, "The Riverway Project: Engaging Adults in Their 20s and 30s in the Process of Transforming the Synagogue," *CCAR Journal: A Reform Jewish Quarterly*, Winter 2009, 47–55.

4. I am indebted to Rabbi David Teutsch (of the Reconstructionist Movement) for the extensive writing that he has done on Jewish communal decision-making processes: David A. Teutsch, "Shaping Communities of Commitment," *The Reconstructionist*, Fall 1995, 16–23; David A. Teutsch, "The Rabbinic Role in Organizational Decision Making," *The Reconstructionist*, Fall 1999, 15–23. Both articles are available for free online at http://www.therra.org/recon_journal_authors.htm.

5. Union for Reform Judaism and the Religious Action Center of Reform Judaism, "On the Farm: A Youth Group Program to Explore our Food System," Union for Reform Judaism, http://bit.ly/farmvisit.

6. One of the fundamental assertions of this book is its claim that a liberal Jewish discussion about dietary matters need not be limited to the parameters of traditional kashrut. Nonetheless, I believe that any discussion of Reform communal dietary policy must *begin* with a discussion about where we stand on matters of traditional kashrut. To skip that step, and limit our conversations to matters of fair trade, environmentalism, and spirituality, would be a significant mistake in my opinion.

7. This exercise utilizes the excellent list of Jewish values found in David A. Teutsch, *A Guide to Jewish Practice* (Wyncote, PA: Reconstructionist Rabbinical College Press, 2003), 15–25.

8. See, for example, the 1989 UAHC study *Worship and Ritual Patterns of Reform Congregations* (which claimed that more than 72 percent of UAHC congregations prohibited pork and shellfish and that more than 26 percent of congregations did not mix meat and dairy).

9. See chapter 8, "Is Dietary Practice Now in the Reform Mainstream?" Based on the survey results, Richard Levy and Marc Gertz observe that 62 percent of respondents refrain from eating pork at home, while only 58 percent of respondents light Shabbat candles at home regularly.

10. Incidentally, this exercise is a great teachable moment for facilitators to empower participants to become self-aware of their own eating habits by getting them to be more mindful of the items on a menu before they order something for themselves. Menu reading can be a spiritual exercise! Who am I? What are my core values and beliefs? What are these menu items? Where did they come from? If I choose to eat this, will that choice complement my value system? Or will it be a personal transgression of who I am/aspire to be?

11. Hence the (partially) ironic notion of the Jewish deli, given that the vast majority of Jewish delis are not actually kosher. David Sax, *Save the Deli* (Boston: Houghton Mifflin Harcourt, 2009), 29–30.

12. Meyer, *Response to Modernity*, chap. 2.

13. Jonathan Sarna, *American Judaism: A History* (New Haven: Yale University Press, 2004), 145. There, Sarna argues that the banquet caterer observed a kind of "proto-kosher style" (my words, not Sarna's) by avoiding pork on the menu. Even this notion of keeping some aspects of the dietary laws, while abandoning others, is anathema to the Pittsburgh Platform of 1885.

14. Teutsch, *Guide to Jewish Practice*, 33.

15. Categories taken from Arthur Waskow, "Down to Earth Judaism: Food, Sex, and Money," *Tikkun*, January/February 1988, 19–24.

16. Or at least decreasing one's consumption of beef, as Rabbi Eric Yoffie advocated in his 2009 URJ Biennial sermon.

17. See, e.g., the Leah Koenig Passover meditation on p. 5 of the document at http://bit.ly/gratitudekoenig.

50

REAL LIFE / REAL FOOD
Kosher Christmas Dinner

Mary L. Zamore

When I first married my husband Terje, I did not think much about the challenges of his parents not being Jewish. After all, they are nice people who seem to accept his life choices with amazing grace and who readily accepted me as part of their family. Plus, they live really, really far away.

My in-laws are Norwegian, Christian by birth, yet never attend church. My mother-in-law retains more of a spiritual connection to the church; my father-in-law is a staunch monotheist who has no place for such institutions. They live in a Christian society that has minimal church-state separation. Until immigration trends recently shifted to absorb Muslim refugees, Norway had been a homogeneous society of white, Christian Vikings. The Norwegian passport application actually asks for your shade of blonde hair.

My husband found his path to Judaism independently, and we met while both studying in Jerusalem. Today, our extended interfaith family finds a beautiful balance. Terje and I call it *sh'lom bayit*; I don't know what my in-laws would call it. However, I am grateful for their efforts to accommodate and support our nuclear family's religion. My in-laws even contribute to my son's Jewish day school tuition. This is extraordinary for Christian grandparents who come from a socialized country in which most education is free.

In some ways, food has been the most challenging part of this equation. Early on, Terje had to tell his parents that he could no longer eat everything. This was a big deal for parents who nurture through food and were in the food industry their entire lives. Over the years, Terje has gently reviewed the rules for them, patiently answering their many questions. I do not know if they really get it, but they love their son, so they accept his needs, although not always easily. They don't serve us pork or shellfish or mix milk and meat in our food.

Striving to find sh'lom bayit and kibud av va-eim, "honoring parents," Terje and I have stretched our boundaries to accommodate my in-laws' comfort zone. For example, Terje and I will not normally eat nonkosher meat. In our non-Norwegian life, we have greatly reduced our meat eating, and the bulk of the meat we do consume is from ethical purveyors of grass-fed, non-factory-farmed, kosher meat. Our concession in Norway, only in my in-laws' home, is that we will eat non-shechted meat. The cuts and animals have to be kosher, but since it is very challenging to get truly kosher meat in Norway, we make this exception in order to make meal preparation less stressful. I think my in-laws intuitively understand the value of sh'lom bayit. They surprised us on our last visit. These two senior citizens traveled 3½ hours round-trip to go to the Oslo synagogue, the only source of kosher meat in Norway, to bring back food for us.

I smile when I think about the Christmas dinners I have attended over the years. My whole Norwegian family gathered around the beautifully set table, kosher-style food sitting side by side with the nonkosher food in perfect balance. This vignette symbolizes the equilibrium we have achieved. Compromise means bending without harboring resentment and certainly not relinquishing one's ideals completely. Compromise means that you are willing to sacrifice at the same time that you recognize what another has sacrificed for your sake. While there are certainly bumps along the way, ultimately sh'lom bayit prevails through elevating the values of love and respect over ego and orthopraxy.

To Learn More

I. Perspective: History and Trends of Jewish Dietary Practices within Reform Judaism

"Commentary on the Principles for Reform Judaism," October 27, 2004. Central Conference of American Rabbis. http://ccarnet.org/Articles/index.cfm?id=45&pge_prg_id=4687&pge_id=1656.

Diner, Hasia. *Hungering for America: Italian, Irish, and Jewish Foodways in the Age of Migration*. Cambridge, MA: Harvard University Press, 2001.

Dreyfus, A. Stanley. "Qedushah in Diet: A Symposium on Kashrut in Reform Judaism." *CCAR Journal*, Winter 2004, 29–37.

Englander, Lawrence A. "Afterward: Some Observations." *CCAR Journal*, Winter 2004, 67–71.

Freedman, Seymour E. *The Book of Kashruth: A Treasury of Kosher Facts and Frauds*. New York: Bloch Publishing, 1970.

Joselit, Jenna Weissman. "Food Fight: The Americanization of Kashrut in Twentieth-Century America." In *Food and Judaism*, edited by

Leonard J. Greenspoon, Ronald A. Simkins, and Gerald Shapiro. Omaha, NE: Creighton University Press, 2005.

Knobel, Peter. "A Reform Perspective on Kashrut." *Reform Judaism*, Summer 1995, 25.

Kraemer, David. *Jewish Eating and Identity through the Ages*. New York: Routledge, 2007.

Nathan, Joan. "A Social History of Jewish Food in America." In *Food and Judaism*, edited by Leonard J. Greenspoon, Ronald A. Simkins, and Gerald Shapiro. Studies in Jewish Civilization, vol. 5. Omaha, NE: Creighton University Press, 2005.

Schaalman, Herman E. "The Divine Authority of the Mitzvah." In *Gates of Mitzvah*, edited by Simeon J. Maslin. New York: CCAR Press, 1979.

Yoffie, Eric. *Toronto Biennial Sermon*. November 7, 2009. http://urj.org/about/union/leadership/yoffie/?syspage=article&item_id=27481.

II. Buffet of Educated Choices: Jewish Ritual Law

Abraham, Abraham S. *Nishmat Avraham*. Brooklyn: Masorah Publications, 2000.

Abramson, Robert, Samuel H. Dresner, Seymour Siegel, and David M. Pollock. *Keeping Kosher: A Diet for the Soul*. New York: Rabbinical Assembly, 2000.

Apisdorf, Shimon. *Kosher for the Clueless but Curious*. Baltimore: Leviathan, 2005.

"A Case for Jewish Vegetarianism." http://www.goveg.com/pdfs/jewishvegbooklet72.pdf.

Forst, Binyomin. *The Kosher Kitchen: A Practical Guide*. Brooklyn: Mesorah Publications, 2009.

Garfunkel, Trudy. *Kosher for Everybody: The Complete Guide to Understanding, Shopping, Cooking, and Eating the Kosher Way*. San Francisco: Jossey-Bass, 2004.

Global Exchange Passover Supplement. http://www.globalexchange.org/campaigns/fairtrade/cocoa/Passover.

Greenberg, Blu. *How to Run a Traditional Jewish Household.* New York: Simon and Schuster, 1983.

Stern, Lisë. *How to Keep Kosher: A Comprehensive Guide to Understanding Jewish Dietary Laws.* New York: Morrow, 2004.

Teutsch, David A. *A Guide to Jewish Practice.* Wyncote, PA: Reconstructionist Rabbinical College, 2003.

III. Environmental Ethics: *Bal Tashchit*

"About the Film." Official *Food, Inc.* Movie Site—Hungry for Change? http://www.foodincmovie.com/about-the-film.php.

"Bal Tashchit: The Development of a Jewish Environmental Principle." Coalition on the Environment and Jewish Life. http://www.coejl.org/learn/je_tashchit.php.

Bernstein, Ellen, ed. *Ecology and the Jewish Spirit: Where Nature and the Sacred Meet.* Woodstock VT: Jewish Lights Publishing, 1998.

Berry, Wendell. *Bringing It to the Table: On Farming and Food.* Berkeley: Counterpoint, 2009.

Bittman, Mark. *Food Matters: A Guide to Conscious Eating with More Than 75 Recipes.* New York: Simon & Schuster, 2009.

Brickner, Balfour. *Finding God in the Garden: Backyard Reflections on Life, Love, and Compost.* Boston: Little, Brown, 2002.

"Community Supported Agriculture 101." Union for Reform Judaism. http://urj.org/life/food/?syspage=document&item_id=27140.

Foer, Jonathan Safran. *Eating Animals.* New York: Little, Brown, 2009.

"Gardeners Sharing Their Harvest with Food Pantries Using AmpleHarvest.org." AmpleHarvest.org. http://www.ampleharvest.org/.

Gore, Albert. *An Inconvenient Truth.* New York: Rodale, 2006.

"GreenFaith Leadership Programs." GreenFaith: Interfaith Partners for the Environment. http://www.greenfaith.org/.

"Greening Reform Judaism." Union for Reform Judaism. http://urj.org/green.

"A Green Table, A Just Table—Program for NFTY & Youth." Union for Reform Judaism. http://urj.org/life/food/ ?syspage=document&item_id=27141.

"A Guide to Synagogue Gardens." Union for Reform Judaism. http://urj.org/life/food/?syspage=document&item_id=27460.

The Jew & the Carrot (blog). http://blogs.forward.com/the-jew-and-the-carrot.

"Jewish Environmental Education, Bike Rides, Sustainable Food." Hazon. http://hazon.org/.

Kingsolver, Barbara, Steven L. Hopp, and Camille Kingsolver. *Animal, Vegetable, Miracle: A Year of Food Life*. New York: HarperCollins, 2007.

Koeppel, Dan. *Banana: The Fate of the Fruit That Changed the World*. New York: Hudson Street, 2008.

Nachman, Candace. "*Bal Tashchit*: Optimism in a Time of Teshuva." Canfei Nesharim. http://www.canfeinesharim.org/learning/torah.php?id=12439&page=12439.

Nir, David. "A Critical Examination of the Jewish Environmental Law of *Bal Tashchit* 'Do Not Destroy.'" *Georgetown International Environmental Law Review*, Winter 2006.

Pollan, Michael. *The Botany of Desire*. New York: Random House Books, 2001.

———. *In Defense of Food: An Eater's Manifesto*. New York: Penguin, 2008.

———. *The Omnivore's Dilemma: A Natural History of Four Meals*. New York: Penguin, 2006.

———. *The Omnivore's Dilemma for Kids: The Secrets Behind What You Eat*. New York: Penguin Group USA, 2009.

———. *Second Nature: A Gardener's Education*. New York: Dell, 1991.

Risa, Alyson. "Waste Minimization, *Bal Tashchit* and Beyond." Judaism and the Environment. http://more.masortiworld.org/environment/space/community/Waste_Minimization_Bal_Tashchit_and_Beyond.pdf.

Schwartz, Eilon. "*Bal Tashchit*: A Jewish Environmental Precept." In *Judaism and Environmental Ethics: A Reader*, edited by Martin D. Yaffe. Lanham, MD: Lexington, 2001.

Waskow, Arthur Ocean. "The Emergence of Eco-Judaism." *CCAR Journal*, Winter 2001.

Stein, David E. S., trans. "Halakhah: The Law of *Bal Tashchit* (Do Not Destroy)." In *Torah of the Earth: Exploring 4,000 Years of Ecology in Jewish Thought*, edited by Arthur Waskow. Woodstock, VT: Jewish Lights Publishing, 2000.

Weber, Karl. *Food, Inc.: How Industrial Food Is Making Us Sicker, Fatter and Poorer—And What You Can Do About It*. New York: Public Affairs, 2009.

IV. Kindness to Animals: *Tzaar Baalei Chayim*

Feintuch, Yossi. "Who Eats First?" *CCAR Journal*, Fall 2008, 48–51.

Foer, Jonathan Safran. *Eating Animals*. New York: Little, Brown, 2009.

Greenberg, Paul. *Four Fish: The Future of the Last Wild Food*. New York: Penguin, 2010.

Grescoe, Taras. *Bottomfeeder: How to Eat Ethically in a World of Vanishing Seafood*. New York: Bloomsbury USA, 2008.

Jewish Vegetarians of North America. http://jewishveg.com/.

KOL Foods: Glatt Kosher Grass-fed Organic Meat—The Way Meat Was Meant to Be. . . . http://www.kolfoods.com/.

Marine Stewardship Council. http://www.msc.org.

Schwartz, Richard H. *Judaism and Global Survival*. New York: Lantern, 2002.

———. *Judaism and Vegetarianism*. New York: Lantern, 2001.

V. Concern for Oppressed Food Workers: *Oshek*

Abolish: The American Anti-Slavery Group. http://www.iabolish.org.

Anti-Slavery: Today's Fight for Tomorrow's Freedom. http://www. antislavery.org/.

The Child Labor Coalition. http://www.stopchildlabor.org.

Equal Exchange: Fairly Traded Coffee, Tea, Chocolate & Snacks. http://www.equalexchange.coop.

The Fairtrade Foundation. http://www.fairtrade.org.uk/.

Global Exchange: Building People-to-People Ties. http://www. globalexchange.org/.

Jacobs, Jill. *There Shall Be No Needy*. Woodstock, VT: Jewish Lights, 2008.

Off, Carol. *Bitter Chocolate: The Dark Side of the World's Most Seductive Sweet*. New York: New Press, 2008.

Satre, Lowell J. *Chocolate on Trial: Slavery, Politics, and the Ethics of Business*. Athens, OH: Ohio University Press, 2005.

UFW: The Official Web Page of the United Farm Workers of America. http://www.ufw.org/.

Unfair Trade. www.unfairtrade.co.uk.

Wolfe, David. *Superfoods: The Food and Medicine of the Future*. Berkeley: North Atlantic, 2009.

VI. *Hechsher:* Who Decides What Is Kosher?

Abramson, Robert, Samuel H. Dresner, Seymour Siegel, and David M. Pollock. *Keeping Kosher: A Diet for the Soul*. New York: Rabbinical Assembly, 2000.

Alroy, Odelia. "Kosher Wine." *Judaism* 39 (1990): 452–60.

Esposito, Sergio: *Passion on the Vine*. New York: Broadway Books, 2008.

European Union: Council Regulation (EC) No. 1493/1999 of 17 May 1999 on the common organisation of the market in wine.

Fishkoff, Sue. *Kosher Nation*. New York: Schocken, 2010.

Gradstein, Linda. "Israel's Wines: A Culture Uncorked." *Washington Post*, June 7, 2009.

Greenspoon, Leonard J., Ronald Simkins, and Gerald Shapiro, eds. *Food and Judaism*. Omaha, NE: Creighton University Press, 2005.

Juravel, Avrohom, and Zev Baruch. "Uncorking the Secrets of Kosher Wine." *Jewish Action*, Spring 2007, 64–68.

Klein, Isaac. *A Guide to Jewish Religious Practice*. New York: Jewish Theological Seminary, 1979.

MAGEN TZEDEK: Kashrut for the 21st Century. http://magentzedek.org.

Plotkin, Paul. "Kosher Enough: A New Look at Kashrut." *United Synagogue Review*, Fall 2005. http://www.uscj.org/Kosher_Enough__A_New6815.html.

Pyevich, Caroline. "Why Is Wine So Fined?" *Vegetarian Journal* 16, no. 1 (January/February 1997). http://www.vrg.org/journal/vj97jan/971wine.htm.

Rogov, Daniel. *Rogov's Guide to Israeli Wines*. Jerusalem: The Toby Press, 2010.

———. *Rogov's Guide to Kosher Wines*. Jerusalem: The Toby Press, 2010.

Silverman, Israel Nissan. "Are All Wines Kosher?" In *Conservative Judaism and Jewish Law*, ed. Seymour Siegel and Elliot Gertel, 308–16. New York: Rabbinical Assembly, 1977.

Uri L'Tzedek: Orthodox Social Justice. http://www.utzedek.org/index.php.

VII. Guarding Our Health: *Sh'mirat HaGuf*

"Eating Disorders." Union for Reform Judaism. http://urj.org/life/health/eatingdisorders/.

Grossman, Marni. "In the Beginning There Was This: Fat . . . and Then I Started Cutting." *Lilith*, Winter 2009/2010.

Preuss, Julius. *Biblical and Talmudic Medicine*, trans. Fred Rosner. New York: Sanhedrin Press, 1978.

VIII. Justice: *Tzedek*

Alexander, William. *The $64 Tomato: How One Man Nearly Lost His Sanity, Spent a Fortune, and Endured an Existential Crisis in the Quest for the Perfect Garden*. New York: Algonquin, 2007.

MAZON: A Jewish Response to Hunger. http://mazon.org/.

Tamari, Meir. *With All Your Possessions: Jewish Ethics and Economic Life*. New York: Free Press, 1987.

IX. Spirituality

Ehrlich, Elizabeth. *Miriam's Kitchen: A Memoir*. New York: Penguin Books, 1997.

"Food Blessings." Union for Reform Judaism. http://urj.org/life/food/?syspage=document&item_id=27462.

Krantz, Douglas E. "Setting the Table: Nuturing a Health Religious Awareness." *CCAR Journal*, Summer 2008, 43–48.

Sax, David. *Save the Deli: In Search of Perfect Pastrami, Crusty Rye, and the Heart of Jewish Delicatessen*. Boston: Houghton Mifflin Harcourt, 2009.

Slater, Jonathan P. *Mindful Jewish Living: Compassionate Practice*. New York: Aviv, 2004.

Spiro, Jack D. "Eating at Bar-Mitzvah Receptions." *CCAR Journal*, June 1964.

———. "What Is a B'rachah?" *CCAR Journal*, June 1972, 38.

Zanger, Walter. "Praying or Eating?" *CCAR Journal*, Winter/Spring 1995, 41–44.

X. Making Your Choices: *Shalom*

Apisdorf, Shimon. *Kosher for the Clueless but Curious*. Baltimore: Leviathan, 2005.

"Food for Thought: A URJ-Hazon Curriculum Guide on Ethical Eating." Union for Reform Judaism. http://urj.org/life/food/?syspage=document&item_id=27461.

"Food Policymaking Guide for Synagogues." Union for Reform Judaism. http://urj.org/life/food/?syspage=document&item_id=27463.

"Just Congregations." Union for Reform Judaism. http://urj.org/socialaction/training/justcongregations/.

"Repairing Eden Guide: Sustainable Food Practices for Faith-Based Institutions." GreenFaith. https://www.z2systems.com/np/clients/greenfaith/product.jsp?product=4.

Sameth, Mark. "The Broad Spectrum of *Kashrut*." In *The Rituals & Practices of a Jewish Life: A Handbook for Personal Spiritual Renewal*, ed. Kerry M. Olitzky and Daniel Judson. Woodstock, VT: Jewish Lights, 2002.

Yoffie, Eric. "Shabbat Sermon: URJ 70th Biennial Convention in Toronto." Union for Reform Judaism. http://blogs.rj.org/reform/2009/11/president-yoffies-shabbat-serm.html.

Responsa

GUIDE TO SOURCES

Each source is identified by page number(s) only, by volume number, or by a leading symbol.

Page number(s) only—e.g.:

Artificial insemination 218–222

Such references are to Responsa of the Central Conference of American Rabbis, *ed. Rabbi Jacob D. Schwartz (New York: UAHC, 1954). (Note: All such citations are taken from the yearbooks of the CCAR and are also included in ARR—see below.)*

Volume number (in Roman numerals, followed by year and page number(s)—e.g.:

Mixed marriage
Three generations of XCIV (1984) 173–174

Such references are to Yearbook of the Central Conference of American Rabbis *(or CCAR Yearbook).*

Symbols—e.g., the appearance of "ARR" in:

Building a Chapel on a Cemetery (ARR 75–76)
Circumcision of Infant (XCII: 1982, 218–219, ARR 141–143)

Such references are to one of the following sources, many of which can be ordered through the CCAR Press website (www.ccarpress.org):

ARR—*American Reform Responsa*, ed. Walter Jacob, 1983
CoRR—*Contemporary Reform Responsa*, Solomon Freehof, 1974
CuRR—*Current Reform Responsa*, ed. Solomon Freehof, 1969
NARR—*New American Reform Responsa*, ed. Walter Jacob, 1992
NRR—*New Reform Responsa*, ed. Solomon Freehof, 1980
RRT—*Reform Responsa for Our Time*, ed. Solomon Freehof, 1977
RRTC1—*Reform Repsonsa for the 21st Century*, Vol. 1, ed. Mark Washofsky, 2010
RRTC2—*Reform Responsa for the 21st Century*, Vol. 2, ed. Mark Washofsky, 2010
TFN—*Teshuvot for the 1990's*, ed. W. Gunther Plaut and Mark Washofsky, 1997
TRR—*Today's Reform Responsa*, ed. Solomon Freehof, 1990

Glossary

am haaretz: In Hebrew, this term literally means, "people of the land," but it is a phrase that has come to mean "the common people." It can be used in a somewhat derogatory way, delineating between certain class groups, especially in terms of Jewish education. More specifically in the context of this book, it is a category created by the Pharisees to refer to the group of people who did not eat properly tithed food and were not careful in matters of purity.

avodah zarah: The Hebrew term for "idolatry," literally meaning "strange work/worship."

Birkat HaMazon: The series of blessings recited after meals.

chaver: A Hebrew word meaning "friend" or "fellow." It is also a category created by the Pharisees to refer to the group of people who only ate properly tithed food and were diligent in matters of purity.

cholent: A traditional Jewish stew commonly made with meat and potatoes or chicken and beans. It is usually cooked overnight and served during Shabbat to conform to the Shabbat prohibition of cooking.

chukat hagoyim: A Hebrew term for "following the ways of gentiles," from Deuteronomy 18:9.

CSA: Community Supported Agriculture, a model of food distribution that relies on the individual support of specific local, often organic farms in exchange for produce, dairy products, or meats.

Food insecure: the state of living in hunger or in fear of starvation because of a lack of socially acceptable access to safe and nutritious food

Gates of Mitzvah: The CCAR published this book in 1979 as a guide for Jewish life-cycle events created for home use by the average Reform Jew. It was preceded by *A Shabbat Manual*, a book intending to increase home Shabbat practice.

Gemara: The section of the Talmud that consists of Rabbinic commentary on the Mishnah.

hafrashat challah: This Hebrew term literally means "the separating of challah." It is the traditional ritual of tearing off a piece of Shabbat challah. It represents the tithe for the priests in the Temple and the maintenance of ritual purity. It is a tradition still followed today in many communities although wholly symbolic; a piece of challah is separated, blessed, and then thrown into fire or burnt.

hechsher: A *hechsher* is a kosher certification. It is a symbol appearing on a package or premises that indicates that a regulatory body has determined that the product or business is in compliance with the laws of kashrut. The Orthodox Union is the largest kosher-certification agency in the country; however, there are now many organizations that have developed their own supervisors and symbols.

heirloom: Vintage varieties of vegetables, fruit, or livestock no longer commonly eaten. There are active movements to preserve these genetic lines.

hidur mitzvah: A Rabbinic term meaning "to beautify a mitzvah or ritual."

kashrut: The compilation of Jewish dietary laws found originally in the Torah and refined and clarified by the Rabbis throughout time.

K'lal Yisrael: A Hebrew term literally meaning "all of Israel," which has come to mean the entirety of world Jewry. It also connotes the intent of different types of Jews to get along despite differing world views.

leket: The Torah provides various ways in which food was to be shared with those in need of which *leket* is one. In Leviticus 19:9 and 23:22, we are commanded that when harvesting in the field, if produce should fall on the ground it should be left there for the hungry to glean.

maaseir oni: Another way in which food was to be shared with those in need in the Torah. In Deuteronomy 14:28, this term, translated as a "tithe for the poor" is explained as the obligation to set aside one-tenth of produce for the poor, grown in the third and sixth year of the traditional seven-year cycle.

mara d'atra: An Aramaic term for the legal decisor of the local community, often used to describe the job of a rabbi.

mevushal **wines:** The process of heating wine to the point where according to halachah the liquid is no longer available for idolatrous use.

This category of wine will also remain "kosher" if used for idolatrous purposes subsequently.

mikdash m'at: When the Second Temple was destroyed in 70 C.E., the manner of service and prayer to God was forever changed from a single central location to many synagogues in a wide variety of locations. *Mikdash m'at* is a term meaning "a smaller temple," designating a synagogue as well as a Jewish home as a smaller representation of the Temple.

Mishneh Torah: A code of Jewish law written by Maimonides, also known as Rambam, a medieval rabbi who has become one of the most well-known rabbis in all of Jewish history.

Motzi: The abbreviated name of the blessing said over bread.

ne-eman: A Hebrew term literally meaning "trustworthy." It is used in this book as the third category created by the Pharisees, referring to the group of people who ate properly tithed food but were not strict about matters of purity. This group of people fall in between the *chaver* and the *am haaretz*.

oleilot: This term refers to small clusters of grapes that are under-ripened or otherwise deemed unfit, which are to be left in the vineyard for the poor to glean.

Oneg Shabbat: This Hebrew phrase has come to refer to the informal social gatherings after Shabbat worship, most often accompanied by a selection of food. It is a time for worshipers to meet and greet one another. The phrase literally means "the joy of Shabbat."

organic: At the most basic level, the term "organic" is used to identify a food product, meat, or plant that has been raised or grown without the use of growth hormones, pesticides, or chemicals. However, the

United States and many other countries highly regulate the use of the term "organic" through a very specific certification process. To learn more about the legal definition of organic, visit the USDA website: http://www.ams.usda.gov/AMSv1.0/nop.

pei-ah: The concept of *pei-ah*, found in Leviticus 19:9 and 23:22, designates that the corners of the field not be harvested, but rather kept open and available for those in need of food. *Pei-ah* literally means corner.

peret: As specified in the Torah, these are the grapes that fall to the ground during the harvest, which must be left in the vineyard for the poor to glean.

Pharisees: The Pharisees were one of the largest Jewish sects during the Second Temple period, approximately the two centuries preceding the destruction of the Temple in 70 C.E. They are often labeled "proto-rabbis" due to the influence they had on the emerging Rabbinic era after the destruction of the Second Temple as well as a desire by the Rabbis to maintain the chain of tradition.

Pirkei Avot: A tractate of the Talmud that is a collection of maxims and teachings dealing almost exclusively with ethics and morals rather than legal issues. In English it is often called the Ethics of the Fathers.

platforms: The Central Conference of American Rabbis (CCAR) has created five "statements of principle," called platforms, throughout the history of the American Reform Movement. The first platform was created in Pittsburgh in 1885, followed by the Columbus Platform in 1937, the Centenary Perspective in 1976, the Miami Platform in 1997, and the latest platform, the New Pittsburgh Platform in 1999. These platforms are meant to express the evolving ideology and principles of the Movement. The text of the platforms can be found on the CCAR website (www.ccarnet.org).

poskim: Knowledgeable deciders of Jewish law.

shich'chah: A quantity of harvested produce that is accidentally left in the field, which the Torah commands be left for the poor.

shochet: A person who performs kosher slaughter.

Shulchan Aruch: Sixteenth-century law code written by Joseph Karo.

sidrei b'reishit: A Hebrew term literally meaning the "order of creation," it is used to discuss the natural order of the universe created by God, specifically in this book in terms of how genetically modified foods may disturb this natural order.

Tishah B'Av: A Jewish holiday on the ninth of the Jewish month Av, commemorating the destruction of the First Temple in 586 B.C.E. as well as the Second Temple in 70 C.E. Subsequent days of particular suffering or destruction are also included in this commemoration. It is traditionally a fast day.

tithed food: The Torah demands that a certain portion of foods produced be designated as Temple offerings, in part for consumption by priests. Once designated, these are forever forbidden for consumption by non-priests or for non-Temple purposes. The remainder of the food from which the offering was taken was permitted to be eaten by non-priests. This remainder was called tithed food. The Pharisees designate three categories concerning the consumption of tithed food.

yayin nesech: A category of kosher wine law that ensures that the wine was not used for pagan or idolatrous purposes.

z'mirot: Jewish songs or tunes most often sung on Shabbat or other holidays. They are sung after meals and range in language and meaning.

Contributors

RABBI RUTH ABUSCH-MAGDER, PHD, received her doctorate from Yale University for a dissertation entitled *Home-made Judaism: Food and Domestic Jewish Life in Germany and America 1848–1914* and wrote a hands-on Jewish food curriculum as a Jerusalem Fellow at the Mandel Leadership Institute in 2007. She has served as the director of Continuing Alumni Education for Hebrew Union College–Jewish Institute of Religion and is the rabbi-in-residence for Be'Chol Lashon. Rabbi Abusch-Magder is a frequent writer and teacher on topics relating to Jewish food. She lives and bakes in San Francisco with her husband David and their two children.

RABBI JULIE PELC ADLER is the director of Jewish Student Life at Santa Monica College Hillel and the director of the Berit Mila Program of Reform Judaism. Previously, she was the assistant director of the Kalsman Institute on Judaism and Health. She received master's degrees from the University of Judaism and from Harvard Graduate School of Education and was ordained as a rabbi by Hebrew Union College–Jewish

Institute of Religion in 2006. She co-edited the anthology *Joining the Sisterhood: Young Jewish Women Write Their Lives*, published by the State University of New York Press in 2003. She lives in Venice, California, with her husband, Rabbi Amitai Adler, who is (among other things) a masterful chef of extraordinary kosher cuisine.

Rabbi Batsheva Appel is senior rabbi of KAM Isaiah Israel Congregation in Chicago. KAM Isaiah Israel's urban vegetable garden produces hundreds of pounds of produce for local soup kitchens and food pantries. Rabbi Appel has lived and traveled all over the country, visiting farm stands and farmers' markets whenever possible. During the winter she dreams of summer, when the CSA starts.

Trisha Arlin recently completed a year's study as an Arts Fellow at the Drisha Institute (2009–10) and is in the sixth cohort of the Davenning Leadership Training Institute beginning in the summer of 2010. She has been a member of Kolot Chayeinu / Voices of Our Lives since 1997 and edits their journal, *VOICES*, which can be seen at http://kolotchayeinu.org/voices/. Trisha received her BA in theater from Antioch College in 1975 and MFA in film (screenwriting) from Columbia University's Graduate School of the Arts Film Division in 1997. Arlin works as a freelance writer and editor. From 2003 to 2005 she wrote and performed her one-person show, *Things I Have Believed In*. Currently she is working on *d'vrei t'filah*, some of which can be seen on her blog, http://triganza.blogspot.com.

Rabbi Carole B. Balin, PhD, is a professor of Jewish history at Hebrew Union College–Jewish Institute of Religion, New York. She has recently joined a CSA and is exploring new approaches to keeping kosher as a liberal Jew. She hopes to get her hands dirty at a local farm some time soon.

Rabbi Deborah Bodin Cohen worked at the Advocacy Institute in Washington, D.C., between college and rabbinical school as a watchdog of the alcoholic beverage industry. Ordained in 1997 from Hebrew Union College–Jewish Institute of Religion in New York, she has served congregations in Potomac, Maryland, Cherry Hill, New Jersey, and Cary, North Carolina. She has published six books for Jewish children and teens, including *Lilith's Ark*, which received a National Jewish Book Award.

RABBI EUGENE B. BOROWITZ serves as the Sigmund L. Falk Distinguished Professor of Education and Jewish Religious Thought at the New York School of Hebrew Union College–Jewish Institute of Religion, where he has taught since 1962. He is the author of many articles and books on Jewish religious thought. Rabbi Borowitz is the former editor of *Sh'ma, A Journal of Jewish Responsibility*, which he founded in 1970 and edited for twenty-three years. For his contributions to Reform Judaism, the Union for Reform Judaism awarded him its Eisendrath Prize at its 2005 Biennial convention. Rabbi Borowitz received his bachelor's degree from Ohio State University. He was ordained and received the first of his two earned doctor's degrees from Hebrew Union College, the other being from Teachers College Columbia University. He has served congregations in St. Louis, Missouri, and Port Washington, New York, and was a navy chaplain during the Korean War. Prior to his academic position he was national director of education for Reform Judaism at the UAHC.

RABBI JEFFREY BROWN has served as associate rabbi of Temple Solel in Cardiff, California, since his rabbinic ordination (at Hebrew Union College–Jewish Institute of Religion in Cincinnati) in 2005. His contributions to this book build on his rabbinical school thesis, which he wrote under the guidance of Rabbis Sam Joseph and Mark Washofsky.

RACHEL COHEN served as a legislative assistant at the Religious Action Center, the Washington office of the Reform Movement, from 2008 to 2010. During her time at the RAC she focused mainly on environmental issues, including climate change, energy, and food policy. She led several efforts to "green" the institutions of the Reform Movement and staffed the Union's *Shulchan Yarok, Shulchan Tzedek* (Green Table, Just Table) 2009 Biennial initiative on sustainable, ethical eating. Cohen holds a BA in political science from Washington University in St. Louis and plans to stay in Washington to pursue a career in nonprofit advocacy and public policy work.

RABBI WILLIAM CUTTER, PHD, is professor emeritus of Hebrew literature and Emeritus Steinberg Professor of Human Relations at Hebrew Union College–Jewish Institute of Religion, Los Angeles, where he has been on the faculty for forty-five years. He is founding director of the Rhea Hirsch School of Education, the MUSE project in museum education of the Skirball Museum, and the Kalsman Institute on Judaism and Health. He specializes in the literary renaissance of the early twentieth century and addresses problems of health and healing from the perspective of group behavior and modern logic. He is the author of the forthcoming book *Midrash & Medicine: Healing Body and Soul in the Jewish Interpretive Tradition*.

RABBI SUE LEVI ELWELL edited *The Open Door*, the CCAR Haggadah (2002), served as the poetry editor and member of the editorial board of the award-winning *The Torah: A Women's Commentary* (2008), and was one of the editors of *Lesbian Rabbis: The First Generation* (2001). The founding director of the Los Angeles Jewish Feminist Center and the first rabbinic director of Ma'yan, Rabbi Elwell has served congregations in California, New Jersey, and Virgina. She currently serves as Union rabbi and worship specialist for the Union for Reform Judaism.

MARC GERTZ, PHD, has been a professor at Florida State University for over thirty years. Among other courses, he regularly teaches research methods and statistics. He is currently an officer of the Union for Reform Judaism and has served on that board since 1995. He has conducted surveys and analyzed data for the Reform Movement on a wide variety of subject matters.

RABBI RAYNA ELLEN GEVURTZ is a native of Portland, Oregon, and is passionate about caring for all of God's creatures. Rabbi Gevurtz has served congregations in Ohio, California, and Melbourne, Australia. She wrote her rabbinic thesis on *"Tsaar Baalei Chayim* and the Issue of Factory Farming."

RABBI NEAL GOLD has been the senior rabbi of Temple Shir Tikva in Wayland, Massachusetts, since July 2005. Neal is involved in the leadership of a variety of Zionist, interfaith, and *tzedakah* organizations. He is married to Heidi Gold, and they have two sons, Avi and Jeremy.

AARON SAUL GROSS is a Historian of Religions specializing in Jewish Modernity. He is an assistant professor at the University of San Diego, co-chairs the Animals and Religion Consultation at the American Academy of Religion, and is the founder of Farm Forward, a nonprofit food and farming advocacy group. His current research interests include questions of ethics, subjectivity, and identity in relation to Jewish dietary practice and animal ethics. Gross holds an MTS from Harvard Divinity School and a PhD in religious studies from the University of California, Santa Barbara.

RABBI ALAN HENKIN is the Union for Reform Judaism's Union rabbi for the West District. Prior to that he was the URJ's regional director for the Pacific Southwest Council. He has served as rabbi for Temple Beth Solomon of the Deaf in Arleta, California, and Congregation Beth Knesset Bamidbar in Lancaster, California. He holds a PhD in social ethics from the University of Southern California.

RABBI PETER E. KASDAN was named rabbi emeritus when he retired in July 2001, after serving as rabbi of Temple Emanu-El of West Essex, Livingston, New Jersey, for thirty years. He continues to be motivated in retirement by social justice, NFTY, JFTY's Mitzvah Corps and the URJ's Kutz Camp, the survival of the Ethiopian Jews, and the People and State of Israel, all of which were a major part of his rabbinic career. He served on the Commission of Social Action of Reform Judaism, on the board of ARZA / World Union, North America, as president of the Scholarship Fund for Ethiopian Jews, and as the rabbinic advisor of the Jewish Genetic Disease Consortium. He was the recipient of the UAHC's Fund for Reform Judaism Distinguished Service Award, a NFTY life membership, and the CCAR's Rabbi Samuel Cook Award for Service to Youth. His lifelong efforts on behalf of the migrant worker community, specifically his support of and personal friendship with Cesar Chavez and the multi-generations of the Chavez-Rodriguez family, was and remains a highlight of his life.

RABBI ZOË KLEIN is the senior rabbi of Temple Isaiah in Los Angeles. She is the author of the novel *Drawing in the Dust.* She and her husband Rabbi Jonathan Klein have three children, who, if they had their way, would prefer their parents to make three different main courses for each of them for dinner.

RABBI KEVIN M. KLEINMAN is the assistant rabbi of Reform Congregation Keneseth Israel in Elkins Park, Pennsylvania. He has a BA from Brandeis University (2002) and was ordained by Hebrew Union College–Jewish Institute of Religion (2009). Prior to entering rabbinical school, Rabbi Kleinman worked as a Jewish environmental educator for the Teva Learning Center, where he met his life partner and wife, Chana Rothman. He also created and directed URJ Kutz Camp's Teva Outdoor Adventure program in 2007 and 2008.

RABBI PETER KNOBEL is rabbi emeritus of Beth Emet the Free Synagogue in Evanston, Illinois. He is the immediate past president of the CCAR and past chair of the CCAR Ad Hoc Editorial Siddur Committee, which produced *Mishkan T'filah.*

TERJE Z. LANDE wrote his doctoral dissertation on the economic geography of Israel and has been enamored by of Israeli wines ever since. A graduate of the Norwegian School of Economics and Business Administration (Dr. Oecon, MA, and MSc), he was a Fulbright Scholar at Hunter College in New York and a visiting research student at the Hebrew University of Jerusalem. He lives in Westfield, New Jersey, with his wife, Rabbi Mary L. Zamore, and their son Aryeh.

RABBI GERSH LAZAROW emigrated to Australia from South Africa twenty-five years ago. He attended a Jewish day school in Melbourne and later completed a completed a bachelor of arts at Monash University. After obtaining his graduate diploma in teaching, he commenced his rabbinical studies at Hebrew Union College–Jewish Institute of Religion in Los Angeles. He successfully obtained his master of Hebrew letters in 2006 followed by a master of Jewish education the following year. Gersh receive his rabbinic ordination in May 2009 and returned to Melbourne with his wife, Michelle, and their two children, Livia and Samuel, to begin his tenure as rabbi of the King David School, Australia's only Reform day school. Gersh is a passionate educator with a strong commitment to Reform Jewish values, tradition, and community. When he is not teaching, Gersh can usually be found standing next to a barbecue enjoying the pleasures of a good grain-fed steak.

BARBARA LERMAN-GOLOMB is the social responsibility consultant for Jewish Community Center Association of North America and the former director of education and outreach at Hazon. She is an author, activist, and Teva-trained experiential environmental educator. For over eighteen years she has been working to create healthy, sustainable communities through awareness, advocacy, and action. The former executive director of the Coalition on the Environment and Jewish Life (COEJL), Barbara originated the nationwide climate change and energy campaign "How Many Jews Does it Take to Change a Light Bulb?" and was featured in *Lilith* magazine as an "eco-revolutionary."

She serves on the Union for Reform Judaism's Commission on Social Action and Northeast Camp Commission.

RABBI RICHARD N. LEVY is the rabbi of the synagogue and director of spiritual growth at the Los Angeles campus of the Hebrew Union College–Jewish Institute of Religion. He served for ten years as director of the School of Rabbinic Studies at the L.A. campus and, prior to that, was for many years executive director of Los Angeles Hillel Council. He served as president of the Central Conference of American Rabbis, during which time he shepherded passage of the 1999 Pittsburgh Principles. He is the author of *A Vision of Holiness: The Future of Reform Judaism*, published by the URJ Press in 2005, and the editor and primary writer of *On Wings of Awe*, a High Holy Day *machzor* published in 1985, which is being issued in revised form in 2010–11. He is also the editor of *On Wings of Freedom*, a Passover Haggadah, and *On Wings of Light*, a siddur for Shabbat evening. He is married to Carol Levy, and they have two daughters, Sarah and Elizabeth.

RABBI SETH M. LIMMER is rabbi of Congregation B'nai Yisrael of Armonk, New York. Five years ago, his synagogue began to explore new directions in kashrut. Those discussions led the congregation to partner with the Roxbury Farm and Neighbor's Link, a nearby immigrant workers' center, thereby creating a CSA model that provides healthy and nutritious food both for those able to affort its cost and also for the working poor. Seth received his doctorate of Hebrew letters in 2008 from Hebrew Union College–Jewish Institute of Religion in the field of Rabbinic hermeneutics, but more importantly is married to Molly Morse Limmer, with whom he is a proud parent to Rosey Esther and Lily Benjamin Limmer, perhaps the future farmers of America.

RABBI ELLEN LIPPMANN is founder and rabbi of Kolot Chayeinu / Voices of Our Lives, a seventeen-year-old progressive community in Brooklyn, New York. Rabbi Lippmann is the former East Coast director of MAZON: A Jewish Response to Hunger, and former director of the Jewish

Women's Program at the New 14th Street Y in Manhattan. She was an active participant in Interfaith Voices Against Hunger. Rabbi Lippmann is co-chair, with Rabbi Tirzah Firestone, of Rabbis for Human Rights–North America and serves on the board of the Shalom Center. She is also on the rabbinic advisory boards for the Hannah Senesh School and Jews for Racial and Economic Justice and served as the first social justice chair for the Women's Rabbinic Network. She is the co-founder of the seven-year-old Children of Abraham Peace Walk: Jews, Christians and Muslims Walking Together in Brooklyn in Peace. She was ordained in 1991 by Hebrew Union College–Jewish Institute of Religion and also received there the degree of master of Hebrew letters. She holds a BA in English language and literature from Boston University and an MS in library science from Simmons College. Rabbi Lippmann and her partner are longtime Brooklyn residents.

RABBI RICHARD LITVAK is senior rabbi of Temple Beth El in Aptos, California, one of the richest agricultural areas in North America. Rabbi Litvak has long been concerned with the plight of the farm workers and has actively been involved in the United Farm Workers Union. He helped the UFW secure the first union contracts for straw-berry pickers. Rabbi Litvak has served on the Kashrut Committee of the Central Conference of American Rabbis. As a committee member he encouraged concern for the just treatment of farm workers be an important part of a contemporary Reform Jewish food ethic.

RABBI ROBERT J. MARX is the rabbi emeritus of Congregation Hakafa in Glencoe, Illinois. He was ordained at the Hebrew Union College–Jewish Institute of Religion in 1951, and earned a PhD at Yale University. He is the founder of Chicago's Jewish Council on Urban Affairs and a co-founder of Interfaith Worker Justice. In both organizations he seeks to bring prophetic values to the problems of contemporary society.

RABBI RACHEL S. MIKVA is the Schaalman Professor of Jewish Stud-ies at Chicago Theological Seminary. Prior to her involvement in academia, Rabbi Mikva served congregations in Chicago and New York. She is especially interested in the intersection of exegesis, culture, and ethics, which gives rise to her exploration of eco-kashrut.

RABBI BENNETT F. MILLER is the senior rabbi of Anshe Emeth Memorial Temple in New Brunswick, New Jersey. He is a member of the doctor of ministry faculty at Hebrew Union College–Jewish Institute of Religion. He was the founding chair of the CCAR Task Force on Kashrut in 2000. He also serves as CCAR representative to the Board of Trustees of the Union for Reform Judaism.

RABBI JOEL MOSBACHER (Hebrew Union College–Jewish Institute of Religion, Cincinnati, 1998; DMin, New York, 2007) is the rabbi of Beth Haverim Shir Shalom in Mahwah, New Jersey. He is married to Elyssa and is Ari and Lev's *aba*. He spent five weeks this past summer volunteering at Kayam Farm at the Pearlstone Center in Reisterstown, Maryland, tending to the farm in the morning and studying Jewish text related to agriculture in the afternoon.

RABBIS LINDA MOTZKIN and JONATHAN RUBENSTEIN are co-rabbis of Temple Sinai in Saratoga Springs, New York. Jonathan, a baker and bread-making teacher, founded Slice of Heaven Breads and operates it out of the synagogue together with Linda, a *soferet* and scribal arts teacher. Slice of Heaven Breads is a component of the Bread and Torah Project, through which Linda and Jonathan offer experiential Jewish learning that combines bread making, scribal arts, Torah making, and awareness of the natural world.

RABBI MICHAEL NAMATH, the program director at the Religious Action Center of Reform Judaism, lives in Potomac, Maryland.

RABBI KAREN R. PEROLMAN was born in Bremerhaven, Germany, and grew up all over the United States as part of a military family. She was ordained by the New York campus of the Hebrew Union

College–Jewish Institute of Religion in 2010 and currently serves Congregation B'nai Jeshurun in Short Hills, New Jersey, as an assistant rabbi. Her rabbinic thesis focused on the legal and ethical issues of eating meat from a Jewish historical and sociological perspective. She is an alumnus of NFTY and URJ Camp Harlam and is passionate about the intersections of food, Judaism, feminism, and social justice.

RABBI OREN POSTREL was ordained by the Hebrew Union College–Jewish Institute of Religion, New York, in 1993 and has served congregations in Paris, New York, and Napa, California. Rabbi Postrel has studied wine at University of California–Davis extension and has written an online wine column merging wine and spirituality called *Wines and Spirit*. In Napa, Rabbi Postrel served Congregation Beth Sholom from 2007 to 2010.

RABBI DEBORAH PRINZ, CCAR's director of Program and Member Service and director of the Joint Commission on Rabbinic Mentoring, also researches connections between chocolate and Jews. At the CCAR she creates continuing education, trains interim rabbis, and administers the mentoring program. Senior rabbi of Temple Adat Shalom, Poway, California, from 1988 until her retirement in June 2007, she previously served as rabbi of Congregation Beth Am in Teaneck, New Jersey, and was assistant rabbi at Central Synagogue in New York City. She has provided leadership to our movement as a member of the National Commission on Rabbinic-Congregational Relations, as a founder of the Women's Rabbinic Network, and as president of the Pacific Association of Reform Rabbis. She blogs at http://www.jewsonthechocolatetrail.org.

RABBI DOUG SAGAL is senior rabbi of Temple Emanu-El in Westfield, New Jersey. He is a graduate of Wesleyan University, Hebrew Union College–Jewish Institute of Religion, and Yale Divinity School. He is a visiting lecturer at the Academy for Jewish Religion.

Rabbi Mark Sameth is the spiritual leader of Pleasantville Community Synagogue in Westchester County, New York. Ordained from Hebrew Union College–Jewish Institute of Religion in 1998, his essays on Jewish diet have appeared in Olitzky and Judson's *The Rituals and Practices of a Jewish Life* (Jewish Lights, 2002) and *Jewish Ritual: A Brief Introduction for Christians* (Jewish Lights, 2004). A landmark paper purporting to reveal the long-long lost pronunciation of the Tetragrammaton "Who is He? He is She: The Secret Four Letter Name of God" appeared in the *CCAR Journal*, Summer 2008. A teacher of Jewish meditation, Rabbi Sameth sends short, daily *kavvanot* (intentions) from http://twitter.com/Fourbreaths.

Nigel Savage is the director of Hazon, which fosters sustainable community, within and beyond the Jewish world. Nigel teaches and writes widely and was named a member of the *Forward*'s annual list of the fifty most influential people in the American Jewish community. He is believed to be the first English Jew to cycle across the state of South Dakota on a recumbent bike. For more information on Hazon's Jewish food programs, go to www.hazon.org.

Rabbi Ariana Silverman is the assistant rabbi of Temple Kol Ami in West Bloomfield, Michigan. She was raised in Chicago, received her AB in history from Harvard University in 2000, and from 2000 to 2001, served as a legislative assistant at the Religious Action Center of Reform Judaism and the Coalition on the Environment and Jewish Life. She has worked for the Sierra Club, Hazon, Temple Beth Israel in Steubenville, Ohio, and Congregation Emanu-El of the City of New York. She was ordained by the Hebrew Union College–Jewish Institute of Religion in 2010 and is an alumna of the Wexner Graduate Fellowship Program. She lives in Detroit with her husband, Justin R. Long.

Rabbi Joseph Aaron Skloot is a doctoral candidate in Jewish history and a Richard Hofstadter Faculty Fellow at Columbia University, as well as a graduate fellow at the Center for Jewish Law and

Contemporary Civilization at Cardozo Law School. His research concerns the history of the interpretation of classical Rabbinic texts by early-modern and modern rabbis and laity. He was ordained a rabbi at Hebrew Union College–Jewish Institute of Religion in New York in 2010, where he was awarded the Tisch Rabbinical Fellowship. He teaches regularly at congregations and institutions in the New York City area.

RABBI LANCE J. SUSSMAN, PHD (Hebrew Union College–Jewish Institute of Religion, Cincinnati, 1980), is senior rabbi of Reform Congregation Keneseth Israel in Elkins Park, Pennsylvania; serves as national chair of the CCAR Press; and is the author of many books and articles, including *Isaac Leeser and the Making of American Judaism* and *Sharing Sacred Moments*. He is past chair of the Judaic Studies Department at Binghamton University and has taught American Jewish history at Princeton University and Hunter College, among others. He is involved in community and interfaith activities nationwide and currently serves as a trustee of the Katz Center for Advanced Judaic Studies at the University of Pennsylvania.

RABBI MARK WASHOFSKY is the Solomon B. Freehof Professor of Jewish Law at Hebrew Union College–Jewish Institute of Religion in Cincinnati. He serves as chair of the Responsa Committee of the Central Conference of American Rabbis, which issues advisory opinions on questions of Jewish practice. He is the author of *Jewish Living: A Guide to Contemporary Reform Practice* and of the newly published *Reform Responsa for the Twenty-First Century: Sh'eilot Ut'shuvot* (CCAR Press).

RABBI DONALD A. WEBER has served as the rabbi of Temple Rodeph Torah of Marlboro, New Jersey, since 1984. He is a chaplain for the Marlboro Township Police Department and a founding member of the Marlboro Ethics Board. His commitment to feeding the hungry led Rodeph Torah to become one of the first partner congregations of MAZON: A Jewish Response to Hunger, and the congregation's food drives average over five tons of food per year. Rabbi Weber is the creator of TRTCares, a nationally recognized volunteer group that seeks to help those needing assistance with employment, legal, financial, and mental health matters.

Rabbi Ellen Weinberg Dreyfus is president of the Central Conference of American Rabbis. She is the rabbi of B'nai Yehuda Beth Sholom, a Reform congregation in the south suburbs of Chicago. She loves to cook and has written and lectured for many years on issues about Jews and food.

Rabbi Josh Whinston serves as spiritual leader of Temple Beth David in Cheshire, Connecticut. Rabbi Whinston's experience slaughtering chickens was a profound, life-changing moment that he will never forget. Although slaughtering is not a part of his regular duties as rabbi, it will forever shape his rabbinate.

Rabbi Eric H. Yoffie is the President of the Union for Reform Judaism, the congregational arm of the Reform Jewish Movement in North America. The Union represents 1.5 million Reform Jews in more than nine hundred synagogues across the United States and Canada. Installed as president in June 1996, Rabbi Yoffie has led the Reform Movement in exciting new directions, moving congregational life toward greater attention to Torah study and adult literacy. In addition Rabbi Yoffie has created two worship initiatives for the Reform Movements and has been a pioneer in interfaith relations with both Christians and Muslims. Rabbi Yoffie has also been deeply involved in issues of social justice and community concern. He has also worked tirelessly on behalf of the Jewish state and the rights of Reform Jews in Israel, and meets frequently with Israel's elected officials. Raised in Worcester, Massachusetts, Rabbi Yoffie was ordained at Hebrew Union College-Jewish Institute of Religion in New York in 1974, and served congregations in Lynbrook, New York, and Durham, North Carolina, before joining the Union in 1980. He and his wife, Amy

Jacobson Yoffie, reside in Westfield, New Jersey, and have two children, Adina and Adam. Rabbi Yoffie is a regular blogger for the Huffington Post and the Jerusalem Post.

RABBI MARY L. ZAMORE was ordained in 1997 from HUC-JIR, where she was the recipient of the Messinger Family Scholarship, as well as fellowships from ARIL and the STAR Foundation. She currently serves as the Associate Rabbi of Temple B'nai Or of Morristown, NJ. She has also served Temple Emanu-El of Westfield, NJ and Temple Beth Am of Parsippany, NJ. Rabbi Zamore is considered to be the first Reform *mashgihah* overseeing a New Jersey Bakery from 1997–2001. A member of Hazon's Jewish Food Educator Network, she frequently writes and teaches on a variety of topics, including kashrut. Rabbi Zamore lives in Westfield, NJ with her husband Terje Lande and their 10-year old son Aryeh.

RABBI IRWIN ZEPLOWITZ is senior rabbi at The Community Synagogue in Port Washington, New York. He has lectured and taught in a wide variety of advanced adult learning settings and has written a series of *divrei Torah* on the Book of Exodus for the Union for Reform Judaism. He has a particular interest in issues of social justice in the area of same-sex marriage, homelessness and poverty, intergroup dialogue, and Israel. Rabbi Zeplowitz loves to cook (and eat!), and he is an organic gardener. He has encouraged a garden at his synagogue, with produce harvested given to local food banks.

RABBI RUTH A. ZLOTNICK has been rabbi of Temple Beth Or in the Township of Washington, New Jersey, since July 2008. She previously served at New York's Central Synagogue as associate rabbi and director of lifelong learning. Upon ordination, Rabbi Zlotnick worked as the associate director of programs at Synagogue 2000, now known as Synagogue 3000. As a rabbinical student, Rabbi Zlotnick was an intern for the URJ's Department of Jewish Family Concerns and coordinated *L'Tapayach Tikvah / To Nourish Hope*, a program for the prevention of eating disorders.